Ancient Greek
Literature and Society

Ancient Greek Literature and Society

SECOND EDITION, REVISED

Charles Rowan Beye

Cornell University Press

ITHACA AND LONDON

First published 1987 by Cornell University Press.

International Standard Book Number (cloth) 0-8014-1874-7
International Standard Book Number (paper) 0-8014-9444-3
Library of Congress Catalog Card Number 86-47972
Printed in the United States of America
Librarians: Library of Congress cataloging information
appears on the last page of the book.

*The paper in this book is acid-free and meets the guidelines for
permanence and durability of the Committee on Production Guidelines
for Book Longevity of the Council on Library Resources.*

For my children
Howard, Willis, Helen, and Gile

Contents

vii

Preface

Let me advise you to study Greek, Mr. Undershaft. Greek scholars are privileged men. Few of them know Greek; and none of them knows anything else; but their position is unchallengeable. Other languages are the qualifications of waiters and commercial travelers; Greek is to a man of position what the hallmark is to silver.

George Bernard Shaw, *Major Barbara*

A long time ago this quotation from Shaw might have held some truth. Nowadays very few people know Greek, and the idea of a gentleman as Shaw meant the term is a laughable anachronism. While it is sad that so few can read ancient Greek literature in the original language, there is the consoling fact that the literature and antiquity in general have lost their snob appeal. A knowledge of them no longer confers respectability and status upon an emergent bourgeois, certainly not in America or for that matter in England or on the Continent. Increasingly fewer people understand the tradition of antiquity which lies behind so many features of Western culture today. In one way this change is not regrettable. It means that people who approach the subject do so for its own sake. Ancient Greek literature is beautiful, and it offers a range of very different experience and observation. Those who discover it will have the greatest of pleasure, inspiration, and insight.

For this second edition of *Ancient Greek Literature and Society* I have taken the opportunity to rewrite extensively. While I have cut some, I also have written much more about Socrates and Plato, New Comedy, romance, and the Alexandrian literary scene. Nonetheless, as I said in the first edition, this is not a systematic survey of ancient Greek literature.

Enormous shifts in emphasis in scholarship and criticism over the last decade have been very helpful to me, and these have been duly recorded in a considerably expanded bibliography. I do not believe that I have changed my essential views or preoccupations much since the first edition was published. One preoccupation is to estimate the implications of the very *public* character of so much of this literature. Another is to try to establish standards for criticism of pieces that are oral or near oral and that were performed for an audience that was preliterate or barely literate. Still another is to consider the continuing influence of the Homeric poems on the subsequent literature.

I remain interested, too, in noting the constancy of certain preoccupations of the ancient Greeks which seem to be revealed in their literature. What we would call their obsession with death is remarkable, as is their insistent awareness of it, which probably gave them some consolation. Their mental habit of seeing things in antithesis—the absolute symmetry that they imposed on life perceived—is a constant in the literary pieces, even perhaps in the arrangement and unconscious selection of that which they preserved. There is even a kind of natural antithesis between the comic and the tragic—categories into one or the other of which almost every piece can be assigned.

In writing about ancient Greek literature I have borne in mind that we know almost nothing of value about the authors and very little about the circumstances in which these pieces were created. The texts are central. The temptation to interpret these works in twentieth-century terms is almost irresistible. Perhaps, indeed, there are no other terms to use, but to my mind it is worth the trouble to try to conjure up as much as one can of the original milieu in which these pieces were produced. We know little about the entire oeuvre of several authors; of others we have texts that may or may not be finished as the authors wished them. Therefore generalizations must always be suspect. The fact of the matter is that our profound ignorance of ancient Greece makes each piece of literature finally the private property of its reader. It is my hope that what I have written here will stimulate, illuminate, and guide, but not distort.

The reader will find a list of important dates in history and literature in the appendix at the end of this book which may help to clarify the context of each piece. The spelling of ancient names, particularly well-known ones, is generally Latinized because that is the form in which they have become familiar since the Renaissance.

I must thank Robert S. Miller, without whose strenuous efforts I would not have been able to make this second edition.

I am indebted to several anonymous readers of Cornell University

Press for their criticisms of the first edition as well as for their suggestions for improvement. To Robert Lamberton I owe thanks for reading the revised manuscript carefully and critically. Ann Rosener and Willard Spiegelman, who read large parts of the revised manuscript, were entirely helpful. William M. Calder III, J. A. Coulter, Michael Gagarin, Justin Glenn, Rachel Kitzinger, David Konstan, Daniel Levine, Gregory Nagy, S. P. Scully, J. H. Tatum, W. F. Wyatt, and F. I. Zeitlin have been most generous in their suggestions for the bibliography. Thomas Flesher was kind enough to help me with verifications in the bibliography.

I thank once again Gail Cabisius, Douglas Frame, Jørgen Mejer, Brigit McCarthy, Barbara Parry, Barbara Knowles, and John Vaio and especially William M. Calder III, Casey Cameron Mesirow, and Richard Sáez for their careful reading of the manuscript of the first edition of this book and Mary Willis Pendleton for her constant encouragement.

Nearly forty years ago G. F. Else, J. F. Gilliam, and T. G. Rosenmeyer inspired me to make the study of classical literature my life work. Their exciting remarks in and out of the classroom have remained with me as a standard and a provocation through the years. The late Mary Powers Beye first taught me what literary criticism was all about, and I remain in her debt to this day. The late John Gardner, who was my editor on a previous book, helped me in matters of style and thought which I see reflected still in every page I write. In the last thirty years I have had a succession of intelligent, thoughtful, and creative students who have asked me questions and suggested answers that have led me to whatever understanding I have of so much of the literature discussed here. It is to them that I am particularly indebted.

CHARLES ROWAN BEYE

New York

Ancient Greek
Literature and Society

Major Greek settlements in antiquity

CHAPTER ONE

The Language

In the beginning was the word.

Gospel according to John

Speech man taught himself and swift
thought, the temper that makes a state

Sophocles, Antigone 354–55

Most people know Greek literature through translation. Contemporary translations, poetic translations particularly, sound alike because English no longer has a poetic diction. The literature of antiquity, however, is notable for the several highly stylized dictions that characterize the various genres. We speak of epic Greek, for instance, or tragic Greek, and philosophic Greek. This variety of conventional usage within what is classified as one language is one of the remarkable features of the literature. Anyone who wants to understand this literature and must read it in translation needs to have some idea of the nature of the language and its history and development.

The Greek language is peculiarly rich and complex as a vehicle for literary expression, in part because of its enormous vocabulary and in part because of the number of dialects that play a role in the literary language. The earliest literary remains already demonstrate a variety of dialects that were produced by the various movements of Greek-speaking peoples over many centuries.

We know very little about the period between the Greeks' arrival in their historic land and the beginnings of their recorded history in the eighth and seventh centuries B.C. They seem to have entered what is now called Greece toward the end of the third millennium, coming down out of the Balkan peninsula from present-day Albania and Yugoslavia. Some settled in northwest Greece and some in the Peloponnesus. The two groups evidently lost contact with each other:

we assume this because each area seems to have evolved a separate dialect of the language. Their cultural achievements were also diverse. The group in northwest Greece has left us little evidence of what is commonly considered an advancing culture, while the group in the Peloponnesus created one of the Western world's first great societies. They are called Mycenaeans by historians because their capital city seems to have been Mycenae and because Homer, who refers to these people as Achaeans, describes the king of Mycenae, Agamemnon, as being the lord over all the Achaeans who went to fight at Troy.

Throughout the second millennium Mycenaean civilization, which dominated the Greek mainland, sent trading vessels throughout the Mediterranean, rivaled in riches the Minoan civilization on the island of Crete, and finally overcame it. The Mycenaeans learned much from the Minoans as well as from the older civilizations of Asia Minor and the Near East. There seems to have been an international culture in the eastern Mediterranean in the second millennium which may account for the elements in the Homeric epics and in Hesiod's poems which are similar to those in more eastern literatures.

The Mycenaeans were not as a whole a literate people, although a system of writing has been found among their ruins. Called Linear B by modern scholars, it is a cumbersome, complicated system of sound notation which, to judge from what has been deciphered of it, was used for trade and military purposes, possibly by a class of scribes, and was hardly of use for the general populace. They, it is assumed, were dependent on some kind of oral transmission of the facts of their culture. The presumed importance of oral transmission is in keeping with contemporary theories about the origin of the *Iliad* and the *Odyssey*. Although these two poems appear centuries later, they recall at times elements of the Mycenaean world. It is theorized that the oral poetic tradition that lies behind these two epics, which were probably created in the eighth century, must have had its beginning at Mycenaean courts. The oral tradition was evidently stronger than the Linear B script; there seems to have been a relatively easy lapse into total illiteracy once the Mycenaean empire disintegrated toward the end of the second millennium. When there were no longer imperial bureaus, there was no further need of clerks and accountants and the script vanished; at least no later trace of Linear B has been discovered.

The political and economic world the Mycenaeans created in southern Greece and the islands came to an end in the twelfth century

B.C. Around the same time the other dialect group in the northwest began to move down into the Peloponnesus. How the two groups at first confronted one another is unclear. The archaeological evidence does not show disruption of culture in the areas into which the new-comers moved, but rather a general diminution of activity. The incoming people settled in the southern Peloponnesus. They are known as Dorians, and their language and culture as Doric. Later language patterns among the Greeks suggest that these Doric-speaking Greeks were followed out of northwest Greece by yet another group from the northwest. These people, too, must have been sufficiently separated from other groups to develop over time a different dialect, which linguists call Northwest Greek. This group never made it to the Peloponnesus, however. Theirs is the language of the people who lived in Aetolia to the north across the Corinthian Gulf and as far east as Delphi. These two linguistic groups—Northwest Greek and Doric—constitute what linguists call West Greek.

The arrival of the Doric-speaking Greeks into the Peloponnesus seems to have caused or coincided with widespread movements of people over the mainland and the Aegean. Other new dialects developed when the people who spoke Mycenaean Greek broke up into smaller units that lost contact with each other. Once the Mycenaean world no longer had a political or economic basis, the lines of communication failed, and the common language (Mycenaean Greek, or Achaean as it it sometimes called) was no longer spoken. It is important to remember the very small population of the ancient world relative to our own and the great natural difficulties of communication. Isolation was the natural state; without political unity there was no linguistic unity. The Greeks spoke in dialects from this time until the late fourth century, when Alexander's conquests brought a political cohesiveness strong enough to create a common tongue.

Dialectal developments suggest that large numbers of Mycenaeans left the Peloponnesus. Some went to the island of Cyprus. The dialect there is most closely connected with that of the inner mountains of the Peloponnesus, the region of Arcadia. Arcado-Cypriote, as this dialect is called, is known only from inscriptions. It seems to be the closest relative to the language deciphered in the Linear B script. Across the Aegean Sea in the middle of the west coast of present-day Turkey is an area the Greeks called Ionia; the settlers there were Ionians and the dialect Ionic. The people of the islands known as the Cyclades and Euboea also spoke Ionic Greek. The land in which Athens was the principal city was known as Attica; the people there spoke an older version of Ionic called Attic Greek. Archaeological excavation shows Attica to have been continuously inhabited without cultural break from the very earliest times. It is tempting therefore to associate their language with Mycenaean Greek and thus to see Ionic as another close and direct descendant of the Mycenaean or Achaean language, but there are problems making a close identification between Arcado-Cypriote and Ionic. Attic is the most important dialect of the Greek language because most of the writing that has survived from antiquity is written in Attic Greek. It is the form of Greek that most people who study Greek encounter first. There were, however, other important dialects. One was Aeolic, which spread through Boeotia up into Thessaly, from there across to the northern coast of Asia Minor. In Asia Minor and on the island of Lesbos, Aeolic was influenced by the Ionic dialect to the south; in Thessaly it was spoken pure, while in Boeotia it was mixed with Northwest Greek and with old Mycenaean, making it very different from the other forms.

Arcado-Cypriote, Ionic, Attic, and Aeolic are the principal dialects that derive from Mycenaean. They are designated by linguists as East Greek. These two modern linguistic categories, West Greek and East Greek, happen to reflect a distinction that the ancient Greeks themselves made between the cultures of the two geographical areas. In the west it was the Dorians who created a way of life that was in clear contrast to that of eastern Greeks. Among the Dorians the people of Sparta are always singled out as representative of the western way of life because of their power and because of the eccentricity of their ways. In the eastern part of the Greek world before the beginning of the fifth century the Ionians were considered leaders of the East Greek language bloc; sparked by their proximity to the highly developed societies to the east, they were quick to innovate. Later the overwhelming literary production and general intellectual activity in the city of Athens gave special prominence to Attic-speaking Greeks, who nonetheless thought of themselves as essentially Ionians.

Differences between dialects did not to any great extent involve vocabulary; pronunciation and variants of form were the important differences. Certainly speakers of one dialect were intelligible to other dialect groups; the largest obstacle to understanding was the difference in pitch in various syllables among the dialects. On the other hand, so separate and isolated was every city from every other that variant dialects proliferated. Among the Dorians, for instance, Corinthians spoke one way, Spartans another, Megarians a third, and so on throughout every village, hamlet, and crossroads.

The common prejudice of antiquity was that the Ionians were skeptical, intellectual, and experimental—quick and radical in their thoughts and emotions—while the Dorians were slow and conservative, if not stupid (from the Athenian point of view). The description of the basic Athenian and Spartan personalities in Thucydides' *History of the Peloponnesian War* (1.70–71; 84) is an eloquent expression of this prejudice. The manner of the Doric dialect seems to have encouraged the prejudice; it was heavy, perhaps slow, with a flat sound. Typical is the man in Theocritus's fifteenth Idyll (87ff.) who asks a woman he meets to break off the Doric accent because the flatness wears him down.

The Dorians, of course, also had their admirers. For those who esteemed the Dorian way of life the dialect evoked conservatism in manners and attitudes, stability, and the old order of aristocracy in a changing world. The Attic dialect, by contrast, was not so stable. By the late fifth century, with the constant presence of so many foreigners in Athens, the Attic dialect was absorbing features of every dialect. It was in this way, of course, that Attic Greek was emerging to become the common language of all Greeks when Alexander's political settlements in the fourth century rendered dialects obsolete.

The dialects of Greece are a hallmark of the literature, Doric, Ionic (Attic), and Aeolic being the principal literary dialects. They, of course, appear in variants. Sappho, for instance, who lived on the island of Lesbos, writes her poems in the Lesbian dialect, a form of Aeolic spoken on that island. Initially all authors wrote in their native dialects, but as certain genres became associated with specific dialects, writers paid at least limited deference to this convention. The first prose writers, for instance, appeared in Ionia. For a long time thereafter history and scientific writing was expected to have an Ionic coloration. Many of the early choral poets were from Dorian lands, and choral lyric thereafter exhibited Doric forms of speech. Even the choral passages set between the predominantly Attic dialogues in Athenian tragedy bear traces of Doric Greek. The many dialects used by the poets amplified the potential for poetic expression. Instead of one poetic diction there were available several dialects and styles, each with its own associations. The Aeolic lyrics of Sappho, the Ionic elegies of Mimnermus, the Doric choruses of Alcman, the Attic iambics of tragedy—in each of these the variation in dialect offers something that does not exist in the literature of Western nation-states. In these Western states each national language is so firmly entrenched that dialects are curiosities or oddities at best. Certainly the effect of the various Greek dialects is not at all like dialect stories or poems in American letters; these dialects are the speech patterns of minorities in contrast to the one common language. In ancient Greece all dialects were equal; only the Attic dialect, the speech of Athens, where most of the literary production took place and where the political and economic power came to be concentrated, was, so to speak, more equal.

In addition to these, however, there was one common poetic language, the so-called Homeric dialect. This was the language of oral poetry, which many poets through centuries of trial and error created from all the dialects for the sole purpose of narrating the events of saga. As such the dialect was artificial; no one, we assume, ever spoke the Homeric dialect. The importance and pervasiveness of early epic poetry, of which the surviving *Iliad* and *Odyssey* are ample testimony, made the Homeric dialect a common basis for poetic creation. Every style of poetry thereafter, particularly the tragic drama of Athens, incorporated epic words, phrases, and formulas.

It is only because they were preserved in writing that we know of the many dialects. Long after the disappearance of the Linear B script the Greeks invented an alphabetic system of writing when they became acquainted with the Semitic alphabet through their trading association with the Phoenicians. Sometime in the eighth century they adapted this script to denote the sounds of their own language. This truly phonetic alphabet proved to be a singularly efficient device that promoted the spread of literacy and certainly was the basis for the formation of the enlightened democracy in Athens in the fifth century.

After the breakdown of the Mycenaean imperial system, the many dialects that emerged resulted from people gathering into small, fragmented groups in hidden, mountain-ringed valleys. Independent political and economic units developed in each area. The mentality of this period exhibits intense locality; because every town spoke the common language in a distinctively different dialect, every person was an alien beyond the borders of his birthplace. The ancient Greeks are sometimes accused of being provincial and parochial, of being too anthropocentric, limited to the terrestrial view of things. The long preservation of dialects and regional distinctions in an area so small (yet so mountainous and difficult to traverse) is testimony to that innate parochialism.

Much of Greek history turns on the absence of a common, unifying view. War between the city-states was commonplace, Greek against Greek. For centuries they could not unite in a common cause. Yet the limits that such habits of mind imposed also made for a kind of communal introspection from which so much of the literature took its inspiration. This literature was largely created in the city of Athens in the small city-state of Attica within one century. It spoke to the citizenry with so firm a common cultural view that it transcended ideas of nationality and in fact transcended finally the temporal, geographic, and spiritual limits of Graeco-Roman antiquity to shape a considerable part of the art and institutions of the Western world. Such was the intellectual and spiritual power of a small, introspective, self-obsessed self-congratulating city-state.

Athens became the superior political power among the Greeks in the fifth century. From tribute paid by subject cities sprang a building program that paralleled the superlative literature in its beauty and grandeur. Coincidentally or not, the end of Athens's imperial dominance in the debacle of the Peloponnesian War came at roughly the same time that her literary fecundity vanished. In the fourth century Sparta and Thebes succeeded Athens's power and hegemony, only to succumb later to the power of Macedonia. Meanwhile in Athens, prose replaced poetry and philosophy replaced mythology. Athens became a university town.

Alexander ended the city-state forever with the creation of an eastern Mediterranean empire. Alexandria, the city he founded in Egypt—an *urbs* not a *polis*—became in the third century B.C. the new literary center. Its creative energy derived largely from scholars who looked back not with nostalgia, but with the intent of making a Greek literary history—codifying, purifying, and commenting upon the facts. The poets of Alexandria and the Hellenistic world thereafter used tradition as inspiration, either radically to reshape it as a kind of commentary or slavishly to imitate it as an act of obeisance.

In Hellenistic literature thereafter, as in most successive literatures of the Western world, the fundamental perspective became a backward glance; something is being said, one way or another, about classical Greek literature. In varying degrees something of the *Iliad* or the *Odyssey,* for instance, lies behind Apollonius Rhodius's *Argonautica,* Virgil's *Aeneid,* Dante's *Commedia,* Tasso's *Gerusaleme Liberata,* Cervantes' *Don Quixote,* Milton's *Paradise Lost,* Tolstoy's *War and Peace,* Joyce's *Ulysses,* and Nabokov's *Lolita,* just to name the very obvious.

This habit of mind marks a real separation of Hellenistic literature from the literature of the classical period and earlier. In the beginning there were no established genres, no genre rules, no models, nothing. In the briefest span of time a small group of people created diverse forms of literary expression, each of which had the means to say certain things best. Somehow their experimentation went immediately to the heart of the literary problems and found the potentials. Despite analysis, the literature of the early centuries, especially the fifth, remains a mystery bordering on the miraculous.

The third century is called the Alexandrian Age. Alexandria remained one of the great cities of the ancient world, but as with Athens, its absolute cultural dominance was short-lived. By the middle of the second century Rome had become the major power in the Mediterranean. Power, wealth, and dominance came to be expressed in the Latin language rather than the Greek. Roman power and the Latin language could not, however, destroy Greek culture. Hellenism, an international Greek culture, spread uniformly over the eastern Mediterranean, lasting until the creation of the Byzantine empire eight centuries later.

The cultural uniformity of the emergent Hellenistic world was reflected in the linguistic unity. Dialects began to disappear. The Attic Greek dialect became increasingly common. From it evolved what the Greeks from the mid-fourth century on began to refer to as the common language (Greek *koine*), which eventually became the standard written language; for instance, it is the language of the New Testament. When dialects are used in the literature of this period, they mark a clever poet's attempt at evoking a special ambience; for instance, when Theocritus uses an amalgam of the various kinds of Doric found in western Greece in his pastoral poems, he manages to establish some very stylized rustics.

From the second century educated Greeks learned Latin, men who wished to get on in the imperial bureaucracy knew Latin, but Greek literary production never flagged. There were men of letters, essayists such as Plutarch, literary critics such as the figure we call Longinus, humorists such as Lucian, and epic poets such as Quintus of Smyrna. Their works display a wide range of observation about the cultural heritage of classical Greece, reworking of old themes, and evocation of prior styles and forms. In addition to these writings the Greeks of this time invented an important new genre, the ancient novel or romance. The literature of the later period is plentiful, but scarcely as well known in our time as that of the much earlier centuries. It deserves greater attention, if for no other reason than its similarity to some of the literature of the twentieth century.

No translation can render the sensual, intellectual experience of the Greek. The language is exceptionally musical because of the high percentage of vowels to consonants. The pitch accent, which renders one vowel in each word at a higher pitch, makes for further variation in vowel sound. Because Greek is an inflected language, in which elements added to the semantic root indicate the relationship between words, it is freed from the tyranny of word order. In English "the dog bites the man" is very different from "the man bites the dog," although the sentences have the exact same words in the exact same form. An ancient Greek would not understand this system of construction. It is possible in the ancient language, in poetry particularly, to create another kind of meaning, in addition to that achieved by inflection, through the juxtaposition of words. This meaning is often irrational and ambiguous, but nevertheless strong. English-language poets such as Gerard Manley Hopkins and Ezra Pound tried and to some extent succeeded in bringing this phenomenon into their poetry despite the fundamental incapacity of the English language for free word arrangement.

Although inflection released Greek writers from the demands of word order, the sentences, especially in prose, generally fell in the order of subject, verb, and object, each element with its attendant modifiers. The earliest style reflected natural conversational narrative patterns—that is, short ideas brought together by the simplest connectives. This style the Greeks called paratactic (from Greek *parataxis,* "placing side by side"). In the paratactic style juxtaposition is the clue to meaning as in, "It was raining hard, and we didn't go on the picnic," where causality is not expressed but implied. While most languages would employ the copulative "and" to bring these two ideas together, in ancient Greek an adversative construction would be used instead. Thus if one were to find the sample sentence expressed in ancient Greek, it would most likely be read, "On the one hand it was raining; on the other we did not go on the picnic." The underlying sense is the same, but a tension of opposites has been introduced where none exists in the English version. This intellectual habit of ordering things in alternatives, antitheses, and symmetries is characteristic of the ancient Greek manner of exposition.

Parataxis had its day. Eventually there came about a style better suited to the demands of logic and abstraction, a style known as *syntactic,* which coordinated ideas so as to subordinate some to the creation of a central point. Clauses particularly make this style. Its most complex form is the periodic sentence in which the meaning is not clear until the final word. Our sample sentence would be transformed to read, "Because it was raining hard, we didn't go on the picnic," or "It was raining so hard that we had to cancel our plans to go on the picnic," depending on the emphasis desired. A periodic sentence could indicate in one intellectual consortium all the ramifications of an idea and in the exposition of its parts could show the logical hierarchy of the whole.

Very few ancient Greek authors completely surrendered their taste for the freer, vernacular style to the rigidity and formalism that periodicity demands. The conventions of formal grammatical usage were there in the language to be ignored as much as observed by writers seeking the immediacy and *vérité* of a simpler, bolder, more conversational manner. Translations fail us because the Anglo-American literary tradition is heavily influenced by the standards of Latin literature, in which a sharp distinction is made between the written and the spoken language. Translations into the English language cannot easily render the exquisite combination of objective, logical grammatical usage with the emotional, playful, popular idiom. Plato's style is one of the most notable examples of this confident, precise, yet relaxed use of language. In translation, however, his words often seems professorial and academic when in fact he is being playful.

Casualness (freedom to originate) and seriousness (a concern for exactness) in combination are constant qualities of ancient Greek writing. These qualities have helped the language survive these thousands of years—always adapting and assimilating while never losing its shape. The Greek people have always had a passionately tenacious grip on their language. When the Romans ruled the world, they obliterated whole cultures in what is now western Europe, but they did not at all challenge the Greek language in the East. Throughout the period of Turkish domination the Greek language remained alive, banked like coals under ash in the Greek Orthodox Church. The Greek spoken today in downtown Athens is closer to the ancient language of twenty-five centuries ago than modern English is to the language of Chaucer. The modern Greek poet Constantine Cavafy achieves in so many of his poems a sense of the marvelous continuity in the Greek language. He uses words and phrases that are at once altogether contemporaneous and at the same time evocative of Homer and the fifth century. In a Proustian way the passage of twenty-five centuries is made to fade, and we are simply in the presence of the Greek language and things Greek.

CHAPTER TWO

Winged Words

They began to serve the meat and mix the wine and the herald came near leading the excellent singer Demodocus, honored by the people. He seated him among the feasters in a chair next to the broad column. Then clever Odysseus said to the herald . . . "Here, herald, give Demodocus this meat so that he may eat and I may offer my respects, miserable though I am. For among all the men who inhabit this earth singers deserve honor and respect since the Muse has taught them their songs and she loves the race of singers."

Odyssey 8.470–81

The Homeric poems are the only complete surviving examples of Greek oral epic poetry. Other epic poems existed, even other kinds of smaller, occasional poems, but we have only the *Iliad* and the *Odyssey*. They, so far as we can understand from the evidence, came at the end of the oral poetic tradition and survived because they were the best of their kind in the midst of the new forms of literary production that sprang up. The *Iliad* and the *Odyssey* are, therefore, not only an end, but a beginning. They are the end of a tradition of oral poetry, but because they are the earliest specimens of Greek poetry in existence, they are also the beginnings of Greek literature and, for that matter, the whole of Western literature.

The ancient Greeks believed that the *Iliad* and *Odyssey* were composed by a blind poet named Homer, who lived on the island of Chios. In fact, the actual circumstances of their creation—whether they were composed by one man or one woman or several, whether each is of different authorship, whether they were written or are specimens of oral poetry transcribed, when and where and why they came into existence—can never be satisfactorily determined.

Most contemporary scholars hold to the theory that the two poems were composed orally. They assume that over a long period of time professional singers of saga worked out and rehearsed routines of story line, language, and characters—all the elements of adventure stories centered around a hero—so that they could render upon demand spontaneously segments of a traditional story. Perhaps at some festivals an entire story was told.

The oral theory for the original composition of the *Iliad* and the *Odyssey* comes first from the observation that there seem to be references in the two poems to things known to the Mycenaeans but forgotten by or unknown to the later Greeks. Second, because no system of writing is known to have survived the collapse of the Mycenaean culture, it is necessary to assume the oral, not written, transmission of this material. Third, these two poems show similarities to demonstrably oral poems from all parts of the contemporary world.

A major stumbling block to the easy acceptance of this theory is that no unquestionably oral poem even approaches the Homeric poems in quality. Then, too, the history of Western literature is made up of individuals of genius who created the masterpieces. It is difficult to accept that generations of oral poets worked over the material that resulted in these two monumental poems, considered by general consensus to be, along with the plays of Shakespeare, the masterworks of the Western World. Critics want individual poets, not some kind of group effort.

More than fifty years ago an American scholar, Milman Parry, first compiled the statistical evidence that seemed to prove that the two poems were the result of oral composition, that they were made up of traditional phrases, lines, scenes, and characters that denied the impress of any one sensibility. Thus there was no poet, only a tradition that stimulated instinctive responses to the demands of making line after line of dactylic hexametric poetry with which to tell an oft-told tale. Recently the pendulum has swung, as indeed it will do, in the other direction; critics are now intent upon identifying the telltale traces of the poet who took the traditional material and made it his own. Of course, we now have the two poems in the form of written texts. They must have been dictated by an oral poet to someone who had learned to write when the alphabet was invented, or perhaps a poet who was close enough to the period of oral composition to have been educated in that manner but who was somehow capable of the new writing wrote them out.

Computerized linguistic studies of all the surviving examples of poetry composed in the so-called Homeric dialect seem to have established proof for the notion that the poems were composed at different times. According to these studies, the *Iliad* was composed first, the *Odyssey* second, then the two poems said in antiquity to have been made by a Boeotian poet named Hesiod, the *Theogony* and a little later the *Works and Days,* followed by the so-called Homeric Hymns. Thus we can posit a youthful Homer composing the *Iliad* and an older Homer the *Odyssey,* a youthful Hesiod composing the *Theogony* and an older Hesiod composing the *Works and Days.* And then again one could argue that each of these works was composed by a different person at a different time. In the ancient literary treatise called *On the Sublime* (author unknown but usually listed as a work of Longinus) we do in fact find the argument for a youthful *Iliad* and an old man's *Odyssey.* It is indeed attractive to imagine that the theme of an impatient young man who will not submit betokens a youthful poet whereas the story of a man of much experience traveling to get home to his wife, his home, and young son is obviously the work of someone in middle years. There are, of course, other arguments for the claim that each poem has a different author. We shall never know—not about the authorship and not about any other of the vexing matters that crop up in the careful reading of the poems. For as the ancient Greek wit Lucian pointed out, the only person who has the answer is Homer, and he is dead.

Because the alphabet was probably created sometime in the latter half of the eighth century B.C., these poems could not have been made into written texts before then. Evidence suggests that they were composed toward the end of the eighth century and the beginning of the seventh. One could argue that if the poem is the work of an oral poet, he was induced to dictate a version of one of his better routines when the value of the written word as a permanent record became obvious. And because this poet would have had to tell his tale far more slowly than usual for his stenographer, he had the chance to improvise more carefully and thus achieve his masterpiece. One could also argue that if the poet could write—which on the surface of things would seem impossible because it is generally argued that a literate and an oral mentality are utterly dissimilar—he must have been so close to the period before the arrival of writing that he still retained the rhythmic technique of oral composition. The notion of an early written text, however, does not account for the dissemination of the *Iliad* and *Odyssey* throughout the Greek world. The materials of reading and writing must have remained clumsy for a long time, thereby necessitating continued dependence on oral communication.

Milman Parry was so intent on demonstrating the *mechanics* of the technique of oral narrative that he was ready to deny the significance of the repetition of lines, scenes, and phrases and indeed to deny any meaning at all to much repeated descriptive adjectives, as though they were no more than what dead metaphors are in the English language. In doing so, he was trying to imagine the circumstances of performance for an oral poet and what he could expect from his audience and what they might be able to catch in his delivery as the hundreds, perhaps thousands of lines were hurled in their direction.

The contemporary reaction to Parry's theory derives from the important fact that today the texts are read, not heard. The contemporary reader can note repetitions, connections, all sorts of architectonics. Some critics will say Homer intended a certain effect; others will say that the effect is simply unconscious, inherent in the manipulation of the narrative. The meaning is there and whether Homer meant it, whether his audience got it, is irrelevant because there is no way to know and it would be an impertinence in the face of that ignorance to deny what readers themselves sense. That the *intent* is irrelevant holds true for a good deal of ancient literature because we really do not know very much at all about the circumstances of its creation.

An important observation for those who hold to the theory of the oral creation of these poems is that, unlike normal human speech, which uses individual words as its building blocks, the lines of these poems are made up of phrases that have metrical value. Greek epic poetry is formed in dactylic hexameters, a meter characterized by six units of timed sound, of which the last is invariably disyllabic. Each of the preceding five units consists of either three syllables—the first long, the second two short (the dactyl, ¯ˇˇ)—or two long syllables (known as a spondee, ¯¯). The words *long* and *short* refer to the relative length of time taken for sounding the syllable. The metrical scheme, even with all the possible variations available through mixing dactyls and spondees, is highly constraining. Because there is such a pervasive system of phraseology which works within these rhythmic rules, scholars assume that over a period of centuries poets who chanted the deeds of the Mycenaean kings gradually developed a metrically controlled vocabulary of phrases which functioned for them as a language does for humankind in general.

The most obvious example of this vocabulary to the reader of epic in translation is the ubiquitous personal name and adjective combination or common noun and adjective combination, a hallmark of Homeric poetry. Everyone knows Menelaus of the loud war cry, swift-footed Achilles, the wine-dark sea, the hollow ships. These commonplace phrases were important to the poet, because by using an adjectival epithet with names and certain common nouns he could gain immediate control over a larger part of the line than if he were using each word individually; he knew in advance how he would fill more of the metrical requirements of the line. In ancient Greek, the nouns and verbs vary in their endings according to the grammatical situation. This variation alters the metrical value of the word. There are a very few vestigial inflections in English; for instance, the nominative case of the masculine pronoun "he" takes less time to sound than the genitive form "his," which also takes longer to sound than the accusative form "him." This variation was an essential tool for the oral poets in creating their metrical vocabulary. For example, in the *Iliad* the name Odysseus is generally qualified with "shining" in the nominative case, "godlike" in the genitive case, "great-hearted" in the dative case, and "like unto Zeus in counsel" in the accusative case. The ending of the Greek form of the name, as it changes for each grammatical inflection, becomes metrically different and requires a metrically different element to make up a common and easily remembered piece of the line.

The poem is a mosaic of these metrical combinations. The poets used the formulaic phrases to generate analogous—whether in sound or in grammatical construction—phrases with a different meaning. The economy of this phenomenon is revealed in the fact that almost never are there two metrically identical phrases that say the same thing. This would be the same as a language having two words that meant precisely the same thing. It has also been observed that the majority of the words of the poem fall into certain metrical slots in the line and avoid others to which they are equally suited. This suggests that as the poet composed, he could instantly, instinctively "feel" where certain key words would fall. So he had the metrical shape of the line instantly. Creating this system must have been the work of centuries. The important fact is that the poet was creating his line not from the individual words of the language as a literate poet would do but from larger blocks of metrically combined words, the combination of which had been worked out over a long time.

The language of these poems seems too highly contrived to have been usable as the everyday spoken language of a people. It is, in fact, an amalgam of dialects. The reason for this peculiar circumstance may be that in the vast movement of peoples and the concomitant creation of new dialects that resulted from the collapse of the Mycenaean empire the poets who maintained the oral poetic tradition were themselves on the move, part of the dialectal process. Then later, when conditions were more settled, the poets traveled from city to city in pursuit of their livelihood, thereby encountering different dialects. As they came upon phrases or words from some other dialect that were superior to or fit the line better than what they knew, they incorporated this material into the stock of their epic vocabulary. Certain words will fit into the dactylic hexameter line only in certain dialectal variations. What had come into being over a long period of time was a language that was markedly dactylic in quality— an artificial language divorced from the vernacular, made for oral narration by professionals. The language is so contrived that one cannot imagine amateurs using it well, although in a lifetime of hearing the recitation of this poetry people must have memorized a good deal of it. The important consideration, however, is that this was a special poetic diction; the audience had to surrender to it, abandon the patterns of speech and thought in which they normally conducted their lives, and enter into another mental, spiritual, and aesthetic state. It must have been hypnotic.

The poet was no doubt further aided by the use of typical scenes. In the *Iliad* there are thousands of lines devoted to describing men in battle, killing and being killed. It is probably the most vivid battle narrative to be composed until Tolstoy, very much under Homer's influence, created the marvelously intimate yet panoramic descriptions of battle in *War and Peace*. Homer's battle narrative varies little; hero encounters hero, sometimes descriptive or biographical detail of one or another follows, and then comes a detailed description of the fatal wounding and death of the victim. A large part of the poem is made up of infinite variations of this typical scene. In a similar way in the *Odyssey* one meets identical phrases, sometimes repeated half-lines, sometimes whole lines in scenes portraying the serving and eating of meals, none of which is finally exactly the same, varying, as each does, in the introduction or omission of some of the stock phrases. It is this variation within extreme repetition which argues against any kind of verbatim memorizing of the poem by the singers who presumably created the narration. It argues for a narrative created fresh and spontaneously out of rehearsed routines.

Just as there are typical scenes, there are typical characters. In the

Iliad, Ajax, Diomedes, and Achilles, for instance, are variations of the same person; physically they are alike, and their motives and values are the same. The minor warriors, although described in far less detail, are also versions of this stereotypic warrior. There is scarcely any idiosyncrasy, and only occasionally is there the barest manifestation of personality. Achilles, although he behaves differently than the others, is really only a radical extension of them. When Agamemnon says as they quarrel in the first scene of the poem that Achilles wants more than all the others, he is only making the point that Achilles is more competitive, more self-aggrandizing than the others. In his own speeches in the quarrel scene Achilles talks with a frankness that no one else dares (except for the low-class lout Thersites in the second book). While he may take a grander view of himself, he seeks, nonetheless, the very same things all the other men seek. His particular misfortune is to be so great a warrior, so close to the power of the universe as the son of a goddess, and yet finally to be no more than an ordinary human being.

The women of the *Odyssey* also seem to be types. Circe and Calypso are particularly similar, but Helen displays her witchlike qualities, too, when she drugs the wine, and Arete, Nausicaa's mother, is described as dominant in the way these other three are. Certainly Penelope could be said to enchant the suitors in her very own manner, and they thus become her victims even as she is victimized by them.

No Homeric character has an inner life; each is a sum of attributes that are consistently assigned to all the main characters. Homer's characters have been described as monoliths; each responds to situations predictably, always in the same manner; but it is in the response that we find the major distinguishing features. Achilles is always complaining; Odysseus is always paranoid. The lesser characters, when they are sufficiently defined, are similarly constructed: Nestor prefaces his advice on strategy with an appeal to the authority conferred upon him by virtue of his long years of experience; Thetis laments the fate of a mother who must lose a son in early manhood; Agamemnon must test the strength of his authority; Penelope laments her absent husband, and so on.

What might be called technique, the poet's mechanical response to the need to deliver line after line of narration without the aid of writing and rewriting, is, of course, also the genius of oral epic poetry. Typical scenes and typical characters may also be described as ideal. So it is that persons, places, and things, by being described consistently by certain adjectival epithets, transcend time and accident. "Swift ships" are always thus, although they may be rotting on the beach from disuse. Achilles is "swift-footed" even as he languishes inactive in his camp. Pylos, which rises from the bay to wooded hills where the ruins of the Mycenaean citadel still may be seen, will remain "sandy" as long as the *Odyssey* exists. In this way the narrator manages to establish in every changing moment of the story the sense of the fundamental essence, or "realness," of each character and place while using a poetic style that is so utterly artificial.

Such poetry is also conformist. Human behavior as Homer depicts it is normative. People come and go, greet each other, eat, fight, always in one and only one way. No character betrays a range of idiosyncratic traits, and no character has private moments or introspections that establish him or her as peculiar, as existing apart from the group. Instead each always speaks out to others and exists only in response to the presence of others. This feature has been described as the natural consequence of an oral culture, in which the poet needs an audience and an audience needs a poet simultaneously. There is a stern symbiosis there that the reading public, for whom the text exists independent of author or reader, will never know. Nonetheless the narrator has constructed a kind of wall of privacy and separateness for Achilles and Odysseus in the one's self-obsession and the other's paranoia which hints at the intimations of person that characters in later European narratives possess.

Typicality insists upon the immutability of things. Homer has created a vision of life as sacred, beyond time, and completed before it was begun. Here lies the source of the ancient Greeks' overabundant sense of irony, which lies at the very heart of the repeated telling of stories. After Hector tells Andromache that he knows Troy will someday be destroyed and the Trojans killed or sold into slavery, he nonetheless returns to the fight. There is no real struggle to escape what lies ahead, no comment of any sort. This is because in an oft-told tale the audience is complicit with the characters in a certain unconscious way. The audience presumes in the characters the same kind of foreknowledge that they themselves possess of the story. So Achilles can say in the ninth book that he has the choice of living to a ripe old age in Phthia ingloriously or dying young with glory on the plain of Troy and that he is going home, and then as the scene progresses—without any motive expressed—he cancels his announced plan to return to Phthia. The easy acceptance of this turnabout rests on the subliminal knowledge that Achilles is soon going to die at Troy. It is not only that the audience knows this, but repeated tellings of the story make them feel that he, Achilles, shares their knowledge. So it is that when Hector rebukes Paris for his seductive beauty and womanizing ways that made him bring Helen to Troy and caused the Trojans such disaster, Paris can reply, "Don't bring up to me the pleasing gifts of Aphrodite. As you know, there is no way to cast off whatever glorious gifts the gods may happen to give, although no one would willingly choose any of them" (3.64–66). Which is to say that the characters are all victims of the traditional story line and the narrator. What will happen, how they will act, what they are has long since been determined. Helen says the same thing when she observes of herself and Paris, "Zeus gave [us] an awful fate, so that we might be the subject of men's songs in the future" (6.356–57).

The oral poet and his audience must be together for the narration; they are, we might say, enslaved to each other. Together they concentrate on each moment as it is described, and then it is gone. There is no way, as there is in reading, to look ahead to see what happens or to go back to check what did happen. The poet compels belief, first because he claims to be telling a story given to him by the Muse ("Sing, goddess, the wrath . . ." [*Iliad* 1.1]; "Sing into me, Muse, the man . . ." [*Odyssey* 1.1]). As such he is simply the vehicle for the story, not its artificer. The audience cannot suspect him of manipulation or of trying to make meaning. Second, the poet overpowers his auditors with details; so rich is the texture of the narrative that they are forced to accept it as it comes to them. The manner is finally no different from that of any brilliant raconteur who holds his audience mesmerized, who plays upon them and captivates them with the flood of language coming from his mouth. It is important for present-day literates to remember the technique of oral poetry as they go back and forth in the text searching for meaning.

Whoever objects to the emphasis in these pages on the conditions of the oral performance, arguing first that we have a written text and second that sustained artistry of the kind found in these poems demands some kind of writing author, must confront the extreme unlikelihood of an extensive reading public, on the one hand, and the great awkwardness of the papyrus roll, on the other. It is important that whether or not the poet wrote his text, the manner of the narration derives from another kind of poet-audience relationship. Very likely, even if he did write the text down (whether as an aid to memory or as a means to achieve posterity for his otherwise only too winged words), the poet ordinarily recited his narrative. Writing on papyrus must have been a cumbersome affair; no less the reading of a roll. It is no wonder that the early specimens of demonstrably written poetry are all quite brief.

The physical limitations of early writing must always be in our minds when we think of books, reading, and composing. There were no scissors, paste, tape, staples, or word processors. Things once written probably remained as is, and if they needed correction, were simply contradicted at a later place; bits and pieces were not moved around. Readers had to unroll a document on which the writing was cramped and there was no word division or punctuation. The Greeks referred to each roll as a "book." But the division of the Homeric poems into what we now call books, which in modern novels are called chapters, was probably done centuries after the poems were written down. Certainly Homer did not compose the continuous narrative with these book divisions in mind. Whoever divided the poems into books tried to make natural divisions, that is, with the close of day or the cessation of some principal activity. More often than not, each book contains one major event. The quarrel and its immediate consequences in the first book, the visit to Achilles in the ninth book, the death of Patroclus in the sixteenth book, and the death of Hector in the twenty-second are examples that come immediately to mind. But the division is not always so easy; episodes sometimes spill over into a second book. Diomedes' big battle scene, for instance, begins at the opening of the fifth book, but continues until he meets Glaucus on the field of battle and exchanges armor with him, a scene that concludes at line 236 of the sixth book. The book divider would have had problems here, of course, because the principal matter of the sixth book is the scene at Troy when Hector returns there, motivated by his brother Helenus's suggestion to do so (77–101). The book divider apparently felt that the essential matter of the sixth book started with Helenus's suggestion and began his book with material that is part of Diomedes' story and that leads into Helenus's advice.

The oral style, which concentrates so much on each moment, sometimes ignores the overview and makes for contradictions or inconsistencies in the story which offend text readers. The keen-eyed, for instance, will find that King Pylaimenes, who dies in battle early on (5.576), returns to cry over his dead son (13.658). Other contradictions suggest to some a corruption in the text, but they are in fact the poet's creative response to his medium. For instance, in the first book of the *Odyssey* (1.271ff.) Athena gives Telemachus instructions that offer a direction to the plot for the next two or three thousand lines and hint at directions far beyond that. As a program, they may be followed, or, for suspense and surprise, they may be overturned. Athena's directions, however, seem to the reader to be so muddled that no action could possibly develop from them. She tells Telemachus to summon Penelope's suitors to a public meeting, to tell each to go home, and to send his mother home to her parents, who will arrange a new marriage for her. Then the goddess tells the lad to sail to the mainland to seek news of his father, and, if he hears that Odysseus is dead, to return to pay funeral honors to his father and to give his mother a new husband, and finally, after all this is done, to consider the means to kill off all the suitors who throng the palace. The reader's response to these directions is to wonder if he got them right; he reads them a second time and notes that they are utterly contradictory. That is a normal response from a literate person.

Athena's speech, however, is the creative act of an oral poet in shaping his story. Recounting events well known requires that every conceivable opportunity for suspense be explored; in so long a poem the poet needs to offer his audience a plot outline of sorts which will still give him room to maneuver. The poet of the *Odyssey* manages to do all these things in this speech. Directions for Penelope's impending marriage tell us that time is running out for the faithful queen; directions for the voyage of inquiry create further suspense, because upon its outcome somehow the fate of Telemachus and Penelope will be decided. In the farther future lies the tantalizing possibility that the suitors may be killed. After reading over Athena's speech, one might argue that the contradictions nullify any impact the speech might have. But the poet had no intention of its being read over. This is a speech clearly designed for recitation. Each successive item may contradict, but there is no going back to make sure. The speech generates uncertainty, crisis, suspense, and expectation; the plot is launched, and various solutions are hinted at.

Sometimes a scene seems to deny the narrative that has gone before. In the sixteenth book of the *Iliad* (49ff.) Achilles angrily refuses to return to the fight because he has been dishonored by Agamemnon, and yet the reader knows that in the ninth book Agamemnon has promised gifts and the return of Briseis as recompense for the insult he inflicted upon Achilles early in the story. Achilles speaks as though this promise never happened. Is one to understand that Achilles has forgotten the great scene in which he rejected the restitution proffered him? Did the poet forget it? It is an omission of this sort which moves some scholars to insist that the text of the *Iliad* is made up of several disparate narratives from different hands in different periods of time. This line of reasoning has also been used, successfully, to explain contradictions in the Bible. The persons who put the different pieces of it together were dealing with a sacred text, all versions of which were equally so and could not be omitted, however incongruent they were. The story of the *Iliad,* however, would have received very different treatment at the hands of its editor because, indeed, it is not sacred text at all but a story that will rise and fall for readers on the strength of its plausibility. It is highly unlikely that an editor would not have caught, as editors invariably do, a gaffe of these proportions. One is thus forced to fashion an aesthetic that accounts for such seeming inconsistencies.

The clue lies in the simile with which this episode in the sixteenth book begins (16.3–4). The simile is repeated from the beginning of the episode in the ninth book (9.14–15). The tears of first Agamemnon and then Patroclus are compared to the waters pouring from a mountain spring. The simile is used in the ninth book as Agamemnon despairs over what to do for the failing Achaean cause and then again in the sixteenth book when Patroclus returns to Achilles' tent to beg him to return to the fight. In both instances the Achaeans are in real danger of losing everything; in fact, the tide that turned against them, so well described in the eighth book, has not been stopped. In that sense, the action of the sixteenth book is as much a continuation or outcome of the eighth book as is that of the ninth. In the ninth book Agamemnon sends Odysseus, Phoenix, and Ajax to Achilles' tent to offer him gifts and honors as compensation and a kind of reinstatement into the role of principal warrior among the Achaeans and to beseech him to return to the battlefield. Odysseus reports Agamemnon's offer, and Achilles refuses to consider it. Phoenix then cautions Achilles against so unyielding a disposition, offering by way of instruction the story of Meleager, who refused to fight when his city was being besieged. Phoenix describes how there came to Meleager's chamber in supplication first the leading city figures, then his father and family, then his friends, and finally his wife, Cleopatra. Meleager denied the requests of the first three groups, yielding finally to the fourth entreaty, that of his wife, although, as Phoenix points out, and this is finally the point of his story, it was too late for Meleager to take any pleasure or receive any reward from his city for his actions. Yield we must, yield we inevitably will, but let it be when the time is ripe, Phoenix seems to be saying.

In the ninth book Achilles is asked three times, and three times he refuses. As has been observed in the folktales of many cultures, there is a certain fatal turn of events connected with the triad (in the sixteenth book of the *Iliad,* itself, for instance, Patroclus charges the Trojan walls three times, only to be struck down to his death thereafter). So, with Achilles' refusal of Ajax, the third speaker in the episode of the ninth book, the poet has poised his narrative for the fatal turn from three to four. But the plot of the *Iliad* is vast and complicated; the poet must retard the development of the story of Achilles until he has managed to introduce a number of other particulars.

When the simile is repeated at the beginning of the sixteenth book, the poet has brought his action back to the same place in which it was when Agamemnon despaired at the falling fortunes of the Achaeans. The same situation exists now—the same simile tells us this—and the same action is unfolding—that is, the petition of Patroclus flows directly from the events of the ninth book. The rehearsal for it was in the story told by Phoenix. Odysseus corresponds to the city officials who begged Meleager to return to the fight, Phoenix to his father and family, Ajax to his friends. It remains only for the equivalent of Meleager's wife to approach him, and this is Patroclus. Even the names—Cleopatra, Patroclus—seem to establish this correspondence. Patroclus's entreaty, then, finishes the action of the scene in which the three Achaean leaders came to Achilles' tent. Achilles' anger in the sixteenth book flows naturally from his obdurate stance in the ninth; Meleager is the model, his refusal the rehearsal. Achilles yields partially to Patroclus's entreaties, sending him out in his own armor and to his death. Like Meleager, he yields to the entreaties of the person closest to him; for Achilles, as well, it is too late. Caught up in the development of this particular story line, the poet cannot acknowledge in the sixteenth book the complexities of Odysseus's offer of reconciliation and Achilles' refusal of it. For him and his audience nothing has changed. Only a reader who could look back would note the discrepancy. Every reader does and complains, proof if ever it was needed that the poet, who was no dummy, never anticipated literacy as the fatal dust that would clog and slow the exquisite, finely tuned gears of his swift machine.

It is structure—the imposition of the Meleager story upon Achilles' refusals, the repetition of the similes—that provides the logic to these events rather than a psychological nexus common to contemporary fiction. Structure also provides the logic in the scene from the *Odyssey* when Penelope suddenly calls for the contest of the bow (19.570ff.). She has just been given every reason to believe that Odysseus will soon return. The stranger, Theoclymenus, prophesies that Odysseus is already in his homeland (17.165ff.). Odysseus in disguise offers powerful proof that Odysseus will shortly be on hand (19.165ff.). Penelope dreams a prophetic dream, which the disguised Odysseus interprets optimistically (19.525ff.). She who has worn out the years in fidelity to her absent husband, lamenting him every day, needs only to cling to her resolve a few days longer and salvation will come. Instead, at this very moment she suddenly decides to hold the contest among the suitors which will decide who will be her next husband. Moreover, a little previously (18.158ff.), Athena had put it into Penelope's head to descend and appear before the suitors, whom she has consistently insisted that she loathes, not only to excite them, but to ask them for gifts, something a woman might realistically ask only of men whom she truly thought to be her suitors. Critics either decry the improbability of this combination of events and attitudes or, to save the surface, assume that she has, in fact, secretly realized that the beggar is Odysseus. This latter option flies in the face of what is everywhere manifest in Homeric narrative: that the poet tells us everything, leaving no thought or gesture unremarked. It is instead the overwhelming logic of traditional story structures which dictates these events.

The poet is playing with a number of well-known storytelling devices to achieve a maximum climax here. One is the winning of the princess in a contest in which all but one of the suitors dies. To set his audience up for this device our poet has described Penelope in the traditional princess-suitor relationship when she descends the stairs and asks for gifts. Another is the arrival of the stranger underdog, who turns out to be Prince Charming in disguise. These two motives have been rehearsed in the episode at Scheria when the unknown and travel-worn Odysseus enters the contest with the young Phaeacian men and wins (8.109ff.). Nausicaa should have been the prize, except that our poet was not ready to let that motif fulfill itself. Finally there is the common device of the Husband Arriving in the Nick of Time. Nothing *but* the contest could come next.

Homeric epic poetry is too often criticized according to the criteria by which we judge nineteenth-century novels, partly because the first serious scholarship devoted to the *Iliad* and the *Odyssey* originated in the nineteenth century, and the novel of the time seemed on the surface of things to be the obvious analogue. Also, novelists often consciously attempt to bring over something of the epic manner into their prose narratives, as Fielding frequently remarks that he is doing in *Tom Jones*. But to talk about the modern novel in terms of ancient epic does not allow one to talk about ancient epic in terms of the novel. The modern prose novel, at least until well into the twentieth century, is marked by its fidelity to psychological realism and by naturalistic chronological development. The novelist strives to portray things as they are. This portrayal, however, is not true to the aesthetic of ancient epic, at least in the few pieces that survive to represent it. The narrative manner of the Homeric poems has much greater affinities with something like the early images of humans sculpted in marble, the young standing males known as the archaic *kouroi* (which, however, date from a century later). For these the sculptor approached his block of stone and carved out a lateral view and a frontal view without specific reference of one to the other. The head, for instance, does not curve around as heads do in nature so that the earlobe is on the same plane as the upper lip. The viewer looks at the statue from the side or from the front, and these are two very separate views. This tendency to look at the components has been well called by Ben Edward Perry the early Greek capacity for viewing things separately.

Every moment in the narrative, then, has its own integrity. Consider the two sets of duels in the *Iliad*, which a reader may feel are redundant. First, naturally enough, Paris and Menelaus, the lover and the cuckold husband, fight for possession of Helen (3.340ff.). The duel ends inconclusively, and battle breaks out in earnest among the soldiers of the two sides. Then, more than two thousand lines later, Hector and Ajax duel to settle the return of Helen and all her possessions (7.219ff.). This later duel is yet again the conventional duel between husband and lover or in more basic terms between suitors of the princess who will win the bride and her dowry. It was relevant to the scene in the third book and to the men who fought it then; it is not in the seventh book. Of course, it is only the reader who remembers the first duel when he encounters the second, only he who has the time to pause or the means to look back and compare. The auditor in an oral performance would be, as usual, completely engrossed in the narration. But whoever compares will see that the differences between the two are real. This time it is another kind of duel, again natural enough, a battle of strength between the most stalwart warrior on the Trojan side and someone his equal on the Achaean side. The two duels reveal two sorts of contesting men. The second duel always raised problems for scholars studying the poem even though so many lines of dactylic hexametric verse separate the duels. Still the aesthetic of the period demands that we experience the one and then the second without any precise reference to each other. The experience is like the many-faceted view that Picasso gives us in *Les Demoiselles d'Avignon*.

A more extreme form of dislocation is the lengthy description of the funeral of Achilles with which the *Odyssey* ends. It is an event that has almost nothing to do with the story line of the poem; even in antiquity the academic critics of the Hellenistic period objected to it. Yet the logic of structure has given it its place at the close of this story. The suitors have just been described going down to Hades, helter-skelter, without proper burials, in death as in life sloppy, violating the social norms. Throughout the poem their way of life has been contrasted to that of men of order such as Nestor, who conducts rites in the proper ways or the swineherd Eumaeus, who makes sandals with a craftsman's skill. Now the poet is ready to close his poem. In a poem that has followed a life from boyhood to traveling man to settled man to a glimpse of senile man (Odysseus's father, Laertes) a funeral is especially fitting at the end. A funeral serves naturally as a finale; a magnificent funeral, done properly (certainly the narrator does not spare the details), is the natural extension of the contrast between order and chaos elsewhere established. One might also remark that a funeral for Achilles while Odysseus still lives underscores the fundamental difference in view between the *Iliad* and the *Odyssey*. The description, as description, works perfectly where it is. Its irrelevance to the immediate story line is a reader's concern and that of a critic who derives his aesthetic from the wrong medium.

Nineteenth-century scholars who denied the fundamental coherence of the narrative of the *Iliad* as we now have it paid considerable attention to the placement and content of the second through the seventh books of the poem. It is here, particularly, that twentieth-century critics applaud the genius of the poet in arranging his material. He was able to do what he did, again because of the capacity for viewing things separately. He has taken scenes from quite different times in the long story of the Trojan War and fitted them into a continuous narrative bridge, thus providing us with all the background we need for his present story. One is not to imagine that he has snipped these scenes from other papyrus rolls and pasted them into his *Iliad* narrative. Instead, we must assume that they formed part of his repertoire. He could on other occasions sing of the early days of the war, when Paris stole Helen away, or when the Achaeans gathered the fleet together to sail against the Trojans. Here he provides whatever he needs as motivation and begins the episode.

In the second book the soldiers run out of control, making their way to the ships to go back home. After the anarchy has been halted, Nestor suggests that the army line up in formation, contingent by contingent, as a means to establish further control. There follows the so-called Catalogue of Ships, several hundred lines listing each unit, its home area, its leaders, and the number of ships in which they came. It is a passage that for the reader completely stops the action. The Catalogue, however, is interesting in itself, a *tour de force* of remembering names and fitting them into the dactylic line. It is panoramic and signals that the *Iliad* is going to be very large-scale. It is like a flashback montage seen through the soft-focus forward action of the present moment; the geography, the ships, and the words for long-distance movement all recall the departure of the fleet from Aulis, although the poet has established that the army muster is in fact taking place on the plain at Troy.

In the third book, Helen appears on the walls and identifies at the request of her lover's father, old King Priam, the major figures on the Achaean side doing battle on the plain below. Now, Priam after nine years of parleys and truce meetings (to one of which, indeed, he is about to go) must have met these men time after time. Yet it is as though they were appearing for the first time. This notion is reinforced by the fact that immediately hereafter the duel between Menelaus and Paris takes place, again an event that most likely occurred in the opening days of the war when the aggrieved duo must have tried to settle their claims before bringing in the entire armies. But the poet has made the scene follow the review of the troops as simply another event. We turn our attention to it, dismissing the dubious claims of the logic of cause and effect, surrendering instead to the storyteller's chronology, which comes in the phrase "and then." In the same way the poet presents a scene in the fourth book in which Agamemnon reviews the troops drawn up for battle, calling out to the various leaders and getting a variety of psychological reactions from them. Like Helen and Priam's discussion of the army leaders in the third book, this review is so selective that it does not accomplish anything in the way of a true review of the major *dramatis personae,* which in any case has already been made in the Catalogue. It seems, in fact, as though the poet has been excessive in his succession of introductory passages. That, again, is the reader's point of view. Just as the Catalogue in the second book portrayed a geographical context for the Achaean leadership at Troy and Priam's questions and Helen's answers focused on them as men of stature and physical power, Agamemnon's review describes their relationships.

The poet achieves many things at once with these passages. There is the subliminal sensation of the succession of events that lead into the Trojan War proper. Moreover, there is a sense of visual movement from distant homelands to a view from the walls at the men below and finally, more intimately, into a close-up, as it were, of the psychology of personal interaction. At the same time, the poet manages to establish the vastness of his narrative by a series of introductions that will lead him to the personal drama of Achilles and the woe he inflicts upon the Achaeans and the Trojans.

The introductions continue into the fifth, sixth, and seventh books, all of them presented as incidents naturally falling in place in a time sequence, one after the other. In the fifth book Diomedes is described in battle in what the Greeks called an *aristeia,* a moment of individual triumph. It is a scene that establishes the kind of role Achilles normally plays in this army, showing what he has forsaken, perverting his natural self by sulking in isolation in his tent. In the sixth book Hector goes from the battlefield to the city of Troy to speak with his mother, his wife, and his brother's paramour. In the seventh book after arranging another cessation of fighting between the two armies, he fights a duel with the great Ajax, which ends in a draw. Thereafter the Trojans in council debate returning Helen and all her possessions; when Paris refuses to give up Helen, the stage is set for the return to general fighting. The refusal is, of course, an obvious component of the scene with Helen on the walls because it follows naturally from the duel of her two lovers. Homer wanted another duel, however, and the refusal had to wait. Instead of the lovers in this second duel, however, Homer has introduced the principal Trojan warrior and one of the several important Achaean warriors, using the duel not only as his vehicle for the introduction of these two men but also as a star showcase for them, which will take the place of the *aristeia* with which he has just introduced Diomedes. The discussion of the offer to return Helen has been made by Homer into the natural response of a war-weary people in the tenth year of a war. It is now time to begin the plot line promised in the very first book when Zeus agreed to halt the Achaeans and to advance the Trojans as a favor to Thetis. Everything has been explained, everyone has been introduced, but in such a fashion as to leave a seamless web of episodes from the very moment of the quarrel until this point. Because the poet is secure in his audience's acceptance of the validity and integrity of each successive action, he does not waste time motivating and justifying them. His control is absolute.

Nowhere is this marvelous control more apparent than in the shaping of the narrative of the *Iliad,* something that becomes apparent to a reader studying the story, but would be hardly noticeable to a listener. The poem is a brilliant balance of symmetries, reinforcing the underlying tragic action—the sense of doom, of inevitable events, of men's lives shaped by an unseen hand. From the standpoint of narrative production, the instinct to episodic symmetries is simply another means by which the oral poet can hold long narratives together without the benefit of written notes, outlines, and the like. When he begins the narrative, he is shaping the end at the same time. A similar device is what is commonly called "ring composition," in which the narrator will return to the point from which he began an action or anecdote. An example is the way the poet gets into and out of the description of the naming of Odysseus and how he got his scar in the nineteenth book of the *Odyssey.* He begins by relating that the old nurse, Eurycleia, recognizes the scar when she begins to wash Odysseus disguised as a beggar. He then stops the action to introduce the story of the scar and picks up the action again by repeating that the old nurse identifies the scar (392–94; 467–68). These devices are helpful to the listening audience because they resituate them in the narrative, something a reader may do for himself by flipping back through the pages.

Symmetries appear both in minor actions and on a grand scale. Consider, for instance, the symmetries between the action of the first and twenty-fourth books. Action in the first begins with an old man (the priest of Apollo) coming to ransom his daughter (Chryseis) and ends with a divine group scene on Mount Olympus, to which Thetis has come from Achilles' side to speak with Zeus. Action in the twenty-fourth begins with a divine group scene on Mount Olympus followed by Thetis going from there to Achilles' side and ending with an old man (Priam) coming to ransom the body of his son (Hector). Similar patterning can be observed in the arrangement of the major episodes of the poem. For convenience I identify the episodes with the books in which they occur, but keep in mind that these book divisions are only an artificial imposition on a continuous story.

Just as the events of the first and twenty-fourth books seem to duplicate each other, so the principal thrust of the second book—that is, the organization and naming of the principals in the war, the Catalogue of Ships—is repeated in the twenty-third with the description of the athletic contests at Patroclus's funeral. At the funeral games once again, and for the last time in the poem, the major Achaean leaders appear as they compete in contest after contest. There is the same listlike quality to the narrative, the same ranking as to who was best, second best, and so on. The principal event of the third book is Helen and Priam's scanning the Achaean forces from the wall, followed by the abortive duel of Menelaus and Paris. In the twenty-second book, Priam and Hecuba watch from the walls in horror as their son, Hector, is chased and killed by Achilles, and moments later, his widow, Andromache, appears on the wall to bemoan her husband's fate. Here we have a particularly vivid instance of the way in which this storytelling device works: there is tragic irony in Hector, Achilles, and Andromache assuming the roles of Paris, Menelaus, and Helen. The fifth book introduces Diomedes in an *aristeia* that may be balanced by the action of the twentieth and twenty-first books, in which Achilles goes on a mad rampage of killing, a kind of surrealistic version of what Diomedes had done. One might find further tragic irony in the parallel between the courtly and life-preserving meeting of Glaucus and Diomedes on the field of battle with which Diomedes' *aristeia* ends and the duel to the death between Achilles and Hector, which ends Achilles' *aristeia*. The first concludes in the exchange of armor, the second in the defiling of Hector's body.

The sixth book brings the audience with Hector into Troy, where the poet introduces the women of Troy—the nurturant mother and a wife and her child—and describes a religious procession. These are also the emblems of a city, the mark of civilized behavior. This description is balanced in the eighteenth book by the long description of the new shield that the god Hephaestus makes for Achilles at the request of Thetis. The poet describes the decoration placed upon it by the god—a decoration that is an abstraction of a city at peace and a city at war. The decoration reflects one of the poles of woe in this poem: on the one hand, the tragedy of humankind expressed in the fall of a great city; on the other, individual man's personal tragedy as expressed in the story of Achilles. At the center of the *Iliad,* in book nine, is the episode in which Achilles refuses the embassy who beseech him to return to the fight. In book sixteen, his intimate friend and alter ego, Patroclus, goes out to fight and die in his stead. The latter episode is both a direct consequence of Achilles' action in book nine and a reflection upon man's inability to escape his mortality, something that may be said to be a preoccupation of Achilles in the ninth book.

The narrative of the *Odyssey* seems to have a much more linear progression, ending somewhere other than where it began. It is, among other things, a kind of parable of human life, beginning with an immature boy seeking his father, the commonplace act of a youth looking for his role model, then focusing on a traveling man whose adventures require physical prowess or quick wits or sexual skill. The story ends with the traveling man returned, outfitted with wife, son, and estate, confronting his aged, senile father with the horrible glance into the chronological mirror that only someone as courageous as Odysseus can take. As a story of growing up and old, the *Odyssey* naturally progresses from one point to another. It differs from the *Iliad* as well by having considerable fairy-tale material. There are witches such as Circe and ogres such as Cyclops. While Odysseus remains the saga hero recognizable from the *Iliad* and many of his colleagues reappear from that poem and the values are more or less those of the earlier poem, there remains something strange about the hero—he lies so much. The general paranoia of the piece is a quality often found in fairy tales, *Hansel and Gretel* being a prime example. Then, too, the narrative shares many characteristics with the Cinderella story. The hero, who disguises himself so disgustingly as a beggar, reminds one of the pitiful stepdaughter sitting in the hearth ashes. Athena is certainly a variant on the fairy godmother. When the underdog begins to try to string the bow (which will win him the queen) amid the sneers of the assembled suitors, the image of Cinderella trying on the glass slipper comes to mind. This is not a story pattern in which Achilles would be comfortable.

There is, to be sure, an occasional reminiscence of the symmetrical digressions of the *Iliad*. In the fourth book of the *Odyssey*, for example, Menelaus describes overcoming Proteus in order to find out about Odysseus—a tale that balances the description in the nineteenth book of the circumstances of Odysseus's acquiring his scar and his name. Both scenes relate directly to the central psychological truth of the hero of the poem. The first describes Proteus as a creature who, when approached, constantly changes his shape, only to reveal his true self when tightly grasped. The second describes Odysseus as physically scarred and having been given by his grandfather, Autolycus, the name Odysseus because of its etymological connection with the Greek verb meaning "I am hated."

The first two books of the poem set the narrative direction: Will Telemachus find his father (and grow up in the process)? Will Odysseus return and save Penelope from the suitors? Will the suitors get what's coming to them? Telemachus goes forth, learns of his father in the third and fourth books, comes home as an experienced young man in the fourteenth, and meets his father in the sixteenth. Commencing with the fourteenth book Odysseus makes his way back to Penelope and finally is at her side and in her bed by the twenty-third. In the seventeenth and eighteenth books the suitors are provoked into the extreme of misbehavior by Odysseus in disguise so that their retribution in the twenty-second will have the maximum moral savor to it. With Odysseus and Telemachus battling the suitors successfully in the twenty-second book, Odysseus in bed with Penelope in the twenty-third, and the suitors described in their chaotic descent into the underworld in the twenty-fourth, all the questions posed in the poem's opening scenes have been answered.

The narrative is accomplished in a highly economical fashion by the reiteration of one theme, the arrival and reception of the stranger. At this period it was the duty of anyone to accept a stranger into his home and wash, feed, and clothe him before asking his identity. In this way the basic vulnerability of all traveling men (in a world without restaurants, hotels, police, etc.) could be addressed before it was discovered that the stranger might in fact be from a family hostile to one's own. Thus was the common fact of humanity served. So important was this code that Zeus, the god of hospitality, was invoked to sanctify its custom. Using this convention of hospitality the poet has fashioned a narrative that in scene after scene turns on someone learning from strange environments while creating a persona suitable to whatever environment he finds himself in.

He uses the device of rehearsal equally well. Time after time events are prefigured in the earlier narrative. When, for instance, the naive and inexperienced Telemachus travels forth from home to learn of his father, he encounters at the courts of Nestor and Menelaus behavior and values that are completely new to him, having grown up, as he has, in isolation among the boorish, antisocial suitors. Somewhat later we find his father, traveling from one fairy tale creature to another, having to learn ways and places that are utterly foreign to a traditional epic hero. Odysseus's meeting with Nausicaa on the beach at Scheria at the beginning of the sixth book is a rehearsal for the erotic encounter between Odysseus and Penelope in the twenty-third book. (The poet uses the same simile in both settings, a highly unusual phenomenon.) Odysseus's participation in the contest with the derisive young men of the island in the seventh book is a rehearsal for the scene in the twenty-second book in which Odysseus triumphs over Penelope's suitors in stringing the bow. Perhaps nothing is so economically handled as the rehearsal of Penelope's behavior by way of the other women in the tale. The failed fidelity of Clytemnestra, the strength of character of Helen, Arete, and Anticleia, the controlling tendencies of Calypso, and the malign eroticism of Circe all make for a complicated, deep, and enriched anticipation of Penelope's behavior far beyond the everlasting tears of yearning for her long-departed spouse.

Whatever differences there may be between the two poems there remains a demonstrable quality common to both: the Homeric manner. It is found in the objectification of humanity through presentation of character types, the dehumanization of character, the abstraction of reality by the rendering of detail in formula, and the persuasive surface meaning achieved by the brilliance of the language. Homer calls out to the Muse to tell him the story and thereafter disappears from the narrative except to complain twice that he has not strength enough to tell the myriad details which in each instance his story demands. Thus the story tells itself and demands absolute obedience. It has been said that the *Iliad* and *Odyssey* need no interpretation. The Muse, who is the daughter of Memory, has told everything there is to tell. Many object to what seems to be a denial of any subtlety in these poems. Of course, Homer does not tell us everything, and we are free to interpret as we wish. Homer, however, gives the *illusion* of telling everything. He overpowers us with detail and alternative stories; the characters bombard us with their observations on everything that takes place. The audience is helpless before their onslaught. This is the poetry of oral presentation: the poet knows his audience does not have the text and cannot reflect. He keeps at them—hectoring, seducing, amusing, but always demanding their submission to his narrative. In that sense he tells them everything. This is the dread inevitability of the Homeric utterance, pretending to be, as it does, and indeed is, the final truth of history in a world that knew no writing.

CHAPTER THREE

The Heroic World

And when the earth had covered over that generation, then Zeus, son of Kronos, made still another, a fourth, upon the much nourishing earth, a juster, braver, godlike race of heroes who are called demigods, the race previous to ours upon this broad earth. Evil war and dread battle killed some of them at seven-gated Thebes, in the land of Cadmus, fighting for Oedipus's flocks, and some, when they had been brought in ships across the great gulf of the sea to Troy for the sake of the fair-haired Helen; and there death's end came over and covered them. But to the others, Zeus, son of Kronos, gave a place to live apart from men at the ends of the earth and there they dwell, calm in heart, in the islands of the Blessed, by the Ocean's deep, happy heroes . . .

Hesiod, *Works and Days* 156–72

Contemporary scholars generally agree that the Homeric poems as we have them are the product of the eighth century B.C. But because the poems themselves make reference to objects as old as the Mycenaean world and as recent as the eighth century, they are not a very reliable index to the times. While archaeological evidence reveals something about the material remains—the houses, the art, the utensils used in religious rites, and so on—there is no other documentary evidence for the world in which the *Iliad* and *Odyssey* were created than what the text has to tell us. The poems, however, present a mélange of evidence, as one would imagine, of poetry that seems to have been shaped over a period of perhaps five hundred years.

Some critics detect a demonstrable passage of time in the depiction of institutions from one poem to the other. For instance, one can say that the *Iliad* describes a power structure dominated by a monarch (Agamemnon) in some kind of symbiotic relationship with other, lesser kings. Despite his power, this overlord is dependent enough upon his colleagues to have to take advice, abuse, and dissension from them as no absolute monarch would. Menelaus, Nestor, and

Odysseus of the *Odyssey,* on the other hand, suggest country squires, each absolute in a fertile farming valley or on a seagirt island, no longer dependent upon a great king in far off Mycenae. Set against that portrayal, however, is the fact that the suitors must marry Penelope to become king. As a minor, Telemachus does not stand in succession. This idea suggests a much earlier period when royal authority passed to males on a matrilinear basis (there seems to be a parallel in the story of Oedipus, who becomes king at Thebes by marrying the queen, Jocasta).

The sometimes humorous or ironic portrayal of deity, as in the quarrel on Mount Olympus in the first book of the *Iliad* or the buffoonery of divine battle fighting in the fifth and twenty-first books, implies for some critics an idea of godhead far removed—whether in place or time—from the stern god of law and order that Hesiod tries to establish, or even from the Zeus of the *Odyssey,* who upholds the principle of human responsibility in a world of right and wrong (1.32ff.). Achilles' passionate analysis of the exploitation that Agamemnon practices upon his subject kings (*Iliad* 1.149ff.), echoed by the commoner Thersites (2.225ff.), seems to other scholars to betray a social critic of a poet who lived at a time when the age-old privileges of monarchy were no longer exempt from examination or even contempt. The women of the *Odyssey* are so bold, free, and dominant compared to their passive, dependent, shadowy sisters of the *Iliad* that some would like to imagine that the poem was composed for a female audience or in a time when the role of women was considerably enlarged and appreciated in the general society. All these hypotheses are interesting and to varying degrees attractive. At the very least, they make one rethink the poems.

In the past century Near Eastern texts have been discovered which show similarities to both the Homeric and the Hesiodic poems. These force the question whether the poets of the Greek tradition were influenced by these Near Eastern exemplars and, if so, when, or whether, more in the Jungian manner, the human mind—more likely here, the male mind—formulates certain problems in typical ways. Critics are particularly struck by resemblances between the two Homeric poems and remnants of a poem that dates from the third and second millennium, fragments of which have been found in the Sumerian, Akkadian, and Hittite languages among others. These have been pieced together into a tolerably consistent running narrative to which the name *Epic of Gilgamesh,* or just plain *Gilgamesh,* is attached. It is the story of King Gilgamesh, a historical personage, as we know from inscriptions, who despairs of leaving any mark of himself to recall him to mind after his death. His is the familiar dilemma of a man who recognizes his own mortality while at the same time he lives his life as though it will have no end. This dilemma is symbolized in Gilgamesh, as it is in Achilles, by having a divine mother and a mortal father, making him so close to and yet cut off from immortality. He acquires a male friend, Enkidu, with whom he has as close a relationship, says the narrator, "as man and wife." These two embark on a series of adventures, the principal one being the killing of the giant Humbaba.

Shortly after they kill the giant, Enkidu dies, and Gilgamesh sinks into utter despair. He sets out on a long journey that takes him through the underworld to meet the antideluvian Utnapishtim. Here he learns that he cannot hope for immortality. Heartbroken, much depressed, Gilgamesh returns home where he dies and is buried with suitable pomp and circumstance.

There are some tantalizing parallels. The mourning Achilles and Gilgamesh are each compared to a lioness bereft of her cub (*Iliad* 18.318ff.; Assyrian recension of the Gilgamesh story, tablet 8, column 2). Elsewhere the ghost of the dead Enkidu comes to Gilgamesh exactly as the dead Patroclus appears to Achilles. Gilgamesh's mother, Ninsun, like Thetis, mourns for her short-lived son. Calypso and Circe, seeking sexual favors from Odysseus, are like the goddess Ishtar, who invites Gilgamesh into her bed.

Grander correspondences would begin, of course, with the Gilgamesh-Enkidu and the Achilles-Patroclus relationships, which seem so similar as to require direct influence, were it not for the consideration that such a relationship seems to be essential to the masculine person, especially in travel or adventure stories. Dante and Virgil, Don Quixote and Sancho Panza, Huckleberry Finn and Jim, Batman and Robin immediately come to mind. Of course, these may be no more than variations of the tradition rather than an innate disposition to cast masculinity in twosomes.

Odysseus's wanderings are paralleled by those of Gilgamesh. When the former describes his disastrous encounter with the Cyclops and with Circe and the journey into the Underworld to speak with Tiresias, who prophesies to him the course of the rest of his life, he is following the Gilgamesh story relatively closely. The enduring enmity Odysseus arouses in Poseidon by wounding the Cyclops parallels the divine hostility visited upon Enkidu and Gilgamesh following the killing of Humbaba.

It is hard to know whether to emphasize a special relationship between the Gilgamesh story and these two Homeric stories. The precise parallels incline one to do so. It may be more to the point, however, to say that the poets were in every instance employing story lines and story elements common to the entirety of the eastern Mediterranean for many centuries. Scholars have gone further afield, collecting from all periods and all places specimens of adventure narrative centered upon a hero. There are remarkable parallels in technique and story.

The fundamental similarity in attitude prompts the designation of this kind of poetry as heroic poetry; it is considered to reflect what is called "the heroic age," conceived as a kind of inevitable stage in human history. Hesiod is the first to give real expression to the idea in his description of the heroic age with which this chapter begins, but the narrator of the *Iliad* already implies as much when he describes Diomedes lifting a stone, "a big thing, which not even two men could carry, such as mortal men are nowadays" (*Iliad* 5.303f.). Elsewhere he ascribes such a feat to Hector and to Aeneas. By making the action inaccessible to his audience, the poet breaks the historical continuity between the present of his contemporaries and the time of his narration. Perhaps the same mentality lies behind his notice that the great defensive wall the Achaeans built about their ships was washed away at the end of the war and the landscape returned to its original look (*Iliad* 12.12–18). In a sense the poet is assigning his story to never-never land—not, however, as emphatically as the poet of the *Odyssey*, who places his hero in the fabulous land of magic and fantastics.

Viewed this way, the poems cannot easily be defined as expressions of a particular time or place or poet or audience. In this way they become less specifically Greek. The abundance of detail in the *Iliad* and the *Odyssey*, which gives the poems a spurious historicity, should not blind the reader to the fact that, just as in the Gilgamesh story abstracted, transcendent action is being described. In various societies the oral poet is often likened to a seer; in ancient Greece Homer was sometimes called "the divine poet." Not only was he the master of a people's history when there was no writing, he was also their visionary, their means to project themselves in relation to each other and in relation to nature and the universe that surrounded them.

The *Iliad* begins with a quarrel, the opposition of strengths and ambitions. The issue—whether Agamemnon, deprived of his concubine, will go without any emblem of his superiority until the army manages to find him another or whether he will take one from a subordinate chieftain, thereby publicly emphasizing the latter's inferiority—is crucial in a society where a sense of self comes from external substantiation. Anthropologists call this kind of culture a shame culture. Others consider it the essence of a preliterate, oral society in which every idea, emotion, and action is externalized and public, not internalized, as is the experience of reading people. Thus Agamemnon's threat to seize Briseis from Achilles strips the latter of the validation of his public self, which is, we may say, his only self. In fact, Achilles himself begins a challenge to this public self in his angry rebuke to the army leader when he cynically analyzes hierarchy, worth, and material rewards (1.148ff.). Achilles' retreat to the isolation of his tent is the natural emotional response of someone who demands to be valued. It is also a perfect metaphor for the vacancy of soul brought on not only by his being deprived of public status but also by his very own denunciation of the system that gives his life shape.

The quarrel can be resolved only by someone's yielding. Nestor, trying to be the peacemaker, tells Achilles that although he is the stronger, he must acknowledge Agamemnon as finally the more powerful. This is the bitter truth of life which in so many guises is the central theme of the *Iliad*. The poet is quick to repeat a quarrel twice over to make this idea stick in his audience's minds. In the second book he has a man of the army assembly, a commoner named Thersites, speak out against Agamemnon in much the same language that Achilles had used. Odysseus strikes him with a staff, and Thersites tearfully and silently yields as his fellows snicker.

Between these two scenes of human quarreling the poet presents an Olympian version with Zeus, Hera, and Hephaestus playing Agamemnon, Achilles, and Nestor. Zeus, in an ugly show of strength threatens his quarreling wife, who shrinks in fear. It is a burlesque of the human scene. For the immortals, though, such a quarrel is no more than a diversion, while it is crucial to the humans. Nothing matters finally for those who live forever; it is death that quickens the hearts of men to need, demand, and quarrel. Paradoxically, as the narration of the *Iliad* shows, it is death that makes for anguish over yielding, and yet it is to death that all men must yield. As Thersites succumbs to Odysseus's sturdy stick, as Hera cringes before her menacing husband, so finally will events force Achilles to relent.

Achilles' self-exile leads him to self-examination so that when the deputation comes in the ninth book to exhort him to return to the fight, he has moved onto another plane of consciousness. It is not that he has changed, but rather that he is more aware. Odysseus lists Agamemnon's splendid gifts that will restore to Achilles the public esteem that defines his superiority. Achilles rejects them in a speech of great passion in which he makes the famous observation that "cattle and sheep are to be had by any rustler, horses and tripods are common enough prizes, but a man's life, once it has passed out beyond the barrier of the teeth of his mouth, cannot be won or captured back again" (9.405ff.). He tells his visitors then of the choice he must make between going home to die in old age ingloriously or of dying young and gloriously on the field of battle at Troy.

Of course, he will go back to fight and thus to die because the logic of heroism finally gives him no option. Heroism is forged in the contest, which defines a man's excellence and shows his true potential. Homer calls this realization of a person *arete,* for which we might use the English word "quality." Homeric characters are defined by their function, by their actions, and by their public reception, as we have seen, rather than by some internal idiosyncratic character or personality. A warrior hero, then, will realize himself, will demonstrate his *arete,* upon the field of battle. The *Iliad* is full of descriptions of individual heroes triumphing over a mass of the foe; such a moment of superiority is called an *aristeia.* At that moment the hero is striving hardest physically and mentally to surmount whatever competing obstacle lies before him; he is striving to be the best (*arist-* is the root of "best" in Greek). Although left unsaid, it follows that this moment of fullest realization, when the quality or *arete* of a valiant male warrior is most apparent, comes in the supreme, final contest with death. In this sense Patroclus's *aristeia* in the sixteenth book is the ideal one.

Death becomes, then, the measure for *arete.* So it is that the *Iliad* concentrates so much on the battle, for only on the field will the participants to this drama find sufficient dimension. The fighting narrative, the *androktasiai* ("the man-killings"), as they are called, must have been a very popular part of oral saga, for they occur in the *Iliad* far more often than one would think necessary to establish a point or convey a mood. The formulaic language is never more prominent than in the *androktasiai.* These must have been the staple of epic tradition, the first and best learned element upon which each apprentice oral poet built his own creations. However formulaic, the battle narratives are explicit in describing how men do the killing, how men are wounded and die. The spearing, the stabbing, the twitching of hands, the failing limbs, the stumbling, the shrieks, the blood, and the gore are never far from the story throughout the poem.

The poet makes his audience empathize with these warriors by interspersing brief anecdotal facts about the victim or the victor. For example, he may describe where a man was born, what kind of marriage he had or what material wealth he left behind at home. These anecdotes also work in counterpoint to the obsession with death that pervades this poem. Their very subject matter is the stuff of optimism, the triumph of life over death, so rarely encountered in the narrative. The same optimism is found consistently in the character of Hector, who is the embodiment of the social and civilized world of the city, which stands in opposition to the army camp of the Achaeans. He is the only hero warrior in this poem who is portrayed with his infant child, that commonplace expression of humankind's optimistic projection of a future. Corollary to this optimism is his misguided faith in himself, which leaves Hector outside the walls when Achilles makes his last, fatal charge, and earlier made Hector exult all too triumphantly over the dying Patroclus. Much earlier, in the sixth book, as he takes leave of Andromache (at what is their final meeting), he can acknowledge that "I know in my heart . . . that someday there will come a time when sacred Troy shall perish and Priam and his people" (6.447ff.). He is no fool, but lives as most men must—with expectation.

The mood of the *Iliad* is painful, bitter, desperate. At the very end Achilles offers to Priam a description of the universe in its relation to humankind. The gods, he says, live in serenity while they plan for mortal man to live in sorrow (24.525ff.). There are two jars at Zeus's doorstep, one filled with evil and one filled with good. Zeus sometimes bestows from the jar of evil, sometimes mixes the good with the evil. Achilles' words portray a universe that is arbitrary, indifferent, and the source of human pain. Man is defenseless in such a world; as Glaucus says, man is like the leaves of the trees, which the wind scatters to the ground and the spring renews upon the trees (6.145ff.).

The similes clustered so prominently in the battle narratives most frequently compare human action to that of animals, predator and prey. As the lion or wolf naturally and inevitably preys upon the deer or sheep, so one man will fall upon and kill another. As Zeus says, when he grieves for Achilles' horses, who must ride the battlefield and stay so close to human suffering:

You poor things, why did I give you to Lord Peleus,
a mortal man, you who are ageless and deathless?
Just to have misery down among wretched mortals?
For nowhere at all is there anything more sorrowful than man
of all that breathes and creeps upon this earth.

[17.433ff.]

Zeus may feel sorrow for mortals at this point. He may mourn for the death of his son Sarpedon, he may regret the death of Hector, Athena may come to earth to restrain Achilles in his rage at Agamemnon, and various gods may join in the human battle, but the final devastating truth of this poem is that the gods are onlookers, indifferent or impotent, as they watch the human spectacle.

The action of the poem turns on Achilles' resistance to the logic of heroic *arete*—by extension resistance to the idea of death—and his eventual submission to it. In the ninth book it is the old man, Phoenix, a stand-in for Nestor, also a reminder to Achilles of his old father, who counsels Achilles to yield to Agamemnon. The advice is particularly fitting coming from an old man who bears witness in his body and manner to the burden of old age to which all mortals must submit. Achilles' refusal to yield in the ninth book results in the death of his companion, Patroclus, in the sixteenth. In this narrative style in which everything is external, the poet has created the intimate best friend as an alter ego, whose death becomes the intimation to Achilles of his own. Patroclus's death—conceived perhaps as Achilles' deep, inner sense of his own mortality—motivates Achilles' return to battle and plunges him into a surreal frenzy of killings that fill the twentieth and twenty-first books. These are the acts of a desperate man, crying to make meaning when his best friend's death has rendered life meaningless. Ironically, as Achilles assumes his armor at the close of the nineteenth book and prepares to go out to the fight, the poet is also enclosing him in the formulaic language of heroic action. He has returned to where he began. This impression is all the more emphatic because Achilles' reentry into battle, which culminates in the duel scene with Hector, stands in symmetry with the fifth book *aristeia* of the hero Diomedes, which culminates in the sixth book meeting with Glaucus, the two scenes being thus bound in a kind of inevitable nexus.

Diomedes' *aristeia* is the longest in the poem. The poet is in the habit of developing a typical theme or scene completely once and subsequently suggesting the form with a minimum of content. Here he establishes Diomedes as the typical hero. He is the measure for the absent Achilles. Diomedes enters battle, his shield and helmet lit by fire, the sign of his superiority. Here as elsewhere he is called "the best of the Achaeans." To some he seems a god (183ff.), and quite rightly. So superlative is his performance that he is allowed a glimpse of the divine world. Athena, who acts as his charioteer, removes the obscuring mist from his eyes so that he can see the gods in the field. He wounds Aphrodite and Ares. Moreover, Diomedes talks to Athena in the language of equals. Yet he prudently yields to the gods' superiority (818) when after three times (surely the enchanted three) he tries a fourth time to rush the stricken Aeneas (436ff.) and Apollo stops him ("Don't try to rival the gods in your designs" [440–41]).

Diomedes has already demonstrated his instinct for yielding in the fourth book when Agamemnon harshly and unjustly rebukes him for unseemly delay before the fight. Instead of quarreling with the leader, as the poet shows both Diomedes' charioteer and Odysseus doing (4.411ff.; 403ff.; 349ff.), Diomedes replies with accommodation and understanding. Diomedes is the norm from which Achilles tries to depart. As Achilles returns to do battle in the twentieth and twenty-first books, as he becomes a construct of the formulaic language describing an *aristeia,* which is set in dynamic symmetry with the much earlier *aristeia* of Diomedes, one may say that he is also yielding to the crushing imperatives of the language and technique of narration in this poem. Formulaic language is destiny.

In the nineteenth book, when Achilles' anguish over his beloved friend's death has turned to relentless fury and he seeks to lead the Achaean troops out supperless against the Trojans, Odysseus encourages a respite for food:

> Men quickly get their fill of battle
> and the harvest is slight, the bronze
> sword cuts mostly straw on the land;
> Zeus, the battle steward, weights the scales so.
> The Achaeans can't mourn the dead with their belly
> for too many fall each day, one after another
> —when does anyone rest from this labor?—
> but we must bury the man who dies,
> keeping a stout heart, after crying for him all day;
> whoever survives this hateful battle, let him
> turn his mind to food and drink, so that
> we will fight the enemy strongly hereafter.
> [221–32]

This passage is echoed in the twenty-fourth book, providing the most telling indication of Achilles' acceptance of the inevitable. At the beginning of the twenty-fourth book his mother, Thetis, at a command from Zeus comes to Achilles to urge him to give up Hector's body. This he agrees to do with a weary air: "So be it; Priam can bring ransom and take the body, if Zeus so urgently wants it" (139–40). The mood is passive resignation. Later, when Priam arrives, he goes up to Achilles and "kissed the hands, the man-slaying hands which had killed so many of his sons for him" (478ff.). It is this act that causes the great hero to break into tears, thinking of his own father. Priam's gesture makes meaning in a meaningless world and finally redeems Achilles. For shortly thereafter, when Priam has sunk into his own torpor of woe, grieving for his son, it is Achilles who urges him to eat, recalling Niobe, who lost so many of her children and yet in her grief proceeded to eat. In this echo of Odysseus's speech in the nineteenth book the poet brings Achilles around to an act that shows his positive acceptance of inevitability. Recent studies of the psychology of terminally ill patients show striking similarities of feeling with that which Homer gives to Achilles. Denial and isolation, anger, bargaining, depression, and acceptance, in that order, pass through the dying person's mind during his final days. These are Achilles' feelings as well. As the story unfolds, Achilles comes to meet his death.

The world of the *Odyssey,* by contrast, is one in which the act of eating is described often, fully, indeed lovingly. Food, sex, and travel have replaced death and destruction. Witches and giants have taken over from heroes on the field of battle. The central character, freed from the ethical constraints of heroic saga, is like a Bronze Age Cinderella as he, a shipwrecked wanderer, at times assisted by a benign goddess, at length triumphs over malignant forces to win the queen by succeeding at the impossible.

And yet it is in the character of Odysseus that there is the greatest consistency between the two poems. In the *Iliad* he is described by Antenor as someone who could strike a deceptive pose of inadequacy (3.216ff.). The narrator recounts Odysseus's cruel deception of Dolon: Odysseus told the young fellow his life would be spared if he told what he knew, and thereafter Odysseus killed him (10.383ff.). Agamemnon rebukes Odysseus at one point with the words, "you, sir, adept at chicanery, with the eye on your profit" (4.339). Achilles begins his reply to Odysseus's speech in the ninth book with the ambiguously directed observation: "I shall tell it all as it comes to me spontaneously; hateful as the Gates of Hell to me is the fellow who says one thing and conceals another thought in his heart" (9.312f.).

In the *Odyssey* Odysseus lies in almost every instance when he is asked his identity; he is not afraid to humble himself in the disguise of a beggar to achieve his ends. He is quite indifferent to the suffering and death of his crew, which he himself causes, and he is swift and cruel in his revenge upon the suitors and their hangers-on. Like his one-time companions Agamemnon and Achilles, he is a heroic warrior—a model of conventional action and speech, a creature of a shame culture who yet has the flexibility of character to pass time with the likes of Circe and Calypso, not to mention outwitting the dread Cyclops.

His capacity for, nay, need for, deceit works together with the constant theme of arrival in this poem, which requires every stranger to identify himself. In scene after scene everyone invents himself anew. The question and the identification play off the same mentality that the preliterate shame culture of the *Iliad* imposed upon its characters—a man is what he appears to be and says he is to the people who surround him and in a sense bear witness to him. The poet of the *Odyssey,* however, seems to be preoccupied with, among other things, making poetry and thereby charges the identification scenes with a special emphasis. By presenting his characters in situations where they must identify themselves he provides them with the means to become poets creating their own narrative.

Poets are given an important place in the narrative. The poet Demodocus is described joining the assemblage at Scheria and entertaining the Phaeacians after dinner with episodes from the Trojan War. One of his amusing songs is quoted entire in that scene (8.266ff.). That poets were important personages we may infer from the fact that it was the court poet to whom Agamemnon entrusted his wife when he left for Troy (3.265ff.). In the earliest scene at Ithaca the poet Phemius sings a song describing the homecoming of the warriors from Troy. The poet of the *Odyssey* (which is, of course, also a poem of homecoming) seems to be working himself into his text in a self-conscious way.

The sense of a poet looking at his material is magnified in an interesting literary discussion between Penelope and Telemachus (1.337ff.) which is provoked by Phemius's song. She asks the singer to desist, suggesting that he is certainly capable of singing many another song, because the theme of homecoming reminds her of her own great loss. In his reply Telemachus makes two important observations: poets ought to let their minds lead them wherever they will, and an audience will always give a heartier reception to what has novelty for them. Both ideas seem to contradict what is so often assumed to be the truth of oral epic poetry, that the stories are so traditional and the narrative elements so conventional as to deny the kind of individual originality and novelty to which Telemachus seems to be alluding. The poet of the *Odyssey* seems to be putting his audience on notice that he is very much in control. He does so again when Odysseus, as he finishes his tale of the wanderings by taking his audience back to the island of Calypso where he had begun his narration, remarks, "But why should I tell you these things? It was only yesterday that I went through the story in this very house for you and your wife, and it is hateful to me to repeat a story once it's been well done" (12.450ff.).

There are even suggestions that he is playing off the *Iliad*, the poem itself, not the story, when he begins his poem with Zeus's observation about human responsibility for suffering, which exactly contradicts the ethos of the jars-of-Zeus speech Achilles gives in the twenty-fourth book of the *Iliad*. He has the poet Demodocus sing of a quarrel between Odysseus and Achilles (8.75) which, because we have next to no other evidence that this is part of the Trojan story, may well represent the author of the *Odyssey* reminding his audience of the inherent competition between two such mighty poems, his and the *Iliad*.

One would like to believe the poet had the *Iliad* in mind in the witty moment when Odysseus, disguised as a beggar, is about to manufacture for the swineherd Eumaeus a fictive account of his meeting with Odysseus. When Eumaeus protests that he will probably be making it up in order to get a good meal, the beggar responds, "Hateful as the gates of hell to me is the man who tells lies because he is so poor and needy" (14.156–57). The first line occurs only once elsewhere, in the *Iliad* in Achilles' reply to Odysseus (quoted above). The close reader will remark upon the repetition and enjoy the irony deriving from both the immediate context and the overall difference in sensibility between the two poems. (Some will argue, of course, that to accept it as anything other than a coincidence is to deny the incapacity peculiar to preliterates of moving from text to text; others would say that the rebuke is so significant in the *Iliad* that any poem coming thereafter might easily play to it.)

The *Odyssey* poet also seems to parody saga narrative—for instance, in the military adventures described at 14.462ff., which have been called mock-heroic, or in the peculiar *androktasia* when the suitors are killed (22.255–329). Some critics remark that the charming scene of Telemachus in impotent rage dashing the speaker's scepter to the ground (2.80) during his quarrel with the suitors is an allusion to the same action by Achilles in his quarrel with Agamemnon (*Iliad* 1.245). Those critics who hold to the most severe kind of oral poetic aesthetics will, of course, gnash their teeth in the face of such a notion.

All these passages suggest a poet who is self-conscious about his narrative art. The poet's self-consciousness is reinforced by the frequently repeated theme of identification in which fictive biographies are given to the unsuspecting. It begins with Athena's arrival at Ithaca, where she fabricates for the suspicious Telemachus an identification of herself as a human. Odysseus gives four fictitious accounts of himself once he is back on Ithaca—to Athena, to the swineherd, to the suitors, and to Penelope. They present an interesting contrast to the lengthy account he gives the Phaeacians of himself and his travels. As many have noted, the events of his fictitious autobiographies parallel each other as well as events in the travel narrative and share the patina of historicity with which the Trojan saga glistens. The travel stories, on the other hand, which occupy the whole of books nine through twelve, take place by and large among humanly implausible beings—the giant Cyclops, for example, or the witch Circe with her magic wand.

The obviously fabulous quality of these tales is enhanced by the narrator's subtly equating Odysseus with a poet. At the close of book eight King Alcinous has lost his patience with the elusive guest who will not reveal his name. Odysseus's uncontrollable grief at Demodocus's song gives him the opening he wants. He begins: "Now then, do not be devious in your answers to what I am about to ask you. It is far better for you to speak out" (8.548f.). The pent-up curiosity of Odysseus's host is dramatized by Homer in Alcinous's long question to the stranger. The suspense is then echoed in Odysseus's eighteen-line introduction to his answer. Everything is poised for a great recital. Odysseus's initial reply emphasizes the majesty and artistry of what he will say. He talks of bards and the pleasure they bring people, which is the greatest joy of banquets. Slowly he builds to the revelation that he is Odysseus. The prelude is so artfully contrived, so obviously and consciously so, that Odysseus seems actually to be supplanting Demodocus. The banquet is finished, Demodocus ceases, the audience remains, and another entertainer begins. Odysseus's propensity for lying raises our suspicions. Even Alcinous seems subconsciously suspicious when later he compliments Odysseus's ability ("You have told it all out in sequence with skill, just like a bard" [11.368]) and remarks how unlike the world's many liars and cheats Odysseus is. Eumaeus echoes this suspicion later on.

The paradox lies in the fact that the travel tales are supposed to be true and yet the poet hedges them in with so many suspicions, whereas the fictive autobiographies, demonstrably false, are in fact mosaics of elements true to Odysseus's own personality and situation. In each of his false autobiographies Odysseus makes himself a prince, a family man, a victim, and a man capable of unheroic action. The psychological facts of these stories fit so well with Odysseus's actual character traits that the hero is finally paradoxically creating truth out of fiction. The poet shows Odysseus exercising the same control over his fictive narratives that he himself does.

Furthermore, certain elements of the stories are veiled allusions to events of the travels. For instance, going to Dodona to consult the oracle of Zeus represents the underworld journey to Tiresias. One sometimes has the impression that the poet is trying to establish the distinction between fiction and reality, something the repeated shaping of traditional stories must have established, particularly in the mind of an especially inventive poet. Hesiod, a short time later, can say that the Muses told him: "We know how to tell the truth and we know how to tell lies as though they were the truth."

The story of the *Odyssey* turns largely on the theme of investigation and identification. Telemachus, the impotent youth, mournfully declares to the disguised Athena, "Nobody really knows his own father" (1.216). The subplot that centers on the lad has to do with his voyage into the world to find news of his father, that is, to find out who his father is and thus to find himself through gaining a role model, the common masculine process of growing up. He does this with visits to Pylos and Sparta, where his father's old associates tell him anecdotes about Odysseus and recount whatever they know of his present situation. When the poet returns to Telemachus much later in the fifteenth book as subplot and plot are about to merge in the reunion of father and son, he demonstrates that Telemachus has matured from what he has learned in his travels by placing him in a commanding position for the first time. He is confronted by a fugitive, Theoclymenus, who enters the narrative for no other reason than to ask Telemachus for protection and passage on his ship. When Telemachus becomes his protector, the boy becomes a man and assumes all the powers, responsibilities, and privileges of heroic manhood.

Odysseus's travels are to some extent shaped by his curiosity. His men fall victim to the Lotus eaters because Odysseus sent out a party to learn what kind of men inhabited the land (9.87); he nearly loses his own life because he goes to investigate the Cyclop's homestead (9.172ff.); he sends some of his crew to their deaths when he commands them to reconnoiter the Laestrygonians (10.100); when they are on Circe's island and he sees smoke rising from a distant clearing which calls for an investigation, the crew, remembering the catastrophes his previous bouts of curiosity have brought to them, break into tears, but, as Odysseus says, "All that grieving didn't get them anywhere" (10.202).

Once Odysseus is back on the shores of his native island, his progress is marked by a series of revelations that successively reintegrate him into the context and persona that make up the king of Ithaca. These scenes are astonishingly subtle and complete in what they reveal about the central figure in this poem. First, his homeland, which Athena had rendered unrecognizable, is made apparent to him immediately following the epiphany of the goddess herself. These two events are the direct result of his lying to the goddess, who, initially disguised herself, asked him his identity on the beach. Her words to him reveal what it is that distinguishes Odysseus from other men and wins divine favor: "It would take someone quite cunning and deceitful who could surpass you in trickery. . . . Stubborn, clever, never tired of falsehood, . . . you are of all mortals best at planning and speaking. . . . I cannot ever desert you when you suffer because you are so smooth, so intelligent, so sensible" (13.291ff.).

Thereafter, at the command of Athena, who transforms him from his beggarly disguise into a man of commanding stature and beauty (just what any young man dreams the father he does not know will look like!), Odysseus reveals himself to his son, Telemachus. The simile that describes their reunion (they cry as birds cry whose young have been stolen from the nest [16.216ff.]) speaks to the immediate truth of their years of separation, but it is not too much to say that it also portrays the alienation that besets father-son relationships in an overly competitive, male-dominated society such as the one that can be reconstructed from these texts and from the mythology. Once reunited, father and son plot the destruction of the suitors. During this scene Telemachus is tested and proves himself to be his father's son.

Later, just before entering the palace, Odysseus, again disguised as the beggar, is met by his aged dog, Argus (Swifty), who rises and wags his tail feebly in recognition and shortly thereafter, having kept the faith these nineteen years since his master went away, falls dead (17.290ff.). It is a sentimental scene, yet it serves to portray something that cannot be conveyed in a character's speech, which is the usual device in this narrative style for comment upon the action. Odysseus's joy at seeing the familiar landscape of Ithaca instantly conveyed the emotion of being at home, as does his encounter with the aged dog.

The last three recognition scenes are the most momentous, as befits the work of a master narrator who knows how to move suspensefully to his climax. They are also the most lengthily developed. As Eurycleia, his old nurse, prepares to bathe the disguised Odysseus at the command of Penelope, she notices the scar, the token of his true identity, which prompts the poet to tell the story of his getting it. Within the story of the scar there is yet another story of naming the baby Odysseus: Autolycus, his grandfather, "the greatest thief and liar of his time" (19.395f.), names him, saying, "Since I come hated [the Greek word for which has a root similiar to that in Odysseus] by many . . . let his name be Odysseus [the hated one]." Here the deep core of Odysseus—his suspicion, his cunning, his paranoia is suddenly revealed; it is the scar tissue upon his soul that makes him different from all other human beings.

The suitors finally recognize him in the celebrated scene when he strings the bow and shoots the arrow through the axes. It is a contest of strength designed to win a princess among many competing suitors. The context compels one to consider a Freudian interpretation of the event as well, that is, the phallic bow, the ejaculatory tension and relaxation of the bow string, and the vaginal orifices of the axes through which the bow passes so successfully. Certainly Odysseus demonstrates that he is by far the strongest male by performing a feat no one else has the physical strength to complete, but the sexual nuance of this scene is perfectly appropriate and leads naturally to the final recognition scene with Penelope, the princess whom the underdog, the prince in disguise, has just won.

Those who insist that Penelope knows all along that the stranger was Odysseus in disguise, besides overlooking the improbability that Homer, who tells his audience everything, would leave that fact unsaid, weaken the wonderful emotions and tensions of their recognition scene. The poet will not have it that Penelope, who has waited so long and been so steadfast, so discreet, and so intelligently careful, will simply take the stranger's word for it or recognize her long-lost spouse's intelligence and capacity for creative deception. No, he makes her recognition of him depend upon conjugal knowledge. She tricks him into revealing quite spontaneously the secret of the making of their marriage bed, something that he alone would know. At one stroke the poet suggests a level of carnal truth upon which conjugal identities rest and reveals a woman who alone in this poem has the wit to outdo her husband. True to the faintly misogynistic flavor of this story, Odysseus is unmanned, made to reveal himself against his will, by a woman.

A principal difference between the *Iliad* and the *Odyssey* is the number of women who appear in the latter. What is more, they are all powerful. The old slave Eurycleia is described at the beginning as a favorite of Telemachus's grandfather, but whom the grandfather had never made love to out of fear of his wife, Anticleia—a sufficiently unusual act of conjugal submission on the part of the male as to require the poet to notice it. Later we meet Helen, who immediately recognizes Telemachus as Odysseus's son while Menelaus has not been able to do so, or at least come out and say so. As the evening at Sparta proceeds and the tears flow at the sad reminiscences shared by the party, it is Helen, the magician or witch, who puts a drug into the wine to cheer the group. A similar commanding or controlling person is Arete, Nausicaa's mother, whom the girl tells the shipwrecked Odysseus to supplicate (rather than her father) when he arrives at the palace. It is Arete who instantly notices that Odysseus is wearing clothes from the palace. Calypso keeps Odysseus on her island for seven years. Circe tries to enchant him sexually, and although he withstands her powers with the help of the god Hermes, she is sufficiently powerful to keep him by her side for a year, until his crew pleads with him to continue on home (10.469ff.).

Penelope is the summation of these characteristics. Throughout the poem the poet has established Agamemnon's story as a possible analogue to the situation on Ithaca to keep up a certain tension of suspense over what Odysseus will find at home. Penelope has made the suitors her victims by encouraging them, as they tell Telemachus ("she makes us hope . . . she sends us messages" [2.91ff.]), and by appearing before them in a seductive guise (18.205ff.). She dominates Odysseus finally, as no one in the narrative has before, when she tricks him into blurting out the secret of the construction of their bed. Nonetheless, Penelope is the great good, along with homestead and son, for which Odysseus has pined these long years of wandering; when he and she are finally together in bed, the poet establishes the depth of their relationship by noting that after they satisfy themselves with lovemaking, they talk the night away (23.300–343). It is true that although all the women derive from a misogynistic subtext, or at least play to the masculine fear of female domination, they are, all of them, presented as peer figures, even Calypso and Circe. These last are malign witches, but when forced to acknowledge that Odysseus must leave, they cheerfully assist him in his departure.

The presence of important women figures, the emphasis on sexuality, and the many descriptions of eating and of material splendors combine to present a world view altogether different from that of the *Iliad*. Critics tend to contrast the tragic sense of life in the *Iliad* with the comic, life-affirming view of things in the *Odyssey*. In the *Odyssey* Zeus declares that humans are responsible for their destinies; Odysseus's triumph over the suitors is the victory of right over wrong. When offered the gift of immortality, he rejects it, insisting that he must go home. The poet establishes his hero as a man who must experience life as it is lived, who will accept suffering as part of that experience, and who rejects the decidedly nonhuman attribute of immortality. Homer uses Odysseus's refusal of immortality to demonstrate the paradox of the adventuresome hero and his craven crew. The chasm that separates Odysseus's lust for life from the crew's concern for survival is vast. At each dangerous turn of the journey Odysseus wants to investigate the new and the strange while the crew looks for escape. Everywhere they seek food, he seeks information. Ironically their pursuit of survival brings on their death. Desperately hungry, surrounded by the cattle of the Sun God, which they have been warned were taboo, they cannot look beyond the physical fact of their own immediate survival to spare the sacred beasts. Thus they perish, while Odysseus, the much-enduring, much-exploring, gambling man, survives. The paradox seems important to the poet because he mentions this episode in the opening lines of the epic.

In his rejection of immortality Odysseus accepts the experience of dying as part of life. No curious man would give this up. Beyond that Odysseus understands man's essential weakness and insignificance. These demand that he accept and live whatever life is his to have. Odysseus's advice to the suitors says just this:

> Of all the things that breathe and crawl on this earth,
> nothing does earth produce of less consequence than man.

For as long as the gods give him manliness and his knees work,
he thinks that he won't suffer evil in the future.
But when, as will happen, the blessed gods make things wretched,
these too he must bear with an enduring spirit though he be suffering.
For man's mind and disposition is no more or less
than what the father of men and gods causes it to be each day. . . .
Wherefore let no man ever ignore the unwritten laws of this universe,
but keep in dignity and silence whatever gifts the gods may happen to
   give.

[18.131ff.]

CHAPTER FOUR

Literature of the Archaic Period

Now then, let us begin with the Muses, who delight the
mind of their father Zeus in Olympus, singing what is,
what was, and what shall be. From their mouths flows
sweet song endless. And the house of Zeus laughs with joy.

Hesiod, *Theogony* 36–39

Although Homer generally outranks all other ancient Greek poets
in the Western world's critical esteem, in antiquity Hesiod was readily held to be his equal. Herodotus makes the claim (2.53.2) that the
Greeks owe to the poetic invention of Homer and Hesiod their common religion from the descriptions of the gods found in the poems of
these two. Although Plato has the habit of referring to Homer as "the
divine poet," both Hesiod and Homer were listed in the canon of
seven wise men drawn up by the Greeks, among whose number are
also found legendary figures such as Orpheus and figures from history such as Solon. In the Alexandrian period Hesiod was perhaps, or
so it seems, the preferred poet; Callimachus calls him "honey-
sweet," and his trademarks, catalogues and facts, appear in all kinds
of poetry.

The ancients considered Hesiod to be the author of the *Works and
Days* and the *Theogony* as well as some minor pieces that have been
handed down along with these two larger poems. The *Works and
Days* is more than eight hundred lines long, and the *Theogony* is a
little over one thousand. Both, of course, are relatively short compared to the *Iliad* and the *Odyssey*.

As Hesiod tells us in the *Works and Days*, he was a native of Boeotia, the territory to the north of Attica. This fact and the lack of
narrative in the Hesiodic poems relative to the Homeric epics have led

53

scholars to theorize a "Boeotian School" of poetry, which stands in contrast to the "Ionic School." Yet Hesiod, reared where the dialect was strongly influenced by Doric, uses the much more Ionic poetic dialect found in the Homeric poems. The similarities in dialect as well as in formulas and line construction in the poetry of the two argue for a kind of "international" style common to oral poets of the time. Perhaps Herodotus is referring to the power of this pervasive style for influencing ideas when he ascribes the invention of the Greek religion to these two poets. What precisely he means is unclear because the poems seem to be speaking to an audience already familiar with the deities in question. It has been argued, however, that the dissemination of these poems throughout the Greek-speaking world caused the local cults and their gods to diminish in importance while the so-called Olympian deities became universally well known.

It is not known whether Homer and Hesiod were coevals or indeed how many poets composed the four poems under consideration. Every conceivable position has been taken and no doubt will be again because no one will ever know for certain. Furthermore, alongside the obvious similarities between the poems of Homer and Hesiod there are significant differences, perhaps the most striking being that Hesiod puts himself into his poems while the self-effacing poet of the *Iliad* and *Odyssey* never does. The *Works and Days* takes its inspiration from the rage and frustration that animates Hesiod against his brother Perses, who, it seems, has managed to cheat Hesiod out of his share of the family farmland by hobnobbing with the local squires, who act as judges. The poem is at once a passionate disquisition on justice and a warning to Perses that justice will eventually triumph in a victory of Hesiod over Perses. The poet addresses his brother throughout the poem and by extension everyone in his audience, while Homer, after calling upon the Muse for his story, becomes merely the vehicle for its delivery, apart from very occasionally indicating that the telling of it is hard work.

The *Works and Days* is saved from being an essay in dactylic hexameters by the Perses-Hesiod conflict; it is their story that provides the armature of drama upon which the poet builds his case for justice. The story of these brothers, however, may be more a poetic conceit than a real-life background. The brother-to-brother and friend-to-friend dialogue is found in other poetry of the era as well. Near Eastern poetry offers the example of an admonitory poem in which there is a dialogue between Good Brother and Bad Brother, which may be a parallel convention. The poetry of Theognis, a mid–sixth century Megarian, consists in the main of reflections and admonitions addressed to his youthful friend, Cyrnus. In the *Precepts of Cheiron,* a poem attributed by the ancients to Hesiod, the poet uses the same device; in this case the centaur Cheiron advises and teaches the boy Achilles. The obvious oral style of the *Works and Days* argues for a relatively long period of gestation. Hence as the Hesiod-Perses story was passed along from poet to poet, the style became more important than any supposedly autobiographical facts.

Hesiod actually names himself when he appears in a passage at the beginning of the *Theogony* in which his transformation from shepherd to poet is described. One day as he is shepherding, he says, the Muses teach Hesiod a beautiful song. They appear to him (and presumably his fellow shepherds because their address is to a plural audience) and announce rather enigmatically:

"Shepherds! you rustics! Embarrassments that you are! Mere
bellies, nothing more! We know how to tell lie upon lie exactly
like truths, and, when we choose, we know how to tell true things.
[26ff.]

When they have spoken, they give Hesiod a staff, like the speaker's staff described in the first book of the *Iliad*—the staff that anyone who wishes to speak in the assembly grasps to signify that he is taking his turn. Along with this emblem of authority they breathe into him, as he says, song, which is the holy voice, so that he can give ubiquity and permanence (the sense of the verb "to make famous") to what has been and what will be.

The passage is interesting for its portrait of the poet both as a holy man and as a seer who by grace of the Muses is privy to the future. It is furthermore important testimony to a growing awareness of the distinction between fact and fiction. The poet of the *Odyssey,* by emphasizing the almost compulsively mendacious personality of his hero, sets up the paradox that what he says when he lies has more truth to it than what he declares to be true. Thus is launched one of the favorite themes of Western literature, the symbiosis of truth and falsehood, appearance and reality, fact and fiction. The *Odyssey* poet even uses language similar to that of Hesiod's Muses once in describing his hero's false autobiography: "He told a great number of falsehoods, making them out to be true" (19.203).

When, however, Hesiod's Muses arrogate this skill to themselves, they are establishing it as a capacity of poetry itself. It seems to be in the nature of poetry in a preliterate society that it is held to be true because it is the only repository of the culture's wisdom and history. Therefore, it *has* to be true. The anonymity of Homer and his dependence—presumed, conventional, or real—upon the Muses, rids him of responsibility for his narrative. Hesiod, on the other hand, by advertising himself so frequently, takes responsibility for what he says, and in so doing proclaims himself the author of his invention. The very fact of invention, then, introduces the notion of fiction. Hesiod may insist on his authority ("Now, Perses, I have in mind to tell you the truth" [*Works and Days* 10]), and certainly it seems clear that the *Theogony* is, if anything, an exercise in categorizing *fact*. Yet the poet has in preface to these catalogues made the distinction between fact and fiction, and this distinction seems crucial. The intensely personal nature of the poetry of the Archaic Age, which is its hallmark, really, and something that persists into the fifth-century choral lyrics of Pindar, is perhaps more than anything else a response to the poets' liberation from inherited truth—presumed, implied or believed—which is the very foundation upon which the Homeric narratives are built.

Some critics discount Hesiod as a poet, insisting that he was a frustrated thinker for whom an evolved prose medium was not yet invented. This idea not only dismisses the peculiar wedding of his thought and style but ignores the very obvious beauty of his poetry. There are indeed several first-rate passages in both his poems. The description of Zeus's fight with Typhoeus is one (*Theogony* 820ff.), the battle between the Titans and Zeus's siblings is another (*Theogony* 617ff.), and there are glorious descriptions of natural life in the *Works and Days*. Here, for example, is a description of a hot summer's day and a recipe for a mild wine cooler:

> When the artichoke flowers, and the grasshopper chirps
> with his wings, pouring down his shrill song from the tree
> constantly, in the season of heat, the wearing heat,
> then goats are plumpest, wines are the very best;
> women are hotter then, men are weakest then.
> The Dog Star dries out the head and knees;
> the heat dries out the skin; shadow is needed then,
> the shadow of a rock and some Biblian wine. . . .
> I'll drink some glistening wine, sitting in the shade,
> turning my face to the west wind coming fresh;
> from the everflowing spring, as it comes out clean,
> I'll pour three parts and from the wine a fourth.
>
> [582ff.]

As Hesiod proclaims, he is a singer, and the medium of poetry shaped him as surely as he shaped it; his ideas therefore derive in part from the exigencies of his medium. In fact, one should reject the very notion of Hesiod's *ideas,* as though he had an outline that he then cast into a poetic mold. There is no "idea" apart from the poem. The poem is more the *evolution* of an idea in the sense that Hesiod seems to be not exactly sure where he will end when he begins. The creative tension lies in Hesiod's juxtaposing traditional elements in his poem and from these juxtapositions creating the sense of his poem. It seems fair to say that Hesiod could have made heroic poetry if he had wanted to. His account of his participation in the singing at a king's funeral (*Works and Days* 654ff.) is thought to be a reference to his career as a heroic epic poet. Then, too, the invocation to the Pierian Muses with which the *Works and Days* begins certainly has to do with epic poetry. In any case Homer's poetry has enough well-integrated, Hesiod-like catalogues and lists and Hesiod's enough seemingly Homeric passages that there is no need to make a sharp distinction.

Hesiod is different from Homer in an important way. Homer builds his narrative from metrically defined phrases and metrically assigned key words. In the *Works and Days,* however, Hesiod uses a longer, semantically more complete building block: the aphorism. These self-contained ideas are combined to make a greater whole. For instance, lines 21–24—

Anyone will want to work when he sees his neighbor
wealthy, who is anxious to plow and sow,
to keep his house in order; neighbor competes with neighbor
going after wealth. This strife [i.e., competition] is good for mankind.

—contain three loosely connected statements that with very little grammatical adjustment can be separated into six observations free of any connection:

1. Anyone will want to work when he sees his neighbor.
2. He who is anxious to plow and to sow is wealthy.
3. Keep your house in order.
4. Neighbor competes with neighbor.
5. Go after wealth.
6. Strife is good for mankind.

Hesiod's aphorisms bear a strong resemblance to the earliest quoted responses of the Delphic oracle. The oracle dealt out sacred wisdom as, we might say, Hesiod seems to be offering secular wisdom. Herodotus in fact quotes one such aphorism of Hesiod, which also resembles an utterance of the oracle (*Works and Days* 285 quoted at 6.86). This aphorism is an example of a large body of self-contained dactylic hexametric lines, each a complete idea, which circulated orally among the poets. What is critically important in such poetry is not the thought in each line, but what the *combination* means; the joining is the poetic act.

Hesiod's poetry is not easy to criticize because it is remarkably varied. In addition to aphorisms there are descriptions of nature, such as that quoted, and definitions, such as that of justice (249ff.). These passages are clearly built from formulaic phrases as in Homer's poems. Then there are the agricultural calendar, the Ages of Man passage, and the Prometheus/Pandora story. These last three seem, like the aphoristic lines, to be Hesiod's inheritance, something received whole by him, or at least in outline.

Scholars have noted that the *Works and Days* and the *Theogony* bear marked affinities with many texts of the Near East. The *Works and Days* brings together elements that are found separately in the earlier Eastern literature. Hesiod incorporates into the same poem on the one hand the protohistorical cosmological or cosmogonic stories, that is, the Prometheus/Pandora story and the Ages of Man story (the story of man's fall), and on the other hand, the wisdom literature, in turn of two sorts: practical/ethical proverbs and an agricultural calendar. There is also the poet speaking in his own voice. While once these similarities were ascribed to some direct influence—perhaps that of Hesiod's father, who came from the coast of Asia Minor—nowadays comparativists note parallels in ancient literature throughout the world and favor the idea that the resemblance is a reflection of a common habit of mind.

The *Works and Days* falls roughly into three parts. The first is the invocation, the description of strife or competition, followed by the Prometheus story, the Ages of Man passage, and the fable of the hawk and the nightingale. In the second part Hesiod strives to give theological coherence to the ideas of work and justice. This portion ends with the triumphant call to work:

> So if in your heart you want wealth, then
> get to it, work and pile work upon work!
> [381–82]

Properly speaking, only the third part is the works and days. A panoramic view of agricultural life is presented season by season. It commences with autumn plowing (383ff.), proceeds to a description of winter (493ff.) and then spring and summer (that is, contemporary February to June, 564ff.), and ends with a description of the harvest (July to October, 597ff.). To this is appended a maritime calendar, rather like a coda, which is followed by a list of maxims, mostly relating the taboos in life, which is a bridge into the catalogue of lucky and unlucky days with which the poem ends.

The juxtaposition of the elements in the third section of the *Works and Days* makes it easier to understand what Hesiod is doing in the earlier portions of the poem. At first, the connection between the agricultural calendar, the general and particular remarks about a sailor's life, the series of maxims relating to behavior, and the list of lucky and unlucky days is difficult to see. The reason is that the transitions are imagistic rather than logical.

The remarks about the sea proceed easily out of the close of the description of the agricultural year. Hesiod ends, as he had begun, with autumn, now late autumn. He indicates the time of year with a reference to the setting of the Pleiades. This celestial observation provides the pivot upon which he turns to his maritime passage, for he again mentions the setting of the Pleiades (619), this time as a sign when to draw up the ships and leave off seafaring for the winter. He then launches into remarks on the life of a sailor.

A similar transitional device is used at the close of the passage on sailing. Hesiod concludes by saying, "Keep the measure; to everything there is a season" (694). Then he turns to say, "When you are ripe, take a wife," and he is off to the list of maxims. Ripeness follows from season naturally, and both ripeness and season, having to do with propriety of one sort or another, are an easy bridge into the proverbial wisdom the list of maxims offers. Finally, because Hesiod concentrates on taboos in this account, it is easy to proceed to a list of lucky and unlucky days, which concludes the passage. This list is a natural conclusion, comprising calendar particulars for which the previous discussion of the agricultural year was the overview. The theme common to each of these passages is propriety, or, looked at another way, necessity.

The first two hundred twelve lines are also characterized by an imagistic juxtaposition of passages. The connecting image is seeking and hiding something within. Containment, concealment, and retrieval are natural extensions of the agricultural world where seeds are planted in the earth and harvests gleaned from it. This is a very hard passage to analyze because the thought rides on the images.

After the invocation the poet redefines and expands the idea of strife or quarreling to include the idea of competition. There is not one kind of strife, says Hesiod, but two; the one brings war and battle, the other Zeus has set in the roots of the earth. Strife stirs even the lazy man to work, for when he sees his neighbor succeeding, this strife spurs him on. Good strife is clearly farm work.

Hesiod continues his distinction between the two kinds of strife by calling upon his brother. Perses, he says, do not let the bad kind of strife keep you hanging around the courthouse listening to wrangling. Quarrels and courts are no good if you do not have a supply of food laid in. Silly lords and judges of the courtroom, who don't know the benefit to be found in mallow and asphodel! Bad strife is in turn associated with city life, found in the adversary behavior of lawyers and judges, city men. The important connection lies in seeking what lies within. It is a natural idea for moral people who plant seeds and store their harvest in the ground.

By way of explaining why these judges are silly, Hesiod says, "The gods have hidden the means of life from mortals" (42). Here Hesiod seems to be proceeding from the idea of the good strife set in the roots of the earth, reshaping it as human sustenance which is found in the earth, but now implying that it was divine malevolence that hid it. So he can both praise hard work and acknowledge its pain. Zeus hid the means of life in anger at Prometheus (47), who stole fire and hid it. From this strong story Hesiod moves to the Pandora story, the gift of woman to men. She brings a box which when opened lets out all the woes of the world; only hope remains inside.

The ideas of containment, concealment, and retrieval hold these lines together. The gods *hide* the means of life; a few lines later Zeus is said to have *hidden* something unspecified in anger; then Prometheus steals the fire from Zeus and *hides* it *in* the hollow stalk of a plant, whereupon the gods adorn Pandora and by this means *conceal* her malevolent nature; Pandora later clamps down the lid on the jar, thereby keeping hope or delusion *within*. The passage seems opaque, and a common critical refuge is to assume that Hesiod passes lightly and allusively over what he and his audience knew well. But it is more to the point to concentrate on the details he does introduce as being significant for his present narrative.

Hesiod's account tells us that man has Pandora (and by extension womankind in general), fire, work, and misery. By his images he manages to suggest that these four are aspects of the same thing. What has Hesiod portrayed for his audience? Survival is linked with that which is hidden—to wit, struggle, fire, food, and hope, which is linked with woman. Survival is somehow a combination of the food man eats, the struggle with which he forces it from the earth, the fire he makes to cook it, and the babies the woman promises by keeping hope in the jar if it is not too much to see the uterus in the image of the jar. It is not clear in Hesiod's account what other function woman has.

It is a malevolent universe, however, and this malevolence accounts for the need to work, the cruelty of the agricultural routine. Hesiod expresses this idea through the anger of Zeus. In other words, the natural world resents being manipulated for man's survival. Civilization comes at a price; fire allows for an advanced way of life, but along with it, at almost the same moment, comes woman and a host of evils. There is no clear progression in this account; it is not so much cause and effect as simultaneity that gives the sense of aspects of the same thing.

Hesiod concludes the Prometheus/Pandora story with the observation, "And so there is no way to escape the will of Zeus" (105). Abruptly and with no imagistic transition he shifts ground with, "If you like, I shall tell you another story." The account of the Ages of Man is a moral chronology, depicting man evolving from the innocence of the Golden Age through bellicosity and violence to depravity in the Iron Age. It is this last that Hesiod mournfully claims for his own. The horrors of Iron Age families are an abstraction of Hesiod's very own quarrel with Perses. The Ages of Man are like a human lifetime—a descent from infantile innocence, goodness, and helplessness to the corruption, compromise, and despair of old age. The story describes the same passage from primal goodness to misery which the previous account of strife, work, fire, Prometheus, and Pandora had demonstrated. It may also be argued that the progression from unearned bread to work and domestic life with a woman is another accounting of humankind growing up (not unlike the account in *Genesis* or of Enkidu's transformation from the child of nature to a pupil of the temple harlot).

It now remains for Hesiod to sum up with a fable, which by its brevity and nonhuman subject matter serves as an abstraction of what has gone before. The fable articulates the desperation that fills the previous two stories. According to the fable, this world in which mankind is the victim is as inexorable as the talons of the hawk, arbitrary ("I shall make you my dinner if I choose or maybe I will let you go" [209]), and amoral ("You're mine to take where I will even though you are a singer" [208]). No one can escape the will of Zeus. In an agrarian culture no one can escape the inexorability of chores.

The concluding passages of this poem—the agricultural works and days, the maxims, and the list of taboos—are refrains of the themes with which Hesiod began his poem. The idea of the right moment, of ripeness, is a continual refrain in Hesiod's poem. One is reminded of Qoheleth, the Bible's Ecclesiastes, for instance, when Qoheleth says, "To every thing there is a season, and a time to every purpose under heaven" (Eccles. 3:1–9). Hesiod manages, however, to escape the melancholia of the cyclical rhythm that Qoheleth conveys. Hesiod does so by taking a positive stance in the central portion of his poem toward the inexorable rhythm of his life, converting necessity into choice. This is perhaps no more than verbal legerdemain, but man has after all very few ways to escape the fact of his elemental nothingness. It has been said that speech is the futile revenge of the disinherited.

The theme of duality is central to the poem from the beginning—for example, in the invocation (man will be spoken of or not, Zeus can make a man strong or bring the strong man down) and in the notice that there are two kinds of strife, good and bad. Furthermore, there is duality in the conflicts between Hesiod and Perses, Zeus and Prometheus, Epimetheus and Pandora, the Gold and Silver Ages and the Bronze, and the hawk and the nightingale. The quarrel of the brothers becomes the means whereby Hesiod saves himself, for if Perses is the bad brother, then Hesiod must be the good. This opposition also saves his poem from the unbearable depths of pessimism and despair of his harsh observations. The first part of the poem is a bleak account of man's fate. It corresponds to the earlier experience of Hesiod's life, the heartless judgment against Hesiod in favor of Perses. In the second portion of the poem Hesiod attempts to make something of this fate and at the same time holds out the expectation of a changed situation in his landholdings. There is thus a psychological correspondence.

In the second section of the poem this theme of duality becomes even more prominent. There is the image of the racetrack, where arrogance and justice compete for victory; an ideal portrait of the good city to which a brief pendant portrait of the evil city is attached; the image of two roads, one leading to virtue, the other to evil; and a composite of the virtues of work, interspersed with aphoristic comments on its natural opposite, the slothful man, which device again legitimates work by the very nature of the contrast.

The descriptions of the good city and the bad city follow from the portrait of the Age of Iron, but relate as well directly to the quarrel between Perses and Hesiod. Healing in the family situation comes from compassion. This notion leads Hesiod to describe a god of righteousness, a Zeus who will not let man eat one another as the animals do, but who has given them justice (275ff.). This conception of Zeus scarcely coincides with the Zeus of the first part of the poem, but true to the nature of the oral poet, Hesiod has contrived this Zeus for the needs of this passage. At this point Hesiod can say, "To him who knows how to speak justly Zeus gives prosperity. . . . for him who lies and injures justice . . . his descendants shall be dim and obscure." This is not a conception of Zeus that sticks. Hereafter Hesiod returns to the idea of a harsh and unyielding universe as the basis for his speculations.

The duality is important. Arrogance and justice compete on the racetrack; good behavior is promised victory. The good city blooms, like any successful agrarian enterprise. The description of the good road and the bad road underlines the importance of work and the more distant goal of agrarian prosperity. "The gods," he says, "have placed sweat on the road to goodness; the road to goodness is long and steep, rough-going at first." Goodness becomes hard work, justice lies in working hard, and working hard is going along the assigned route. The image of the two roads is a partial restatement of the racetrack image, but minus the idea of freedom. Hesiod returns to the fundamental idea of inexorability. The road is a closed system and, as an image, a natural corollary to the control and rigidity implicit in the fable of the hawk and the nightingale. The important difference is that man may *choose* his road. But the road itself is fixed.

Now Hesiod is able to portray him whom the gods love as the hard-working man. "Gods and man hate him who is idle. . . . If you work hard you will grow rich. . . . Goodness and honor come to him who is rich." But it is not enough to work hard; one must comprehend the way things are: "The really best man is the one who thinks through everything and comes to knowledge, next best is the man who will trust in the advice of one who knows. He who won't listen is useless." Justice is finally simply a word for the way things are supposed to be, the rhythm of the universe. Knowing this, just like knowing where the hidden things are, is salvation. This is the theme of the racetrack story and of the right and wrong roads story, but, more important, justice as salvation is the binding link between the stories and the aphorisms and the agricultural calendar.

The earlier portion of the poem sets forth the inevitability of man's life, but Hesiod, by establishing the ideas of Good and Evil, Right and Wrong, imposes a notion of freedom and choice upon the basic sense of the stories. Like the nightingale, we are caught in the talons of the hawk, but if we know it, we can learn the nature of this power and in some sense use it to our own advantage. To the ideas of Good and Evil and Right and Wrong, Hesiod conspicuously adds and often reiterates the temporal dimension of "timely" and "untimely." The hawk's talons are symbolic of agricultural life, from which there is no escape. If one can live by it, accepting the inevitability and necessity of work, he becomes rich, god-blessed.

The third section of the poem at first seems only to restate the basic premise of the first section, the necessity of work. But it does more than that; it proves the justice of life. It is not at all a guide to agriculture or clean living, as some critics have thought. The calendar is much too incomplete, and the maxims are random and incoherent. Rather, Hesiod is saying that by accepting the inexorability of work, man can triumph.

Whether Hesiod is the author of both the *Works and Days* and the *Theogony* and which is the earlier work remain debatable. At the start of the former the poet says, "Now then, there is not one kind of strife, but two in existence out on the earth," as though correcting the *Theogony* which says, "Deadly Night . . . bore . . . hard-hearted Strife" (224–25). The style of the two is much the same, although the *Theogony* is more a collection of catalogues than the other. Certainly the *Works and Days* is more ambitious in attempting to formulate a coherent account of the workings of justice in man's world. Yet the *Theogony* is a breathtaking overview of the composition of the universe.

The genealogical catalogues of the *Theogony* create a picture of a marvelously complex and diverse world and its history. The enormous scope of space and time in the *Theogony* contrasts sharply with the narrower focus of the steamy domestic relations that characterize Homer's Olympian deities. Yet Hesiod starts with the same anthropomorphized gods as his premise. The hymn to the Muses, which serves as a prelude to his poem, invokes a divine order as human as Homer's, as, for instance, the scene when Hesiod describes the Muses and the unending sweet song that flows from their mouths in the quotation with which this chapter begins.

The genealogical catalogues that make up the *Theogony* provide the natural point for Hesiod's inquiry into the nature of god. Family after family appears in his listing; the sheer volume of names seems often confusing, yet unmistakable patterns emerge. In details, too, Hesiod is sorting and ordering experience. His list of the offspring of the sea

(233ff.), for instance, is made up of names that symbolize various mythological and meteorological facts of sea life. The first several hundred lines of the poem detail the family lines of divine beings who are neither cult figures nor much anthropomorphized nor central to mythology. They are instead the natural facts of the universe—heaven, earth, mountains, and so on. The children of Night (211ff.) also are more representative of the human condition than individually realized, personalized figures of myth. The natural and physical quality of these phenomena is still clearer in the list of the children of Ocean, Sea, and Heaven. These children represent astronomy, meteorology, geography, and geology.

Hesiod's material—the genealogies, the very idea of change, growth, progression, or evolution in some supraterrestrial sphere—is not unique. Traces of this interest can be found in the *Iliad*—for instance, when the poet mentions the dispensation of divine powers and touches on divine genealogy (15.187ff.). Babylonian and Hittite documents, too, show similar ways of organizing human experience in environmental metaphors and the same intimations of supernatural forces. The parallels are not sufficient to suggest direct borrowing, but rather, as we saw in the *Works and Days,* suggest a common human tendency.

The *Theogony* is sometimes considered a handbook of mythology for the poets of Greece. True, Hesiod's interest is antiquarian, and he is devoted to codification. But even more important is his revelation of Zeus as an all-powerful and eternal god, apart from all other deities.

Moreover, his cataloguing and genealogies represent the first experiment in analysis. After the natural phenomena with which the poet begins, the story of the generations of gods prepares for the central fact of the poem, the analysis of the life of Zeus. Not only does this primitive mythology concentrate on divine births, reflecting a cult interest in the divine child, but the stories reflect the hostility between divine father and son. Uranus is castrated and cast into impotence; Cronus, in turn, loses his power at the hands of his son, Zeus. What seems to be a natural Oedipal construct of the archetypal family—that is, son destroying father—is converted by Hesiod to a fact of evolution. The earlier generations of gods are essentially characterized as monsters, fabulous creatures of one sort or another, far removed from the Greek standard of myth, which rejects the inhuman and the unhuman. The gods of the Greeks are born into this world as humans are. And although they are immortal, they are much like humans in other respects. The poet of the *Theogony* parades a procession of monsters in his catalogues, but there is nothing quaint or primitive in this, as there might appear to be. Rather, the poet is intent upon isolating the superior strands in the divine fabric, and true to the Greek view of things, these are distinctly human. So it is that the *Theogony's* generations of gods cleanse the tradition, so to speak, of supernatural elements that are alien to the human dimension. The monsters are banished; Zeus reigns supreme.

Hesiod has fashioned a kind of grand epic narrative in the celebrated Titanomachia (battle with the Titans) and the battle against the monster Typhoeus. These two passages, which have been called one great *aristeia* whose hero is Zeus, serve different ends. The Titanomachia is a collision of two world systems. The descriptions of the fighting emphasize the vastness, and as Zeus and his cohorts win out over the older order of gods—the monsters, ogres, and implacable demons—the vision is that of a change in world orders, the movement of eras. Like Karl Barth's sense of the birth of Christ, Zeus's victory is the beginning of history. The battle with Typhoeus seems to some critics to be redundant and thus an interpolation. To others it seems an example of Hesiod's lack of discipline and of the characteristic garrulity of the epic poet. True, the picture of the single figure of Typhoeus pitted against Zeus represents a formal piece of epic—the climactic duel between two heroes, no different from that of Achilles and Hector before the walls of Troy. More than that, it is the realization of the individual power of Zeus, now the new king of the gods. The poem is historical because it is genealogical; the Titanomachia is part of the history of the gods. The poem is also analytical in that it is an attempt to define the mythological and religious phenomenon of Zeus. The fight with Typhoeus is part of that analysis.

Having brought Zeus, the single victor, into a new moral dimension, the poet is not afraid to introduce a story of primitive religiosity—the story of Zeus swallowing Metis—which seems to contradict the essence of the new dispensation. Such stories are the strength of Hesiod's account, however, because their relative incongruity with the more humane conception of Zeus he is creating seems to show that he speaks the truth. The *Theogony* is built upon the theme of birth and generation. Surpassing, eclipsing, or outstripping is inherent to that theme, even without the Oedipal notion of overthrow. Hesiod has expanded the theme to cover the whole nature of things. It is the earliest expression of the idea of progress and an expanding universe. The overthrow of Zeus is inevitable in such a scheme and also intolerable. That is why the Metis story is needed. The description of Zeus swallowing the goddess Metis, who is pregnant by him with an offspring destined to overthrow him, is grotesque, yet it strikes at the heart of the problem; for in this act Zeus assures himself of eternal power. His victory is the triumph of good over evil; it allows him to foster moral absolutes and eternal justice. The Zeus of the *Works and Days* depends from this conception.

As Herodotus says, Homer and Hesiod made the theogonies, listing the powers and titles of the gods. In time the Greeks grouped twelve together and called them the Pantheon. These are the gods that every city-state enshrined in its temples. These are the twelve that appear as the central group on the Parthenon frieze. They are Zeus, Hera, Poseidon, Athena, Aphrodite, Demeter, Apollo, Artemis, Dionysus, Hephaestus, Ares, and Hermes.

Zeus is the sky god, god of the shining day, yet more important as a bringer of rain to the parched Mediterranean land than as the sun, as the Homeric epithets "cloud-gatherer" and "thunderer" suggest. His thunderbolt is emblematic of his terrible, swift power, as is his great sexual energy, with which he produces so many progeny with mortal women as well as goddesses and nymphs. As befits a god who won his power, Zeus is the god of victory and as such is oftened hymned. He is also the father of mortals and gods and, like a father, the impartial judge of all. He is also the king, and as such the patron of kings, hierarchies, and governments. He does not appear in battle; indeed, the Athenian dramatists who brought various deities before the spectators did not bring Zeus into the action. Zeus is truly the universal god, the god for all the Greeks.

Hera is commonly associated with Zeus as his wife and sister—a relationship that, despite the incest taboo, makes her his equal and by extension makes all females equal with all males. She had important cults at Argos and Mycenae, but she was worshipped everywhere as the Great Goddess. The earliest temples are dedicated to Hera, in keeping with the Greek notion of the female as the indoor creature (the women of the *Odyssey,* for instance, with the exception of Nausicaa, are all met indoors). Homer's portrait of Hera as a contumacious, jealous wife may well reflect the natural disposition of repressed, angry women of the time or the fundamental hostility between the religion of the invading Indo-Europeans with their male sky god and the indigenous agricultural peoples, who worshipped the female reproductive deity. In contrast to Homer's mocking scene of

Hera's seduction of the unsuspecting and easily aroused Zeus, in cult and art the sexual union of the two is a solemn and sacred affair. Hera is often the presiding deity in weddings and marriage, yet she has little role as a mother. By Zeus she gave birth to Ares; Hephaestus she produced by herself. Her jealousy and hostility toward Heracles, Zeus's child by Alcmene, is the stuff of much legend and no doubt reflects the anxiety of wives of the time, whose principal justification was motherhood. Although Homer's portrait of her has strongly influenced the literary tradition, it is not clear whether it relates at all to her cult, either influencing it or being influenced by it.

Poseidon is an ancient god; his name appears on Linear B tablets of the Bronze Age. In the *Iliad* Homer has Poseidon tell of the inheritance from father Cronus, with the Underworld going to Hades, the sky to Zeus, and the sea to himself, with earth and Mount Olympus to be held jointly. His lordship of the sea extends to the ferocious storms that sometimes rage on the Mediterranean. Sailors, as one might imagine, are special to Poseidon, as are fishermen. Called Earthshaker in Homer, Poseidon is also held responsible for the many earthquakes that devastate the Greek lands. A principal form of his cult involves him with horses; some legends describe him as the actual father of the horse. Scholars consider that his association with the horse has something to do with the introduction of that beast into the Greek lands. In any case, his role in literature is that of the elder statesman—grave, authoritative, but rarely acting. He appears in Euripides' *Trojan Women* discussing with Athena the impending sea disaster of the home-going Greeks, who are dangerously elated in the triumph of their victory. Worship of Poseidon was widespread from Italy to Asia Minor.

Athena (also called Pallas) is closely connected with the city of Athens; which is named for the other is still conjecture. Her birth is curious. Hesiod declares that she was the fetus that the pregnant Metis was carrying when Zeus swallowed her and that she sprang forth from his head. According to some versions of the legend, she is the product of Zeus alone, and Hephaestus split Zeus's head open with an axe to get her out. Her special relationship to Zeus is a constant theme. Linear B tablets attest to her antiquity. In many places she was considered the protector of cities and citadels, a common type of female deity throughout the Near East. She is pictured with a shield and a spear, which suit her role as the adrenal rush in battle action. She wears over her shoulder the *aegis,* or goatskin, which, when she raises it, causes her enemies to panic. As befits a virgin, she is also patroness of women's work in the making of fabric. The loom and the spindle are her emblems. Every year the women of ancient Athens made a new robe for the statue of the deity on the Acropolis. In the Panathenaic festival a procession took the garment up to her in her virgin's chamber (Parthenon). She also has in her care the olive trees. Olive trees, which take decades to bear fruit, are a mark of an advanced society, and it is fitting that the guardian of cities should be closely associated with the source for the basic oil for eating, cooking, cleaning, and lighting and for the preparation of fabrics from sheared animals.

Athena is a major character in the *Odyssey,* appearing as Odysseus's constant helper when he returns to his homeland. As she says, it is his lying and cunning that appeal to her, and she assists him throughout as he insinuates himself into the palace and intrigues for his revenge. She appears more than any other deity in extant drama, which is reasonable enough since the dramas are enacted in her city. Not unlike Portia, she manages the trial in Aeschylus's *Eumenides,* casting the deciding vote for Orestes. She maddens Ajax in Sophocles' *Ajax* and invites the unwilling Odysseus to join her in witnessing Ajax's humiliation. She talks with Poseidon of the disasters that lie ahead for the triumphant Greeks in Euripides' *Trojan Women.* Euripides is fond of bringing her in toward the close of the drama to settle the action, resolving the conflicts and outlining the future. She does so in his *Ion, Supplant Women,* and *Iphigenia in Tauris.*

Aphrodite is the goddess of sexual pleasure and as such is related to the Near Eastern goddesses Ishtar and Astarte. The dove is her sacred bird. She is often accompanied by her son, the boy Eros, who represents sexual desire. Some of her temples housed sacred prostitutes, who devoted their earnings to the goddess. She was born in the foam from the lopped-off genitals of Uranus, which fell into the ocean. Greek culture did not repress the open expression and admiration for human sexuality; consequently, Aphrodite held a high place in worship. Eventually, however, there arose the distinction between heavenly love and plebeian love, which is already made in Plato's *Symposium.* While plebeian love was expressive of experiences such as lust and prostitution, heavenly love, or the Heavenly Aphrodite, is more associated with the principle of reproduction and regeneration. She appears in the *Iliad* in a slightly ridiculous posture when Diomedes wounds her in battle, to which she is obviously ill-suited. In Euripides' *Hippolytus* she is the cause of much misery as she sends Phaedra into the madness of love. In Hellenistic times she is the major deity; the sculpted likeness of her naked—a novelty after the conventionally clothed figure in the classical period—became a cliché. Apollonius presents her in his *Argonautica* as the elegant, beautiful, bewildered mother of truant Eros.

Demeter is most of all associated with the growing of wheat. Almost invariably she is connected with her daughter, Persephone, who spends part of every year below the earth in the company of her husband, Hades. If Demeter is the earth, the female growing principle, her daughter is the seed that is stored for four months from the spring harvest until the September planting. Demeter's festivals are everywhere, the special province of women. The rites practiced at her sanctuary at Eleusis were kept secret from those who were not initiates. What little we know of them indicates that they re-created the miracle of her daughter's descent and return from the Underworld in conjunction with the end and beginning of the growing season. Demeter is little treated in literature, but in reliefs she is often shown joyful, with her daughter returned and sitting on her lap.

Apollo, the "God from afar," is a most important god, worshipped both in state and private cults. He is represented as a youth, always aloof and cool. He is patron of music and poetry. The oracular shrine at Delphi is sacred to Apollo, as is the island of Delos, although archaeological excavation shows that in both instances his cult supplanted that of an earlier female deity. He also has a healing function, although his ever present bow and arrow are responsible for innumerable deaths among the Achaean troops, for instance, in the first book of the *Iliad*, and for the deaths of all the children of Niobe. The god of disease and the god of healing are, of course, naturally componential figures. The oracular responses given in his name at Delphi come the closest in ancient Greece to the ethical, moral, and religious pronouncements of an established church. Despite the consistent and clear persona of the young man, there is something less distinctly anthropomorphized about Apollo. In Aeschylus's *Eumenides* he appears as a major character to plead the case for Orestes. He is prologus in Euripides' *Alcestis,* outlining the plot, and he appears *ex machina* in his *Orestes* to settle the action at the end. He is the offstage bad guy in Euripides' *Ion,* having seduced and abandoned the heroine, and is too cowardly to appear at the end, when Athena must make apologies for him.

Artemis, sister to Apollo, daughter of Leto and Zeus, is the virgin goddess of the hunt and the forests. Possibly she represents the eternal promise of fertility which forest and meadow, unplanted and unplowed, indicate. For this reason her virginity is important in her cult as it is not with the asexual virgin Athena. Her association with animals is again representative of a store of power and nutrition yet untapped. The goddess is complex, for she is also cruel in her revenge upon humans with her arrows. In art she is often represented between two rampant beasts. Her lasting literary persona is that of a young girl. In the *Odyssey* Nausicaa is compared to her, as are Apollonius's Medea and Virgil's Dido. In Euripides' *Hippolytus* she and Aphrodite are the two deities establishing the field of action for the hero in an almost allegorical struggle between sexuality and asceticism.

Dionysus is a nature god, the god of wine and intoxication. The Greeks were not interested in simple drunkenness but in the psychological and physical state of abandonment, ecstasy, and madness, all of which are the means to free oneself from the body while still alive and at the same time to lose one's identity. Inebriation can be both liberating and frightening as can be seen in the Euripidean drama *The Bacchae,* in which Dionysus is a major character who wreaks havoc on the principals as he is all the while adored and approved by the chorus of his women followers. Dionysian worship is found in state cults and private ceremonies. There were major festivals dedicated to this god in Athens and among the Dorians. In all of them the common theme was exceeding spiritual liberation, liberation from customary behavior, drunkenness, and madness, if not hysteria. It was the Greater Dionysian festival at which the dramas were presented in Athens. The masks of drama themselves express the psychological state of displacement because those who don them are no longer themselves. Archaeology has established that the worship of Dionysus is very old, yet he is little mentioned in the early literature such as the *Iliad*. He was said to have been born from Zeus's thigh, into which his fetus had been secreted following the death by explosion and fire of his mother, Semele. As a subject for art Dionysus was very popular with the vase painters together with his retinue of female maenads, the ivy tendrils, the animal pack, and the satyrs, often with their distinctive erect phalli. The Dionysian phallus was not emblematic of procreation but of sexual excitement—like wine and hysteria, another means to ecstasy.

Hephaestus is the god associated with metalworking, god of the metal smiths. The working of metal, first bronze, then iron, was the major skill apart from agriculture and properly sanctified. In Homer Hephaestus is lame and laughable, reflecting both the contempt of the aristocratic warrior class for metalworkers and the natural hazards of

work around a forge. His moments of triumph occur in the eighteenth book of the *Iliad* in the description of the shield he forges and
decorates for Achilles and in the eighth book of the *Odyssey* in the
song of Demodocus, who describes the marvelous revenge Hephaestus exacts on his wife, Aphrodite, and her lover, Ares. His cult is
closely associated with fire. He appears but once in extant tragedy, in
the prologue episode of Aeschylus's *Prometheus Bound,* in which he, a
hesitant lackey of the new great power, supervises the attachment of
the Titan to the rocky cleft.

Ares is the god of war; his name, as is it used in the *Iliad,* seems to
mean "battle," or "war rush." As an abstraction both in noun form
and as a qualifying adjective ("warlike") applied to other gods and
objects, this god is less anthropomorphized. There are no interesting
myths attached to him. In the *Iliad* he is called hated by his father,
Zeus; Homer describes him as a coward. In the *Odyssey* he is Aphrodite's afternoon lover who gets caught in the metal cage that her
husband Hephaestus causes to spring up and over their adulterous
bed, much to the amusement of all the other gods, who are called in
to laugh and jeer. War as an art was the province of Athena. Ares is
brute force, a thug.

Hermes is the messenger of the gods, sent by Zeus to Calypso in
the fifth book of the *Odyssey*. He is the psychopomp, the one who
leads the souls of the dead into Hades. In the twenty-fourth book of
the *Odyssey,* he leads the suitors there. He accompanies the aged
Priam to Achilles' tent in the twenty-fourth book of the *Iliad*. His
name stems from the semantic root meaning "a heap of stones."
Boundaries were determined by a pile of stones; later this pile was
stylized and affixed with an erect phallus, a universal and very early
means to ward off unwanted intruders. (The larger primates are said
to drive off primate intruders by facing them with erect penises.)
Although Hermes does not appear in literature as the god of boundaries, this very important function would be in the minds of any
writer and his audience. He appears in the *Prometheus* as the lackey
messenger of Zeus, coming insolently to demand of Prometheus his
secret, and as the prologus in Euripides' *Ion,* in which he tells among
other things how it was who saved the exposed baby and brought
him to Delphi. Like the Norse god Loki, Hermes had a function as
trickster. Cunning and furtiveness are important features of his divine
persona. The Homeric *Hymn to Hermes* describes his theft of Apollo's
cattle.

The Homeric *Hymn to Hermes* is one of a group of pieces composed between the eighth and sixth centuries which has survived as a collection. Hymns were a recognized genre, metrical songs to be sung in honor of a god. In the *Iliad* (1.472ff.), when Odysseus returns Chryseis to her father, the priest of Apollo, the Achaeans offer sacrifice to propitiate the god and sing a hymn to him. Extant specimens show that the conventional hymn recounted the god's various names, epithets, and powers as well as outstanding deeds and then concluded with a prayer. The so-called Homeric Hymns vary in length and style, but the more elaborate among them are clearly literary variants of the more religious, conventional ones. The longer Homeric Hymns emphasize the myth and thus contain more narrative. Because they are sometimes clever and charming, it has been thought that they were a diversion for the aristocracy, something produced for a competition of singing skill rather than as part of a religious agenda. The *Hymn to Hermes,* in which the cunning baby Hermes outdoes his older, more pompous brother Apollo, is indeed quite amusing. The *Hymn to Demeter* contains the most complete version of the story of the rape of Persephone by Hades and her recovery by her mother after the latter's anguished wanderings.

The *Hymn to Aphrodite* is probably the most successful. It is a charming story. The love goddess, who never falls in love but only brings love to others, is made by Zeus to succumb to love for Anchises, a tender, handsome shepherd youth. (Anchises is brother to Priam, who later becomes king of Troy. Anchises himself becomes the father of Aeneas and through him founder of the royal line at Rome and remote ancestor of Julius Caesar, according to Virgil in the *Aeneid*.) Aphrodite disguises herself as a mortal young girl and, decked out in seductive finery, goes to Anchises' tent. Though he is wary of her and is indeed afraid that she is a goddess, he finally gives in to her blandishments. After their lovemaking she prods him awake, standing there revealed as the goddess she is. She tells the fearful and trembling young fellow of the future of the son they have just conceived. In contrast to the Homeric poems, there is heavy emphasis here upon sensual details. The poet luxuriates in Aphrodite's preparations for love, her ointments and jewels, which are then described again when she removes them in Anchises' tent. There are also descriptions of flowers and trees and of Aphrodite's and Anchises' physical beauty.

Structurally the story in this hymn is a variant on the theme of the Great Goddess and her male consort. Aphrodite takes Anchises, uses him, and discards him. "Tell no one that you slept with Aphrodite," she cautions him (281ff.). "After going to bed with you," exclaims the enthusiastic Anchises, "I would gladly die" (153–54). And when he discovers who his bedmate really was, he says in fear, "Don't leave me to lead a feeble life among men, but pity me" (188–89). Aphrodite describes the fate of Tithonus, who was granted immortality but not eternal youth and was thus doomed to eternal senility: "His voice flows on without end, but there's no strength to him" (237). She says, "If only you could live on as you are now in shape and looks and could be called my husband, then no sorrow would enfold my heart; but soon enough old age will enfold you, ruthless old age, which stands near mankind, deadly, destructive, which even the gods hate" (241–46). So the melancholic note, which ever lurks about youths in their prime, intrudes into this charming tale. Although this hymn is made in the language and formula of the Homeric epics and indeed the Anchises seduction closely resembles in part the scene in the fourteenth book of the *Iliad* in which Hera dresses up and goes off to seduce Zeus, there is a coherence and control, an adjustment to brevity which reminds one of Theocritus.

Because Thucydides and Pindar use the word *prooimion,* "introduction," in describing them, these hymns are thought by some scholars to have been used as a kind of prelude to a recitation of part of the Homeric epics. This theory seems highly improbable, at least for the longer hymns, which would compete by virtue of their own narrative power with the subsequent recitation of Homer.

How the *Iliad* and the *Odyssey,* or the *Works and Days* and *Theogony* for that matter, were passed down from the time of their presumed composition to the moment when they are known to have been committed to written texts is not known. That the poems are the product of an oral poet or poets, living in a preliterate culture or one in which writing was a very new technology, is held to be true by most scholars. For a long time there reigned the hypothesis that the *Iliad* and *Odyssey* were dictated by their author, the preliterate poet, to someone skilled in the new writing. That they were immediately written down and circulated is a highly problematical supposition given the utter inadequacy of early writing surfaces for easy reading and dissemination, not to mention the difficulties of manuscript copying. So perhaps they continued to be transmitted by word of mouth and were dependent more and more upon memory. Slowly they came to be poems memorized verbatim rather than narratives spontaneously created by an experienced poet from the traditional story line, stock characters, situations, phrase formulas, and narrative turns.

As time went on, a class of professional reciters, as opposed to creating poets, emerged in response to the demand to hear the poems as they were. The ancients called them *rhapsodes,* men whose profession it was to recite the Homeric epics. There remains a portrait of one from the late fifth century, probably fictional but no doubt realistic, in the Platonic dialogue *Ion.* Here the rhapsode Ion is made to undergo Socrates' interrogation (one's sympathy goes to Ion immediately—Socrates can be so tiresome!) in order to demonstrate that his talent for reciting great poetry does not mean that he knows anything about it or anything else.

Tradition has it that Peisistratus, the strong man of Athens in the sixth century, enlarged and enriched the local Panathenaic festival by introducing among other things the recitation of the *Iliad* and *Odyssey.* For this purpose texts were established and strict attention was paid to the sequence and integrity of the recitations. Thus it was that the Homeric poems became institutionalized. Perhaps it was this event that ratified the text version of these poems.

It must be remembered that the Achilles story and the Odysseus story were only two of many narratives having to do with the events surrounding the Trojan War and that there were also epic narratives about Heracles, Jason and the Golden Fleece, and so on. There is a hint of how this poetry formed an evening's entertainment in the *Odyssey* when Demodocus sings about the Trojan Horse episode (8.499ff.). Most narratives must have been relatively brief, like Demodocus's song, rather than long and monumental like the *Iliad* and the *Odyssey.* Few fragments of the other heroic narratives survive. Aristotle dismisses them when he praises Homer in the *Poetics* for the unity of his plots and for managing to bring all the myriad relevant details of his stories together in a coherent fashion. The Hellenistic poet and critic Callimachus rages against the early so-called cyclic poets, whose principal poetic device, as Callimachus says, is the tiresomely reiterated "and then . . . and then. . . ." These are the poets who in the seventh and sixth centuries created what are called the epic cycles, poets who tidied up the flotsam and jetsam of traditional stories, such as one Demodocus sings in the *Odyssey,* making them into continuous narratives. All the events leading up to and subsequent to the Trojan War were contained in a series of poems. This collection began with the birth of the gods and ended with the curious—if quite conventionally Oedipal—story of the death of Odysseus at the hands of a son, Telegonus, whom he fathered with Circe and who had left his mother's island in search of his father, only to meet him and fight with him, each unknown to the other. Telegonus then marries Penelope, and Telemachus, no doubt feeling himself a wee bit *de trop,* retires to marry Circe! And where could the saga tradition go after that extraordinary minuet of loose ends tied up?

The poetic invention in these pieces, to the degree that the fragments and later ancient opinion allow for a substantiated judgment, seems to have been weak; one might say that epic poetry was tired. Certainly the seventh and sixth centuries were a time when many poets, individuals well known, created shorter poems in a variety of meters, thus getting away from epic. These were centuries of great change on many fronts. The growth and development of villages into cities was accompanied by an increase in immigration out of the Greek mainland due to the rise in population on what was very minimal farmland already impoverished of topsoil. New settlements of Greek-speaking people sprang up from the Black Sea to the southern part of present-day Italy and to the island of Sicily. In these new settlements land was owned individually rather than arranged in family holdings, a trend that was exported back to the mainland. The invention of money allowed for the growth of a monied class, a group of savers and lenders, who both challenged the power of the landowning aristocracy and enslaved impoverished debtors.

All these conditions weakened the strength of the extended family, the clan, a development that slowly, very slowly, increased the emphasis on the individual, a perception new to Greek thinking. Individual as Achilles and Odysseus may seem, they are nonetheless representative of types and so treated, at least subconsciously by the poet. In these centuries the new individualism is perhaps most obviously reflected in the literature by the sudden appearance of a group of poets who are named and who moreover tell their audience about the circumstances of their lives and their innermost feelings. Unfortunately, this rather large group is represented by the most meager fragments, so that critics are able to make only minimal judgments about the quality of each poet. The reputation, for instance, of Sappho, the early sixth-century poet from the island of Lesbos, was very high in antiquity and for that reason remains so today, but it is sustained by so few extant pieces and fragments that as serious judgment it is ludicrous. The same holds true for almost all the rest.

The new movements in poetry, all of them, employ elements of the diction and style that are characteristic of oral epic poetry. There were, however, other kinds of rhythmic language at the time of Homer and his contemporaries. Both the *Iliad* and the *Odyssey* describe pieces with singing or chanting. Examples are the little boy singing the Linus song, a song of grief, while his friends dance, a scene represented on the shield of Achilles (*Iliad* 18.570), and the wedding song, again on the shield (*Iliad* 18.493ff.). And there is random singing, such as that of Calypso as she works (*Odyssey* 5.61f.).

Evidence for poetic development in this period is so meager that only generalizations can be made. One new invention was the so-called elegiac couplet, which was made up of a line identical in form to the lines in Homer or Hesiod (that is, dactylic hexametric), followed by a variant on it which was shorter and commonly completed the thought begun in the first. Possibly poems made from such couplets were chanted or sung to the flute. Because of the metrical similarities with epic, the poets used the language of epic. More important, the ethos of epic poetry, of the heroic world, colors the elegiac poems. Probably for this reason elegiac is the medium for epitaphs. The most famous of these is probably that composed by Simonides for the Spartan dead at Thermopylae:

> Tell the Lacedaemonians, stranger, that here,
> obedient to their commands, we lie.

It was also the natural medium for martial exhortation. The Spartan poet Tyrtaeus, for instance, wrote a long poem of Homeric character on the virtues of dying in battle in defense of one's city. It begins:

> To die is beautiful, falling in the foremost rank,
> when it's a good man fighting for his fatherland.

The Athenian political figure Solon uses elegiacs to lecture his fellow Athenians on his personal philosophy as well as his political program. But elegiac was also used for more personal statements, although these again are in the nature of pronouncements, such as this of Mimnermus on love:

> What is life, what is joy without golden Aphrodite?
> May I die when these things no longer move me—
> hidden love affairs, sweet nothings and bed,

you know, the blossoms of youth there to be snatched
by man and woman both. For along comes painful
old age, makes a man repulsive, feeble, to boot . . .

or Theognis on social change:

Kyrnos, my boy, it's the same city, but different people;
who formerly knew neither justice nor laws,
who wore to shreds goatskins around their ribs,
who went about outside the city like deer.
Now they are the gentry, Kyrnos. Those once noble
are the lowly now. Who can bear seeing it?

The earliest known lyric poet is Archilochus, born on the island of
Paros, who lived between 680 and 640, more or less. He made elegiacs, but also created poems in the iambic meter and its reverse, the
trochaic. He uses these meters well, which implies that there was a
tradition behind him. Archilochus plays off the conventions of epic,
mocking some of the values and pretensions of heroic poetry. For
instance, unlike the epic hero with his excessive anxiety over keeping
and taking weapons in battle, Archilochus can cheerfully say:

Some Saián is enjoying the shield, pretty little thing
that it was, I ditched by the bush, quite against my will.
But I myself escaped death. And that shield, to hell with it!
Tomorrow I'll get me another no worse.

Or, Archilochus describes his ideal general—quite a contrast to the
heroic general, the Homeric "lord of hosts":

I don't like a great general, one walking legs astride,
nice hair, shaved, proud of it.
No, give me a little fellow, legs you can see between—
that bowlegged!—standing firm on his feet, full of heart.

Most of all, Archilochus's poetry reveals the man. Although it is for
the public, his poetry is private, marked by an intimacy of expression, unlike that of Hesiod, Solon, or Mimnermus. In the following lines, for instance, he describes both the loneliness and the
aloneness of the soldier of fortune:

In my spear is my bread kneaded, in my spear wine,
Ismarican wine, I drink leaning on my spear.

Archilochus sounds like Odysseus on his storm-tossed raft when he cries out:

> Heart, heart, stirred round in sorrows beyond repair,
> up, escape, press your chest against the evils
> in the enemy ambush, take your stand nearby.
> Steady. Neither in victory rejoice too high,
> nor, beaten, fall down at home and grieve.
> Take pleasure in delights and at evils grieve
> not too much—get to know the rhythm that holds mankind.

The same intimacy is brilliantly displayed by Sappho in one of the very few pieces surviving. Her sensuality is matched by the wide variety of meters she uses, far more sensual themselves than the conventional meters of her poetic colleagues. Here she sings of her feelings at seeing a woman whose company she wants, talking and laughing with a man:

> Seems just like the gods
> that fellow sitting across from you
> and near, hearing you
>   sweetly talking
> and your sexy laugh. Makes my
> heart fly up in my breast
> looking at you even a second, my voice
>   won't come any more,
> but my tongue breaks, all at once
> a little fire runs up and over my skin
> my eyes can't see, my ears,
>   they roar.
> Sweat starts pouring down, trembling
> comes on all over. I am greener
> than grass, and I seem like
>   I could die.

A fragment of one of her poems found written on a third-century potsherd, is a series of sensual impressions. It is addressed to Aphrodite:

> Come to me here from Crete to the holy temple,
> to your sweet grove of
> apples, altars smoking
> incense.
> Here the water is cold, it rushes

through the apple tree leaves, roses
make shadow patterns everywhere, quivering
leaves stop in sleep.

Sappho uses language self-consciously, deliberately breaking the epic linguistic patterns. This must have fallen upon her auditors' ears as twelve-tone scales once did on ours. For instance, she uses the common epic phrase *gaīă mĕlaīnă*, "black earth," in the accusative grammatical case, *gās mĕlaīnās*, creating a metrical unit, the cretic ‾ˇ‾, impossible in dactylic hexameters. To hear the accustomed phrase in that hitherto impossible metrical shape is to make the language new again, to rediscover the *words* in the phrase. Similarly, she separates the common phrase *ptera pukna* (which is hard to translate exactly: "thick wings" or "wings rapidly") into *pukna dinnenter ptera*, "thick/rapidly flapping wings." Suddenly the traditional phrase is gone, and yet it is still there. These are subtleties, but they fracture and recast traditional language.

The poem from which these two examples are taken is Sappho's most famous and possibly only complete poem. She has taken two moods and brought them together in an unusual way in twenty-eight lines. She begins with the typical elements of prayer to a goddess, using epithets and getting a sense of great size and space:

Clever-minded immortal Aphrodite,
child of Zeus, cunning, I beseech thee
don't break with worries and cares my
    heart, lady,

but come here, if ever another time
you heard my cry and came from
afar, leaving your father's golden
    house, you came

hitching up a chariot. Beautiful sparrows
brought you swift over the black earth
rapidly flapping wings out of heaven through
    the middle air.

Swiftly they came, and you, blessed one,
a smile on your immortal face,
asked what I was suffering, why
    I had called

and what most I wanted for myself and my
crazy heart. "Whom should Persuasion
bring to you in love, who, Sappho,
    hurts you?

For if she now flees, soon she'll pursue.
If she refuses gifts, nevertheless, she'll give them.
If she won't love, soon she will love
    even against her will."

Come to me even now, free me from
harsh cares, get me what my heart
tells me get, you yourself
    be ally.

In the third and fourth stanzas she has a bit of narrative. Then the pace changes to staccato questions, first in indirect statement, then in direct quotation, then the more breathless sixth stanza. One feels the power of the goddess, and yet as the seventh stanza returns to the prayer, it is clear that the intensity of the sixth was the increasing passion of Sappho's fantasy. In this way Sappho has endowed the formality of the prayer with the emotion that initially motivated it.

There is no doubt that throughout the seventh and sixth centuries poetry was the important medium of social communication. This is more obvious in the poetry of elegiac poets such as Solon or Tyrtaeus, but, as the fragments of Sappho demonstrate, even the personal poets were revolutionizing language and perception as well as describing their feelings. A more philosophical poet was Xenophanes, who wrote during the middle of the sixth century. Some fragments of his poetry question the human authority for anthropomorphized gods. If cows had hands, said Xenophanes, then they would portray god as a cow. He further castigates Homer and the other epic poets for portraying gods as so much like humans that they are flawed with all the unattractive traits humankind possesses. In some of his poetry he poses the notion of a kind of eternal consciousness. In place of the polytheistic universe of Greek tradition there is an Infinite governed, one might say, by brain waves. Although Xenophanes lived out his life in southern Italy in so-called Magna Graecia (the Romans called it "great Greece" because of the preponderance of Greek colonists) and Sicily, he was born in Colophon in Asia Minor, where it is thought he first came in contact with the kind of thinking found in his poetry.

It was at this time and in Asia Minor, particularly at Miletus, that prose first began to be used for systematic thinking—a hint of the future when prose eventually eclipsed poetry as the medium for intellectual communication. What little we know of the thinkers of Miletus comes from the merest fragments and the often obscure comments of Aristotle and other students of philosophy from centuries later. The Milesian School, as it is called, is exciting because it presages the strenuous rationalizing of the fifth century and because these men were the first to conceptualize in a fashion that suggests scientific method. It is true that their prose is not stylized art and that these thinkers are not exactly literary figures. They betray habits of mind, however, that later become common enough to be reflected in the literature.

The Milesian School is associated with the names of Thales, Anaximander, and Anaximenes. Thales, it is said, declared water to be the primary stuff of all things. This idea is explained as his belief that water is present in everything, that growing things depend on water, and that the different ways in which water manifests itself make it the prime candidate for consideration as the single substance to which all visible creation can be assigned. The importance of Thales's thought, of course, lies not with water, but with his determination to refine the perceived world to one principle and to define phenomena as so many changing aspects of this one material substance. It is the first and essential step on the way to a scientific view of things.

Anaximander improved on the ideas of Thales by conceiving that the one substance underlying all perceived reality could not be something in that perception. Instead of something like water, he called it "the boundless," that is, an entity outside of time and space and definition. In sum, Anaximander had the instinct to reach for an abstraction rather than an image, thus making the move away from the metaphorical nature of all Greek thinking up to his time and toward the philosophical language of Aristotle.

Anaximenes, his younger contemporary, turned again to an element of this world, naming air as the basic matter of the universe. While this might seem a step backward, Anaximenes seems to have been interested in another aspect of the problem of perception. His theory of air emphasizes the importance of condensation and rarefaction in matter and paves the way for the atomic theory of Democritus, a man from Abdera in Thrace who lived in the fifth century. With Anaximenes the importance of the Milesian School comes to an end. It did not survive the fall of Greek cities of Asia Minor to the invading Lydian army of Croesus. But it established the importance of adjusting between the authority of human empirical experience and what the mind thinks, between the thing perceived and the thing described.

The great power of language, the possibility that a statement is as real as something perceived, intrigued the Athenians throughout the fifth century. Parmenides, for example, wrote a poem in hexameters (a kind of latter-day Hesiod, perhaps) devoted to a discussion of reality and—if the fragments are a true index—the function of the verb "to be" in defining reality. Because the commonplace Greek verb of being does not make the distinction between "to be" and "to exist," the rhetorician Gorgias of Leontini was able to make a series of witty and paradoxical statements starting with, "If there is nothing, then nothing exists." Clever as he is, underlying his words is the serious assumption that whatever can be said is in some sense real or true. This assumption forms the basis of Socrates' lifetime pursuit of precise definition. It is the seriousness of this notion that redeems in Socrates what sometimes seems to be nothing more than mere preciosity.

The greatest body of surviving poetry written before the Hellenistic period—apart from the work of the tragic dramatists—comes from the hand of Pindar, who was born in 518, just under a decade after Aeschylus's birth, and who died in 438, the year Euripides brought out his *Alcestis*. Although he is not of the same time period as the poets already mentioned, his medium—choral lyric—and his favorite themes are sufficiently old-fashioned to make him seem to be a poet of the late archaic period. He lived elsewhere than in Athens, and it is not unreasonable to say that he therefore did not have to cater to the avant-garde—hence the old-fashioned flavor. Born in Boeotia, he spent his professional years constantly traveling; he was a poet for hire, and he went where the commissions were. His major clients were on the island of Aegina not far off the coast from Athens and a number of the tyrants of Sicily. Which is not to say that he was not lionized everywhere in the ancient Greek world. His celebrity during his lifetime was unmatched by any other ancient poet. In modern parlance he was very definitely a star. The seventh *Olympian Ode,* for example, was inscribed in gold letters in the temple of Athena at Lindos.

Choral lyrics are poems sung and danced by an ensemble. They were an aristocratic art form characterized by aristocratic values among which the great importance of community was symbolized by the chorus. There are fragments of the choral pieces of Alcman, a Spartan poet of the late seventh century, which celebrate Spartan festivals and other public occasions. These seem to have been designed for a chorus of Spartan maidens who sometimes seem to be given personae in the lyrics themselves. The choral ode was popular in the sixth century and is associated with Dorian societies. Thereafter it died out, surviving as only one of the features of Athenian tragic and comic drama. The Dorian origin of the choral ode is evident in the presence of features of the Doric dialect in Athenian tragic and comic choruses, while the language of the dialogue is in the Attic dialect.

Pindar's output was exceedingly large and varied. It was collected into seventeen books by category—hymns, paeans (a special kind of hymn originally addressed to Apollo in his role of healing god, later to other gods and other situations, but always with a special emphasis on imminent improvement of a situation, that is, a good luck hymn), dithyrambs (narrative songs of the life of a god or hero), processionals, songs for girls' choruses, songs of praise, funeral songs, and victory songs. By coincidence the victory songs have survived. Sometimes called epinicians, from the Greek word for victory hymn, there are forty-four divided into four groups depending on the athletic contest at which the victory was won. These contests were the Olympian Games, the Pythian Games, the Nemean Games, and the Isthmian Games.

Athletic contests were important occasions in ancient Greece, always occurring in a religious context. They were an extension of the heroic ethos found in Homeric epic, that is, that peculiar translation of highly charged aggression into the pursuit of lasting glory and honor. Thus it is not remarkable that the end goal of these ancient contests was always and simply winning. In modern times, by contrast, the nature of the physical achievement—a new time record set, for instance—is an equally important part of the competition. But the ancient Greeks seem to have had considerably less interest in progress than we have.

The Olympian Games were the most important of these events. They were held once every four years from 776 B.C. until well into the Christian era in the precinct of Olympian Zeus in the central Peloponnesus at the river Alpheus. The Olympian Games became a five-day affair with running, wrestling, chariot racing, horse racing, and so on, divided into men's and boys' events. The games drew participants from all over the Greek world. So important was this festival that the Greeks numbered time by the four-year intervals between Olympian Games, that is, first Olympiad, second Olympiad, and so on. The Pythian Games, second in importance, evolved from a very early festival at the oracle of Apollo at Delphi which had been centered upon a musical competition. Later this event was regularized to occur in the third year of every Olympiad and enlarged to include athletic events. The prize was a crown of bay leaves. The Nemean Games were a minor local event until the early decades of the fifth century when they too became Panhellenic. They were held in the sanctuary to Nemean Zeus, south of Corinth, every second and fourth year in each Olympiad. The prize for the competitions, which were much the same as those held at Olympia, was a crown of wild celery. A similar crown was the reward for winning at the Isthmian Games, which were held in honor of Poseidon at Corinth. Starting in 581, they, too, became an international event, held every second year and much patronized because Corinth was considered to be fun city in antiquity. (The saying "It is not for every man to make the voyage to Corinth" was the ancient Greek way of saying that life is unfair.)

The winner in each event was not always the actual contestant. Cities that backed the local hero who won the prize claimed the victory for themselves. This intense identification of city with hero is not unlike that between today's athletes and their audience, city, or country. In addition to civic backing, some contestants won their prizes on behalf of some magnate, often one of the Sicilian tyrants. This practice was common in horse racing and again is not unlike modern jockeys wearing the colors of a great stable. It was these affluent, well-situated backers who paid to have Pindar compose a victory hymn, and it is their role in the triumph, rather than the actual winning of the contest, that Pindar celebrates.

Pindar has enjoyed a mixed reputation over the centuries. Friedrich Hölderlin, for example, valued him highly and translated his lyrics into German. Ezra Pound, by contrast, called Pindar "the prize windbag of all time." For any critic Pindar presents enormous problems. The circumstances of performance raise questions about the accessibility of the performed text. It is known that the chorus sang the words while dancing, yet Pindar's language, grammar, and arrangements are extremely complicated. His strong, concrete images are often quite difficult (for instance, Pindar on aesthetics: "The forehead of every work begun must shine forth from afar" [*Olympian 6*, strophe 1]). How much of this dense text passed from the chorus to the audience? No doubt the audience was helped by the metrical scheme. While no two surviving poems have the same metrical form, Pindar uses a scheme in which each stanza or *strophe,* as the Greeks called it, is answered by a metrically identical stanza, known as the *antistrophe.* Presumably the choreography was made up of parallel dance patterns to match these stanzas. This structure may have helped the audience elicit the meaning.

Then, too, Pindar's themes are limited. He talks of nobility, grandeur, glory, brilliance, fame, beauty, and immortality. The presentation of these themes in a series of platitudes from ode to ode no doubt facilitated the process of writing under pressure, eased the burden for the chorus of learning their part, and made the poem more accessible to the audience. By weaving his poems out of the unsurprising, conventional values of his patrons, Pindar provided a solid fabric for the brilliance and variegation of his images and his sentence structure. Nonetheless, much of Pindar's poetry *is* difficult. As he himself says, "There are arrows in my quiver which speak to the *cognoscenti,* but the many need interpreters. Wise is the man who is born knowing much. Those who have learned what they know chatter like crows" (*Olympian* 2, strophe 5). This distinction between innate understanding and acquired knowledge is commonplace in aristocratic thinking, an expression of their monopoly of the culture, which continues throughout the fifth century into the dialogues of Plato in the fourth.

The convention of the epinician ode demands the name of the victor and his city, as well as some details describing him, then some references to the place of the victory and its occasion. There is also a myth. Sometimes it is told fully, as in the fourth Pythian ode, which has a very long narrative of the Argonauts; sometimes the myth is simply mentioned, as in the first *Olympian,* in which Pindar simply alludes to Poseidon's relationship with Pelops. There are aphorisms as well. There is often a prayer at the beginning or the end. And Pindar often speaks in his own person in these poems.

The content of many of these surviving odes is not unlike the speech of Phoenix in the ninth book of the *Iliad.* The old man begins with a personal appeal to Achilles to gain the young man's attention and validate Phoenix's authority for speaking. He then sets forth the thesis that "to yield is best." He next presents this idea in imagistic terms: "Entreaties are the daughters of Zeus, lame, halt, squinty-eyed." Then he translates the present situation into an example, a *paradeigma* (our word "paradigm"), describing the misfortune that befalls Meleager for not yielding soon enough.

Pindar enters his poems to mention his fees, to decry his critics, and to offer aphorisms, often noting the immortality of glory that his poetry will confer upon his clients. His performance is in fact a dramatization of the very glory of poetry to which he is so passionately committed. It is argued that in presenting maxims, Pindar is not offering his own philosophy but rather using a convention of the epinician, signaling a transition from one part of his poem to another. The argument is perhaps an apology for the simplicity of thought in these poems. But thought is not what Pindar is about.

At one point (*Pythian* 3, antistrophe 4) he offers a kind of emendation to Achilles' description of the jars of Zeus in the twenty-fourth book of the *Iliad,* which bears materially on his poetry:

> Gods give men two evils for every good.
> Fools can't handle this with grace.
> But nobles, they turn the beauty to the outside.

Pindar's harsh view of a bleak and indifferent universe was commonplace in the Archaic Age. He understands that the aristocratic class, freed from the necessity of forcing a living for themselves, have the leisure and education to contemplate this woeful truth. Those who understand what they see will know that living well is the best revenge, that beauty is the only justification. This certainly is the great aristocratic code that endures down into the democratic Athens of the fifth century, which makes possible both the grandeur of the tyrants' courts throughout Greece and the public works projects in Athens. Pindar is part of that process. He is a maker of beauty; he will adorn his clients' lives. His language, rhythms, and images will ennoble their actions, and, by giving them celebrity, give them permanence.

His constant reference to the world of the epic heroes and his poetic dialect, which leans so on that of the Homeric epics, suggests that Pindar sees himself as a poet in that tradition. He also fancies himself a seer and prophet. He is as gnomic and allusive as any oracular response from Delphi. He does not write epic poems. Rather, he takes images, ideas, bits and pieces from saga narrative and makes his own beautiful mosaic. In so doing he is anticipating the Alexandrian period, when the poets played off the great tradition of fifth-century Athens as well as the heroic poems. It is possible that the similarity derives from a like insecurity of ideas. Pindar was born just about when Athens began the enormous cultural thrust forward, fueled by the new democracy. The issues of that society—the new freedom, the conflict between individual and city, the relative strengths of convention and human nature, ideas of progress and conservatism, haves and have-nots—do not appear in his poetry. He speaks to a time long gone by, just as he comes from a city that misses out on the energy of the fifth century. The beauty of his contrivance, unfortunately, is lost on those unfamiliar with the Greek language; they will notice only the superficiality of his ideas. But, as Oscar Wilde once said, "All bad poetry springs from genuine emotion." Pindar's exquisite poetry, on the other hand, springs from decorum and contrivance.

Anyone interested in trying to experience a Pindaric ode will do well to compare Pindar's first *Olympian Ode* with the fifth ode of Bacchylides, Pindar's contemporary and rival. Both poems were composed on commission from Hieron, the tyrant of Syracuse, on the occasion of the victory of his horse, Pherenikos ("Victory-bringer") at the Olympian games in 476. (Pindar's first *Pythian Ode* and Bacchylides' fourth *Ode,* both composed for Hieron's victory at the Pythian games in 470, are also worth comparing.) Some wag, after working his way through Pindar's epinicians, once remarked that Hieron had to commission two poems each time so that at least there would be one he could understand.

In the fifth *Ode* Bacchylides recounts the meeting in the Underworld between Heracles and Meleager. Meleager died when his mother, in revenge for his killing her brother (by accident), took an enchanted stick from a chest and set it afire, an act doomed to end Meleager's life. Here as elsewhere in his surviving pieces Bacchylides is concerned with telling a story. Yet he will not resort to the massive, detailed lines of the typical epic narrative. Instead, he sets forth his story in brief phrases and images, here translated literally.

> Thestios' fierce daughter
> for me a mother of evil fate
> plotted my destruction, fearless woman that she was;
> from the carved chest
> she took the stick of quick death,
> burned it, the stick fate once had ordained
> would be the end of my life.
> At the time I was in the act of slaying
> the blameless body of Klymenos, Dapylos'
> bold son, before the walls;
> for they were fleeing toward
> the well-built city

of Pleuron. My sweet life grew short.
I felt my strength decline.
Oh me, breathing my last, I cried,
wretched at leaving my glorious youth.

As in epic narrative the epithets are there and the action is there, but the details are not. In this poem Bacchylides *suggests* the meaning of his narrative in a way quite unlike the explicit epic. After Meleager describes his death at the hand of his mother, Heracles shudders, then says, "It is best to speak of what man has the potential to do," that is, let the past alone, look to the future. He then asks, "Have you any sisters at home?" Meleager replies, "Dejaneira," and here the narrative part of the ode ends. Extraordinarily condensed, with much implied and much unsaid, the poem speaks to an audience that knows that Heracles will marry Dejaneira and that she, through jealousy, will be the cause of his death (however unwitting). Another woman, another destroyed male—it is Meleager and his mother all over again. Bacchylides seems to be saying, look to the future with caution, expect little. Success is failure. For the victory ode these are the proper, commonplace cautionary tales. Bacchylides maintains the suggestion of narrative in his poem, whereas Pindar extravagantly departs from his story.

Pindar's first *Olympian* begins:

Water is best, but gold like shining fire
that stands out in the night is man exalting wealth's high mark.
If, my heart, you will
sing of contests,
look no further than the sun,
no other star hotter in the day
shining through the desert of the air,
or sing no contest greater than Olympia
whence comes the oft-sung hymn
thrown around the wisdom of the wise,
to sing of the son of Cronus
as the wise arrive at the blessed hearth of Hieron.

With a grand flourish typical of his opening lines, Pindar announces that his theme will be preeminence. He uses the images of the Milesian philosophers' first principles, the most valuable metal, the brightest planet, the greatest god, the supreme athletic contest, the chief form of singing, and the greatest ruler, not to mention the wise who will be gathered at his table, preeminent among whom will be the poet himself.

When he turns to introduce his myth, the story of how Pelops in the first chariot race was helped by the god Poseidon, who loved him, he continues to interrupt the telling of it, really the suggesting of it, for a series of commentaries on related matters. For instance, he says:

> here in the colony of good men, colony of Lydian Pelops
> whom the Earthshaker, great in his strength
> Poseidon once loved and wanted, whom Clotho seized out of the caldron
> outstanding with his shining ivory shoulder.
> Yes, there are many wonders, and somehow
> some way stories tricked with glittering cunning
> lies deceive the talking of men beyond the true account.

His audience would know that the ivory shoulder is a reference to the story of Tantalus cutting up his son, Pelops, to serve as dinner for the gods. All refrained from eating so grisly a meal except Demeter, who absentmindedly ate the shoulder piece in her grief over the lost Persephone. This primitive detail offends the poet, and he stops to speak against it. Yet why, one may ask, does he include it in the first place when it seems only to complicate and obscure? Pindar brings in the ivory shoulder to raise the subject of decorum, which leads to the subject of the beauty of poetry, which will be translated into the love Poseidon felt for the beautiful boy. Beauty and love he can equate with excellence and fame, which will come to Hieron partly by victory but more by the victory hymn. Pelops, who won because of his beauty, which made Poseidon care for him, is succeeded by Hieron, who wins the race and then immortal fame with the help of Pindar (who, while elevating himself to equivalency with Poseidon, casts Hieron's power and station as the latter-day equivalent of Pelops's beauty). In contrast to Bacchylides Pindar had gone far away from his story. The poet concludes:

> The fame of the Olympic contests looks out afar from
>   the racecourse
> of Pelops, where swiftness of feet is in the contest
> and the high points of boldness and the struggle of strength.
> The winner all the rest of his life
> has honey-sweet good weather

because of the contests. Nobility that goes on day after day
is the highest for all mortals. And I must crown
this man with a horseman's song
in the Aeolic mode.
I know no man knowing
  more of beauty, holding greater power
of those whom I adorn with noble folds of hymns.

These lines are held together by "the fame," looking out "afar," "the high points," "winner," "rest of his life," "good weather," "nobility," "day after day"—all true to the exhilaration of winning, which, it is to be remembered, is the object at hand. In the poem Pindar addresses what is fleeting and what is imperishable; he does so by moving between personal comments, remarks on the poet's craft that speak to the occasion, and the eternally true maxims of the group and the myth.

The year in which Hieron's victory occasioned these two poems also saw the performance in Athens of Aeschylus's *Persians*. Unlike other tragedies, the *Persians* dramatizes a historical fact, the Persian defeat at Salamis. Because the action of the drama consists of the reaction of the Persian court at Susa to this doleful event, a situation about which Aeschylus would have known nothing, it is probably just as well to call the *Persians* a fiction. But the way in which Aeschylus uses geographical distance and stresses the exotic nature of Persian culture, together with his refusal to refer to the contemporary Greek world, mythologizes the real event. "Sea-washed Ajax's isle, soil bloodied, holds all there is of Persia," sings the chorus of Persians (595ff.), using the style of epic poetry to give epic proportion to the topical reference to the corpse-strewn beaches of Salamis following the naval battle in September 480.

The chorus enters singing a lyrical catalogue of the Persian forces. Unlike Homer's catalogue, however, reminiscences of which give this choral ode that typically Aeschylean "epic" flavor, the Persians' song combines the names in a way that suggests vastness, rather than simply supplying a register of place names:

And they, Susa and Agbatana
and the ancient bulwark of Cissa,
leaving, went on horse,
on ship, by foot they went,
bringing war's close array of men,

> Amistra and Artaphrenes,
> Megabates and Astarpes,
> lords of Persia,
> kings, to the great king subservient,
> they rush, overseers of a great army,
> bowman and cavalry,
> fearful to behold, terrible to fight
> in the show of their courageous heart.
> Artembares, horseman lustful of battle,
> Masistes, archer, conqueror,
> the noble Imaius, Pharandakes,
> Sosthanes, driver of horses.
> Others the Nile sent, the great
> and greatly nurturing Nile; Sousikanes,
> Pegastagon, Egyptian-born
> ruler of holy Memphis,
> great Arsames . . .
>
> [1ff.]

So the chorus continues proudly, boastfully until they are in place in the dancing area of the theater. Then the meter changes to lyrics cast in Pindar's usual strophe-antistrophe choral structure, which was also used by the tragedians. The chorus grows more reflective, switching from language that recalls Homer to maxims in the style of Hesiod as they pose questions:

> God's deceit and deception—
> what mortal man avoids this?
> Who masters his flying leap
> with swift enough foot?

Throughout this opening chorus Aeschylus translates the historic fact of the Persian expedition into a sacral truth in the same way Pindar removes himself from the immediate victory of Hieron's horse to something transcendent in that event.

Fourteen years later, in 458, Aeschylus won first prize with his Orestes trilogy. The first play, the *Agamemnon*, has lyrical choral passages of unusual force and grandeur reminiscent of Pindar's epinician poems. There are significant differences, however, for Pindar created relatively brief, occasional poetry, whereas each choral ode in the *Oresteia* is an integral part of a large dramatic whole. The first two choral odes of the *Agamemnon* are unusually long and relatively obscure. They suggest oracular responses, a suitably prophetic tone for the narration of events that are made by the poet to exist simultaneously in past, present, and future. Their length establishes the grand architecture of the entire trilogy, which will take the audience from the sullied sheets of Atreus's bed to the citizens' court on the Areopagus at Athens. The chorus begins:

40 This the tenth year since Priam's
        great plaintiff
    Lord Menelaus and Agamemnon,
    two-throned, Zeus-born, two-sceptered
    stout yoke of honor in Atreus's line,
45 launched from this land
        myriad ships in expedition
        a defense of soldiers
    crying great Ares from their heart
        like eagles
50 in grief at the nest departing of their young
    high over their beds wheel about
    plying the oars of their wings
        child care gone now
    which kept them to their beds.
55 Someone on high whether Apollo
    or Pan or Zeus heard
    the high-pitched cry, bird lament
    of these visitors to god's domain
    afterward sent punishment upon the transgressors.
60 So Zeus, the Lord, protector of the stranger, host
        and guest,
            sent Atreus's sons to Alexander [Paris]
            because of a woman of many men
            great wrestlings, weighing down of limbs,
            when the knees are planted in the dust, and
65   the spear snaps at the outset,
            laying it all on Trojans and Danaans
            alike. Now things are
    where they are. It will fall out to what was fated.
    No sacrifice, no libation
70   of wine or of tears
        will soften stiff wrath.

The choral ode is complex at the beginning and continues that way, so much so that from time to time editors of the text must assume that there are errors of copying in the lines. The complexity seems appropriate, though, for expressing the manifold faceting of human experience. The initial ambiguities in the metaphors and other images build to a powerful impression of the cruel contradiction and complexity of the universe. This is an impression sustained throughout the trilogy as Clytemnestra is transformed from a mother seeking revenge into an adulteress, as Orestes, the avenger of his father, becomes the murderous son, and as the Erinyes, the dread Furies, are transformed into the Kindly Ones, the Eumenides.

Aeschylus dresses Menelaus and Agamemnon in epic costume. Lines 42–44 have the quality of Homer's language, particularly line 43, which sounds like a drumbeat as the three main words in that four-word line (all beginning with a *d* sound in the Greek) are heard. In lines such as these the chorus seems to be singing an epic. Throughout this choral ode and the next Aeschylus alludes to the war at Troy as the high adventure Homer describes. But at the close of the second ode, in his characteristically ambiguous way, he reiterates the epic motif with a totally altered significance. The grand epic sense remains in such phrases as "Ares money changer of bodies and weigher of spears in battle" (437), but the value of war is undercut by other words. For behind Ares with his scales of death stands the commonplace notion of Zeus, weighing upon his scales the fates of the fighting men, just as he does in the twenty-second book of the *Iliad* with the fates of Achilles and Hector. Like the image of Ares, the words that follow are bitter: dust exchanged for bodies, beautiful young men buried at Troy, the parents angry. The motif of concerned parent/endangered child is repeated from lines 49ff., also from another, ironic perspective.

Agamemnon and Menelaus are "plaintiff" (41), a word from the law court, as is "defense" (47), although less specifically so. The war is fought for justice; the gods have heard Agamemnon and Menelaus and aid them (55ff.): justice will be done. The images forecast the triumphal end to the trilogy in a court of law. Along the way, ironically enough, justice will be sought in more than one murder. In several of Aeschylus's plays he establishes the theme of the ending with the initial choral ode. Here the sons of Atreus are instruments of justice before a city-state's legal machinery has been established. The word translated as "punishment" (59) is *Erinyes,* the Greek name given to the grim spirits, the Furies, who avenge family murder and who will later hound and pursue Orestes after he has murdered his mother, until he is set free by Athena's court and the Furies are transformed from the irrational spirit of vengeance into benign deities.

Where the ode is most exciting is in the image of the soaring eagles. Next to the net image that begins the next choral ode (355ff.), the eagle-parent image in all of its complexity is the most important in the trilogy. The eagles are, as the chorus says (58), entrants into the gods' world, shrieking for their young. Eagles are traditionally associated with Zeus. They will avenge Paris's seduction of Helen, who has left the nest. But there is also the true child gone from the nest, that is, the slaughtered Iphigenia, a notion reinforced when the chorus describes the portentous omen of the eagles who rip open a pregnant hare (114ff.). The second eagle image alters the initial impressions. The avenging eagle, the proud father, and the war lord are cast now as murderers. In the prayer to Artemis which follows shortly thereafter (139ff.) the poet poses things in terms of male and female: Artemis, the pregnant hare, Clytemnestra, and Iphigenia against the sons of Atreus and Zeus. What man has done to women will be done again.

> Holy Artemis in anger and in pity
> at her father's winged hounds
> eating the unborn children of the hare
> hates the banquet of the eagles.
>
> [125ff.]

This image calls to mind the banquet of Thyestes, at which Atreus, having killed the adulterous Thyestes' children, served them to him unsuspecting. As always in this play the one image evoking another points to the inexorable return of events. Specifically, Artemis will demand through Calchas the sacrifice of Iphigenia, a scene for which this dread slaughter of the eagles is a rehearsal. A similar demand will be repeated when Clytemnestra forces Agamemnon to walk upon the carpet as a kind of reiteration of the killing of Iphigenia.

The choice Artemis forces upon Agamemnon and his subsequent sacrifice of Iphigenia are treated by Aeschylus in the allusive manner so common to Pindar and to Bacchylides. Because the ode is part of a drama and the context explains much, the chorus describes only briefly and abstractly the ships becalmed, Calchas's answer, Agamemnon's response, and Iphigenia's death. Without mentioning names, the chorus refers to the prophet, the father, the chieftain, the child, the daughter. Flashback openings are windows onto an action that the abstracting choral lyric makes greater than its participants, action that has become mythology. In a brilliant moment of theater Aeschylus uses these two opening choral odes as a kind of backdrop against which Clytemnestra, the mother and wife, moves back and forth, performing her acts of thanksgiving at the altars. Like the action the chorus describes, she herself becomes a symbol. The abstraction of these odes is intensified with a number of gnomic passages, reminiscent of Hesiod, many of them exceedingly dense, for example:

> There is no defense in money
> for the man who insolently
> kicks at the altar of Justice
> into his own disappearance and destruction.
>
> Dread Persuasion, powerful child
> of premeditating Destruction crushes him.
> All remedy is vain.
>
> [381–87]

Aeschylus gives a theological and philosophical perspective to the events of the play in these odes. The odes are a view of the action, while at the same time Clytemnestra's movement is the only dramatic action and in combination with the choral lyrics stands as a complete statement of the events so far. Such is the economy of Aeschylean theater.

Dramatic choral lyric is not usually so ambitious as it is in this play. Sometimes it seems to be mainly ornamental. It is not clear how accessible the choral odes were to the audience. They were both sung and danced in production. When read, however, the best choral odes in tragedy are not only dazzling verbal arrangements, but are also a view to a parallel world of action, more complicated, profound, or abstract, of which tragic action is the merest tip of the iceberg.

CHAPTER FIVE

Athens in the Fifth Century

O, glistening, violet-crowned and awful,
bulwark of Hellas, famous Athens, holy city

Pindar, fragment

. . . if any ambassadors come to town to trick you the first thing they
call out is "violet-crowned." If anyone says that, then you sit right up
on the crowns of your ass. Then if anyone adds "glistening Athens,"
they've made it on account of that "glistening," although it describes
sardines better.

Aristophanes, Acharnians 636ff.

Athens is the teacher of Greece.

Pericles (quoted by Thucydides 2.41)

The history of ancient Greek literature of the fifth century B.C. is
the history of the city of Athens. The fifth century was one of those
rare times in human history when circumstances in one small city
produced, attracted, and inspired a group of writers who turned out a
stunning range of universally acknowledged masterpieces. It is remarkable how the city itself, obviously or implicitly, intrudes into
this literature. Tragic and comic drama, of course, were produced
and performed as civic events. Their political flavor is unmistakable;
that is, the sense of a public forum, social communication, or whatever we want to call it is never absent. But it is scarcely less pronounced in all the other writings of the time.

We talk of the fifth century. A historical period is hard to pinpoint;
the details are so many, the perspectives so various. Narrative historians let wars or political events inform the structure of their story.
One could set the boundaries of the period of Athens's literary glory
as the birth of Aeschylus (545 B.C.) to the death of Socrates (399 B.C.)
or Plato (347) or Isocrates (338). Or one might say that when Eu-

ripides and Sophocles died in 406, the poetic Muse went with them, just as the tutelar goddess Athena deserted her city in its defeat at Aegospotami at the end of the summer in 405. The latter notion has the kind of stagy quality that historians sometimes use to reinforce artificial temporal categories such as these.

In fact war and politics *do* establish this period best. The burst of cultural energy is coincident with the reforms of government by which the democracy was established around 510 and with the victory of Athens over the Persians in the first decades of the new century. In the same way the decline of literary activity (at least as we see it on the basis of our scanty evidence) can be related to the economic and human loss and the spiritual fatigue brought on by the long-fought Peloponnesian War and the Athenian defeat in 405.

Historians, literary or otherwise, from antiquity on, take an organic view of this period, treating it as a person who ages and dies after a glorious youth. The more common metaphor is seasonal: so it is that with the fateful battle of Aegospotami in 405 and so perfectly *at the end of summer,* Athens entered her autumnal years, which culminate for literature in the so-called New Comedy of the late fourth century, which is to the drama of the fifth century what Noël Coward and Neil Simon are to Shakespeare. This autumn is then followed by a long winter as Athens becomes the ancient world's university town, dead, caught in the amber of its ancient perfection. Looked at in this way, fifth-century Athens seems an exceptionally lively, healthy organism or a particularly beautiful springtime. The danger in this approach, one that besets literary historians continually, is that it tempts us to look for the first telltale wrinkle of age or the first falling leaf. Critics of Euripides are particularly susceptible to this temptation because so much of his surviving work differs, sometimes radically, from the less numerous extant pieces (we have so little to base our generalizations on!) of Aeschylus and Sophocles. Of course, we are helped in this view of Euripides by the ancients themselves, the comic dramatist Aristophanes in particular, who is often rather hard on Euripides.

We must always protect ourselves from the ancient tendency to view all things as in decline. To succumb to critical notions based on inevitable decadence is to ignore how scanty our evidence is and, more important, to deny the infinite repertoire of responses to the human condition, some of which will resonate more deeply or sympathetically in one epoch than in another. There are fashions in taste in literary history, too, not to mention the constant adjustment of interpretation. In the nineteenth century Sophocles was an Anglican bishop; in the twentieth he is more like Camus.

Athens became the natural site for a population center because of the Acropolis, the high outcropping of rock that provided easy defense. As Athens grew in size, it became dominant among the settlements that sprang up at the crossroads throughout the countryside. These rural groups were eventually amalgamated into the city, their men given access to the assembly, their religious rituals made part of the city ceremony. The land mass, roughly the size of Rhode Island, of which Athens was the center was called Attica. It consisted of farmland, not much of it very fertile.

As time went on, economic dislocations in the farming community threatened the social fabric of this emergent city-state. Men who had gone into debt and failed to meet their payments were sold into slavery to satisfy their creditors. Men of the people who had grown prosperous on their farming still did not have access to public office, which was open only to aristocrats. As the crisis grew, a man named Solon was appointed to a special office to try to resolve the economic problems. He redeemed the Athenian citizens sold into slavery, redistributed some of the land to the landless, and established categories of privilege and responsibility among the citizenry based on their material wealth rather than on any hereditary aristocratic right. Throughout this period Athens remained a small place, really a large village, still dominated by the great landowning aristocratic families. The *agora,* for instance, the large area containing the public buildings and the major shopping centers at the base of the Acropolis, was not yet in evidence.

Athens began to change into a true city (Greek *polis,* from which our word "political" comes) when Peisistratus seized control of the government in 561. Born into an aristocratic family, he ruled in the manner common to tyrants in Greek city-states of the sixth century; that is, suppressing the power of the traditional aristocratic ruling class, he looked to the soldier class for his support. These soldiers were not the soldiers of the contemporary imagination. Called hoplites, which means "men outfitted for battle," these were men who had the means to outfit themselves with the necessary weapons and amenities of military life and thus were men of some property. Before this time community security had rested upon the men of the aristocracy who fought from expensive horses and chariots. The hoplites represent a new class whose group service gave them cohesion and a desire for a recognized role in the political life of the community.

At this time the word "tyrant" did not have the pejorative connotations that later history has given it. A tyrant was simply a man who held the supreme ruling power in a community illegally. That is, he was not the son of the king or the choice of the aristocracy. Peisistratus, like the other tyrants of the time, improved the lot of the nonaristocratic people and brought the cultural amenities of the aristocratic life to the public, making the whole city his court. He embarked on land reform and building programs; he started festivals and imported artisans and artists. After his death his sons lost control of the city in 510. The aristocratic cliques wanted to take back the power, but the Athenians, having been given so much attention and stimulation under the tyranny, could not tolerate their domination again.

Cleisthenes was voted by the people to an office of political reform, and, thanks to his stratagems, political chaos was avoided. Himself an aristocrat, the leader of an aristocratic faction, Cleisthenes had political ambitions. These he satisfied in a radical way by initiating a series of reforms that placed further power in the hands of the people, providing for a participatory democracy that has been the world's model ever since. "Power in the hands of the people," of course, meant something very different from what it means now. Only adult males had any access to power. While enlarging the group who could vote, Cleisthenes retained adulthood, ethnic integrity (that is, Athenian parentage), free birth, and the male gender as prerequisites for citizenship. It is important to bear in mind that the preeminence of these qualities is an underlying assumption in ancient Greek literature throughout the fifth century.

Before the tyranny of Peisistratus, the strong, rich, and well-born from the three principal sections of Attica—the coast, the plain, and the uplands—were in constant rivalry for domination of the city's political life. After the Peisistratids were gone, when these same groups threatened to return Athens to a state of political chaos, Cleisthenes undertook to destroy the access to power of any person or group so as to return the power continually to the people. He instituted ten new tribes made up of voting units known as *trittyes*. Each of the *trittyes* was made up in equal parts of men from the coast, the plains, and the uplands. This mixture denied any one area the chance to dominate in the voting or to form a geographical bloc.

Other equally ingenious schemes were devised by the Athenians as time went on, which demonstrate the city's characteristic rationality. What follows is a synthetic account of the Athenian governing system once it had evolved over a period of thirty or forty years.

The popular assembly was the sovereign body. It was open to all adult, freeborn males over eighteen; this was perhaps forty thousand out of a population of two hundred thousand to three hundred thousand. When voting time came, of course, only those who could get to the assembly voted; there was no notion of representation. (During the Peloponnesian War the temper of the assembly changed when the Spartan invasions of Attica forced so many conservative farmers into the city of Athens for security. The assembly meetings grew increasingly tense, as city folk and country folk polarized.) Five thousand was an average attendance figure, an unwieldy number for the planning or execution of anything. In fact, a kind of steering committee had been instituted prior to this time. Called the *boule,* or council, it was now established at five hundred, with fifty men chosen from each of the ten tribes. Five hundred being still too large to be thoroughly effective, the process was further refined by the introduction of the prytany, an executive subcommittee of fifty, which rotated its membership ten times a year. Each rotation brought a new group of fifty men from one of the ten tribes that sat in the *boule.* In this way all five hundred men of the *boule* had the opportunity to take a more effective role in the management of the city. The prytany was sufficiently intimate for the members to discuss among themselves the affairs of state. The assembly, however, remained the final political power. It met once in each successive prytany, that is, ten times a year, to deliberate and to vote legislation and action. Each day the actual head of state, holding the keys to the treasury, the seal, and having absolute power in emergency, rotated among the fifty in the prytany. In a year, then, three hundred and sixty-five men out of the five hundred men who at different intervals sat in the prytany held office as head of state, and, if the assembly met that day, president of the assembly. Membership in the *boule* was for a year and could be repeated once, although not in the consecutive year. So it was that most Athenian men in the course of a lifetime sat in the *boule* and in the prytany, and many held executive office. This meant that the real exercise of considerable power could and did fall to many men randomly and distributively. Most Athenian males, we may assume, lived heightened political and social lives by virtue of this experience.

The method of choosing men to serve as government officials, those who were in the *boule* and those who sat on juries, evolved in a curious way toward the purest democratic practice. By 487, candidates to these positions were all elected by lot, that is to say, randomly and arbitrarily, as American civil juries are chosen. By eliminating popular elections the Athenians were able to eliminate also the influence of prestige, charm, personality, intelligence, talent, and expertise. In addition, the annual rotation of these offices denied to anyone the opportunity to build up a fund of knowledge so as to become indispensable, as is the case with entrenched bureaucrats, the tyrants of the modern state.

Corollary to this democratic system was the law for ostracism, a vote for exile. A man voted into exile had to leave the city for a decade (although neither his family nor his possessions were affected by the decree against him). Ostracism was another civic check upon anyone who in any way might prove dangerously superior and thus powerful. Early in the year the assembly voted on whether a vote for ostracism should be held. No debate was allowed; it had to be a matter of instinct or previous consideration for each voter. If a majority of the assembly voted favorably, then during one of its earliest successive meetings the vote for ostracism was taken. In the interval no public debates were held, and no accusations against anyone were made. At the time of the voting each man decided for himself. It was not a matter of party, bloc, or faction, although there is great temptation to see it that way from the modern perspective. It was, instead, each man's private political decision. Whoever received a majority of the vote went into exile.

Political strife and factionalism found expression not so much in the assembly as in the system of law courts. Litigation was a constant feature of Athenian life. A great part of the population sat on juries, which met almost daily. Juries consisted of up to 6,001 men, depending on the importance of the trial. Members were elected by lot; a simple majority ruled. Eventually jurors were paid a small sum, which converted jury duty into a kind of valuable daytime occupation for the older members of the community. Juries were little hampered by observing the niceties of law in finding for or against the defendant. A man's worth to the city and his esteem among his fellows were considerably more decisive factors. The trial of Socrates on charges of impiety and corruption has been made memorable by Plato's account of Socrates' defense (*Apology*). It is clear—despite whatever fictional liberties Plato may have taken—that the defense finally rested not on guilt or innocence before the law, but on the jury reaction to Socrates' singular public personality. So it must have been in many another trial.

This extraordinary democratic system allowed for a certain kind of direct leadership, the exact nature of which is much in dispute. The assembly popularly elected ten generals for a year's term; what is more, the generals could stand for reelection. This curious body, called the *strategia,* is hard to define. What power did they have? More to the point, what power did Pericles have? We know that he was reelected to a generalship often and finally without interruption from 443 to his death in 429. Nineteenth-century historians likened him to the British prime minister, the nine other generals being his cabinet. This interpretation subtly colors accounts of the period to this day; yet it is not a good analogy.

While it is true that men became generals by popular election, they were not elected as a group. Therefore they owed no political debts to each other and did not represent a political party; they could not function as a cabinet or presidential council. More important, they did not initiate or realize policy. This was the assembly's function. Each time the assembly met, it could embark upon new policy, start a war, call for peace, and so forth. The generals had to carry out whatever was voted.

The generals were elected originally to lead men into battle. It is easy to see why popular election persisted for men in this capacity, although many elected were clearly amateurs in military matters. Who, after all, wants the random neighbor elected by lot to be in command when catastrophe impends? The generals remained military men, whether it was Themistocles improving the Piraeus harbor as a general or the civilian Cleon losing his life at Amphipolis when he led troops against an infinitely superior soldier and strategist, the Spartan general Brasidas.

Their main political function, however, seems to have been to stand as a projection of the popular will. Ancient evidence suggests that the generals spoke a good deal in the assembly, urging one course of action or another. Insofar as they articulated what the people wanted to hear, not necessarily consciously, but instinctively, they were successful. Plato describes how the assembly hooted down those who did not know what they were talking about (*Protagoras* 319d). Aristophanes' most political comedy, the *Knights,* portrays the people (Demos) as master in the household and the major political figures of the time—Cleon, Demosthenes, and Nicias—as the servants below stairs who will try any wile or stratagem to stay in

Demos's good graces. Thus he portrays the generals as essentially expressions of the common will. Far more than power or money the Athenians valued glory and fame, or so it seems. These were the rewards the generals received, but they needed the people to bestow these upon them. Furthermore, in any large assembly of men there has to be the few who manage the talking. There is anarchy otherwise. Pericles was probably elected general again and again because he said what the Athenians wanted to hear and he encouraged them to do what they wanted. Is this not finally the mark of any truly great leader? The debates in the assembly do indeed seem to have aired the essential positions on any subject so well that the assembly could vote from conviction. The power of the generals, therefore, was something that had to be renewed constantly by the people. Sovereignty was never delegated in any real sense.

We may assume that this intense political life had its effect on the literature of the fifth century. Athens was a community where the men actively participated in the management of the city on many levels, making ethical and moral decisions affecting a whole society. The fate and purpose of the community were matters of constant discussion. Political debate in tragic drama must have had great meaning by virtue of this experience. The debate in the *Antigone* between Creon and Antigone over the primacy of religious law or city law and the obligations owed to siblings and the punishments deserved by traitors reflects the kind of argument and decision making the men of Athens were used to.

Whether listening to Herodotus read from his *Histories* or Gorgias, the rhetorician, lecturing, or whether watching a tragedy or comedy in the theater, every man of the audience was a social person, a political person, intensely involved in the city, closely relating to the fellow members of the audience. The ancient Greeks had no real concept of the private person. Their word for it, *idiotes,* the root of our "idiot," means someone withdrawn from his true self, which is the public man.

Social cohesion is the basis of a remarkable anecdote about Socrates. When Aristophanes presented the *Clouds,* which parodies Sophistic teaching, the character of the Sophist was represented by an actor wearing a mask made to resemble the face of Socrates, who was notorious for his ugly countenance. At the moment when the character made his first appearance, Socrates is said to have stood up so that the audience could note how well the mask maker had done his job. This intimacy and camaraderie among so vast an assemblage is frequently apparent in Aristophanic comedies, in which the actors often speak to the audience. We must remember that there was no proscenium arch and no raised stage and that the chorus, situated between the actors and the audience, becomes by metonymy the entire group seated in the amphitheater. These circumstances are often vividly effective in tragedy—for example, in the opening of *Oedipus the King* when Oedipus addresses the suppliant populace of Thebes, who are represented by the chorus but to which by extension the entire audience is joined. The same effect is achieved in the *Agamemnon* when Clytemnestra defends her actions before the chorus. In the drama they represent the townspeople, but finally no more so than the entire audience of Athenians sitting watching the spectacle.

Athens was like a giant family, you might say. The family and the *polis* are, in fact, remarkably intertwined, forming one of the major metaphors from which all Athenian life flowed. Sophocles plays to this idea in the *Antigone,* in which the tragic conflict between Antigone and her uncle and king, Creon, is both political and familial. In the same way Plato has Socrates defend his allegiance to Athens in the *Crito* by likening the city's laws to the parents who raised him. In earlier centuries, when Athens was a mere village with little political or social structure, the extended family was the major cohesive force in the society.

Other social groupings reinforced the idea of the family. The migrating Indo-Europeans came divided into tribes. Each tribe was made up of brotherhoods, each a giant family because everyone—man, woman, and child—was officially enrolled in membership. Finally there were neighborhood organizations based on geographical association. Each of these units had special cults, rites, religious leaders, and celebrations; each offered its members some kind of assistance and protection. Because there were no city-sponsored agencies promoting their welfare, these societal groups were valuable. At the same time they reinforced the social aspect of each person. We do not hear of the isolation and alienation that mark urban life in the twentieth century. No wonder it was unusual to be considered a private person.

Within the family husbands and wives held different roles. What Hector says to Andromache in the *Iliad* remained true: "No one can escape his fate. . . . Go back to the house, take up the loom . . . and leave war to me" (6.488ff.). An Odysseus or an Orestes travels; a Penelope or an Electra waits at home. The household was arranged to serve the interests of the group who had rights in common to inherited land. Children were desired to maintain the family's ownership of the land and also to succor their parents in their enfeebled old age. The commonly expressed horror of parents surviving their children was not sentimental but practical.

A woman was needed to produce these children and then to rear them and manage the house; her life was defined by these needs. Because children were the key to landownership, a girl's virginity and later the legitimacy of a wife's offspring were of paramount importance. A girl's life was passed in the home and in the women's quarters. Once pubescent, she had to be confined and quickly married. In the early years of marriage the young wife was again confined so that her contact with males would never be suspect. She was even kept from eating with her husband and his male friends. Nowhere in the literature do we find any particular concern for the feelings of women in these strenuous domestic arrangements. Once the family's progeny were born, women had a far easier time of it. They could divorce, retain their dowries, and even have adulterous relationships (especially because there was no scruple against killing unwanted children at birth).

A man of property or from the aristocracy normally married after active military service, around the age of thirty. His wife might be only half that age. His experience outside the house and his formal education put impossible barriers between himself and his naive, house-sheltered, teenage bride. In any case he would already have habituated himself to passing time in the company of foreign-born courtesans who earned their living in Athens. These were women who for some reason had to find their security outside the family— women who had physical charms, style, personality, and social and cultural attainments, which they used to give pleasure in return for rewards with which they could buy the security their sisters derived from the conventional family situation. While it is true that this form of sexual and psychic service has its obviously degrading aspects, these women were nevertheless free in many respects—to exercise their minds and to discover a great deal about the world—privileges that their respectable sisters never knew. There is a theory that the relative emancipation of women in the early Hellenistic period stems from the example set by courtesans.

In the fifth century greater competition for a woman's husband's interest came from his homosexual affections. Respectable aristocratic and monied males sought the company of handsome teenage boys.

Emotional, intellectual, and physical ties grew strong, and, if we can believe our sources, this relationship was the most serious in a man's life. This does not seem unreasonable on the face of it, because both wives and courtesans were not considered peers with males. Conjugal relationships ensured a lifetime of household well-being; courtesans provided wit, gaiety, and sexual proficiency; boys were the source of self-esteem and personal improvement. The commonplace attitude toward this practice appears in the speech of Phaedrus in Plato's *Symposium,* who argues that a male's impulse to superior behavior derives from his need to seem a superlative person in the eyes of his male beloved.

Male relationships, however, are rare in myth and in tragic and comic drama. One reason may well be the censorship exercised in successive centuries, when homosexuality was considered odd or immoral; materials on this theme may have been destroyed. Tombstone epitaphs also show strong affection between husband and wife. Aristophanes' comedy *Lysistrata* is strong evidence that Athenian men as a group preferred heterosexual intercourse and were generally sexually interested in their wives. The play is about a fantasy stratagem whereby the women of Greece deny their husbands sexual relations until a peace treaty is signed. Much of the humor turns on the physical distress of men who have been kept from their wives too long. Of course, comedy demands simplification; thus there would be no room in the play for courtesans or boys. At the same time one gets the sense from the play that in ancient Athens as in other societies most men wanted conjugal heterosexual relations as a staple of their lives whether out of habit or from indolence or timidity—perhaps even for love, although this seems doubtful.

Homosexuality, however, was not reprehensible or ridiculous, unless it was coupled with effeminacy. As a social institution, much encouraged, it provided a male with the narcissistic delight of coupling with a youthful version of himself. Such a relationship not only distanced old age and death but gave a man a chance at a later age to remake himself. It gave him a reason to live up to his highest standard. In a society in which males were so competitive it provided him with masculine intimacy. Male children were traditionally raised in the women's quarters as strangers to their fathers; homosexual relationships gave to men surrogate sons and allowed an emotion and passion fathers and sons rarely know.

We must also consider that ancient Greek society, not having prohibitions against homosexual activity as the Judeo-Christian societies do, did not threaten males who tried out what is probably a perfectly natural alternative or supplementary experience. Mediterranean teenage males can often be, as ancient statuary attests and modern example shows, both breathtakingly beautiful and strikingly androgynous. In a society in which young girls were not to be seen, it is no wonder that teenage boys became objects of sexual interest.

Male homosexuality, it sometimes seems, carried an ideological message for conservatives. To the conservative aristocrat who preferred landowning to seafaring, who believed in superiority by birth rather than by amassed wealth, who encouraged quiet power in the hands of his class and despised the vociferous democratic assembly, the social system of Sparta seemed superior. And Spartan life was characterized by the socially approved, indeed desired, practice of male homosexuality. Male homosexuality also reinforced the aristocratic emphasis on exclusiveness. While kinship is a major mode of achieving this, homosexuality can further it, too. For one might say that the young passive partner in anal intercourse is tamed and bonded in a certain sense.

Ancient tragedy has always been a mine for psychological speculation because so many of the dramas play on relations within the family. The male-female relationship in tragedy, as one might expect from the facts of Athenian family life, is often one of conflict or even disaster. Creusa's betrayal and exploitation by Apollo in Euripides' *Ion,* Dejaneira's unsuspecting gift of death to her philandering husband, Heracles, in Sophocles' *Trachinian Women,* Medea's killing of her children to avenge the husband who deserts her in Euripides' *Medea,* and Clytemnestra's seduction and killing of her husband, Agamemnon, in Aeschylus's *Agamemnon* are examples. Against these family conflicts we might set Jocasta's loving concern for her husband, Oedipus, only remembering that it is ironically also the love of a mother for her son. Whatever the relation between the sexes, ancient ideas of decorum inhibited realistic love scenes; they would be difficult in production because males took all the roles.

Many plays portray dominant females and inferior males, the latter generally the victims of the former, this in a society in which women were very much dominated by their powerful fathers, husbands, or brothers. The explanations for this phenomenon are numerous. One is that myths that are associated with a cult of the strong female goddess and her inferior male consort who dies following his association with her are transmuted in the drama of a society of dominant males and repressed females to express the latent rage of the latter and the fear of that rage or a projection of it by the former. Another is that children growing up in a home in which the father was generally absent, as was the case in Athens, if only in the sense that he was not in the women's quarters as the children were, tend to have the notion of a strong, dominant mother and a weak father. Added to this notion is perhaps the child's sense of the mother's rage at this rejection.

If one were to remonstrate that I am foisting twentieth-century psychological notions onto another time and scene, I would answer that there are plays that rather starkly portray women's rage. Euripides' *Medea,* in which the chorus joins with Medea in depicting woman's plight in that society, is probably the best example. Euripides' *Bacchae* gives a frightening (from the male's point of view) portrait of female hysteria mixed with hostility toward males. Despite the strong sense of family in the fifth century, an increasing individualism encouraged people to think of themselves apart from their roles in the family. This phenomenon perhaps gave or forced upon women more of a sense of self, more of a chance to act out their reactions to male repression.

If women were admitted to the tragic theater festivals—and we are not sure whether they were—how did they react to these plays? Did the Athenian woman always play a passive, weak, introverted Electra to her husband's decisive, wise, and seasoned Orestes? Was she always the alien Medea in the self-satisfied Jason's house? Did tragedy teach her something or confirm what she already knew? How is it that males would choose such scripts, pay to have them produced, act in them, and watch them? Would they see Euripides' *Medea* as the story of a woman victimized by her husband and male society, or as the tragic dilemma of the conflicting roles and needs of both parties in the conjugal situation, or as the story of a man victimized by a bizarre, foreign sorceress wife for whom he has already done enough?

It is tempting to compare Aeschylus's *Agamemnon* with Euripides' *Medea* to chart a change in concept of individualism and in the role of women. Clytemnestra in the *Agamemnon* is pretty much defined by her function. She kills her husband to legitimate her role as mother. Later, she appears to exult over her act, *in this one moment defining it as hers.* Aegisthus, her lover, her murdered husband's cousin, enters to remind us (to remind her?) that her passion for him has redefined her function from an avenging mother to a murderous adulteress. This suggests that she is the victim first of Aegisthus as some kind of *ate,* the seduction sent to goad her into murdering Agamemnon, and, second, of the House of Atreus, which in generation after generation causes the destruction of children and marital betrayal by blood relations. In sum, Clytemnestra is a creature of her story as well as of her husband's family. In Euripides' *Medea,* however, the female character who kills her children to remind her indifferent husband of her importance to his dynastic ambitions can be also read as the woman who refuses to be imprisoned by motherhood when her husband walks out on her and so kills the impediments to her own freedom and walks out herself. In either case, Medea is concerned throughout the play with her rights to some kind of marital happiness as a wife, an individualistic stance inconceivable in Aeschylus's Clytemnestra.

In the course of the fifth century, as the city grew more powerful relative to the family, the city usurped some of the functions of the family. We can see this phenomenon reflected in Aeschylus's *Oresteia* trilogy, which ends in a civic trial by jury for the matricide Orestes, and in Sophocles' *Antigone,* in which Antigone's personal familial act is suppressed by the city. In both cases traditionally family-sanctioned action becomes the prerogative of the state. The city took on some of the family's attributes as well. The executive body, the *prytaneion,* for instance, ate a common meal like a family. There was a community hearth. The city worshipped Athena just as individual families had a household cult. Athena was translated from the keeper of the household to keeper of the city. Her virgin chamber (the Parthenon) was situated upon the Acropolis. Her people, Athenians, were named after her, not after a place. Beyond the family, beyond the city as family, lay the universe itself, peopled with deities, many of whom were themselves depicted in myth as members of a family.

The mythology of the gods which we find in the literature is not a reliable index of the daily religious practice of the ancient Greeks. More reliable are the details of the cult rituals and the festivals throughout the year, occasions when the people enacted traditional, communal attitudes toward the divine beings that filled their universe. As one might expect in a polytheistic society, the rituals were many and diverse. Most common was the slaughter of an animal as an offering to a god, followed by the burning of the inedible parts as the offering and the eating of flesh by the community. Animal sacrifice can inspire feelings of awe in the face of death, continuity of life in death in the eating of the animal's remains, guilt in the act of killing, community in the act of eating, and so on; which feelings were aroused in each instance depended on the focus of the ritual.

There were also fire rituals relevant to the hearth, a symbol of the continuity of life and civilization, just as fire is also a symbol of life. Offerings of the first fruits of the harvest were made to the gods in the same spirit as the dash of wine splashed on the ground as libation to the god prior to eating and drinking. For these activities there were priests, often members of aristocratic families who inherited the office but were not priests by profession. Professionalism was more common among the seers. For a religious institution that more closely resembles what we know as an established church one must look to the oracle at Delphi at the shrine of Apollo with its priestly staff rather than to the civic temples.

The festival that is best known to us is that in honor of the god Dionysus, which was the annual occasion for the presentation of tragic and comic dramas. A portrait of another festival has been left to us, originally sculpted in marble for the frieze of the Parthenon, now fragmented in the pieces known as the Elgin Marbles which are in the British Museum. This frieze depicts the procession of Athenians as they make their way up to the Acropolis to present, as they did annually, a newly woven robe to the goddess Athena. The festival was the Panathenaea, a celebration of the new year (which came in midsummer after the harvest) and also the birthday celebration for the city of Athens. It was the major political festival of the city, and in time it served as a unifying festival for Ionians as a group.

Another festival in honor of the god Dionysus came in the springtime. Called the Anthesteria or Old Dionysiac Festival, it was a three-day celebration of the arrival of spring and the maturation of the new wine. The first day was for gathering the jugs of new wine, which had been laid down at the grape harvest the previous fall. The second was a day of drunkenness and gloom. There was a contest to see who could finish a two-liter jug of wine fastest. Ritual preparations were made at the houses that day to receive spirits of the dead. Ghosts were thought to roam the city as the human inhabitants reeled about in a stupor. At the close of the day the citizens went off to deposit their wine casks in a designated area, where a ritual holy marriage took place between a priestess and the god Dionysus. On the third day a porridge of grain and honey was cooked and eaten in memory of the first meal taken after the primeval cataclysmic flood. At the same time a ritual cry bade the ghosts to depart. The day following the festival was devoted to contests; vase painting shows repeated instances of children swinging. As commentators have pointed out, the

Anthesteria bears similarities to the Christian Good Friday–Easter celebration, an analogous agrarian calendar holiday marking the end of winter and the beginning of another growing season.

There were also festivals in celebration of gender, the best known probably being the Thesmophoria, if for no other reason than the survival of the text of Aristophanes' comic drama, *Thesmophoriazusae* (*Women at the Thesmophoria*), which has the festival as its dramatic setting. In honor of the goddess Demeter, this festival was found throughout ancient Greece, a festival for and celebrated by only women. Its principal ritual act was the slaughter of pigs, which were thrown into a chasm filled with snakes. Then, after the snakes were scared away, the putrified remains were retrieved. Different localities had different procedures. Blood seems to have been associated with this festival somehow, as well as ritual obscenities in word, action, and image. Our sources are meager and sometimes fragmentary; to make sense of these details is difficult. Ideas of fertility and reproduction are represented in the juxtaposition of women and pigs, the animal most commonly associated with fecundity. Is menstruation symbolized in the blood? The chasm into which the pigs are hurled to their death perhaps represents death itself. Perhaps the snake is phallic; perhaps its presence in the chasm is an equation of masculinity with death, just as the female is always so clearly associated with giving and maintaining life (one thinks perhaps of the female Persephone being carried away under the ground by the male Hades, which action stops the growing process until she is returned). "Perhaps" is the key word here; our evidence could not let it be otherwise.

Religion and drama probably indoctrinated more than the school. Formal education in the fifth century was simple, but it did much to instill an appreciation of poetry. The aristocratic ideal was a combination of athletic exercise to create a beautiful body and of music and poetry to create a beautiful personality. While there were reading, writing, and arithmetic, the emphasis was on the development of a noble young man. Nobility depended on beauty. The ancient Greek word *kalos* means both "good" and "beautiful." In the Greek mind there was always what we would consider a confusion between physical beauty and moral worth. They simply did not make the distinction. Moderns make a distinction, derived from the Judeo-Christian tradition, between beauty and goodness and label those who equate the two as decadent, but in the fifth century B.C. the two were simply different aspects of the same thing. This idea is fundamental to understanding Plato's search for "the good."

A beautiful boy is a good boy. The subliminal motive in education was partly pederastic. Education is bound up with male love, which inspires the educator to appear at his best before the student, his beloved, and the student to emulate the teacher, his lover. Obviously, Athenian educators had little to offer women and in fact did little or nothing for them. Iphigenia, for instance, in Euripides' *Iphigenia in Tauris,* is illiterate. Doubtless, thoroughly uneducated women were better able to accept the narrow life imposed on them than they would otherwise be.

Aristocratic education was also based on the premise that the quality of goodness was something with which a man was born. This was thought to be true at least of aristocratic males, the only really educated people in the society. The aristocracy was known as "the good" (thus "the beautiful" as well). Education, therefore, was to promote and encourage that innate goodness. Memorizing poetry and practicing music were exercises to formulate actions and thoughts in the young in accordance with the native impulse to goodness with which they were born. Formal education simply reinforced the habits of mind and behavior learned in childhood in the home. The poetry of Homer, which was memorized by the boys, is pedagogically ideal because it is so conformist. Aristocratic education was an activity of leisure that revealed the person, who might be thought of as a static work of art rather than an evolving or developing individual. This premise is the opposite of the educational practice that sprang up in the latter half of the fifth century in Athens.

Literacy was common in Athens in the fifth century, but books were not. Those who were not aristocrats were cut off from a great deal of traditional knowledge and experience. An aristocracy controls best when it has a monopoly on culture. In the early period only the aristocracy held office at Athens; they alone understood the laws and the operation of the government. The wisdom accumulated over a century by this class became an invaluable exclusive oral tradition passed down in these families, not available to outsiders. But as more and more freeborn males were called upon to take part in government, as more and more litigation arose, the outsiders needed and wanted to know how the system worked. Furthermore, they wanted to know how to function in it—how, for instance, to speak effectively in the many arenas for debate. And they wanted to know whatever there was in the form of accumulated knowledge about humankind and the world. The educational system was not prepared to show them. This desire for education was the impetus for the creation of a class of professional educators known as the Sophists. The education they offered was pragmatic and not overtly ideological; they taught men how to speak and what to talk about.

Our word "Sophist" comes from the Greek *sophistes,* which might be translated as a "professional wise man," or an "intellectual"; the tone could be pejorative depending on the speaker's viewpoint. A man who dealt in wisdom could make good money. In a society in which one drachma was an average day's wage, the Sophist Protagoras was said to have charged ten thousand drachmas for a three- to four-year course; prices had fallen half a century later, the rhetorician Isocrates complains, to a thousand drachmas.

The major Sophists were celebrities, and their lectures were thronged. Plato, however, had great contempt for these men; his disdain fills his dialogues. In them Socrates continually asserts that it is fraudulent to claim that goodness (his conception of socially and politically positive behavior) can be taught. Socrates, in Plato's dialogues, is forever disabusing the people he meets of the notion that they know anything technical about goodness and telling them that goodness cannot be taught as woodworking or any other craft with a set of standards and rules can. The Sophists who have the misfortune to meet Socrates in Plato's pages never have the chance to retort that the science of man was in its infancy, that much could be done if Socrates and Plato would stop trying to idealize man and ignore empirical evidence, stop proceeding from *a priori* truths that were not found in fact, give over the principle of education by indoctrination, and get on with the business of developing a sociology and psychology of man.

Perhaps the aristocratic Plato's indignation sprang from the same source as the wrath of the judges of the Areopagus court when they saw their power eroded in the 460s. In the early days of the court these men were aristocrats; the court was a visible expression of the aristocracy's exclusive hold on law and custom. Similarly, before the arrival of the Sophists, education was the province of the aristocracy. As an extension of the aristocratic tradition, education was something available to the aristocratic young. The Sophists challenged this situation by opening education to anyone willing to pay. Protagoras's dictum that man is the measure of all things is a direct challenge to the aristocracy, who legitimated their claim to knowledge by making it as transcendent, metaphysical, and god-given as their own traditional social status.

The major popular philosophical debate of the fifth century over the relative value of *nomos* (custom) and *physis* (nature) was inspired in part by the aristocratic belief that the traditional culture that had produced them as a privileged class was natural, hence inevitable. The wider horizons and experience derived from expanding trade and immigration introduced to Athenians the possiblity that cultural values were all relative, that *nomos* played a larger role in the arrangement of human lives than had hitherto been postulated. The Sophists who lectured objectively about human behavior, offering diverse facts and establishing alternative theories, were saying in effect that nothing is fixed, that human behavior is various, that every man has a right to create himself, and that no one class has a monopoly on standards of thought and behavior. Besides being a constant source of philosophical speculation and argument, the debate appears quite often as a theme in tragedies and comedies and is of central importance to Herodotus in his history writing.

Critics like to identify what they believe to be the effects of Sophistic teaching. Analytic thinking and generalities on psychology and social behavior are particularly noticeable in later tragedy. One thinks of Creon's speech in *Oedipus the King* (583–602) on the role of a prince regent or Ion's speech on country living in the *Ion* (585ff.), both of which are highly analytical. Thucydides' generalizations on the nature of revolution (3.82ff.) are a particularly good example of the influence of Sophistic thinking in his work, but it is everywhere in Thucydides' speeches, which are elegant analyses, either psychological or sociological, of human action.

Entire plays show Sophistic coloration—Euripides' *Hippolytus,* for instance. Phaedra, dying of desire for her stepson, Hippolytus, represses this emotion, true to her instincts of decorum. But she confesses the situation to her old nurse and confidante, whose reaction is brilliantly done by Euripides. At first she is shocked, horrified, assuming the same values that led Phaedra to be silent. She goes off, but soon returns to say, "Second thoughts are sometimes best" (435–36). She then delivers a speech saying in effect that sex is natural, it is good for the body, and its positive aspects far outweigh ethical and moral considerations that are in any case conventional rather than natural. Euripides has presented an interesting contrast. Phaedra has acted out of right instinct, that code of behavior inculcated in the aristocracy which passes for natural. The nurse, by changing her mind, demonstrates the possibility of rational rather than instinctual reactions to the situation.

The arguments that the nurse marshals are what we find written in the fragments of a fifth-century Athenian Sophist named Antiphon. Man, said Antiphon, is subject to natural law. The law of nature is that man seeks life and avoids death. Man-made law coerces and therefore is opposed to natural law. Each of us must disregard man-made law as far as he can in pursuing his own needs. Euripides at the very beginning gives a Sophistic tone to *Hippolytus* by posing Aphrodite and Artemis as the two symbolic poles, making them not so much goddesses but allegories of Sexuality and Abstinence. Hippolytus is as much a symbol of repression as a tragic hero.

Sophistic teaching, however, was finally antipathetic to the art of tragedy and to a tragic sense of life. Analysis is alien to the kind of symbolic language and action that is acutely necessary to ancient tragedy. Furthermore, to have its effect tragedy depends on a belief in the inevitable. Sophistic thinking, on the other hand, is optimistic, given to problem solving and to denying the inevitable. One might see this conflict as between a belief in the superiority of the past and a belief in progress or between aristocratic thinking and emergent middle-class thinking. In theater these two points of view are represented by tragedy and melodrama.

It is interesting to observe the way Euripides, who began by writing conventional tragedy and whose last play, the *Bacchae,* is one of the most powerful expressions of it, could often slip out and over to the other perspective, sufficiently warping the tragic frame to pave the way for the theater of New Comedy, which was to dominate a century later. In the ancient biography of Euripides it is written: "Plot reversals, the abduction of young maidens, substitutions of children, recognition scenes with rings and necklaces—these are the very stuff of New Comedy and it was Euripides who developed them." These are not tragic events; they are reversible elements of the optimistic world of melodrama, whose outcomes hang in the balance until the eleventh hour. They are the ingredients of problem solving. They are also what folklorists identify as fairy-tale motifs rather than the stuff of heroic narrative. We can find them in Herodotus as well. However one may choose to define it, there is a perceptible shift in thinking in the latter half of the fifth century.

The art and literature of Athens in the fifth century corroborate what the evolution of its democracy suggests, that is, an intensification in the belief in the value of humanity. Never was a society so completely anthropocentric. The paradox is, of course, that this self-obsessed, self-congratulating passion did not extend to women, who were excluded from so much societal privilege. Also excluded were resident aliens, called metics, who lived and worked in Athens, usually as traders. A far larger category of the excluded were the slaves, who were property before the law, although their persons were protected. Chattel slavery in Athens was fed by war captives, sold almost directly from the field of battle to traders who followed the armies; children born to enslaved parents; and barbarians sold from their homelands, particularly unwanted children. Slaves, male and female, performed the same tasks as free workers in the household, in the field, in the atelier, and in the houses of prostitution. This practice inhibited the development of a wage economy or a working class. It has been argued that the low esteem in which artisanry was held by the Greeks, certainly by the philosophers, is due to the fact that so many artisans were slaves. Apart from the slaves who were brutally worked in gangs in places like the silver mines at Laurium, slaves were usually few and working side by side with free people in most other locales. The intimacy that seems often to have resulted may have improved their lot. Certainly slaves in tragedy seem often to be trusted, respected persons of wisdom. Although enslaving fellow Greeks was not common, its effect must have been startling—a constant and fearful reminder of the utter insecurity of life.

Another paradox is that the men who talked so much of freedom and exercised their freedom in the assembly consistently voted for their city's economic and political domination and exploitation of all the peoples who were once their associates in the Delian confederacy but who had become no more than subjects of an Athenian empire. This league was the outcome of the Greek victory in the Persian War, which enlarged the Athenian presence and power among the Greek cities. Perhaps it can be argued that Athens's increasing power and hegemony grew more or less imperceptibly from the first decade until by the middle of the century Athens was an empire without knowing it.

At Marathon in 490 Athens played a major role in the defeat of the Persian invasion force led by Darius. A decade later Xerxes' invading army was stopped for the first time in the bay opposite Salamis, where the Athenian navy utterly routed the Persian fleet, inflicting massive casualties and causing the fleet to withdraw. A subsequent naval engagement at Mycale, in which the Athenians were again superior, and a land battle at Plataea favorable to the Greeks collapsed Persian pretensions to power in mainland Greece.

Athens entered the period of peace as a military power equal to Sparta, whose army had traditionally commanded the respect and fear of the rest of Greece. More important, Athens was a naval power. The strategic necessities now were to keep the Persians from coming across the Aegean and to make lightning expeditions into Persian territory to make away with enough plunder to pay the expenses of the war. These goals required ships. The Peloponnesians, either because they looked to the west or because they were, at least the Spartans, not adventurous, limited themselves to a land army and retreated from all overseas action. And so the balance of power shifted toward the Athenians.

The politics of Athens was also altered by the victory over the Persians. Traditionally, the hoplites, the infantrymen of property who could afford to outfit themselves for battle, had provided the community's security and thus constituted a politically imposing class. Now with the prospect of a continual naval presence in the Aegean the future defense of Athens rested on the rowers, a class of men of the most limited financial means. The movement during the next two decades to open all political offices to every man and to establish payment for public service was the outcome of the new political strength of the rowers.

In 477 Athens and most of the island communities formed a league of mutual assistance and protection against the Persians and head-quartered it on the island of Delos. The member cities were for the most part Ionic-speaking Greeks for whom Delos, a major site of religious festivals for Ionians, had important associations. Therefore, the Delian League (as modern historians call it), whatever its purposes, constituted an Ionic bloc, a tangible antithesis to the traditional, much less effective league of the Dorian city-states of the Peloponnesus. Thus the cultural polarities, hitherto muted, now became more visible and more acute. Athens insisted that member cities in the Delian League have democratic governments; conservative, oligarchic governments were suspect. Persia was not the only official menace to Athens; Sparta was increasingly becoming the focus of hostilities in the rhetoric of the Athenian assembly.

The city of Sparta, which lay in a fertile, mountain-ringed valley and was remote and isolated—significantly with no outlet to the sea—formed the perfect contrast to Athens. We must remember, however, that we are at the mercy of our meager ancient sources and that the ancients, with their deep and pervasive need to see things in symmetries and antitheses, may have carefully, if unconsciously, selected materials for posterity that offer a structure of perfect contrasts.

The Spartans were conservative people known for their skill in battle. Economically they were self-sufficient. As befits people with rich land and no harbor, most Spartans were farmers, not traders. Their government system was stable, their society little open to change. Those Athenians who could not stomach their democracy, the empire, or the rapid changes in their own society looked to Sparta as the ideal. Sparta's way of life was hard; Spartans prided themselves on their endurance and the simplicity of their lives—minimal talk, minimal baths, minimal indulgence of any sort. The conflict between Athens and Sparta was always partly political, between a democracy and an oligarchy, but it was also between two ways of life, two value systems. At its heart the conflict rested on Athens's acceptance of change and Sparta's rejection of it. Of course, from the contemporary viewpoint the Athenians would seem highly conservative. On the whole the ancient Greeks had little faith or interest in change. It is reported that the town of Locris had a law, which, however extreme it may have been, is indicative of the deep bias against change. Whoever proposed a new law in the assembly had a noose around his neck. If the law failed to pass, he was hanged forthwith. Other states had monetary punishments for the urging of what by subsequent vote proved to be a minority view.

The Spartans controlled a land where over three-fourths of the people were serfs, tillers of the soil for their Spartan masters. Serfdom was the consequence of the Dorian peoples' arrival in the Peloponnesus when they overcame and dominated the local population. Later, when an enlarged population required more land, the typically conservative Spartans conquered and enslaved the neighboring Messenians instead of sending colonies abroad as their fellow Dorians did. Fear of slave revolt molded the society; Spartans devoted themselves to soldiery as an instrument of repression. From childhood men were trained to fight. They lived in barracks until thirty years of age and thereafter continued to eat at a common soldiers' mess, each contributing to the food supply. Men were bonded into a tight emotional unit by the barracks homosexuality, an essential feature of Spartan growing up. Rites of passage from boyhood into adulthood, many of them demanding extremes of endurance, further bonded the males together.

Spartan women, in contrast to those in Athens, were relatively free. They lived much of their lives separate from their men, managed the farms, and had considerable responsibilities. The promiscuity of Spartan women was a subject of much speculation and gossip throughout the rest of Greece, prompted in part by the Spartan concern for eugenics, which placed a higher premium on the physical superiority of the breeding partners than upon marital ties. Old, infirm men, for instance, with vigorous young wives are reported to have found for their wives males by whom they could conceive superior children.

Just as they declined to enter into overseas colonization, the Spartans avoided the temptations that new ideas and commerce might bring by choosing a system of coinage that made extensive trading in or out of the country well-nigh impossible. Thus they escaped the waves of social and political change that the invention of money brought to other parts of Greece. Social unrest was also inhibited by the fact that every landholder could vote. Spartan stability, single-minded purpose, and patriotism were attractive in antiquity and still are for many persons. Probably the single motive that produced this seemingly poised and excellent society was fear of serf uprisings. Over the centuries Sparta's cultural sterility became physical as well, and by the second century B.C. there were few Spartans left in that little backwash valley of the Peloponnesus.

The Delian League was established as a common defense against Persia. However, because Athens was the greatest power and because the ten treasurers of the league were to be Athenian citizens, it was not exactly a mutual arrangement among member cities. Every city contracted to contribute ships to a common armada or, if this was difficult or a city's proportionate share was less than a full ship, the city could contribute money. Most favored the latter option. Thus, whether innocently or by design, Athens's shipyards and navy were busy turning out ships and maintaining them. The vagueness of the law and contractual arrangements governing the league made the ships *de facto* and probably *de jure* Athenian property.

Very soon after the league's formation the arrangement began to appear more empire than league. In 472 Carystus, a city on Euboea, an island just off the mainland coast of northern Attica, was forced by the league fleet to join because the city was too strategically located to be neutral. More ominously, in 467, when Naxos chose to opt out of the league, the fleet laid siege and broke the will of the city on the argument that no city could withdraw until the league was dissolved by common consent. Carystus and Naxos were nakedly made subject states of Athens, were forced to pay tribute, and thus lost their autonomy. The other Greek city-states viewed this development uneasily. Things got worse; more cities revolted, and more were subdued and made subject to Athens. In 454, a pivotal date, the treasury was transferred from Delos to Athens to the safekeeping of the goddess Athena. The city unashamedly began a building program with this money that made it the glory of the ancient world. The league was twenty-three years old; a generation had passed.

Relations between Athens and the Peloponnesian states ruptured in 431. The outbreak and subsequent events of the Peloponnesian War are available in Thucydides' account and do not need retelling here. It was a long war fought in a desultory fashion by land forces (Spartan) that could not effect any real damage to a city-state (Athens) that could safely import its food, and by a navy (Athenian) that could only sail around a land mass (the Peloponnesus) effecting minor skirmishes. The city of Athens with its long walls stretching to the harbor was relatively immune to the ravages of war. Throughout the war men came and went at Athens, and the dramatic festivals continued without interruption.

The damage seems in some ways to have been more psychological than real until the defeat of the Athenian fleet in October of 413 at Syracuse. The Athenian loss in Sicily was a calamity for the city. Suspicion and hatred were rampant. Fear of the Persians, always latent, became overt. Athenian allies revolted. The political situation was growing increasingly tense when the conservatives in Athens decided to test their strength in the absence of the fleet (ever the bulwark of the democracy) at the island of Samos. In May of 411 a provisional government took over, charged with establishing a body of four hundred men who would choose a group of five thousand to replace the unstable, unreliable assembly. To get the people out of power, pay for public offices was abolished. Oligarchical suspicions were such that no one body would yield to another. Every newly established council or body wanted equal executive power; the government became unwieldy. The revolt of Euboea in September alarmed the city, and when the rebuilt fleet won two important victories, the traditional constitution was restored. But the illusions and the enthusiasm were gone. Almost a century after it was begun, Cleisthenes' political experiment was severely shaken.

The literature of the fifth century generally reflects Athenian culture of the time. While it is tempting to try to discern a reaction to specific events, dating the plays is hazardous. We can securely date all of Aristophanes, all of Aeschylus except the *Prometheus*, about half of Euripides' plays, and only the *Philoctetes* and the *Oedipus at Colonus* of Sophocles. Sometimes the connection between a play and historical events is obvious, as when in 472 Aeschylus celebrated the Athenian victory over the army and fleet of Xerxes with his *Persians*. To heighten Athenian self-congratulation the dramatist set the scene at the court in Persia, putting the description of Athenian triumph into Persian mouths. In 461, when the court of the Areopagus, whose aristocratic bias had already been much reduced by the law of election by lot, lost jurisdiction over many categories of crime, the last visible power of the aristocracy was diminished. With the establishment of numerous alternative courts and the publication of a law code, the power of dispensing justice became widely dispersed, and legal matters were settled upon open statute rather than according to the un-written—hence disputable—code of an aristocracy. Between 462 and 460 a law was passed which provided payment for members of the juries and gave to males who needed to earn a living the necessary support to serve. These political events are reflected in Aeschylus's *Oresteia,* presented in 458, which is a trilogy about crime and punish-ment ceasing to be prerogatives of the family and being handled instead by the state through jury trials and the law.

Also in 458 the Athenians seized control of a Dorian city, Megara, immediately to the west and made an alliance with Argos, a major Dorian city on the Peloponnesus. Having secured somewhat their position with the Dorians, the Athenians embarked on a greater se-curity measure; they resumed building the long fortification walls from the city to the harbor. This project was favored by those who sought power for the rowers, money for the traders, and empire for everyone; now no matter what happened to their land the Athenians' umbilical cord to the sea was safe. For the farmers, however, and the great landowning aristocratic families, the building of the great wall from Athens to Piraeus was folly. The wall symbolized the city's increasing dependence on foreign food supplies and the declining importance of the grower class at Athens. The tension between these two attitudes is frequently expressed in the literature, especially in Aristophanes' plays, in which the conservative point of view (hostile to trade, favorable to local agriculture) is often given voice. Di-caeopolis, for example, the small farmer in the *Acharnians,* is just such a one, the kind of person who suffers most from empire and benefits least, seeing his beloved land ravaged by the Spartans (the play was produced in 425, in the early years of the war), himself forced to live in the city.

There seems to be a remarkable shift in Aristophanes' plays from political seriousness to fantasy as the political and military situation in

Athens worsened. In 425 and 424 he presented the *Acharnians* and the *Knights*. Both plays are sharply defined political statements, attacks on policy and on the political maturity of the assembly, both suited to a critical time when wits needed sharpening to confront the city's many problems. Thereafter we note a change. In 423 in the battle of Amphipolis Cleon, one of the leading men of the assembly died, as did the great Spartan general Brasidas. In the same year Aristophanes presented a parody of the Sophists in his *Clouds*. His *Peace* was presented in 421, the same year Nicias concluded a peace treaty with the Spartans. References to the treaty are there, but utterly tame for a writer whose dialogue is usually sharp-tongued (the treaty was so unsatisfactory a political arrangement that war began almost immediately). In 414, when Athenians were facing defeat in Sicily, Aristophanes put on the *Birds,* his most delightful fantasy, in which an Athenian decides to join the birds and build a city in the clouds. In 405, several months in advance of the disastrous battle of Aegospotami, the end of all Athenian hopes, he produced the *Frogs,* which is marvelous literary analysis, yet topical only metaphorically in his presentation of Dionysus, god of theater, who seeks to bring back Aeschylus for the moral rejuvenation of the Athenians in their decline.

More harrowing than any event of the actual war was the plague that came in 430. It decimated the population that was crowded into the city, which was under siege by Spartan invasions, as we can learn from Thucydides, who describes the plague in some detail (2.74ff.). Strangely enough, the plague is scarcely mentioned elsewhere. Here is an event that should have played upon the latent fear of punishment (*nemesis*) for their highly assertive action (*hubris*) that appears everywhere in the literature. The Athenian adventure in empire was alien to Greek thinking—an obvious instance of excessive, possibly self-deluded, action. The plague seems such an obvious example of divine displeasure and the empire an equally obvious instance of human arrogance that one would expect them to be so linked in literature. Yet the Athenians had built up an extraordinary edifice of self-justification upon their heroism at Marathon and Salamis. Patriotism has marvelous powers of self-delusion. Only in *Oedipus the King* is there a plague that suggests the actual event. Because of the plague in the play, many critics date the play to the plague period. Because Oedipus and Jocasta appear as the kind of rationalist, energetic, overachievers that we presume Pericles and his extralegal consort, Aspasia, to have been, the same critics read the play as some kind of

Sophoclean rebuke to the pride of intellect that lives at the expense of pious humility.

The most catastrophic event of the Peloponnesian War was the Athenian expedition against Sicily in 415, which began with such high hopes and ended so disastrously for the Athenians with the battle in the harbor of Syracuse in 413, as we can read in the detailed and moving account by Thucydides in the seventh book of his *History*. Euripides' *Trojan Women* was produced in 415, the same year the Athenians sailed for Sicily. That was the year after the Athenians had brutally forced the citizens of the island of Melos into submission, killing or enslaving all of the population. It is remarkable that Euripides chose to address city sacking, the decimation and enslavement of a civilian population, and the victors' high hopes dashed at that juncture of events. Literary historians like to style him as a social critic, but somehow this label seems too easy, not to mention unlikely. The tragic theater was so public an affair that it is hard to imagine its audience paying for and accepting such overt criticism. The major theme of the play is, in any case, the devastation of women treated as objects. It is only our historical hindsight, prompted by Thucydides, who uses the event thematically, which makes so much of the sack of Melos and its juxtaposition to the ill-fated Sicilian expedition.

Although we may dismiss so topical a reading of the *Trojan Women,* there is, nonetheless, evidence to show that the early, archaic fear of overachievement had not disappeared in the face of Sophistic rationalism. The publication or the public reading of Herodotus took place in the 420s. His narrative is a sustained demonstration of the inextricable link between human greatness, wealth, and high achievement on the one hand and blindness, stupidity, and destruction on the other, the first condition inevitably leading to the second. If the plague did not set off Athenian fears, then surely the disastrous Sicilian expedition must have been seen as the work of jealous gods striking down Athenian pretensions. The general uneasiness produced by Athens's defeat at Aegospotami no doubt touched latent religious anxieties which brought about Socrates's trial. Among the charges brought against him in 399 was impiety for having introduced new gods. Once before, in 450, Pericles' teacher and friend, the philosopher Anaxagoras of Clazomenae, was tried for impiety because he taught naturalistic interpretations for meteorological phenomena, a practice calculated to put seers and soothsayers out of business. Historians remark on the increase of rationalism in the fifth century, but that is only relative to the preceding and subsequent periods.

It was not the rationalism of the Sophists' teachings as much as the failure of the city-state, to which the gods of the Pantheon were so closely linked through cult and ritual, which destroyed the traditional religion. The gods of the Pantheon were political gods, and they failed their *polis*. Because they were so thoroughly anthropomorphized, the crises of events and the defects of life could be laid to their machinations. That they were supernatural beings with exceedingly nasty human psyches is evident again and again in Euripides' portrayal of wanton and vicious deities.

Athens's vitality did not die in the fourth century, but reality could not vie with legend. Plato, for instance, looked to an ideal city and turned his back on the actual. Ironically, his search for the ideal foreshadowed the destiny of Athens. The city was to enter the mythology of history, to become the symbol of ancient Greece. There have been many persons in the last twenty-five hundred years who have insisted that mankind's finest hour was lived in fifth century B.C. Athens. It is a place we can never enter or really know. As Thucydides said, "If the city of the Lacedaemonians were deserted and there remained their temples and the foundations of the buildings, I imagine that after the passage of time there would be considerable doubt on the part of successive centuries as to their greatness in relation to their fame, . . . whereas if Athens suffered the same fate, one would consider their power to be double what it was on the basis of the sight of the city" (1.10). Even then Thucydides foresaw that Athens had at its command money, talent, cultural vitality, and, if we can believe Pericles' funeral oration ("Athens is the teacher of all Greece"), a sense of its place in history which made of the city and its achievements a myth in the heroic tradition from which its culture had sprung.

CHAPTER SIX

Tragedy

Art is not an imitation of nature, but a metaphysical complement to it—something created with the express purpose of dominating it.
Nietzsche, The Birth of Tragedy

Greek tragedy, my dear, decorum; the ultimate gesture is performed offstage.
Genet, The Blacks

To sit in the ruins of the Theater of Dionysus at Athens brings home with a shock how remote the tragic drama of the ancient Athenians is from us. The spectacle, actors, voices, and dance are gone; only the words remain. Yet these have survived the intervening twenty-five centuries with such authority that what they portray has become as much a staple of modern culture as elements of the Judeo-Christian mythologies. Sophocles' Oedipus has become very much *our* Oedipus.

Is it legitimate to speak of "Sophocles' Oedipus"? This is a real problem in criticism. Sophocles and his world are long gone; only a printed text remains which only we can bring to life. Sophocles and his fellow tragedians presented plays that spoke to their audiences from a shared experience. We can recover only a bit of their common past and present. Anyone reading or watching one of these dramas will, naturally enough, react to what the play seems to be saying directly. While watching or reading, we can ignore the fact that we and the Athenians of the fifth century B.C. come from two very different worlds. These tragedies have survived partly because people, actions, and motives are presented in a sufficiently stark, abstract fashion to evoke responses century after century. On the one hand, they are spare enough to allow and encourage an audience to read into them what it will; on the other hand, they speak simply to the fundamentals of the human condition, which does not change, or so it seems, over the millennia.

Yet it is also reasonable enough to want to set the plays as much as possible in their historical context so that we can sense the nuances that this context provides. The distance in time is so vast and our evidence is so fragmentary, though, that the task can never be done to satisfaction. Yet to dismiss the background makes us vulnerable to striking misinterpretations of the text. One thinks of Shelley's *Prometheus Unbound,* or the simple-minded Christian tendency to assign sin, guilt, crime, and punishment where none exists.

Most persons encounter ancient tragedy only in the printed word. It takes an effort to imagine tragedy as theater, in which the circumstances of production and the expectations of the audience were altogether different than with reading. Contemporary experience of drama comes mainly from film or television. The latter, presented on so small a screen in the privacy of the viewer's world and exhibiting programs of stultifying vacuity based on a view of things deriving from the utmost banality, is completely alien to the manner and content of ancient tragic drama. Most people reading a tragedy will find their analogue in film and unconsciously apply the aesthetics of this medium to their reading. This analogy will not do, however. Intimacy in community is the essence of the film-viewing experience. Consider the darkened auditorium which, because it contains the group, demands conformity, yet because it is dark, allows for solitude. The large vision on the screen in the darkened chamber overwhelms and demands total submission of the viewer. In his rapt absorption he has thrust upon him from the screen the smallest details made emphatically large.

Ancient tragic drama was, by contrast, a public event, done on large scale. At Athens the Theater of Dionysus, built against the steeply rising east slope of the Acropolis, was large enough to accommodate fourteen thousand to seventeen thousand people. This group sat together on benches without divisions so that as arms, legs, and haunches touched, emotions could race through the audience. A large crowd is characteristically animal. Probably it was in reaction to the natural volatility of a crowd that the Athenian assembly passed a law making an outright and provocative disturbance during a performance a capital offense. The setting offered little form of crowd control. Performances were out of doors, in daylight, continuous, starting at dawn in a large arena where there must have been constant movement, as at present-day sporting events or at Chinese opera.

People leaving to relieve themselves, hawkers selling food, these were moving elements of the panorama as much as the actors and the chorus.

The chorus performed in front of the rise of benches on the flat area known as "the dancing place" (*orchestra* in Greek, which is the reason for the present-day practice of calling the ground floor of theaters the orchestra). Behind them was the area where the actors performed. They were probably on the same level with the *orchestra* of the chorus; a raised stage was a later development.

Behind the actors and chorus stood a building known in Greek as the *skene* from which evolved our word "scene." Originally *skene* meant "tent"; in the early days of Athenian theater the actors presumably used the tent to change masks and costumes and, when the script called for it, as a place into which to withdraw. Later the tent was replaced by a two-story building that formed a rudimentary backdrop and also a sounding board. Many of the plays take place before a royal palace, probably to accommodate the permanent installation of the *skene*. It had doors into which actors could go and windows from which they could speak. Furthermore it supported a device that conveyed aloft those actors representing divine figures. It is this mechanism that gave rise to the phrase *deus ex machina*, "the god from the machine," a Latin translation of the original Greek expression. This machine may have been suspended from the side of the building like a crane and may have run on a track on the roof.

Our scanty evidence suggests that settings were not elaborate or necessarily very realistic. Sophocles' *Philoctetes* required a cave, and the *skene* served for this. Probably the notorious tendency to maintain the same scene throughout the play ("unity of place") derives from the difficulty of making changes, given the presence of the permanent *skene* (although Shakespeare was not inhibited by a similar problem). Perhaps the physical limitations to scene making are also the reason for the convention of narrating scenes of disaster and physical mayhem in a messenger's speech rather than portraying them. They often take place in more than one setting and need more movement.

On the other hand, the messenger's speech may reflect the ancient Greek tendency to present things in speeches. The Homeric poems show an unusual preponderance of dialogue over descriptive narrative. Whole books of the *Odyssey* are first-person narrative. The historians in turn rely upon monologues or dialogues in the place of simple third-person description, a practice taken up by Plato for his exposition of ideas. In tragedy there is more commentary on action than action itself. This peculiar abstraction of reality would call for settings that were symbolic or suggestive rather than realistic.

The abstract quality of ancient drama is also implied by the very size of the theater. The distance from the middle of the tiers of seats to the middle of the orchestra was in most theaters considerable. Given the fact of uncorrected myopia in the ancient audience, the spectacle must have been viewed in the abstract, not in detail. Consider too the complete absence of mechanical aids toward creating focus: no darkened auditorium, no lighted stage, no proscenium arch, only the semicircular seating arrangement.

It is common to find ancient theaters built with a splendid and compelling view beyond the *skene*. The size of the theater itself would make it hard for the audience to concentrate; still more, the spectator seats were built to look out upon hypnotic vistas—at Delphi across a deep valley to a facing mountainside, at Pergamon to a breathtaking, vertiginous drop to a far-off valley, at Taormina to the rugged coast, at Segesta to the distant valleys between mountains. These spectacular views result partly from the necessity of carving the seats of the theater into a hillside from which generally there was more to view than the *orchestra* below. But a slightly different siting in most instances would have severely limited the panoramic sweep. Taking in the view is inescapable; the diffusion of focus makes the performance part of a process rather than an end in itself.

Tragic drama was, as we have said, a public event. Performances formed part of the festival in Athens that we call the City Dionysia or Greater Dionysia. The plays must have been popular; by the second half of the fifth century another city festival of tragedy appeared, and from time to time festivals were put on in the countryside of Attica. Of course, the custom spread to most other cities in the Greek-speaking world.

The City Dionysia took place in late March shortly before the April harvest. This is the time of year when the rainy season ends, a fact that lends support to the notion that tragedy originated as a kind of celebration of the death of the year god. But it is more likely that the date of the festival was set in late March because the winter storms that make the Aegean unsailable were over and rain was less likely to ruin this outdoor festival. The Greater Dionysia was open to all Greeks and was also attended by foreigners who had diplomatic or commercial business in Athens. Before the day's performance the children of those who had died in Athens's service were paraded, honors to outstanding citizens were proclaimed, and ambassadors

were publicly received. More than a religious event, the festival was a
state holiday; even prisoners were released from jail for the festivities.

Tragedy was only part of the festival. At a later date comic plays
were added and from the beginning there were dithyrambs, a kind of
chorus of young men and boys singing lyrics not unlike the choral
passages in the tragedies. The dithyrambs were much more narrative
than drama, at least initially. Later the words were overwhelmed by
the music, which seems to parallel what we are told about Euripides'
increasing interest in the music of his choruses.

Each of the three tragedians who competed in the festival presented
three tragedies and one satyr play in one morning on three successive
days. Initially one comic drama followed in the afternoon of each
day. Later the number of comedies was increased to five, and they
were presented together on one day subsequent to the days for tragedies. The last two days were allotted to the presentation of the
dithyrambs. Ceremonies began at dawn; the playing time of tragedies
is about an hour and a quarter, and they seem to have been presented
without intermission. Probably the satyr play that followed was
among other things a psychological device to break the tension of the
three nonstop tragic dramas.

The audience seems to have arrived at the festival with little or no
foreknowledge of what they were to see. That is to say, there were no
advertisements, no critical reviews, no friends who had previously
seen the plays. New plays were put on each year; revivals—except
perhaps some pieces of Aeschylus—were not common until the
fourth century. On the day before the festival it was customary for
the playwrights and actors to appear before the public to announce
the stories of the coming plays. Because the arena where these an-
nouncements were made was small, they probably did not reach
much of the prospective audience. The playwrights were certainly
able to rely on the general public's knowledge of the pool of myth
and saga from which they drew their material. Perhaps this consideration explains the tendency of the tragedians to use certain stories
repeatedly. As Aristotle points out, they tended to limit themselves
to events in the history of the royal house of Atreus or that of Labdacus, the most famous offspring being, respectively, Agamemnon
and Oedipus. While it is readily apparent how little effort the dramatists made to bring their audience into the story, Euripides is conspicuous for sometimes using complicated and little-known stories,
which he outlined and explained in his prologue. His use of new

stories may explain why Euripides won fewer first prizes in competition than Sophocles or Aeschylus.

The playwrights competed for first, second, and third prize, natural enough in so competitive a society. First prize was a gold crown, awarded for reasons as political and social as they were aesthetic. The choice of the three poets who presented plays was up to the archon eponymus, who was simply an official in the Athenian government, a kind of alderman chosen by lot to his office, not a drama critic or an academic. (One archon, for example, is known to have refused a script of Sophocles.) Nothing makes clearer that ancient tragedy was not the property of an elite or a literary group. How the archon arrived at his choices, whether scripts were read to him or parts acted out, we do not know.

The determination of the prizes had scarcely more authority. The judges were chosen by lot, in this case from a pool drawn up from each tribe by the council, who were free to choose persons formerly connected with theater: actors, *choregoi,* playwrights. The producers (the wealthy *choregoi*) of the current tragedies made every effort to get friends and supporters onto the lists. Once established, the judges' names were placed in ten urns, one for each tribe. The urns were then sealed and stored until the day of the performance when one name was chosen from each urn. These ten judges made lists of their preferences. From these ten lists five were randomly chosen which constituted the basis for ranking the victor. Such a system makes victory a random matter, but a good deal of significance must be attached to frequent victories. The considerable number of victories given to Aeschylus and Sophocles is remarkable.

Public reaction was considerable. There are stories that the Athenians fined the dramatist Phrynichus, whose play on the Persian capture of Miletus in 494 upset them too much, that women miscarried in fright as the chorus of the dread Erinyes appeared in Aeschylus' *Eumenides,* that the audience walked out of an earlier version of Euripides' *Hippolytus,* scandalized by a scene in which the queen openly propositioned her stepson. There was a custom that on the day following the Dionysia a meeting of the assembly was held to determine if any impropriety had occurred during the festival, and upon this occasion the judges who awarded the prizes could be attacked for faulty judgment.

That Aristophanes' comic dramas presented parodies of Euripides' characters and his theatrical manner suggests an audience that exercised considerable critical judgment. His *Frogs* is evidence of a more penetrating critical intelligence in the audience. The parodying of so many lines from the plays of Aeschylus and Euripides in the *Frogs* suggests an audience that was conscious of style and, moreover, that could remember lines from many pieces, some of which had not been produced in the previous decade. Social communication at this time was still oral, of course, which implies a populace with acute memories. It is remarkable that the Athenians assimilated so much of their theater so thoroughly. If an Athenian remembered in detail the language of tragedy, a style and diction used for the most serious topics, it is reasonable to imagine that whenever his mind turned to such topics, the tragic language and manner may have seemed to him the natural vehicle for his speculations. The Athenians may thus have been self-consciously immediately involved in tragic style.

When at the end Dionysus decides to bring Aeschylus back because the tragic theater needs his moral earnestness, we may assume that Aristophanes is playing to the Athenians' high expectation of tragic theater. To imagine that tragic drama constituted entertainment for them is a mistake. The Athenians probably approached tragedy with utter seriousness, expecting it to fulfill social needs and to project something of the community. All criticism must take this idea into account. Frequently the tragedies present attitudes and actions that are unspeakable although not unthinkable. Thus they provide in a socially acceptable way a chance to give vent to feelings that individuals must repress as too destructive socially. Dramas of parental cannibalism (the banquet of Thyestes), incest (Oedipus), matricide (Orestes), suicide (Ajax), infanticide (Heracles), treason (Ajax)—not to mention the commonplace marital betrayal—are examples of the wide range of human expression with which the audience could identify in a safe way. Some dramas present alternative ways of confronting a situation. The idealism of an Antigone or Oedipus, for instance, is contrasted with the pragmatism of a Creon or Jocasta; the quietism of an Ismene, or Jocasta's brother, the prince Creon, or the acceptance of Tiresias, Cadmus, or Phaedra's nurse, is contrasted with the rigid refusal of Pentheus or Hippolytus.

Philosophers might say that tragedies are verbal constructs of the reality that surrounds us. Through empathetic response with characters the audience is led through a psychological, nonintellectual experience, a kind of logic not based on reason. Tragedy was highly abstracted and symbolic in a time when the apparatus of logical inquiry and formulation was not in use. Plato's vehement rejection of the poets for his ideal city in the *Republic* is more his insistence upon the absolute superiority of an *intellectual* over an empathetic apprehension of reality than objections to the content of the plays. The fourth century's turn away from poetry of any kind to prose and to abstraction and logic represents a major shift in the use of the mind by the Athenians.

The three tragedies a playwright offered in competition were sometimes a continuous development of the same story line. The only surviving example is the *Oresteia (Agamemnon, Libation Bearers,* and *Eumenides)* of Aeschylus, the only tragedian to write dramas connected in this way. The word "trilogy" is sometimes applied to this concept, although, as used by the ancient scholar Aristarchus, it means only the three tragedies presented on a given day. Often there was some sort of thematic connection between the three plays, as we can tell from the surviving titles. Thus we must use caution when interpreting any single play if we do not know how it fit in with the others in the group. A common misuse of the term "trilogy" is to label Sophocles' *Antigone, Oedipus the King,* and *Oedipus at Colonus* "the Theban trilogy." These three plays, whatever relation they may have with each other because they deal with the fortunes of the same set of people, were not produced at the same time and *in no way* have the kind of relationship that the plays of the *Oresteia* have.

The structure of tragedy remained constant throughout the fifth century. Generally a *prologos* starts the dramatic proceedings either by setting the mood, as the watchman does in the *Agamemnon,* or by delineating the problem, as Antigone and her sister Ismene do in the *Antigone,* or by outlining subsequent events, as the goddess Artemis does in the *Hippolytus.* The *prologos* is followed by the entrance of the chorus, called the *parodos.* Subsequent to these is a series of dialogue passages, called episodes, set between choral odes. Dialogue normally consists of a longish passage of iambic lines by one actor to which another actor responds in a passage of the same length. Often there appears something more abrupt, more like conversation, known as stichomythy (speech in rows), a series of one-liners exchanged between two characters. Because of the insistent parallelism of the stichomythy, the lines are highly epigrammatic and self-contained. Stichomythy usually involves competition or conflict and is thus very much in keeping with the nature of tragic drama. The last choral passage that accompanies the actors' departure from the theater is called the *exodos.*

The relationship between the odes and episodes is much disputed.

Do the dialogue passages advance the plot, while the choral odes are a pause in its movement? Are the choral odes lyrical restatements of what the dialogue developed in the episodes? Are they reactions to the dialogue passages? Is the chorus a metaphor or projection or representation of the watching people of Athens, the ever-present group who must comment on the proceedings? It may be argued that the choral odes, which are characterized by the beauty of their lyrics and very frequently by the generality and platitudinous nature of their content, represent a decided solution or resolution to the tension. They put a halt to the ambiguity and horror of the dialogue passages, intervening with art to distance woe, functioning as a kind of aesthetic proscenium arch of words to keep the audience separate from the dramatic proceedings. Perhaps in a society for which religion provided little comfort against the cruel truth of life, it was art that through form and beauty granted some solace.

Initially the poet acted in his own plays; later the state paid for the services of three professionals, one assigned to each tragedian, awarded by lot. Only males were actors; as the fifth century progressed, the audience grew more attentive to the quality of the acting. Actors became celebrated—by what criterion it is unknown, possibly by the sheer technical skill required of them. The job was indeed hard because it meant playing the protagonist role in all three tragedies and the satyr play. This would mean, for instance, switching from Clytemnestra in the *Agamemnon* to Orestes in the *Libation Bearers*.

Apart from the chorus there were never more than three actors in a play, which meant that no more than three speaking parts could appear together at any one time (although we know of up to eleven roles in one play). Lightning changes must have been required at times. In Sophocles' *Antigone,* for instance, the actor playing Creon goes out at line 1114 and returns as Eurydice at 1180, departs at 1234, then returns as Creon at 1255. The practice works against subtleties of characterization; Theseus in Sophocles' *Oedipus at Colonus* may have been played by three different men. Costume and mask evidently supplied sufficient surface.

There are a variety of possible explanations for the limit of three actors. Three has any number of metaphysical attributes. It is the perfect expression of the family (father, mother, child) seen through the eyes of a child or recollected by an adult. It is the neatest expression of the group (two's company, three's a crowd; one, two, several). It is the sum of the persons of the Indo-European verb (I, thou [you], he [she, it]). The ancient Greek obsession with symmetry may account for the bias toward dialogue, which prohibits general conversation in the tragedies (compare the plays of Shakespeare, who often presents a whole group with speaking parts). There may simply have been few men capable of throwing the voice adequately. And, to the conservative ancient Greek, once a limit of three, always three.

The actors were noted for their voices, which had to be strong enough to project a great distance (150 feet at Epidaurus from center orchestra to the top row) in an open-air arena that brought no sound back, against clothing that muffles sound. Furthermore, the actors wore masks through which they had to project their voices. Clarity, volume, lack of strain, the ability to change the voice to suit the character—these are the matters ancient critics looked for in the actors' voices. Little or nothing is known of gesture and body movement other than what can be seen on vase paintings, which may be stylized and in any case are immobile. Certainly whatever was done had to be large and simple in order to be seen and comprehended in so vast a space. Descriptions of physical manifestations of emotional states were common in plays probably because the actors could not convey the emotions adequately to such large audiences. The mask, which was a constant feature of ancient tragedy, is yet another response to the problems of enormous space. Borrowed from religious ceremonies, in which putting on a mask symbolized putting on the god, the tragic mask was originally individual, but later standardized to represent a range of conventional expressions. The mask is yet another means to project a surface without depth, so characteristic of this art form.

It is still more difficult to imagine the function of the chorus. We know next to nothing of the dance and the music. Only the words remain. How well were the lyrics understood when sung in unison? Sometimes choral lyrics seem so superficial or banal that it seems the playwright was more interested in the music. Evidence shows that the music became more exotic and the rhythms more complicated and forced. Aristophanes' parodies of Euripides show that the tragedian was interested in musical effects such as trilling. Does this trend signal the ascendancy of music over words?

As music grew in importance, the chorus waned and in the fourth century disappeared. In Aeschylus's plays the chorus is well delineated entering into and affecting the action. For instance, the chorus portrayed the hysterical women in the *Seven against Thebes* who so upset Eteocles and the Erinyes who pursue Orestes in the *Eumenides*. In Euripides' plays, however, they often seem to stand about, little

delineated, there simply to sing odes. According to Arisotle, Agathon, Euripides' contemporary, started the practice of writing choral
passages that could be transferred from play to play. Thus, finally,
the chorus became a mere entr'acte. Yet in the last two extant plays,
Sophocles' *Philoctetes* and Euripides' *Bacchae,* the chorus has an
amazingly powerful role. The isolation of Philoctetes is no better
demonstrated than by the choral remarks on the loneliness of Lemnos, more specifically by the chorus lying to him, becoming in that
moment the fundamental hostility of his environment. The Maenads
in the *Bacchae,* while exhibiting the range of passion which the worship of Dionysus inspires, constantly interact with Dionysus.

The production of the tragedies was an obligation—a kind of in-
come tax—laid upon Athens's wealthier citizens, who nonetheless
were pleased to have yet another occasion for covering themselves
with glory. The tragic poet might act in his plays or direct them, but
the cost of the production was borne by the *choregus* ("he who leads
the chorus"). Costumes for the chorus, training for the chorus, their
salaries, their trainer, the flutist—these were the responsibilities of
the *choregos.* Each playwright had his *choregos,* who strove to mount
the most brilliant production. The *choregoi* were wealthy men; they
must have been powerful. One wonders if, as powerful men are wont
to do, they attempted to influence the playwright. We know that
they tried to influence the judges, obviously for reasons of prestige.
Did they take an interest in the content of the plays? Did they ever
find them morally offensive? Did they try to introduce political ideas
and ideologies into the plays?

It is not altogether clear who constituted the audience for these
plays, but it is safe to say the vast majority were Athenian males, men
who participated in the fullest sense in their government, just as some
of them did in the choruses themselves. It is reasonable to assume,
and important to remember, that they brought to the theater the
issues, values, and theories that they were in the habit of discussing.
We who look at ancient tragedy over the span of twenty-five centuries, for whom the original setting is well-nigh unknowable, tend
to look for abstracted universals in the plays. Perhaps, however, the
original audience was too involved in social and political life simply
to look for universals.

A crucial factor of ancient tragedy is the common culture to which
the playwrights could refer. Adult, freeborn Athenian males were
educated little but alike. The history, mythology, philosophy, ethics,
religion, literary style, and so on that they learned came from memo-

rizing the *Iliad,* the *Odyssey,* and the poems of Solon in their early years. The Homeric poems portray an aristocratic culture, and Athens of the seventh and sixth centuries was itself dominated by an aristocracy. Neither the change to democracy nor the rise of trade challenged the aristocratic ideology. The frequent aphorisms for which ancient tragedy is famous are really part of the consensus, allusions to a stable and complete view of life held by the entire audience. Those who try to establish the viewpoint of any one of the playwrights are probably engaged in an exercise in futility. Apart from the absolute paucity of the evidence, the ideas expressed in the plays are so safe, so conventional, so commonplace—and, what is more, lodged in an art form so dependent upon public approval— that anyone who thinks to discern the profile of the author has most likely chanced upon a mirage.

Over the last two millennia the criticism of tragedy has changed many times. Yet it always began with the hero. As tragic drama developed through the fifth century, the hero and the dialogue grew more individualized, while the role of the chorus diminished. In political terms these changes can be explained as a movement away from the aristocratic concentration upon the group, where the physical, social, and sensual values of music and dance were emphasized, toward the nonaristocratic (shall we call it bourgeois?) concentration upon the individual. The increasing despair of the extant tragedies may as well reflect the individual's emergence from a society made up of extended families, the *oikos,* which has a continued existence beyond the lives of any of its members, to the isolated world in which each of us in dying individually faces total extinction.

The tragic hero, like the Homeric hero, is a self-aggrandizing, self-centered, narcissistic figure, an expression of the ancient Greek capacity for exalting the ego, which has remained a distinctive characteristic of Western culture ever since. It is remarkable therefore that in their drama there cannot be found any characters with developed personalities, any figures deeply felt. When the heroes of Shakespeare are compared to the Greek heros, the latter seem two-dimensional, more type figures than individuals. Their personalities do not affect the action as, for instance, Othello's jealousy does, or Macbeth's ambition. Attempts to say that Oedipus's fits of anger influence things are merely pallid readings of a would-be Shakespearean drama and in actuality highly irrelevant.

Critical concentration upon the hero has, in fact, been challenged in the last decades on the view that Aristotle's emphasis upon action in tragedy implies that drama is best understood as a structure of events. The characters, while not incidental to the action, are not, on the contrary, the reason for the action. Rather, action exists independent of the characters. Critical emphasis upon the action has opened up tragedy to structural interpretations, that is, to breaking down the action into its essential elements. In these interpretations, the action of the drama is associated ever more closely with the myth from which it is drawn. Often such an interpretation can be confusing because the dramatic presentation of the myth and its abstraction, the bare story, are not at all the same thing. Jung and his followers have for a long time read into the dramas archetypal persons and acts. The danger in this approach is that it tends to diminish the particularity of any drama.

Certainly the extraordinary universality of ancient Greek tragedy is one of the reasons it has endured. Tragedy can be manipulated and distorted to accommodate differing views on life, as for instance, in Seneca's Stoic re-creations of the Greek tragedies, which paved the way for the Christian tragedy of Shakespeare. Still, there remains a base structure that speaks to human beings at all times. It consists of the *hamartia,* the human frailty or failure, the *metabole,* the reversal, and the *anagnorisis,* the realization. Humans seem to be the only animals who realize they are doomed. But tragedy is not pessimistic, as some would maintain, or gloomy; the concentration is not on the *metabole,* but on the glorious, hard-won, hard-to-hold *anagnorisis.* It is this act of unblinking clarity that justifies man to himself, and always shall, in a world of puny gods and senseless fate.

The impulse to generalize about tragedy is irresistible. Because the form remained constant over the years, it is easy to believe that something essential is repeated from play to play. Aristotle's *Poetics* reflects that viewpoint by talking in the abstract about tragic art and tragic drama, as if there were such a thing independent of the actual pieces composed by the playwrights. In fact, the only feature shared by all the extant plays is the fact of their performance at the Greater Dionysia festival; beyond that it is difficult to define tragedy.

Contemporary ignorance of ancient tragedy, although often ignored, is central to our criticism of it. To speak of "ancient tragedy" is, in fact, to discuss the extant pieces of three Athenian playwrights of the fifth century. Other playwrights are known to have existed, as are many other plays by the famous three as well as productions in other cities and centuries. Generalizing about the plays of the surviving three is perhaps a useless enterprise. There survive seven plays of

Aeschylus, who is known to have composed between seventy and eighty. Sophocles is thought to have composed one hundred and twenty-three plays, of which but seven are extant. Euripides composed between eighty and ninety plays, of which nineteen still exist. Even with the addition of the great number of fragments of other tragedies, the sample for generalizing is very small indeed. And works of art even by the same person are always unique, making even the most tentative generality pretentious.

The history of the surviving Euripidean plays shows still further the hazards of generalizing. The *Alcestis, Medea, Hippolytus, Andromache, Hecuba, Trojan Women, Orestes, Bacchae,* and *Rhesus* were preserved as a school anthology in use around A.D. 200; the others are known from a surviving part of the alphabetized collection of Euripides' plays made in Alexandrian times. This latter random sample is infinitely more valuable for assessing the totality of the playwright's work. It is surmised that the seven extant Aeschylean plays and seven Sophoclean plays represent an anthology of the Roman period. In addition we have manuscripts from the Byzantine period of Aeschylus's *Prometheus, Persians,* and *Seven against Thebes,* which is an even smaller anthology and presumably suitable for a Christian student. Anthologies represent a great threat to valid generalizing because they are created by an intelligence with a point of view; one can generalize safely only about that viewpoint. In the case of Euripides, however, the larger sample and the contrast between the anthologized group and the random group does allow for some true insight into his entire production. Certainly the exclusion from the anthology of plays that demonstrate several other tendencies in Euripides' dramaturgy, notably plays one might call creatively untragic or antitragic, shows concretely the existence of, if not the nature of, the bias of the anthologizer.

The danger of generalizing on the basis of such slim evidence is illustrated by Aeschylus's *Suppliants.* The play was long thought to be the earliest extant tragedy because the dramatic role of the chorus is large, because their odes, which fill much of the play, advance the action, and because the individual characters have relatively minor parts. A common theory of the origin of tragedy has it that drama began in choral pieces in which the leader began to interact enough with the chorus (questioning them, perhaps) that a kind of dialogue began. Tragedy is thus thought to have evolved from the continually emerging dramatic roles of the actors at the expense of the chorus, which eventually faded into inconsequentiality, singing nothing more than what are beautiful songs. The *Suppliants* is taken from the story of the fifty daughters of Danaus, fugitives from Egypt seeking asylum in Greece, who are pursued by their male cousins. The fifty daughters imply a chorus of fifty persons, equivalent to the fifty-member chorus of dithyramb from which tragedy is thought by some to have evolved.

Throughout the play the chorus, singing of their plight and their hopes for the future, overwhelm the two actors who appear as their father, Danaus, and as Pelasgus, the Greek king whose protection they are seeking. Pelasgus, it is true, has a certain pivotal role. He must face the crisis of war if he accepts the girls into his country or risk an impiety if he rejects the suppliants. He is damned if he does, damned if he doesn't. This situation is probably an accurate representation of the Aeschylean tragic vision; it is also the fate of Eteocles in the *Seven against Thebes* and Clytemnestra, Agamemnon, and Orestes in the *Oresteia*. The similarity suggests that Pelasgus is also a tragic hero. Nonetheless, Pelasgus is never around long enough, nor does he say enough relative to the women, to establish himself. Thus the *Suppliants,* which emphatically belongs to the chorus, is, as the theory went, the earliest surviving play.

Some thirty-five years ago, however, a newly discovered papyrus fragment suggested that the *Suppliants* was brought out in the 460s. This would be some time after Aeschylus's *Persians*, which shows the so-called "later" development of chorus and actor and is known to have been performed in 472. Either Aeschylus wrote the *Suppliants* early and brought it out later unrevised, or he archaized, or—and this is surely what the discovery should tell us—stylistic evolution is not so sure or rigid as previously imagined.

The theory of consistent choral diminution is also weakened by the fact that some late choruses are very significant. In Euripides' last play, the *Bacchae,* for example, the chorus has an unusually strong role. They are the worshippers of the god Dionysus, who is a main figure in the story. Throughout the play they sing of the blessings of the worship of the god, while both their aggressive hostility to Pentheus and their warm encouragement of the cause of Dionysus make them so partisan that they seem to be actors in the drama. Sophocles' very late play, the *Philoctetes,* has a chorus that enters the action to the point that they lie to the hero. They are far from insignificant and far from the commonplace notion of the chorus as "the ideal spectator" (that is, one who looks on but is not affected by or involved in the proceedings).

The tragedies differ sufficiently from one another to render precarious any generalization. Various similarities, though, inhibit theories of long-term change or trends in tragic viewpoint. Some Euripidean plays portray situations very similar to those of Aeschylean plays. Hippolytus, for instance, clings to his chastity in an obstinate and prideful way that reminds one of Aeschylean *hubris*. Aeschylus's *Eumenides* is talky in the same way that has caused critics to label Euripides the fifth-century B.C. George Bernard Shaw. The structure of Sophocles' *Oedipus at Colonus* is very much like the *Prometheus;* in each play a stationary hero is visited by a number of persons who react to him as he talks of the past and the future until finally he suffers a dramatic change—Oedipus disappearing in a thunderclap, Prometheus cast down into Tartarus.

The *Prometheus* is possibly the more unconventional. It is hard to stage, being lyrical rather than dramatic, and the very long speeches do not work as dialogue. It is static; the motionless Titan is approached by the Oceanids, Oceanus, Io, and Hermes. They react to him and in that fashion explain him; but they do not interact with him. There is conventional action only at the beginning and end when Prometheus is nailed to the rock and when he is cast into Tartarus. Within what is really a pageant—the passion of Prometheus, so to speak—there is the sense of action, first through the arrival and departure of the many characters, then by the vast range of space evoked in the numerous geographical references, but most of all through Prometheus's prophecies and recollections, which bring the audience back and forth through a great passage of time. This is indeed a *big* play.

The *Prometheus,* in fact, is a good example of a play that will not fit neatly into anyone's theory. If it is structurally like the *Oedipus at Colonus,* it is very unlike most other surviving tragic drama. Its somewhat anomalous character becomes easier for generalizers to deal with because there is some doubt whether Aeschylus was its author. Yet this doubt means that any consideration of the Aeschylean oeuvre really ought to leave the *Prometheus* out. Part of a lost trilogy, the other parts of which are only imperfectly known, the *Prometheus* is particularly liable to be misunderstood. The play, insofar as it is open to interpretation, is interesting for the many ambiguities and conflicting meanings that the playwright has ingeniously forced to work together.

Prometheus's crime of stealing fire from Zeus for humankind, which is recounted in Hesiod's *Works and Days* and in his *Theogony,* is the immediate background to the *Prometheus*. The playwright also assumes his audience's knowledge of the overthrow of the previous generations of the gods, Uranus (Heaven) by his son Cronus and Cronus by his son Zeus, which is also recounted in Hesiod's *Theogony*. There, besides the story of the generations of gods and of Zeus's victorious fight against the older generation of Titans (in which the Titan Prometheus sides with Zeus), there are hints of the story known from other sources of the potential overthrow of Zeus by his son born of Thetis. Prometheus alone knows this destiny, and he reveals it to Zeus only at the end of the trilogy, thereby endowing his rule with eternity.

One of the more difficult aspects of the play is the sympathetic portrayal of Prometheus set against a Zeus who is almost a wicked villain. Other Aeschylean plays, as well as the writings of Hesiod and Solon, show that the common conception of Zeus at the time was as the guardian, if not the creator, of the moral order. Here, in contrast, he is depicted as a tyrant. Io, who has been lusted after by Zeus and persecuted for it by Hera, is described by the chorus (88ff.) as a simple girl who has been destroyed by getting involved with people too powerful or grand for her. Oceanus speaks as an old-fashioned aristocrat who has learned to yield quietly to the new, violent power (311–12; 329), and Hermes is described as the tyrant's lackey (941ff.). Because an Athenian tyrant's rule commonly engendered strong antipathy, the Zeus figure must have been unsympathetic. It is worth noting that Zeus does not actually appear in the action as a character.

The ambiguities in this play are bold, setting up contradictions that any honest contemplation of the workings of the universe will discover (see lines 515ff.). All-knowing Zeus paradoxically does not know the secret Prometheus knows. He did not in fact know that Prometheus was intent on stealing fire. Prometheus, in turn, who knows all the future (see lines 97ff.), chose to serve Zeus in the battle against the Titans even though he foresaw his own ill treatment at Zeus's hands (224ff.). Yet elsewhere (267ff.) he seems *not* to have realized what suffering lay ahead. This ignoring the future is reflected in Io, for when Prometheus has revealed her pain-filled future and she says that suicide is her only alternative (750), she nonetheless continues on into that grim future. Her persistence, her instinct for survival, is the dramatic realization of the hope Prometheus gave to man. He himself possesses it (187ff.)—hence his suffering. Hope, says Hesiod, is what was left in Pandora's box when all the horrors of this world were released. One thinks of Brecht's *Mother Courage*.

Prometheus is man's protector. Suffering for man, identifying himself with man's suffering, he, a god, stands more to the side of man than god. As he says, he has given man hope and skill. Man ameliorates his lot with skill and intellect; he confronts his doom with the hope that it will be overturned. Prometheus describes a kind of ascent of man which is directly contrary to the more common pessimistic view of man in decline as described in Hesiod's Ages of Mankind. Science and technology and the pursuit of the better life are optimistic. Prometheus, who succeeds through craft and guile (intelligence and skill), allies himself with Zeus, whose victories, as Prometheus foresees, will come to him through intelligence (see Themis's prophecy, 214ff.). When Prometheus becomes Zeus's victim, he survives on the empty (as the audience well knows) hope that he will see Zeus overthrown. Does he not sense that this is a vain hope? Is hope, however illusory, nonetheless necessary?

In this play Prometheus almost plays man to Zeus's god. Theirs is a symbiotic relationship. What distinguishes god from man is immortality and the quality or attribute, the magic one might say, each god has. Man is born helpless. Prometheus bestows technical skill and hope. But just as Zeus needs Prometheus because he has a secret that will destroy Zeus, mankind has what the gods need. This relationship is implied in the identification of Prometheus with man throughout this play. In Aristophanes' *Birds*, when it is proposed to block the passage of smoke from sacrifice on earth as it goes heavenward to the gods, the playwright offers a humorous observation on divine dependency on man. But the fact of the matter is that god is created not only in man's image, but in man's imagination. The mutual dependency to which the *Prometheus* addresses itself is very real.

The unsympathetic portrayal of Zeus in this play may cause us to forget that, according to conventional wisdom, Zeus ushered in a new moral order, while Prometheus was part of a vanquished race of deities. Surely the trilogy as a whole took this position; we know that Prometheus and Zeus were reconciled at the end, probably more on Zeus's terms. The common metaphor of the play is disease. Disease, in the ancients' view, is anarchy. Disease was thought to be an imbalance of the body's humors, and imbalance is everywhere in this play: in the tyranny and victimization on the historical level; Promethean insolence and daring; Zeus's harsh and overweening authority; men's presumptions. Balance, the healing of disease, presumably came at the end of the trilogy with the reconciliation.

Aeschylus's *Oresteia* is the one surviving trilogy. It is instructive to see how ideas or images begun in the first play resonate throughout until the end of the third play. At the very beginning Clytemnestra is referred to as "planning like a man." The gender distinction persists—for example, when she says, "These things you learn from me, just a woman, of course" (348), delivered surely ironically, to which the chorus of males arrogantly respond: "Madam, you speak very well, like an intelligent man" (351). The male-female issue continues through the play until finally it becomes the central argument in the court scene in the *Eumenides* as the chorus of women argues for the condemnation of the child who killed his mother against the defense that the child was avenging his father. The greater action of this trilogy is justice moving from the hands of women to the courts of men. That idea, too, has been enunciated from the beginning. The very first great choral ode of the *Agamemnon* begins:

> This is the tenth year since Priam's
> great plaintiff,
> Lord Menelaus and Agamemnon . . .

as though the Trojan War were a legal action.

The playwright sets up important parallel action in the plays. The first two plays begin with long choral odes that establish the action in the past. Then in the first play a husband returns home and is lured into a cozy bath and murdered by his wife, abetted by her paramour, his cousin. In the second a son returns home and murders his mother, abetted by his sister, her daughter. In both scenes a silent witness reveals the significant "truth" about the event. The prophetess Cassandra, silent in the homecoming carriage, the unwilling concubine and spoil of war, watches Clytemnestra invite her husband to his destruction. When the royal couple have withdrawn, Cassandra begins a kind of hallucination before the horrified and fascinated chorus in which she sees the entire history of the House of Atreus as its principal events are about to be played out once again: the adultery of Thyestes, Atreus's murder of his brother's children have returned in the killing of Iphigenia, the adultery of Clytemnestra with Aegisthus. In the *Libation Bearers* as Orestes, who has been ordered to this dreadful deed by an oracle of Apollo, hesitates at murdering his mother, he turns to his heretofore silent comrade Pylades for advice. "What shall I do?" he asks. In a brilliant *coup de theatre* Aeschylus employs the newly invented third speaking part to utter just these three lines in the entire 1076-line play.

What will become of the oracles of Apollo then,
what will become of oaths? If enemies you must
have, let them be men, not the gods.

[900–902]

It is as though a voice of a god comes out of the silence.

Orestes is caught in one of those Aeschylean damned-if-you-do,
damned-if-you-don't situations. The ancient Greek tragic sense of life
consistently poses man in circumstances not of his own making from
which he will find no exit, but Aeschylus, like all the great artists of
his culture, manages to dignify this view of man's lot. Early in the
Agamemnon the chorus articulates one of the great religious truths of
this play:

Zeus shows man the way to think,
setting understanding securely in the midst of suffering.
In the heart there drips instead of sleep
a labor of sorrowing memory;
and there comes to us all
unwilling prudent measured thought;
the grace of gods who sit on holy thrones
somehow comes with force and violence.

[176–83]

The word "to suffer" in Greek also means "to experience." Knowledge gained through suffering is considered the complete experience
of life. The inevitable harshness of life is the means whereby humans
realize themselves utterly. The extreme, violent, willful action of
tragic drama is on the one hand doomed and on the other conscious
self-destruction. Depending on one's perspective, it is either the gesture of self-awareness or the preparation for it.

The poet sets up the action in a pattern that allows for inevitability
and choice at the same time, a pattern Herodotus frequently uses to
explain action. The idea is that great men, exhilarated by their greatness and prosperity, are vulnerable to seduction, which leads them to
miscalculate in making choices, to err, and hence to invite catastrophe. With the fleet becalmed at Aulis, Agamemnon, leader of the
armada against Troy, is forced to choose whether to get the expedition underway by the sacrifice of his daughter, seemingly demanded
by the goddess Artemis as explained by the seer Calchas, or to give
up his plan. Whether to be father or generalissimo—that is the
choice.

The crucial moment in this play is the so-called carpet scene. Clytemnestra comes forth to greet her lord, an ironic speech of welcome and longing on her lips (she did long for him, she does welcome him with passion, for she wants so much to kill him!), and begs him to enter the house on a purple carpet she has had the household servants lay out for him. Visually, this great tongue of blood extending from the door, the orifice of the house beckoning him to sexual delights and death within, is extraordinarily powerful. Agamemnon scruples to walk upon the carpet, hesitant to crush such luxury underfoot. Clytemnestra insists; he demurs. It is a sexual duel and also a contest of powers that reminds one of the final encounter between the dazed, speared bull and the matador awaiting his charge. Clytemnestra needs this moment to justify the killing of her husband. He must reenact his killing of their daughter. Agamemnon, now victorious in war, is seduced by Clytemnestra into the prideful act, and he mistakenly walks on the carpet against his better judgment, at the same time mistaken in his arrogance, both forgetful of his dead daughter in front of her mother and indifferent to his wife, asking her to be kind to the concubine he brings with him.

It is at this moment that the playwright brilliantly begins the shift in Clytemnestra from mother betrayed to betraying adulteress. Clytemnestra's welcoming words with their sexual suggestiveness, her verbal duel with her husband as she seduces him to walk on the carpet, together with the presence of the silent, watchful concubine Cassandra remind us of the sexual bond between the royal couple. Later, when Clytemnestra displays the corpse of Agamemnon and she is joined by her paramour, Aegisthus, the adultery completely obliterates the memory of the sacrificed daughter. In this way Aeschylus prepares for the rest of the trilogy. The first play is conventionally called *Agamemnon,* but it is Clytemnestra's play. Her livid satisfaction at her husband's murder is evoked in these marvelously sexual lines. She tells of stabbing him dead and what is really the final satisfying orgasm for which she has waited so long.

> He gave birth to a sharp stream of blood,
> hit me with black drops of dead man's blood,
> and I rejoiced no less than the corn does
> at god-given rain's sparkle in the birthtime of buds.
>   [1389–92]

The action of the last play of this trilogy, the *Eumenides,* does not parallel the action of the other two, perhaps because Aeschylus wants to show some resolution as the jury puts a stop to generational crime and betrayal. Things will no longer repeat themselves; juries made up of male citizens will replace the incestuous, hothouse vendettas carried on by the old crones of the family. Thus the tragedy might be said to have a "happy ending," except that Athena must cast her vote to break a hung jury. The tragic gender conflict remains. Males will continue to destroy their children for the sake of their careers and negligently bring home their concubines; wives will seek revenge upon them to validate their existence as childbearers and adulterously accept males twixt their sheets. Children will be asked to betray one parent or the other and in doing so will destroy themselves. The family remains; the city has emerged to provide stability and protection.

The generalizations in Aristotle's description of tragic drama in his *Poetics* rest largely on Sophocles' *Oedipus the King*. The play has come to mean the perfect tragedy, although Aristotle was in any case only being descriptive, not prescriptive. It is, however, only one kind of tragic experience; no other play is exactly like it. The reason for its enduring great popularity, apart from Aristotle's use of it, may be that more than any other extant tragedy, the audience experiences the play as a revelation, as one surprising new truth after another, just as Oedipus does. The difference is that while for both Oedipus and the audience it comes as a surprise that each person who confronts the king has a new clue to tell him about the murder of Laius or about his origins, only the audience knows the final hideous revelation toward which Oedipus is innocently moving closer and closer. The audience marvels at the courage of the king who wills himself closer and closer to a truth that slowly but surely becomes dimly apparent to him. Sharing the surprise and feeling the horror the king only dimly senses at first creates the greatest empathy. Pity and fear, Aristotle says, are engendered by tragedy. Nowhere is this truer than in *Oedipus the King*.

The play appears to be about awareness; its action involves coming to know something. It is a dramatization of the Aeschylean "knowledge through suffering" as well as the Socratic "the unexamined life is not worth living for men." It is not about crime and punishment, as so many critics believe. The ancient Greeks did not have much notion of sin, the transgression of known laws of god. First, there were no divine laws, no commandments to transgress. Second, although elements of the Orphic cult suggest it, the ancient Greeks seem not to have a strong belief in man's depravity; there was no original sin in the Promethean theft of fire to match the eating of the apple. Socrates, it seems, speaks for his countrymen when he insists that man by nature will always choose the better course if he is not hindered by his ignorance. There is no Iago, no villain in Greek thinking.

The myth of Oedipus could be approached from any number of positions. Sophocles passes over the oracle that told Oedipus he would kill his father and marry his mother, Oedipus's desperate attempt to evade this doom by heading toward Thebes instead of home to Corinth, his killing of the old man on the road—a killing, by the way, that in a society without a police force is a neutral collision of force, not to be judged as murder—and his marrying a woman who reason tells us must have been sixteen to twenty years older than he and very recently widowed. There are lots of other plays in this myth, the obvious one being about an arrogant young man who is so obtuse as to kill a man old enough to be his father and marry a woman old enough to be his mother. Indeed, because Sophocles' Oedipus gets into such a rage with Creon and Tiresias (just as he was probably too impatient with the old gentleman at the crossroads who was trying to force his carriage through), critics fasten on his temper as though it were Othello's jealousy or Macbeth's ambition, as though Sophocles himself were privy to the Renaissance mistranslation of Aristotle's *hamartia* as "tragic flaw." But that is not what this play is about. Sophocles never introduces these prior events into his play until they become part of the revelation. Note how cleverly he manages to leap over the improbability that Jocasta has never told Oedipus in all these years about how her first husband died. (André Gide's dramatic version of the story is very funny at this point.) Sophocles' evasion makes it all the clearer that his play is not about Oedipus's actions and the consequences of them. The play is about discovering the truth of these actions. To repeat, there is no crime, there is no punishment. True, Oedipus puts out his eyes, Jocasta kills herself. But there are some things so horrible that one wants to blot them out. Oedipus, of course, blinds himself so that he can see the things that matter rather than the externals. Tiresias has shown the way.

Oedipus is optimistic, a problem solver; as such he is ambitious and aggressive. He solved the problem at the crossroads, killed Laius, and drove through; he solved the riddle of the Sphinx, took the throne, and now will solve the problem of Thebes' pollution. The will of Oedipus is so strong that he determines to torture a man so that he will admit a truth that will destroy Oedipus, something

Oedipus already senses. This quality has many times over been demonstrated in the play, not least when juxtaposed against Creon's self-
proclaimed parasitism and Jocasta's straining of logic to obscure what
is unpalatable. In almost an allegorical counterpoint Creon offers
indifference, she evasion. The bigger contrast, however, is between
Oedipus and Tiresias, whose blindness is a kind of knowledge beyond intellect. When Oedipus, who knows nothing of the truth but
who is so proud of his intellect and problem-solving abilities, says
contemptuously to the old man, "You are blind, blind in your ears,
your mind and your eyes," a frisson of horrified fascination runs
through any audience. Oedipus is like the maddened bull, stupid and
heavy, looking out from strangely unseeing eyes, facing the agile
matador kneeling before him with the sword hidden in the folds of
the cape.

As Oedipus moves toward the fatal self-realization, he is several
times baffled by his intellect, which formulates the facts falsely. The
first time is when he accuses Creon of political intrigue, the last when
he assumes that Jocasta's sudden, desperate desire to avoid the truth is
based on her fear that he will prove to be slave-born. When Oedipus
suspects Tiresias and Creon of plotting against him, Sophocles shows
him to be using his intelligence to *avoid* the truth; Tiresias says
enough for any rational man to understand if he wanted to. But
Sophocles also portrays Oedipus as somewhat paranoid. Paranoia
and the darting intellect return in his speech of 1062ff., when he
suddenly fancies himself to have been slave-born. There is a personal
characteristic here. Oedipus in his own and everyone's eye is not the
legitimate ruler of Thebes; no one (except the audience, of course)
knows him to be the son of the late king, but rather a traveling man,
an adventurer who by his wits ascended the throne. Set against Creon, Jocasta, and Tiresias, the very establishment of Thebes, he is
naturally suspect and alien from time to time. His celebrated temper
flows naturally from his aggression, his ambition, and his insecurity.

It is the irony in the experience of the play that works the greatest
effect upon the audience. Oedipus seeks to learn what is already
known to the audience. His seeking, their knowledge, is the point at
which destiny and free will merge. These are but two aspects of any
event, of course. Every line of the play lives for the audience in this
double temporal field. When Oedipus formally declares the killer of
Laius to be taboo in the Theban lands, he is showing the free and
vigorous use of kingly power, but is really describing himself as he
will be at the play's close. In fact, he has already committed parricide

and incest, the inherently taboo acts. Sophocles manages a brilliant stroke in this play when Jocasta comes upon the quarreling brothers-in-law, Oedipus and Creon, and scolds them as any mother would. Compassionate wife and sister though she may be, the audience senses the maternal note at this moment; her behavior is an ironic relevation of what Oedipus is and always has been.

The tragedians rarely invented plots but found them in the stories handed down from the sagas of the oral period. As Aristotle points out, these came to be concentrated on the doings of certain illustrious families. Several plays deal with events in the royal family of Atreus: Aeschylus's *Oresteia*, Sophocles' *Electra*, and Euripides' *Electra*, *Orestes*, *Iphigenia in Tauris*, and *Iphigenia in Aulis*. The house of Labdacus is celebrated in Aeschylus's *Seven against Thebes*, Sophocles' *Antigone*, *Oedipus the King*, and *Oedipus at Colonus*, and Euripides' *Phoenician Women*. Very few tragedies are set in Athens because the Athenians had little local mythology.

Saga inhabits a curious realm between history and fiction. The ancients had sufficient appreciation of the fictive nature of traditional stories that they allowed their poets considerable latitude in shaping them; at the same time the *traditional* quality of saga—its historicity together with the insistence of the narrator—projected an authority that fiction could not possess; after all, the oral poetic tradition constituted the Greeks' cultural heritage, their only history handed down from the prehistoric period. Furthermore, characters who are already part of a people's cultural consciousness, who appear and reappear from drama to drama, acquire a kind of substance. Creon, for instance, brother to Jocasta, uncle of Antigone, appears in three of Sophocles' extant plays as well as Euripides' *Phoenician Women,* which altogether span almost thirty years of playwriting. Creon has a life of his own beyond any author's creation. This is not true of ephemeral beings such as Caliban, Nora Helmer, and Blanche Dubois, all of whom owe their existence to their author's imagination. The saga figures lived in a world that no single author could control.

Aeschylus's *Persians* is the one extant play based on a true event. The action of the play takes place in the aftermath of the battle at Salamis, where Athens destroyed the Persian fleet and along with it Xerxes' dreams of conquering Greece. Aeschylus has contrived a play that is remote from this immediate fact. The scene is innermost Persia, the characters have strange-sounding ("foreign") Persian names, and no individual Greek is mentioned. In sum, the historical event of September 480 B.C. is moved to the background; it functions as the reversal in the action so common to tragic drama, announced in a messenger's speech. The play centers upon Xerxes' expectations in mounting this expedition and how his defeat relates to these. In this way Aeschylus has transcended the historical facts to look at the workings of pride and its delusion. This becomes the "truth" of these real events.

Despite the enormous popularity of the Homeric poems, or perhaps because of it, the tragedians did not generally take episodes from these epics and turn them into tragedy. Nonetheless, the influence of Homer is everywhere—in the slow-moving, majestic catalogue of warriors in Aeschylus's *Seven against Thebes* (375ff.), for instance, or in Sophocles' two sublime, Achilles-like egotists, Ajax and Philoctetes, or in the tragedy of Agamemnon's epic-style ambition in Euripides' *Iphigenia in Aulis*. Still none of these playwrights reworked any of Homer's stories.

The stories from saga or epic that appear in tragedy are much abstracted. Saga—quasi-historical, traditional, and presumed to be true—is a story in which there is interaction between people, places, and events. Tragedy, on the other hand, is distilled saga. The details are gone; only the myth remains. Our word "myth" comes from the Greek *mythos,* "story." Myth is the narration of acts. Character, personality, locale, prior events—none of these factors that normally qualify the action in a story is essential to myth. It is action undiluted, distilled from antecedents, coincidents, and posterity. When a poet uses a myth, he can tell the story as he will, but the details do not affect the action.

Many tragedies portray family situations, probably because in a society in which an individual could find no support or protection outside the family, each person was "doomed" to his or her family, its conflicts, joys, and miseries, for life. These plays present in various external dress certain key relationships: husband-wife, brother-sister, father-son, and so on. The principal social value of many plays may be that they articulate deep-seated, difficult-to-express urges and conflicts individually or culturally felt. A common relationship is the destructive conjugal one: Clytemnestra-Agamemnon in Aeschylus's *Agamemnon,* Dejaneira-Heracles in Sophocles' *Trachiniae,* and Medea-Jason in Euripides' *Medea* are conspicuous examples. The relationship of Phaedra to Hippolytus in Euripides' *Hippolytus,* although actually stepmother and stepson, is remarkably similar as is in certain respects the Alcestis-Admetus relationship of Euripides' *Alcestis.* In each instance, the male rejects or resists the woman, and she retaliates overtly or unconsciously. Agamemnon kills Clytemnestra's daughter, abandons the mother, and resists before stepping on the ceremonial carpet and entering the house (a situation with sexual implications). Heracles resists his wife's embrace as he returns with a new concubine. Jason plans to abandon Medea and marry anew. Hippolytus rejects Phaedra's advances. Admetus is willing to see his wife die in his place. Clytemnestra plots to cut her husband down, Medea kills Jason's children, Phaedra dooms Hippolytus in an untruth, whereas Dejaneira innocently kills her husband with a love potion, and Alcestis piously imposes upon Admetus a lifelong obligation of mourning, which is a kind of living death.

That Agamemnon seems to be a tired, failed general, Jason a heartless opportunist, Admetus a pompous egotist, Heracles a misogynist bully whose only interest in women is carnal, and Hippolytus a prude and a prig is beside the point. Critical attempts to attach personality to the characters in tragedy derive from Christian emphasis upon personal responsibility and lead to facile and faulty interpretation. It is more profitable to think of roles. Agamemnon, for instance, is general, king, head of the house, and father. The collision in Aeschylus's play comes in acting out these roles; Agamemnon, then, is not a personality, a character making a personal choice, when he does what he does. The range of the roles that may be associated with each character can be extended to get at the richness of suggestion in tragedy. Some, of course, might equally well call it creative ambiguity. Agamemnon is also a sacrificial victim, a year god, an embodiment of excessive pride, and a wayfarer, just as Clytemnestra is a victor, a high priestess, emblem of the Great Mother Goddess, the embodiment of *ate,* divine seduction, and a welcoming host (and, as some have noted, ready with her knife in the bath, an incarnation of the male fear of the *vagina dentata*). Above all they are husband and wife battling for their place in the house. Neither is a realized personality. One cannot imagine them in the routine of their life away from this horrific moment of the drama.

Although the characters of ancient tragedy do not reveal any depth of personality, it may be argued that tradition and their reappearance in so many pieces of literature endow them with a substance upon which the poets build. Sophocles' interest in the house of Labdacus covers a generation of its family members; there are extant three plays about it: the *Antigone,* probably produced in 441, *Oedipus the King,* soon after 430, and *Oedipus at Colonus,* which was brought out posthumously in 401. Antigone and Creon appear in all three, Oedipus in two. The critic may wonder whether the principals in this story existed in meditated form in the poet's mind. Perhaps neither playwright nor audience needed extensive characterization.

It is instructive to look at Creon, who has a considerable role in all three Sophoclean plays. Brother to Jocasta, he is not meant to rule, but to remain instead a prince of the household. This is the role Sophocles gives him in *Oedipus the King,* in which to defend himself against charges of political intrigue, he delivers a speech describing the pleasure of the life of privilege without responsibility (583ff.). Sophocles has made the amiable, pleasure-loving, passive Creon a contrast to the energetic, insecure Oedipus. Another facet to Creon, an aristocratic trait, is his instinct for privacy. He twice urges that action or talk take place within the palace away from the public, but Oedipus, who exhibits from his very first speech an inclination to self-advertisement, denies him. Creon's measured calm remains even after the hideous revelations have left Jocasta dead, Oedipus cast from the throne, and himself king. In the colloquy between Oedipus and Creon at the play's very end, Oedipus is still impetuous and commanding ("Send me from Thebes," "Lead me away," "Don't take the children"), whereas Creon is platitudinous and passive ("Everything in due season," "Make that request of god," "Don't try to control everything").

The Creon of the *Antigone* is the earliest preserved Sophoclean conception of that character and also the most fully realized. He is king, pitted against his niece Antigone, who has committed crimes against the state which he takes to be also against himself. In his arguments with her and with his son he is angry, vehement, and intransigent. At the end, when Antigone and Creon's wife and son have all killed themselves—she to bear witness to her belief, they to commit themselves to her cause—he is humbled and fallen, aware too late. Misguided, grown tyrannical in his desperation, Creon is nonetheless never malicious.

A similar Creon appears in Euripides' *Phoenician Women,* which covers the action of both the *Antigone* and *Oedipus the King.* Creon is the same peripheral royal thrust onto the throne and into conflict with Antigone at his nephew's death. It is her disloyalty and intransigence that make him harsh, not something in his character.

In Sophocles' *Oedipus at Colonus,* however, Creon is a monster of a man—a liar, sanctimonious, alternately brazen and wheedling—who will use any ruse, lie, or show of force to get Oedipus back to Thebes from Athens where he has taken refuge. He is the natural foil to

Theseus, king of Athens, who is Oedipus's protector. Historians like to point out that Athens and Thebes were bitter enemies at the time of the play's production, which may have influenced this portrayal of Creon. Whatever the reason, this last Creon is not made from the same mold as Sophocles' other two. One cannot imagine him evolving over the years out of the other two conceptions Sophocles had realized. Creon seems to be a product of the action in each play rather than a manifestation of a rounded figure held in the author's imagination. Just as the Creon character is used variously to suit the temper of each play, so the same story material of the five extant plays whose action derives from the events in Oedipus's family following his self-blinding is manipulated to express differing meanings.

The traditional Orestes-Electra story survives in three plays. They are instructive in showing how the playwrights used myth in creating plot. The result is different from fiction because of what is familiar and what is assumed. Aeschylus brought out his *Oresteia* trilogy in 458, the second play of which is called the *Choephori* (*Libation Bearers*) and deals with Electra, Orestes, and the slaying of Clytemnestra. Sophocles and Euripides each brought out a play entitled *Electra*. Euripides' version came out somewhere between 417 and 413. One of the more tantalizing scholarly games is dating Sophocles' version. It is thought to be roughly contemporaneous, but the question is interesting, for to some minds it is a corrective to Euripides' conception, whereas to others Euripides' *Electra* is a parody of Sophocles'.

The legend of the House of Atreus contains certain elements with which the dramatist must work and some that he may or may not include. The part of the legend relative to Orestes and Electra is, in the barest outline, as follows:

Agamemnon, chosen overlord of the expedition against Troy, faces military failure when the fleet is becalmed in Aulis's harbor. Winds are promised by the seer Calchas if he will sacrifice his daughter, Iphigenia. This he does, and the fleet departs. His wife, Clytemnestra, in grief at her daughter's death (real or feigned motive), takes a lover, Aegisthus (her husband's cousin), and plots Agamemnon's death. Upon his return, caught by deceit, he is struck down. Clytemnestra and Aegisthus now rule openly, casting from their rightful position Clytemnestra and Agamemnon's daughters, one of whom is the royal princess Electra. She continually laments her father's death and prays for the return of her brother, Orestes, who, sent away at the time of his father's death by sympathetic household figures, has grown to manhood in foreign lands.

Finally Orestes returns at the command of Apollo to exact vengeance upon his mother. Because he has been gone since infancy she does not recognize him. He is revealed to his sister, and there follows a joyful scene of recognition between brother and sister after which they lay plans for killing their mother. There is then a tearful, horrible recognition scene between son and mother, and then she is killed. After her death and that of her paramour, Orestes suffers a violent emotional reaction. These are the events of Electra and Orestes' story proper, but the playwrights assume knowledge of the details of the family story mentioned above.

The essence of this story is the son's revenge killing of his mother; closely related is the daughter's humiliation and the yearning for revenge; and perhaps equal in importance is the reunion of the siblings. Psychologists who have analyzed this story find it analogous to the Oedipal situation, changed from incestuous intercourse to the less taboo matricide. In one variant of the myth, however, Orestes' "punishment" is harsher. Pausanias records (8.34.1–2) that after killing his mother, Orestes bit off his thumb, an act that has been interpreted as a more obvious form of castration than Oedipus's self-mutilation. Clytemnestra's often expressed fear of Orestes is similar to Oedipus's parents' fear of their baby son. Social psychologists note that the house of Atreus story projects a child's fear of parents; that is to say, Atreus dismembers and cooks children, Thyestes eats children, Agamemnon kills his daughter, and Clytemnestra spurns her daughter and wishes her son dead. In addition to the familiar mother-son relationship, the story portrays the close bond between siblings, the isolation of children in the family, the daughter's sexual jealousy of her mother, and the mother's rejection of her daughter.

While free to find his own emphases, the playwright has the following items to work with: the return of the brother; the disguise of the brother; the oracle of Apollo; the lamentation of the sister; the recognition of the siblings; the confrontation of son and mother; and the son's reaction. It says something about Athenian values that the viewpoint never tried but certainly possible is Clytemnestra's defense of her action stemming from her position as outsider, a victim crushed by the fateful forces of the House of Atreus. There is a hint of the inherent attraction of this interpretation in her moderate response to her hotheaded, absolutist, quite puritanical offspring, especially in the Euripidean version. But then Euripides could see Medea as the victimized bride in her stranger-husband's house.

Minor variations in the story are unimportant and do not constitute commentaries upon the story itself. They merely change the focus slightly. For instance, the Euripidean Clytemnestra has had children by Aegisthus (62). This is a "normal" domestic detail in an intensely domestic play, but drains the tension off from the rigid triangle of mother, paramour, and daughter. The rejection is no longer willful and vicious, but rather the absent-minded negligence of a carnally preoccupied mother.

Aeschylus's treatment of Orestes and Electra is different from Sophocles' and Euripides' treatment of them because their story is part of a larger whole, a trilogy that dramatizes the events from Agamemnon's return through to Orestes' absolution in a court of law, with stops on the way for lyrical reminders of everything from Thyestes' adultery to Iphigenia's death. In the grand Aeschylean manner the events of these three plays are made part of a larger process. Orestes and Electra are symbolic figures caught up in the universe's rhythm of crime and retribution, which like the tide, ceaselessly figures and organizes human affairs, so that Clytemnestra's revenge upon her daughter's murderer becomes a crime against her husband, and her son's revenge upon his father's murderer becomes in turn a hideous matricide. The *Libation Bearers,* though, was conceived as an independent unit and can therefore legitimately be taken out of the trilogy and compared with Sophocles' and Euripides' version of the story.

Aeschylus's *Libation Bearers* is the story of Orestes and the matricide. Electra exits for the last time at line 584, a little over halfway through the 1076-line play. The theme of gender conflict that pervades the entire trilogy is enacted in the male Orestes coming alone to seek his father's revenge against the woman, wife, and mother. The action of the play is relatively slight. The brother arrives, meets his sister, and they both lament and pray to their dead father. Disguised, Orestes seeks out his mother, kills her, and is pursued by the Furies. The lyrical lamentation and prayer at the tomb of Agamemnon, Orestes' killing Aegisthus, the confrontation between mother and son, and his subsequent religious pollution constitute the major dramatic movement of the play. The action in a sense repeats that of the *Agamemnon;* after a lengthy lyrical passage recalling some grim past history (in the earlier play the scene of Iphigenia's death, here Agamemnon's death) a traveler is offered the hospitality of the house, and an unsuspecting victim is killed.

Orestes is an instrument of justice acting on command from an oracle of Apollo's Delphi. Indeed justice is the central theme of the trilogy. He is nemesis visited upon Clytemnestra, who in her turn has brought retribution upon Agamemnon. For Orestes the perspective is different. He is led along, seduced into this action by Apollo, who functions as *ate,* a kind of divine deluder, just as Clytemnestra deluded the exhausted Agamemnon, wheedling and commanding him to step upon the carpet. Orestes obeys the god and kills his mother. He too, therefore, faces nemesis, which comes in the form of the pursuing Furies, who drive him mad.

It is Orestes' play and a religious play. Although the chorus often reminds us of the prospect from Olympus, Orestes is more than the voice of the god. "He who does not avenge his father's death is cast adrift," he declares (291–92). Revenge alone can give some ethical basis and form to his existence. The killing of Clytemnestra should be the cleansing act, but ironically for Orestes and Electra there is no resolution. At the end they are wanderers, still adrift, destroyed people.

Electra is central to the long lyrical lamentation. In this play she is almost the personification of grief, especially familial grief. The chorus describes her sorrow (17–18) with a word that has many shades of meaning: "She is conspicuous/outstanding/fitting in her grief." This Electra is little characterized, scarcely differentiated from the chorus. While Sophocles' Electra goes on for one hundred lines in joy at seeing her brother, ten lines suffice for the grimmer Electra of Aeschylus, just enough to express her woe and her love for her family. The often expressed idea in the lyrical lamentation and prayer that Agamemnon was denied the true honor of burial is an expression of a family destroyed, roles forgotten. Electra, the daughter, keens for her dead father; Orestes, the son, kills for his father. His tragedy is that his victim must be his *mother,* just as his mother had to kill her *husband,* just as Agamemnon had to kill his *daughter.*

The reunion between Electra and Orestes is mechanical. Based on tokens of identification (matching strands of hair, matching footprints), it is a brief moment of joy, not developed dramatically, set in the midst of the lengthy expression of grief shared by the chorus and Electra. In this way Aeschylus has focused on the event and minimized its effect on the participants; it is more a key being turned, a piece of a puzzle falling into place, some rhythm of the universe asserting itself in the human scene.

Sophocles' *Electra* is the same story, but certain changes in emphasis materially alter the idea of the story. Orestes appears very little, the recognition scene is delayed until the last part of the play, the oracle of Apollo is scarcely mentioned, and Clytemnestra is killed first, before Aegisthus. Sophocles reverses the order of Clytemnestra's and Aegisthus's deaths because he does not have, as Aeschylus did, a subsequent third play. The matricide excites if not revulsion, then some uneasiness: it is Orestes' tragedy. Aeschylus needs the *Eumenides* to work it out. Sophocles neatly shifts things, thereby allowing gratification at the death of Aegisthus, a completely unsympathetic figure, to dilute the feelings evoked by Clytemnestra's death. This shift allows for a considerably more ironic conclusion to the play, that is, the positive resolution of Aegisthus's death has been bought with Electra's spiritual destruction.

In any case Orestes' diminished role in Sophocles' play makes the morality of matricide less important. Electra is at the center, and she is not affected by Apollo's oracle or disguises or moral confusion. She laments her dead father and hates her living mother and wishes her dead; such is the action of the play. Sophocles introduces into this long, static, one-dimensional lyrical expression of grief a thrilling moment of action—the two-hundred-line false account of Orestes' death in a chariot race (679ff.). Its drama, suspense, and excitement give expression to all the hopes raised and dashed in the breast of the long-suffering Electra, a perfect straw to break the camel's back.

The drama moves at a fast pace from the beginning as Orestes, in talking with his old tutor and traveling companion, gives the details of Apollo's oracle, then plans a stratagem for his companion and one for himself. In this brisk fashion Sophocles rids the play of surprises. Everything is settled and known in the first hundred lines. Early on Orestes poses the prospect of meeting Electra, and the old man vetoes it. Sophocles thereby openly reminds his audience of one of the staples of the plot and then indicates that they will not be getting a drama of recognition and revenge. The story as story is laid to rest; the playwright may linger with the person of Electra and concentrate on her grief.

Electra, instead of being part of the choral lamentation, is at the center. She calls upon the sun and sky to bear witness to her woe (86ff.), and she vows to cry as long as she can see the night and the day (103ff.). The mourning Electra is testament to her father's murder, as the celestial phenomena testify to the universe and the order of things. Clytemnestra's plan to imprison Electra underground out of sight and hearing is a response to her emblematic role (see 108–9: "Before the doors of my father's house I weep"). To the chorus's remonstrance that impotent grief might as well be abandoned, that there is more to life than the expression of sorrow, Electra compares herself to the nightingale (the bird of mourning) and to the mourning Niobe turned to rock; in short, her grief is not *part* of her, but all of her, natural as the instinctive animal response, permanent as the petrified Niobe, regular as the sun and stars.

The chorus in its usual fashion is reasonable, talking of moderation, proportion, change, healing, and acceptance. Electra will not accept or wait for the passage of time that brings change to all things. The chorus warns her against forever creating new ugliness in her tortured soul (215ff.); she cannot see an end to evil. She argues that if the dead indeed are dead and nothing more, then the religious awe surrounding death is nothing (245ff.). She cannot let go her grief. In the long (over two hundred lines) lyrical exchange between her and the chorus, Electra's character is established. At the last she sums herself up in these pitiful lines: "While I wait for Orestes I myself am being destroyed. . . . When one is set in evil circumstances there is strong pressure to practice evil, too" (303–4, 308–9).

Grief-stricken Electra stands in contrast to the chorus, to her sister, Chrysothemis, and to Clytemnestra, all of whom seem to have resolved things better by comparison. Then, too, Electra does some mean things—for instance, ordering Aegisthus's corpse to be thrown to the dogs. This is not the mark of an ugly character but rather an indication of the extremes to which her mood of grief and the attendant morbidities of resentment, bitterness, and vengeance have brought her. In the stichomythy of 1014ff., Chrysothemis appears to be sensible and Electra raging, the natural result of her psychology, as is her assumption that Chrysothemis will betray her (1033–34).

Sophocles' Clytemnestra is not admirable, yet not to be despised either. Critics influenced by Christianity are too quick to set up categories of good and evil. Characters from myth are neutral until the dramatist endows them with attitude. In talking to Electra, for example, Clytemnestra appears reasonable ("With Aegisthus gone, you wander about, pay no heed to me—although you tell everyone I control you brutally. . . . I have no malice, but I'm certainly ready to give back to you what you say to me" [514ff.]); firm ("That's how I see it even if you don't agree. . . . Therefore, what has happened has not broken me down" [547ff.]); civilized ("Of course, I'll let you speak. If only you had always entered into conversation with me in this way, you would not have been so impossible to listen to" [556ff.]); and feeling ("It's awful to save one's life by the misfortunes of someone [she means Orestes] who is really one's very own self" [766ff., 770ff.]). Electra is the typical fifth-century old maid, just as her brother Orestes is the typical young male. She is housebound and emotionally bound to the family—an impotent, sulking person. He is free, a man on the move, a decisive figure who acts, whereas Electra can only suffer. As Chrysothemis says to her, "Don't you see? You were born a woman, not a man" (997).

Recognition does nothing to mitigate the lamentation in this play. Woe is all that has voice here—once at the play's beginning, once at the messenger's speech, and once over the urn; nothing thereafter cancels it. Recognition and reunion are instead used ironically. Orestes does not wait at the beginning of the play for Electra to come out. Electra believes in the false tale of Orestes' death, greets the false urn of ashes, and denies the authority of the true tokens reported by Chrysothemis. Orestes, when he meets Electra, fails to recognize her—a scene to which Aegisthus's false identification of Clytemnestra's corpse is chilling counterpart. Sophocles makes the point that Electra is so tightly gripped by the passion of her grief that nothing will pry her loose, not even the joy she feels at the arrival of the long-sought brother.

Euripides' play is immediately a challenge to any modern critic. It is so difficult to get the tone of this strange play that it is hard to read it with confidence. Euripides is an intelligent playwright, although sometimes sloppy and indifferent to tragic proprieties. Everything he does is for a purpose. Like Sophocles, he creates a heroine ravaged by grief, but with a difference. Instead of being the victim of a spiritual condition, his Electra is the victim of a lurid living situation. She is in rags, living in a rustic hut and—most extraordinary—married to a simple farmer. Her initial appearance comes as a shock, surely a calculated one. The farmer acts as the *prologus;* his speech is in the Aeschylean manner of exultation. It moves from the glory of the Trojan War down the long passage of time, to the doom, murders, and sorrows of the House of Atreus to the particulars of Aegisthus's attempts to keep Electra a virgin, to a thump in line 34: "Electra he gave to me," says the farmer. The statement is shocking certainly, possibly humorous.

Electra the farm girl makes her entrance shortly thereafter. The contrast between Electra, daughter of Agamemnon, and Electra, wife of the farmer, already outlined in the *prologus's* speech, is extravagant in her opening speech. "O black night, nurse to golden stars," she begins in the elevated diction common to tragic figures, then follows in another vein: "in which I go about with this jug set upon my head, carrying water from the spring." As the conventions are violated, or seem to be, the effect is again unsettling and possibly humorous.

One could say that Euripides is speaking to a different audience (although it seems he created this play roughly at the same time Sophocles created his) or more to the point, to different concerns of the same audience. He seems to be addressing domestic sensibilities by defining alienation and woe in social (a bad marriage) and material (a hovel, patched clothes) terms. This is not the aristocratic point of view common to tragedy; some would label it middle-class. It anticipates the world view of late comedy.

Again when the chorus offers cheer and common sense (167ff.), exuding good will like an Ismene or Chrysothemis, Electra's rehabilitation means to them new clothes and finery. And she rejects the chorus in those terms. When she speaks to Orestes of her suffering (305ff.), material deprivation is the principal concern. Similarly, in the initial exchange between Electra and her husband, they talk of the barnyard and housework. Tragic heroes do not think about domestic details, nor do they mouth the platitudes Electra's husband is fond of sending in her direction, for instance, "It's a disgrace for a girl to stand around talking to young men" (343–44), or "If a woman puts her mind to it, she can always find something to set on the table" (442–43).

Unkempt Electra among her pots and pans reduces the celebrated grief once so lyric and tragic to something more like a snivel. This notion is reinforced by Orestes' distaste at entering the farmer's shack after he has praised the nobility of his soul (391ff., esp. 397). Nobility of soul is all very well, but the smells of a barnyard shack make a deeper impression. How then is Electra to maintain her tragic stance, always but one remove from caricature? If Euripides is playing this straight, it is a rather mean little play. Perhaps Euripides is going for laughs. Would an audience sitting in tragic theater tolerate this? Would the archon eponymus have chosen such a script for the festival? Probably Euripides intended the play to be *unsettling*. Laughter is said to be the product of a confrontation with the unknown or unusual. The action of this play may well have provoked uneasy laughter as does the biting sarcasm of the brother/narrator in Tennessee Williams's *Glass Menagerie,* a play that is at once sad, horrible, and funny.

There are interesting moments of conventional writing in this play which set off still more sharply the unusual nature of Electra's situation. The farmer *prologus* touches most of the obvious clichés while giving Electra's background, but these clichés seem in part calculated for their juxtaposition to her present state of ignominy. Electra's initial lyrical lamentation (112ff.) is conventional; there are the expression of grief, the apostrophe to her father, the allusion to his murder—all the things one expects from Electra. Considerably more personal anguish is expressed in this version than in the other two; there is more grieving Electra than grief. Yet the audience is distanced by the complicated word order of the lyrics, a very fancy diction for this barnyard setting.

Equally disquieting, mildly amusing, downright hilarious—it is hard to know from this distance—is the way Euripides plays with the traditional tokens of recognition. A servant announces that someone has left a lock of hair at Agamemnon's grave. Could it be Orestes' hair, he asks. Nonsense, replies Electra; Orestes would not sneak into the country, and furthermore how can one match hair? The old man persists, mentioning the footprints that match her own. Electra sniffs: the ground is too rocky for footprints, and furthermore, how could siblings of such different sizes have similar footprints? The old man falters: Would you believe a piece of clothing? Electra cooly reminds him that Orestes could scarcely still be able to fit his baby clothes.

Why does Euripides play up the recognition scene so much? The rejection of these unlikely tokens is followed by the identification of Orestes by a scar on his brow (558ff.), realism's stern rebuke to the fairy-tale quality of the traditional elements. More than a criticism of the Aeschylean scene, as some critics believe, this scene is the dramatization of a new sensibility. Aeschylus offers the basic fact of recognition divorced from the realistic details of method so that the audience concentrates on the fact, not distracted by the cunning inherent in the manner. Euripides presents this scene instead to show how the nature of myth conflicts with the contemporary needs of drama, storytelling, and character.

Drama, the "thing done," is human action, which when unpredictable is suspenseful. Suspense is a chief ingredient in many forms of theater, but not so in that of the ancient Greeks. Traditional tales can turn on surprise but hardly on suspense. The action of myth and saga proceeds from the known to the known; in the telling all is anticipated. In fact, suspense is antithetical to the tragic mood or to tragic irony. Yet in Greek tragedy freedom of will of some sort or other has been manufactured to give the dignity without which human existence would be unbearable and drama surely aesthetically repellent. With will man contrives his death; ideas such as *hubris* and *hamartia* derive from an instinct for endowing human nothingness with proportion.

But as the fifth century proceeded, there emerged in Sophistic thinking a progressive and optimistic alternative to the tragic sense of life that is the hallmark of the Archaic Age and the early fifth century. This was rationalism, another kind of free will by which problems could be identified and solutions found. Euripides' recognition scene is based upon this. He denies its inevitability by showing a free human intellect that is not passive before the tokens of recognition, but instead analyzes them. The moment is fluid and variable; it is not in the least tragic.

The Euripidean idea of character is equally important in changing the nature of this scene. The fifth century witnessed the growth of human individualism, the very antithesis of the typical character. Euripides' plays often turn to the psychological truths of personality that lurk beneath the surface of a typical character of a traditional story. A marvelous brief instance of this kind of insight comes in the *Electra* in the description of Aegisthus, drunk at the grave of Agamemnon, his lifelong hatred grown impotent with its object gone (325ff.). From the start of the action Electra has been given hints of character. She acts from personality; events do not create her. Thus it is Electra who controls the recognition scene rather than the recognition scene dominating her as it does in Aeschylus's version.

This play effectively dramatizes the essential paradox of appearance and reality by presenting the myth somewhat askew; neither participants nor events quite conform to expectations. The appearance and reality theme recurs throughout the play, as in the discussions of true goodness. In praising Electra's farmer husband, Orestes offers the conventional suggestion that external appearances do not always reveal the nobility that lies within (367ff.). The farmer, who is indeed the only really decent principal in the play, counters by stressing that material comfort, a full belly, defines a man's character: "I think of the power money has, money to entertain with, money to pay the doctor bills; a little bit will buy the food and a man with a full belly is the same whether rich or poor" (426–31). Appearance and reality are clearly very different for these two characters. Euripides compounds the irony when he has Orestes offended by the "good" farmer's poverty while preparing grimly to accept his hospitality and later, in

a contrast full of ambiguity, when he has the messenger describe the
lordly and gracious invitation to the disguised Orestes from the play's
bad man, Aegisthus (774ff.).

Ambiguity colors the scene between Electra and Clytemnestra.
Aspects of the daughter's character have been well established. Her
rather prurient observations on the adulterers' sexual life (918–24,
945–51) recall the references to her own ripeness at the play's beginning and her awareness of her mother's sexual satisfaction compared
to her own neglect as a virgin ("breeding children in Aegisthus' bed"
[62]; "mother in bed with another man" [211]; "women love their
men, not their children" [265]. Now as she gloats over Aegisthus's
corpse she speaks of money again, of his comfort and her own priva-
tion. She is a rather ugly, emotionally deprived, and tortured person.

Clytemnestra is tired; her thoughts stay with Iphigenia, a woman's
rights, and sex. One has the feeling that she has had to defend these
positions too often. Indeed, for the traditional Clytemnestra these are
the standard thoughts that come from her lips rather mechanically.
But Euripides endows her with sensitivity and rationality, which
combination suddenly projects a personality from out of the well-
rehearsed positions of Wronged Wife and Mother ("Don't hate until
you know what you are hating" [1015ff.]; "There is a fool thing in
women and when their men cheat on them they'll go right out in
imitation and get a friend themselves" [1035ff.]; "My child, you were
born to love your father; that's just the way it is. Some love their
father more, some their mothers. I quite understand and sympathize
with you" [1102ff.]). At the end of their exchange she seems bored:
"O me and my strivings and schemes—perhaps I hated my husband
too much" (1109f.).

Electra's reply shows the other side of Clytemnestra, and it is not
very pretty. The revelation of this other side does not wash out the
previous impression, but rather complicates the situation, increasing
the ambiguity. That is the feeling at the play's end, which is not at all
dispelled by the arrival of the Dioscuri *ex machina,* who impose an
arbitrary ending to the story. Electra and Orestes remain two humans
who have acted out something given them by Apollo and fate. It is
not their fault, but then they enlist no sympathies. They are just as
ugly as Clytemnestra and Aegisthus. What Euripides has done is to
build characters. Electra, the force of grief, the eternal nightingale,
emblem of her family's destruction, becomes the depressed, emotionally starved, and angry person that anyone so obsessed by grief
suggests.

The notion that moments in this play may have provoked laughter or at least profound uneasiness rests on the belief that late-fifth-century audiences were becoming self-conscious, just as the poets who wrote for them were. The ancient Greek instinct for convention and repetition could very well encourage comparison, allusion, and creative imitation. Euripides often seems to be asking his audience to see his drama in terms of another work, particularly the Homeric epics. These are the beginnings of a literary sensibility upon which Aristophanes depends for the effect of several of his plays, notably the *Frogs,* produced in 405, eight years after Euripides' *Electra.* Creating action within the frame of reference of other theater or other literature calls for a kind of intellectual response that does not generate empathy. The playwright and the audience become too self-conscious. Sometimes even the characters do, as in the *Electra,* in which the chorus has its doubts. They sing of Thyestes seducing Atreus's wife (699ff.) and how Zeus therefore changed the course of the sun, an event they admit is highly unlikely, but, as they conclude, the kind of myth that is worthwhile because it inspires man to fear and hence to worship. Euripides makes thoughtful plays, but sometimes weaker theater by introducing ideas so nakedly into them.

This dramatist has left us one of the very best commentaries on tragic drama in the form of drama itself, his remarkable play *Orestes,* in which he shows the consequence of the tendency to treat myth self-consciously. This intellectualist dramatization of a critical stance hints at why the art of tragedy lost its strength roughly around the end of the fifth century. The *Orestes* was produced in 408. The ancient scholars indicate that the plot was Euripides' invention, an unusual act of creation which resulted in a highly imaginative development of the affairs of Electra and Orestes after they have killed Aegisthus and Clytemnestra. Some nineteenth and early twentieth century critics have been harsh in their condemnation of the play because, when judged by the canons of realism, the story seems ludicrous. The *deus ex machina* ending especially offends because the resolution Apollo commands is so boldly antagonistic to what has gone before. But contemporary predilections for the absurd have made this play suddenly more accessible. The impossible conflict created in the ending becomes in itself the more valid resolution.

The familiar brother and sister appear again in this play, yet much changed. He has gone mad, and she is burned out, as though dead. His madness does not come from the pursuing Aeschylean Erinyes. Orestes thinks he sees them, but the audience and Electra know that they are phantoms of his depression. The externalized reaction to a shame culture has been internalized to guilt. "What is your sickness?" his uncle asks, to which he replies, "My awareness, that I am conscious of having done dreadful things" (395f.). His sickness is more a disease of the soul coming from a way of life and associations than the consequence of his actions. At one point (793) he warns Pylades that it is catching. The advice is too late, for Pylades is equally infected.

At the beginning of the play Orestes has an attack of madness. When it subsides, he speaks, rational once again. Now after the attack ("the calm after the storm" [279])—in the larger view after the matricide—he speaks of his weariness (301ff.), his depression and loneliness (296ff.), and his despair (218ff., 288ff.). Euripides has created this state of mind for Orestes as the natural psychological expression of his traditional weakness, his natural impotence (in the *Libation Bearers* he is the creature of Apollo, and it is Pylades who gives the decisive command [900–901]; in Sophocles' play Orestes is no more than the flesh-and-blood manifestation of Electra's resolve; here again it is Pylades who finally must speak decisively [1105]). Euripides' Orestes is vulnerable, much like Hamlet, here more so than in the earlier versions. Deceit and disguise have turned to confusion and madness, impotence and irresolution to guilt and despair.

Electra is a destroyed person. "You are among the dead," she says to the memory of her mother, "and I pass my time in groaning and crying, tears all night long, unmarried, barren" (201ff.). Clytemnestra has escaped into death, her life complete, leaving Electra impotent. The heroic resolve of the Sophoclean Electra, whose grief and self-sacrifice are constant testimony to the outrage her mother and Aegisthus have committed, makes no sense after Clytemnestra's death. The Euripidean Electra has moved into *history,* into the aftermath, where she is a burned-out shell. Myth, where she formerly dwelt, like art, has no aftermath. The nervous tension of the *Orestes* quickens in the collision of intellectual attitudes that marks the late fifth century. By emphasizing history Euripides suggests that myth is obsolete.

Myth is cyclic; the action, whether understood to be ritual, formulaic, or archetypal, is essentially repetitive. Mythic action is not lodged in time but has beginnings and ends from which and to which everything moves on the same route endlessly. This mythic sense of time and activity conflicts with historical perspective, which is linear and progressive; time and events move forward along a time span and nothing is repeated. Sophistic ideas of progress in the late fifth century, reflected in Thucydides' analysis in his opening chapters of the growth and development of the Greek people, represent the major challenge to the tragic mode of thought.

Myth's suggestiveness also clashed with the prevailing intellectual temper, which was moving toward logic, categories, and all the other tools of the practicing philosopher. Myth allows for illogicalities to be resolved in a way impossible to the intellectual mind. Hesiod's conception of work as punishment and virtue at the same time is an example of the synthesis of illogicalities. The *Prometheus* is another example: Prometheus is a god who somehow represents both *human* progress and his own rebellion; he is at once a Titan whose crude age must pass in the evolution of godhead toward Zeus's eternal order of justice and a Christ-like divine victim of an Olympian tyranny that destroys goodness to maintain power. The fifth century saw Athens move toward a rational society in which the increasing presence of logic tended to make the symbols inherent in myth more orderly, more specific; the movement was toward allegory. Herodotus's rationalization of traditional stories is an example of this process.

In the *Orestes,* the collision of myth and history is most clearly expressed in the words of Tyndareus, grandfather to Orestes and Electra (491ff.). As is so often the case, Euripides settles on almost a prose exposition of his dramatic idea, yielding to an untheatrical convention of the time, the debate. He often creates stern old-timers who tell some home truths. Pheres in the *Alcestis* is another example, as is the nurse in the *Hippolytus* and Hecuba in the *Trojan Women* and again in the *Hecuba.*

Tyndareus makes the telling point that there are courts of law for redress in Orestes' situation and that it was senseless for him to kill his mother. Stripped of his symbolic value, the mythic freight unloaded, Orestes stands in history as a murderer, nothing more. The story, when denied its symbolic or archetypal truths, cannot exist as a piece of action independent of time, whose meaning and implications reside in and are forced from the action itself. Lodged in history, the story must have consequences; its "problems" demand solutions. Tyndareus goes on to say that because murder begets murder, some solution must be imposed (507ff.). Again the playwright attacks the mythic mode, whose essence is the cycle—Thyestes seducing Atreus's wife, Aegisthus seducing Agamemnon's wife, Atreus killing Thyestes' children, Agamemnon killing Iphigenia, Clytemnestra killing the man of the family, Orestes killing the woman of the family. The events of the house have a fixed rhythm, returning always in the outcomes to the origins.

In Homer's account there is nothing of Orestes' madness and absolution. This must have been created later. The story of Orestes' madness and trial comprises the last part of Aeschylus's trilogy, which the tragedian ends with a hung jury from which a decision can be extracted only by the extraordinary additional vote of Athena. In this way the playwright seems to be saving the myth while at the same time acknowledging the jury system. Euripides has done something else; he has brought the matricide out of myth and into history. Aeschylus has used the matricide as the seed for the arguments of Orestes and the Erinyes before the court at Athens. But he has transferred the Athenian jury system and the philosophy behind it to the timeless plane of myth, whereas Euripides in the *Orestes* allows myth to disintegrate in the forces of history.

"I shall defend the law," declares Tyndareus in the *Orestes,* "as far as I am able, and put down this brute savagery and murderousness that always destroys land and cities. Indeed, what could you possibly have been thinking of with your mother there beseeching you, showing you her breast?" (523ff.). Again Tyndareus goes to the heart of the matter. Greek myths contain so many unspeakable family relationships—incest, infanticide, patricide, matricide, murderous sibling rivalry—that story and legend make tolerable in the telling. When these stories are subjected to rational analysis, when the facts of the myths are isolated and inspected, when the immunity that time and symbol confer is withdrawn, there is left no more than sordid criminal behavior. Orestes did in fact come back to Argos and in a kind of unblinking way killed his mother while his sister cheered him on from the side. These are not nice people or nice myths; they are repositories, in fact, of "brute savagery," irrational animal behavior to which Tyndareus opposes the law. Myth, it can be argued, is a kind of prerational operational code, a system of admitting and settling claims analogous to the legal codes and statutes enacted by societies. And Tyndareus is claiming that myth is obsolete.

Clytemnestra, Orestes, and similar figures of myth are distillations of society, symbols of humankind, but they are never part of society. Historically such mythic figures reflect an aristocracy that does not acknowledge the rest of society, or society as such, and thus does not in fact constitute a conscious class. Before the reforms of Solon the people did not exist as such, and thus there was no society, certainly not before the tyrants gave them notice. Members of the aristocracy did not reckon the effect of their actions on persons outside their families. This attitude accounts for the inverted, narrow world of these persons, the sense of hothouse closeness. There is no escape into society. In this particular myth the special closeness of Orestes and Electra (see her speech at *Orestes* 307ff.) expresses this attitude. In the *Orestes* the aristocratic position is challenged by the ever present threat of the people of Argos. Euripides demonstrates the inadequacy of the apolitical myth by showing the impossibility of Orestes and Electra's almost solipsistic position. He further shows other principals in this story to be vulnerable. Helen herself must sneak through the streets of Argos, and Menelaus is equally wary throughout. Most important, Orestes must defend himself and Electra before the assembly. Orestes has always acted in myth as a paradigm. Now he must defend himself analytically, rhetorically, logically. It is not enough that he has acted out what he is. He must advance his cause as an idea. The people reject him, and at the same time, Euripides seems to be saying, they are condemning the function of myth. When law becomes the articulation of an increasingly rational society, then Orestes' mythic, symbolic act is reduced to murder. Law defines the needs and dilemmas of society and robs traditional stories of their symbolic value. They are thereby reduced to their crudest, simplest truth, and often, as here, that truth is repellent.

Who, then, is to blame for what has happened? Or, is it blame that is to be attached? "Apollo," says Orestes, "went astray, not I. What was I to do?" (596). Yet it is not that easy. Tyndareus remarks that Orestes is hated by the gods for what he did (531), which is another way of coming at what Orestes' remark about conscience suggests. As Orestes comes to understand that he himself is responsible for his acts, Euripides dramatizes this new awareness in a brilliant and devastating way. Orestes acts out the character the myth has given him, first as a violent madman, then as a murderous delinquent advancing on his aunt and cousin.

The plotting to kill Helen (1105ff.) parallels the traditional killing of Clytemnestra. It seems to be Euripides' own invention, and a brilliant one indeed. Here in the suspenseful land of absolute fiction, where at last Orestes and Electra ought to be *free,* they can do nothing other than act out the imperatives of vengeance, of a young male's murder of an older female relative, all out of context. To underscore this idea, Euripides creates a Helen who is no noble victim as Clytemnestra is, but catty ("still a virgin, dear"), vain ("only cut the tips of her hair for mourning"), overelegant with her retinue of Trojan slaves, and vulgarly proprietary as she goes about putting owner's signs on the furnishings (1108). Her murder could only be petty and squalid.

Toward the play's close the moral and theological ambiguity is resolved in the invocation to Agamemnon (1225ff.), in which the blame is placed on the dead king ("It is because of you that I suffer" [1227]; "I offer up to you my tears . . . and my lamentation" [1239]). Euripides is not launching an attack on Agamemnon or any other single element within the story. The call to Agamemnon, himself conspicuously a victim and remote as a source of his children's immediate woe, summons the entire story to mind. The myth itself becomes the agent of this grief, a grief that has been both a prop and a mainstay of their lives and the force that annihilates them. In the end Orestes and Electra appear to be victims of their story. While this is true for everyone and hindsight tells us that history is inevitable, the traditional nature of myths conveys an irony, the sense of foreknowledge that "real life" lacks. Mythical characters seem doomed; crushed by the relentless logic of their story.

The finale of this play is particularly brilliant. The murderous trio—Pylades in his bravado, Orestes in his meanness, and Electra in her bloodthirstiness—having been egged on cheerfully if mindlessly by the chorus, turn their attentions to burning the palace (1353ff.). Throughout the play there have been references to it, both as a building and as the seat of the family of Atreus (see particularly the choral ode at 807ff.). Historically, aristocratic families occupied grand houses that stood before the populace, like the stage palace before the audience. They and their houses were emblems for the people. Orestes speaks to this idea when he makes his defense before the people of Argos turn on the symbolic value of the matricide (see 565ff.), really his worth as living theater and symbol. His very act of defense is indeed theater. Pylades' arguments for murdering Helen— "We'll punish her in the name of Hellas," "You won't have the title of matricide but killer of Helen" (1132ff.)—reinforce the idea of Orestes as emblematic. Ironically, Orestes happens to be the first paradigmatic figure in extant Greek literature, functioning as the perfect role model for hesitant Telemachus in the *Odyssey*.

Allied to the idea of *house* are ideas of family and inheritance, which also come up often in the play. These ideas are inseparable, and they constitute the matrix of the myth. Electra's first speech is a typical rehearsal of the mythic history of the House of Atreus. Euripides has interjected an unsettled, tentative quality into the commonplaces that he gives her to utter. Electra is strangely halting as she speaks, unsure or weary or both. She tells it all in an odd way:

> Tantalus, known as the lucky one—and I am not being
> ironic or bitter—born to Zeus, or so they say . . .
> paid the penalty, as they tell it. . . .
> Why should I list all these unspeakable things . . . ?
> Atreus? . . . Well, I'll pass over his fate. . . .
> Then that famous, if indeed he was famous, Agamemnon.

The story is told, but the reluctance in the telling is unmistakable. Electra's aversion to her story and to her family is obvious and natural, but Euripides invests it with new significance. In the course of the drama myth itself appears faulted. So it is toward the close of the play, having acted out the murderous natures given them by the story, Electra and Orestes turn on the house, the incarnation of the myth of the House of Atreus and still more the symbol of the myth, to destroy it.

The destruction is reinforced in the peculiarly absurd directions of Apollo, the *deus ex machina*. This scene has caused untold confusion among scholarly critics because it is so outrageous, so incongruent with what precedes. Yet that incompatibility exactly describes the inadequacy of myth. The cyclic nature of myth is reflected in the neat and arbitrary way events and persons are arranged in violation of the dynamics engendered in the preceding scenes. For instance, what is more marvelously ridiculous than Apollo's saying, "Hermione there, at whose throat you have your knife, is destined to be your bride"? Cyclic action is static, but Euripides has allowed the characters to evolve. The collision between myth and history could not be greater. Myth is shown to be irrelevant.

Euripides' most telling dramatic device is the Phrygian eunuch slave who appears toward the close of the play, surely the most curious figure ever in extant ancient theater. The slave's speech is a messenger speech of sorts; thus he stands before the audience as the very representation of tragic convention as he tells of the horrendous events going on within the palace. The slave's way of mangling the language is completely shocking. It is important to realize that he is trying for tragic diction and style. He manages a number of literary or mythical allusions (e.g., "bull-horned ocean," 1376), and he gropes for ornamental language in the common epic convention

(1577–79). The chorus has to ask him to speak more clearly (1393); he agrees to give each detail, but then can't resist the imagistic: "All right, ladies, if you want the details, then in came this pride of lions [Orestes and Pylades]" (1400–1401).

The crude, confused, half-educated, ignorant language of the Phrygian eunuch is perhaps the most shocking element of this strange and unsettling play. This language portrays the *reality* of this state of mind rather than a coherent, articulated, hence abstracted depiction of the state as was customary in ancient theater. At the same time the eunuch's poetic tag lines caught up in broken Greek seem to make a mockery of the stilted, elevated diction and style peculiar to tragedy. As Euripides has called in history to challenge myth, he summons reality to suggest the irrelevance or absurdity of the tragic-lyric linguistic convention. Art is denied for truth.

Comedy

A hard man is good to find.

By the time of the Persian War the Athenian assembly had voted to include what they called "comic" drama alongside tragedy, satyr plays, and dithyrambic choruses at the Greater Dionysia festival. The English word "comic" derives from the Greek *komikos,* but the meaning is not necessarily the same. It is not exactly clear what the word means in Greek—humorous, certainly, serious as well, and probably religious, too. The institution of comedy at a major state festival with state support supposes something more serious and socially valuable than mere humorous entertainment.

There are various religious traditions among the ancient Greeks that call for obscene and abusive language and for drunkenness; perhaps these were the inspiration for comic theater. A commonplace of comedy is the phallus, whether worn, exaggerated and erect, by members of the cast or the center of the joking. This may come to comic theater from religion. Religious ritual employed the phallus as much as religious art objects depicted it. Anthropologists have found that in some cultures an erect penis is thought to be apotropaic, that is, to have the magical property of warding off malignant forces. In ancient Greece a representation of an erect penis was sometimes carried in religious procession. There exist to this day on the island of Delos the remains of gigantic sculptured penises, the testicles and ruptured trunk sitting on stone bases several feet off the ground, mute testimony to a religion that sanctified the mystery of human sexuality and reproduction as much as succeeding religion has repressed it.

Whatever else it may mean, it seems clear that *komikos* means something more than laughter-provoking. The word is used, for instance, by an ancient writer to differentiate the *Odyssey* from the *Iliad*. Ancient critics of Euripides have left the opinion that his *Alcestis* and *Orestes* are "relatively *komikos.*" That description might refer to the fact that both have more or less happy endings—no one dies—although this seems a misreading of both plays. Or it may refer to the roles of Heracles in the *Alcestis* and the Phrygian eunuch slave in the *Orestes,* both of whom resemble characters from the comic theater. Belly laughs were more likely to be provoked by the popular burlesque of mythological stories than by Aristophanes' plays. Those of his plays that survive are more shrill, sharp, and nasty than funny. "Comedy," as an all-inclusive term, may define a sense of well-being. There is a phrase in epic poetry that suggests this. In moments of exuberance, joy, or beauty, there often appears the epic phrase "the whole earth laughed."

It is hard to know what makes different people laugh. Over the centuries it changes so very much. Each set of three tragedies, for instance, was followed by a satyr play. Only one has survived: Euripides' *Cyclops,* a humorous version of the Homeric account of Odysseus's meeting with the Cyclops. It seems to be typical of satyr plays in that the plot was a gross distortion of a mythological story. As one ancient critic said, satyr plays are tragedy at play or tragedy making jokes. In Sicily early in the fifth century a certain Epicharmus wrote plays, only fragments of which survive. These seem to be more complicated and serious than satyr plays, but again were parodies or burlesques of mythological and saga themes. It seems fair to say that parody and burlesque are principal forms of ancient Greek humor. The early fifth-century *Battle between the Frogs and Mice,* largely a parody of Homeric battle narrative, is an amusing distortion of the heroic perspective, as though the characters in *The Wind in the Willows* were to take on major roles in the *Iliad*. The *Margites,* which does not survive, seems to have been an epic adventure story in which the hero was a fool or simpleton, not unlike Don Quixote. The immediate appeal is clear. Epic and tragedy take themselves so seriously, the characters are so one-dimensional, and their attitudes are so exaggerated that these literary forms fall only just a bit short of caricatures. Thus they are immediately vulnerable to being cast in a ridiculous light.

Little is known of fifth-century comedy apart from the examples furnished by the eleven surviving plays (out of forty or more) of Aristophanes, the first of which, the *Acharnians,* was produced in 425 and the last, *Plutus* (Wealth), in 388, that is, sixty years after the inclusion of comic plays into the festival. Ancient literary scholars created three categories of comic theater: Old Comedy, Middle Comedy, and New Comedy. Aristophanes' pieces are representative of the first, but only of the end of the period; the second category survives only in fragments, and the third is defined largely by the recently discovered plays of Menander (342–c.290 B.C.).

Born about the middle of the fifth century and living into the second decade of the fourth century, Aristophanes was only one of several important comic poets in the fifth century. The two most often linked with him, Cratinus and Eupolis, are known only by fragments of their works, but these and accounts of the content of their plays make clear that their plays were very much like those of Aristophanes. Cratinus may have tended more toward mythological travesties, but he seems to have been just as political as Aristophanes. Their subjects all seem to have been topical. The surviving titles of their plays show coincidental themes, just as the cover stories in contemporary newsweeklies do. Philosophers, for instance, were the subject for both Aristophanes (*Clouds*) and one of his competitors in 423, tragic poets for Aristophanes (*Frogs*) and a comic poet named Phrynichus in 405. This latter date was, of course, the year after the deaths of both Sophocles and Euripides. That two comic poets should be inspired by this event makes clear that the future of tragic theater must have been an important popular concern. Tragedies were a thoroughly political institution—as much as the comic theater that discussed them.

The last two surviving Aristophanic comedies were produced after the turn of the century and seem different from his earlier pieces. *Plutus* particularly has been held up as an example of a trend toward the New Comedy, exemplified by the works of Menander. Literary historians tend to organize things organically as though each successive genre or piece of literature perceptibly grew out of what came before. The remarkable dissimilarity between what Aristophanes and Menander created perhaps should inhibit the tendency in this instance. But *Plutus* has come to be thought of as the connecting link, and, true enough, it displays several features that are found in Menander's theater. There is no important choral function in this play, no passage in which the poet addresses the audience through the chorus on topical matters. The role of the slave is enlarged so that he becomes as significant as his master, a common phenomenon in later comedy. The absence of choral lyrics immediately makes the play more realistic. This realism is increased by the introduction of characters with commonplace attitudes and characteristics and who are concerned about private, social matters instead of public, political ones.

Comedy of the fifth century, by contrast, was thoroughly public, political in the grander and more original sense of that word. Aristophanes often plays to the notion that spectators and actors are united when he has actors address the audience, sometimes with pointed and personal questions as in the *Clouds* in which the following dialogue relating to anal intercourse occurs:

> "Do you see anyone with an elastic asshole among the spectators?"
> "Yup."
> "What? Really?"
> "By god, almost all of them have elastic assholes. This one, for starters; and that one I recognize; and that one with the hair." [1096ff.]

In Aristophanes' plays there is frequently a long choral passage filled with pungent observations on the events of the city and the quality of tragic drama and its dramatists. The chorus together with the comic hero, a fellow often devoted to some fantasy stratagem, seem to represent a lunatic version of the Athenian assembly, its passionate crowd and the dominating speaker urging on his ideas. Aristophanic comedy is often termed political comedy; critics scan everything down to the throwaway lines to discover the author's platform. An ancient source indicates that in 426 or 425 Aristophanes was prosecuted for "having brought disgrace upon the city" with his attack on its magistrates in a play that has not survived. Critics note his attacks upon Cleon in the extant plays and imagine that his theater had an activist role in guiding Athens. But this idea is to misconstrue the force of state comedy. Although seeing prominent persons ridiculed was an accepted part of the festival, it is reasonable to assume that as with tragedy, so with comedy, the city official responsible for choosing the competing comedies chose dramatic pieces that were expressive of public sentiment. In the years in which Aristophanes so ridiculed Cleon, Cleon was the most popular speaker in the assembly. If comedy does indeed derive from, among other things, a religious practice in which abusive language plays a part, then it can be argued that the attacks upon Cleon were supportive rather than destructive. In any case, Aristophanes and his colleagues survived Cleon, his successors, and two political revolutions. That survival betokens an establishment institution, not a rebel. In any case, the idea of political power in comedy runs counter to the strong bias against all power bases in the Athenian democracy.

Aristophanes' most politically topical play is the *Knights,* produced in 424. It is on one level a violent attack upon Cleon; contemporary critics with aristocratic pretensions have praised Aristophanes for his courage in the attack on the nouveau-riche Cleon. Oddly enough the play was introduced about a year after Aristophanes is alleged to have been brought to court by Cleon himself for some kind of lèse-majesté; either Cleon had grown indifferent, or the charge was not as we imagine it and personal insult was really not an issue, or, as one so often suspects with ancient scholarship, the notice of this event was an ancient scholar's wish-fulfillment realized in the writing.

The play is actually a rather funny statement about the body politic in a democratic society. The character of Demos (People) is the central figure; two leading contemporary generals, Nicias and Demosthenes, both of them well born, are this sluggish dolt's slaves. The backstairs slave household has been augmented by a crude Paphlagonian tanner (Cleon), who is later ousted by a sausage maker. The play turns on the efforts of these men to compete for control of the household and their master. The play is an account of the enslavement of the generals to the people and the nature of this servitude. It is true to the underlying fact of Athenian political life that the assembly never surrenders its sovereignty. "Just keep serving them sausages. . . . Use that coarse voice of yours," says Demosthenes to the sausage maker (213ff.).

The year before (425) Cleon had won an amazing victory over Spartan forces at Sphacteria on their own territory, and he was now at the height of his popularity. The truth of the matter is that in a society where so much emphasis was placed on public honor Cleon had to pander to the assembly to receive it; his achievements, such as this utterly unlikely and quite by chance military victory (he, amateur soldier that he was, later died in another military engagement) were so many tidbits that he was forced to feed the people. The *Knights* is first a comic vision of the political and social system in which popular esteem requires slavery, masters are in fact slaves, slaves are masters, glory requires pandering, and class distinctions make for angry accusations. The young, well-bred men of the chorus are viciously hostile to Cleon; many of their complaints turn on misused money. The choral anger means that the moneyed classes are hostile to the average citizens who benefit financially from empire rather than that Cleon is a crook. The angry censure of the chorus is yet another burden that anyone in public life must assume.

The play does not seem to be meant principally as an attack on Cleon because Aristophanes seems to ally himself with the slaves of Demos, of which Cleon is one, when he speaks about the problems of being a comic playwright (507ff.). The manner in which the competing plays were chosen and then judged would lead the playwrights to consider themselves the slaves of their audience, at their mercy. Aristophanes speaks through the leader of the chorus, who says that the audience is changeable by nature and betrays its earlier poets when they grow old. Aristophanes makes his audience just another Demos, which is, of course, exactly what they were. The play does not so much attack Cleon as recognize the symbiotic relationship between leader and governed, between manipulator (poet) and manipulated (audience). It is a tribute to the Athenians that they were able to look so honestly at the nature of governance in an arena so public as theater. Contemporary critics used to considerably greater public hypocrisy confound this honesty with political attack, but perhaps it is not there at all.

Comedy's social function lay in offering another perspective on the familiars of Athenian life. By making consequences absurd, grotesque, or fantastic, comedy nullified the power or authority of change. In that sense comedy was conformist, as can be expected in a state-sponsored institution. Aristophanic comedy relies heavily on burlesque, parody, and travesty, displacing the balances of the known world, and releasing the spectator from the gravitational forces of common sense and prejudice so that he may float by and around familiar objects. The extant plays mock war, peace, intellectualism, avant-garde dramaturgy, sexual roles, philosophical conservatism, the assembly, and the jury system. Comic humor allows the audience to get closer to these subjects than their fear or uneasiness about them might otherwise allow.

Figures are both demonstrably real and grotesquely perverse in Aristophanes' creation. The reality elicits a response from the viewer; the deformity nullifies the issue. One eats his cake and has it, too. The poet can portray for his audience the inherent viciousness of thwarted idealists, whose capacity for change has been stymied by the rusty machinery of their minds. The chorus of old men in the *Wasps*, who aptly describe themselves as wasps endowed with stingers, represent such idealists. In *The Women at the Thesmophoria Festival*, he makes a caricature of Agathon, an effeminate exquisite, both sweet and complicated, who is the very portrait of the avant-garde theater, itself threateningly seductive.

In briefer moments as well the poet achieves this reaction. Dicaeopolis in the *Acharnians,* for instance, is a truly pathetic figure at the play's beginning. Gazing out upon his beloved farmland, now lost to him and damaged, the character must have instantly evoked an empathetic response from the Athenian audience, immured within their city's walls, their land subject to Sparta's annual incursions. Just at this moment, however, Aristophanes dispels the emotion by rendering Dicaeopolis frail and trivial as he talks of his farting. Again in the *Lysistrata,* when the heroine delivers a plea both serious and emotional for an end to war, talking of the bloodshed between Greek-speaking peoples, the men standing before her are portrayed as consumed with passion for the goddess Peace, who is also present in the scene. Grotesquely and ironically their passion for peace is actually a lust for the woman so that they can speak only of the pain of their erections. The tragic dilemma of internecine war is voiced and then silenced, as it were, by the playwright's art.

Much as it addresses the overriding horror of the times, the *Lysistrata* steers clear of any precisely Athenian topic—this in 411, a year of Athens's loss of Euboea and its own political turmoil in which shortly after the festival a revolutionary oligarchic government overcame the democracy in Athens. That same year Aristophanes presented *The Women at the Thesmophoria Festival,* the subject of which is Euripidean dramaturgy, safe enough in troubled times. Aristophanes' most beautifully fantastical play is the *Birds,* produced in 413, the year the Athenian army at Syracuse was in the process of ruining their rather good chances of winning the war. The play is about creating a new city in the sky, with birds for inhabitants, and then subduing the Olympian deities to the power of the new city, called Cloudcuckooland. The play looks to the heavens, away from humans and their terrestrial problems, to a new start, a utopia. It cancels history by denying the religious system upon which that history rests. It is remarkable for the brilliant lyric poetry of the choral odes and for the many references to happiness throughout, a notion little entertained by the ancient Greeks and perhaps the most fantastical element of all in the play.

The structure of Aristophanic comedy is loose, yet what there is seems formed on the model of Attic tragedy. Whereas the latter's form is rigid, the comic poet places enormous demands of imagination upon his audience as his story races from vignette to vignette and lurches through time. Aristophanes' use of fictional plots made the prologue highly important as the means for outlining the story. It is here that the comic hero is struck with the mad idea or stratagem he pursues through the play. Thereafter the chorus arrives in opposition to the hero. The atmosphere of hostility and conflict that the chorus introduces is characteristic of Aristophanic comedy. It, too, reflects the essentially conflictive or dichotomous action of tragedy, if not the fundamental sense of contest or antithesis, which everywhere informs Greek culture.

After a certain amount of hostile interaction between chorus and hero the chorus proceeds to what is technically known as the *parabasis,* the "going aside" or "stepping aside." This is the time when the chorus steps forward and speaks to the audience, often out of character, and often as though speaking for the poet. Through the chorus Aristophanes complains about the lot of the comic playwright in the *Knights,* defends his political position in the *Acharnians,* and pleads for political amnesty in the harshly polarized atmosphere of the last decade of the fifth century in the *Frogs.* Sometimes the *parabasis* keeps to the theme of the play as in the *Birds* when the birds sing of Procne, recount the early history of the world from the birds' point of view, and tell the reasons people worship birds. The musicality of the birds is enhanced by birdcalls interspersed throughout. Paraphrase and description, however, cannot get at the extraordinary delicacy of thought and image as well as the exotic sound in this *parabasis.*

Following the *parabasis* the drama resumes more or less. The rest of the play is generally episodic as the hero acts out the bizarre idea or fantasy that he has planned earlier on. In the course of this action he meets a variety of characters who respond variously to him. An exception is the *Frogs,* however, the latter part of which is taken up with the celebrated debate between Euripides and Aeschylus over the relative merits of their plays. While the literary criticism met here is generally exaggerated, as is the demand made on the audience's literary knowledge, the verbal play and parody are subtle enough to require considerable attention. That subtlety is unusual in Aristophanes, and so is the fact that the scene does not fulfill the expectations raised in the prologue (the stratagem of Dionysus fetching Euripides from the Underworld). Indeed there is a surprise—Aeschylus is brought back instead!—something little found in ancient Greek literature. The *Frogs* was, however, well received, winning first prize at the Lenaea festival and, according to an ancient scholar, so much admired that it was put on again, a most unusual honor.

Most of the extant plays end with a celebration of food, drink, and sex. These are the constituents of the comic view of life, an affirmation of life in the living of it and of the life force that creates and nurtures humankind. It is his appreciation of food, drink, and sex which makes Odysseus a comic hero, a man who counsels Achilles to eat before he fights (*Iliad* 19.221ff.), who seeks to return to his wife and their shared bed, who enjoys the favors of the women he meets on his homeward journey. Characteristically Odysseus rejects Calypso's offer of immortality so as to have the pleasure and challenge of this life. If the *Odyssey* can be called comic, then the *Iliad* seems to stand in perfect symmetry as the tragic epic poem. Characteristically, Achilles rages against having to yield, against the inexorability of his lot, yet finally does. As Odysseus yields to life, the other yields to death; in that sense the *Iliad* is tragic, and the *Odyssey* is comic.

The comic hero does not face death, but he goes to his own peculiar comic doom, to a banquet or marriage, to a full belly and exhausted loins. The triumph of will he displays in conceiving his fantasies and imposing them upon the chorus does not desert him at the end. He goes out drunk and bellicose (the old father, Philocleon, in the *Wasps*) or with a girl on each arm (Dicaeopolis in the *Acharnians*) or burning down the Sophists' lair (Strepsiades in the *Clouds*) or marrying the girl (Trygaeus in the *Peace* and Pisthetaerus in the *Birds*). These men are always energetic, hurling insults to all and sundry, defending themselves against attacks. The most memorable Aristophanic hero is a man of years; he creaks, groans, laments the passage of time, contemplates his youth with nostalgia, and yet is comfortable in his age. Yet not all Aristophanic heroes are like these. Dionysus in the *Frogs* is a sentimental, vague, and confused person of great good will; Mnesilochus in the *Women at the Thesmophoria Festival* is little characterized beyond being nervous and gossipy.

If with so small a sample one can generalize, then Dicaeopolis in the *Acharnians* is an outstanding example of the more common type of Aristophanic hero: a country man, simple, direct, honest, without pretension. These men do not like the city. Strepsiades in the *Clouds*, for instance, objects to the values and attitudes of his city-bred wife. His son has been ruined by them. Can it be said that the rustic hero represents the *good* man? Certainly Strepsiades is stupid and ridiculously excitable and the old man of the *Wasps* ends up as lunatic in his pursuit of pleasure as he had been with jury duty. Yet the distinction between Strepsiades and his extravagant, pretentious wife and mindless son is that he is good, even as the chorus turns on him. Whether the bias for agriculture and rural life carries the additional ideological freight of conservatism, allegiance to the aristocratic ideal, and hostility to shipping and trade is not clear. The commonplace nostalgia for a simpler, rustic past is perhaps a value judgment as well.

The war benefited the traders and oarsmen especially; it harmed the farmer, keeping him confined to the city and away from his beloved countryside. Aristophanes' plays reveal a curious love for nature and the country that might almost be called the beginning of the pastoral sensibility. The joys of country life are mentioned in almost every play. The description of the rural world in the *Peace* (566ff.) and the contrast with the city (602ff.) are pastoral in mood. The sentiment parallels that of Euripides' sweet, simple temple boy, Ion, whose pleasure in working close to nature and away from the city is the principal feature of his personality (*Ion* 82ff., 585ff.).

The ancient Greeks are notorious for their indifference to nature. Homer, for instance, has no descriptions of natural settings apart from the gardens that surround Calypso's cave. The epithets he uses to describe places are always the vaguest and most general, and his similes from nature are confined to depicting animal behavior. Later poets are the same, except Hesiod, who refers to a farmer's positive dislike of the tyranny, the insults that the countryside can inflict upon a working man, and an aesthete's acknowledgment of its beauties. Sappho's description of a grove of trees is unusual and remarkable. When Socrates walks with Phaedrus outside the city walls of Athens to lie on the grass and talk, it is described as a rare occasion. Parks and gardens were foreign to the Greeks; indeed, they had to borrow a word for them. Xenophon, Plato's contemporary, imported the Persian word *paradeisos* to supply this want in the language. Perhaps during the Peloponnesian War, when the cramped living quarters of the city became exceedingly oppressive, country life naturally became more attractive throughout the populace for virtues real or imagined. Yearning for the countryside may have been the motive as well for the unusual choral ode in Sophocles' *Oedipus at Colonus* which praises the olive groves of Attica.

The battle of Marathon is yet another prop for the men of Aristophanes' comedies. Marathonioi, as they are often called, are dedicated to a moment sacred to them and their country, a moment expressive of the ideals that they believe their city to possess. The battle of

Marathon (490) was an extraordinary Athenian military triumph, now sufficiently shrouded in the mists of passing time to have become uncomplicated and pure as patriotic myths must be. Aristophanes' surviving plays come from the time when Athens was past the glorious prime memorialized in the funeral oration delivered by Pericles in Thucydides' pages. Thus the victory at Marathon seemed all the more glorious. The chorus in the *Wasps* are Marathonioi. Their song (1061ff.) relives the glorious moment when they killed and repulsed the Persian invader. Their strength and ferocity have become irascibility, petty nastiness, and grumbling, represented by the wasps' stingers.

This song should easily refute the notion that Aristophanes defends the views of the conservatives of Athens. The passage is an effective caricature of the decadence inherent in unswerving allegiance to a former moment of military might. Aristophanes has the remarkable skill of portraying thoroughly unsympathetic persons in a nonjudgmental way. There is no affection but much understanding. When, however, Strepsiades burns down Socrates' "Thinkery," there is a certain intensity, a certain unmistakable viciousness. Is Aristophanes taking sides? Is it the artist in him who foresaw that poetry was about to be eclipsed by the unpoetic, nonimagistic, analytic prose of Socrates' disciples? Or is the burning simply another example of Strepsiades' stupidity? Because Plato presents Aristophanes in sympathetic conversation with Socrates at an evening drinking party in his *Symposium,* it seems Plato might be saying something about their relationship in terms of this play. It could mean that they were indeed friends and mutual admirers, or it could mean that Plato wanted it to seem that way for reasons inherent in his story.

The Marathonioi and every other stout old man of Aristophanes' plays fuel the vigor of their enthusiasm and their successful stratagems with the conviction of their ideas. Their conviction is part of their success, of course, and is the reason they can march resolutely to their weddings and banquets. They have earned them. But Aristophanes has the genius to turn conviction inside out and reveal it as *une idée fixe;* that is why old men are perfect for his purposes. Energetic, exuberant, triumphant at having survived life, they are also eccentric, vulnerable to the revenge that life exacts upon their golden youth, and laughable. What is more, they are the perfect foil to the Athenian cultivation—adulation, really—of beautiful youth founded upon the premise of tragedy.

The creaky limbs, the faulty eyesight—these inadequacies are

brought together by Aristophanes in the ever present theme of farting. As a sneeze was thought in times past to loose the soul from its
moorings, there is no stronger reminder that we are vessel not monolith, creatures of muscle and nervous response, not cerebral, than a
powerful breaking of wind. Farting is absolutely basic to fifth-century Athenian comic sensibilities; not only does it appear in every
extant Aristophanic comedy, but also in the one surviving satyr play
as well. A measure of the gap between Aristophanes and Menander is
in fact the disappearance of the body as part of the comic vision. No
one farts in Menander's extant plays.

Moreover, every male in Aristophanic comedy must confront his
penis. Erect, cumbersome, painful, the phallus of the Aristophanic
plays is a constant reminder of the beast in the human male. More
than that, the phallus is an instrument of self-awareness which makes
the comic hero an analogue—through the looking glass—to the tragic hero. The hero of comedy, like his tragic counterpart, proceeds to
awareness, in his case, an awareness that comes from sensuality. Like
the tragic hero, he must confront inevitability, but it is in the form of
an erection that has a will of its own. The banqueting and lovemaking
with which comedies often culminate are the realization of something
akin to Homeric *arete* but from the comic perspective. The triumph
of life that eating and sex embody produces its own pain and thus its
own comic awareness—a parallel to the Aeschylean notion that learning comes through suffering. This pain is represented by the uncom-
fortable, embarrassing farts and erections. Erections and flatulence
are the human truth, the frail foundation upon which the ideal edi-
fices of banquets and lovemaking are reared. Males pursue sex and
food in rich fantasies, and in their realization the penis comes up in
pain, and the gas emits its trumpet sound.

Aristophanes is graphic in describing various physiological pro-
cesses. It is only now that the Victorian shackles of prudery are
beginning to be removed sufficiently to allow a contemporary audience to appreciate Aristophanic humor in this connection. Most
moderns can handle belching easily, farting perhaps with a blush.
Sexual intercourse is a common enough subject these days, but staged
masturbation will not play outside of New York, nor will detailed
descriptions of cunnilingus succeed in popular literature. It must be
remembered that the comic theater in which these topics were commonplace was for the general public, or at least the male members of
it (it is not clear whether women went to the festival). Fifth-century
vase painting is filled with scenes of heterosexual intercourse, fellatio

and cunnilingus, and homosexual anal intercourse as well as occasional scenes of bestiality. The Judeo-Christian ethos has robbed sexuality of its beauty and joyousness, has made sex shameful to an extent that the proper appreciation of the pagan attitude toward sexuality will probably never be possible, if for no other reason than that the transmission of the tradition has been largely carried in Christian hands and thus on Christian terms. Sexual desire of whatever sort makes a male vulnerable, and it is this vulnerability that no doubt principally engaged Aristophanes when he fashioned his comedy. He could not, as a modern comedian necessarily would, appeal to his audience's prurience. They had no reason to have any.

Sexuality is joyous in these plays. At the close of the *Acharnians* the pompous general Lamachus goes to the doctor to heal his battle wound while Dicaeopolis takes his girls off to bed to cure his great erection (an early dramatization of the slogan "Make Love Not War"). More than that, sexual desire is ultimately animal, spastic, and compulsive. It is the opposite of that serious, deliberate, self-consciously cerebral and stylized stance that is so typical of the Greek self-image in the fifth century. Their statuary poses man as sublime, awesome, beautiful. One thinks of the Charioteer at Delphi or the Apollo in the pedimental sculture at Olympia or the bronze Zeus-Poseidon in the National Museum at Athens or any one of the *kouroi* statues to be found around and about. They are the visual rendering of what in the verbal representation of man in tragic theater becomes almost caricature. Comedy goes exactly to the other extreme; man descends from pedestal or frieze, begins to masturbate, to fuck and fart. Aristophanes insists on these particular human attributes because they *are* sensual. They are the way stations to the corporal satisfaction, if not satiety, promised in the feast and in the bed at play's end. So it is necessary to emphasize and to begin with, as Aristophanes did, the anus and the genitals as comedy's common ground, the source of joy and laughter.

The Greeks admired, indeed adulated the human body. Their reverence for a young beautiful male body knew no limits. Nothing offended, as we can tell from Aristophanes and from vase painting. There are several examples in painted scenes on the vases of a young man who has drunk too much in the process of vomiting it all up again. The subject reveals that the Greeks were not offended by anything humanly possible; the treatment shows that they had the capacity to turn anything, no matter how potentially unseemly, into art. Their sense of propriety, however, was such that they were offended by *formal* innovation. Picasso's surreal or cubist paintings would have enraged the men of the fifth century, whereas they would have viewed his realistic ink drawings of men in groups on whom prostitutes are performing fellatio as small jewels from the master's hand.

The Greeks were conservative people with a well-developed sense of propriety—*to prepon,* they called it, "that which is fitting." It is like the English word "decorum," but the idea in Greek is both more powerful and more pervasive. *To prepon* lies behind the measures and volumes of the architectural members of the buildings, the judicious stance and composed gaze of the statues, and the changeless balance and harmony of the tragic choral odes and dialogue passages. Comedy can easily play off this instinct, and the satyr plays seem to have done so. The only surviving satyr play, Euripides' *Cyclops,* follows the Homeric account of Odysseus's visit to Polyphemus's cave, his entrapment, the blinding of the giant, and Odysseus's escape from him. In the play Odysseus remains true to his epic character; he is the serious figure whose long speech, a messenger speech in effect (382ff.), gives a more detailed version of the blinding event than Homer puts into Odysseus's mouth in the *Odyssey.* The Cyclops is big, clumsy, and crude, a grotesque figure who would be impossible in tragic theater. Euripides has done nothing to make him as sympathetic as Homer has done. For instance, he does not include the tender and mournful speech Cyclops addresses to his ram as it unwittingly carries Odysseus from the cave.

The third important figure in the *Cyclops* is Silenus, a woodland figure, who often accompanies the satyrs who form the chorus in this kind of play. A companion of Dionysus in his triumphs and his revels, the man-beast Silenus often appears drunk, but also makes wise, pithy comments on the action. The chorus and Silenus are ridiculous, at the opposite pole from Odysseus, who represents reality in the drama. With his messenger speech and his epic action, he is the core epic-tragic literary experience against which the chorus and Silenus play. The elegant choral lament on the absence of drink and sex (63ff.) and the chorus leader's curiosity about whether all the conquering Greeks had a chance to rape Helen (179) are the distortions that make Odysseus's part amusing. The same incongruity emerges when the chorus prepares to take a stand in aid of Odysseus only to discover that they are too lame or that there is too much dust in their eyes (632ff.).

Silenus is drunk through most of the action, incongruously talking of his physical charms (evidence suggests that Silenus was always represented as ugly). He inflames the Cyclops, who yanks him off scene to satisfy his erotic desire. Silenus is exceedingly flexible. He is willing to trade with Odysseus, although the Cyclops would punish him if he were to find out. He is willing to lie about Odysseus to save himself. He gets drunk and decides that he wants to stay and drink rather than escape. In contrast to the tension that is so prominent in both comic and tragic dramatic figures—the former so angry, so excitable, the latter so obsessed, vehement—Silenus is passive, agreeably yielding, and tolerant. The Silenus figure constitutes a distinctly different type from the more common representations of humankind in early Greek literature.

Euripides' *Alcestis,* the ancient scholars inform us, was presented as an alternative to the traditional satyr play. If true, the information is surprising; the ancient Greeks do not seem to have been keen on variation, innovation, or deformation. Based on a fairy-tale theme, itself unusual among the saga-based tragedies, the *Alcestis* has a remarkably incongruous scene in which Heracles is presented more as a comic than as a tragic figure. The Heracles figure is interesting in being exploited both for comic and for tragic potential. True to the ancients' penchant for propriety, the two conceptions were kept separate. Heracles, the heroic doer of deeds, slayer of giants, tragic killer of wife and children, is never confused with the gluttonous, drunken, oversexed buffoon. Thus in this play of mourning it is startling when Heracles arrives, blithe and unconcerned (true, he does not know of the household's sorrow), and remains to eat, drink, and philosophize into the unwilling ear of the grieving slave who must serve him. Does his presence allow or encourage the audience to find the events of this play humorous, or at least unsettling?

Apart from the humorous potential of his acting contrary to the genre requirements, Heracles shows himself to be generous, sympathetic, a man who says yes to life in a play in which the other principals have yielded to death. Alcestis has gone to her grave, Admetus to perpetual mourning. In a society in which women were meant to serve the dynastic ambitions of their husbands—bearing their children, maintaining their households—there could be no finer paradigm of wifely self-denial than Alcestis's legendary willingness to die in her husband's stead when the fates decreed his untimely death. Iphigenia echoes conventional Greek thinking when she says to her brother in *Iphigenia in Tauris,* "If a man dies, there is a real loss to the house, but a woman is a weak support" (1005–6). Phaedrus in the *Symposium* tells Alcestis's story as the supreme act of love. Told in the context of a speech in praise of homoerotic love, the story seems to mean to him that men will find their self-esteem in the love offered them by another male, while women will realize themselves in dying for a male. In social terms, Alcestis's sacrifice answers the real problem in Athenian society of the desolation and insecurity of a widow: better dead and with glory. According to the tombstone clichés and the choral refrain, Alcestis won herself the highest reputation by acting out the fantasy in which women can ignore the squalor of their lives while dreaming of a funereal, marmoreal celebrity.

Euripides gives this material a new perspective, which is perhaps why the ancient critics saw the play as something other than conventionally tragic. The dying Alcestis demands of Admetus that in return for her sacrifice he never marry again—and in terms strikingly legalistic and free of any sentiment of the heart. It is unclear whether Admetus is overcome with guilt or with self-pity, but he agrees never to have a woman in the house again, indeed to conduct his future life as though in perpetual mourning. The request is cruel and must be seen as, if not revenge, then a dying person's determination to dominate from the grave. It was customary for males to remarry within a relatively short span of time and certainly to keep company with women as soon as possible. "Get yourself a woman," advises Thetis to Achilles grieving over the death of Patroclus.

Heracles' arrival minutes after the death and just in time for the funeral is a crisis for Admetus, who must balance the masculine claims of hospitality against the dubious domestic virtue of mourning his dead wife. He tries to do both with the inevitable collision. At the close of the play Heracles escorts the veiled Alcestis, whom he has rescued from death, to Admetus, asking him as his host to take the woman into his household as a further gesture of friendship for Heracles. Again Admetus, caught between the domestic obligation to his late wife and his public role as host, chooses to honor the latter. Nonetheless, all's well that ends well. Alcestis is returned to him. The *Alcestis* may be a burlesque of a tragic theme after the fashion of the Sicilian Epicharmus or faintly like the regular satyr play. Yet the *Alcestis* is never really funny because the characters are so mean and the dialogue so sharp and bitter at times, as when Admetus's father tells the son how selfish he is and how foolish his wife is (614ff.).

Euripides first competed in 455 and won his first victory in 441. The *Alcestis,* produced in 438, the earliest surviving play of Euripides, is evidence that he was inventive quite early on. Toward the close of his life, around the beginning of the last decade of the century, he wrote three plays that are a departure in tone from all other extant tragic drama: the *Helen,* produced in 412, the *Iphigenia in Tauris* slightly earlier, and the *Ion* slightly later. Neither the strange *Alcestis* nor his *Electra,* which has been considered humorous and unsettling but nonetheless deeply serious, matches the tone of these three. Many critics contend that the true roots of later Athenian comedy are to be found here, more than in Aristophanes' late plays. It can also be argued that these dramas foreshadow the principal concerns of the one major literary invention of the Greeks in the centuries following their absorption into the Roman empire: the novel.

The *Ion* is a play with a truly happy ending. It is the story of a woman ravished by the god Apollo. She bears a son whom she exposes at birth, who is reared as a temple boy at Delphi, and with whom she and her husband are later reunited when she identifies the clothes in which he was exposed. Euripides has abandoned the sacral, genealogical, and dynastic elements of this story for domestic and personal significances. A young woman's reputation, a husband's claims to a position into which he has married, a barren wife's fears of being superfluous, a boy and his mother finding each other—these are the reiterated themes. The difference between the *Ion* and, say, the *Oresteia* is obvious. Aeschylus's trilogy is also a domestic story, but completely subordinated to the larger themes of evil, inherited guilt, god's intervention in man's world, the vulnerability of grandeur, and so on. Euripides has painted so intimate a scene that when it is time for Apollo to effect the resolution, he is too cowardly or self-centered to make amends and so sends Athena instead, who says, "He did not choose to appear before you since blame for what happened in the past might come out in the open" (1557–58).

The *Ion* is a play of intrigue, surprise, identifications, false discoveries, and, most of all, details. That these are also distinctive features of the narrative of the *Odyssey* lends support to the view that the Homeric epics derive from two entirely different sensibilities, tragic and comic. Into the second of these categories fall the *Odyssey,* certain Euripidean plays, later Attic comedy, and the novel or romance, as it is perhaps better called.

Details fill this play. The initial choral ode is sung by women tourists who exclaim over the sculpture and architecture of the temple of Apollo at Delphi. It is an example of what the Greeks called *ekphrasis,* the verbal description, accurate and stylized at the same time, of a work of art. Details are emphasized again as Creusa describes so exactly the golden bracelet with the poison in it (1005ff.). Later in the play in the messenger's speech describing Xuthus's preparations for sacrifice there is another *ekphrasis* (1146ff.) about the embroidery on the banner. Finally, in the moment of recognition between Ion and Creusa the embroidered cloth in which the infant Ion was exposed is fully described (1421ff.).

Because there is no reason to believe that theater at this time was equipped with elaborate sets or props, careful descriptions were useful. Still, they have a more important function in this play. The identification scene turns on material details. The earlier descriptions are used to place the characters—Ion at Delphi, Xuthus as king. The details are important to the identification scene as they are not in a similar scene in Aeschylus's *Libation Bearers*. The reunion of Electra and Orestes is part of a tragic or mythic movement for which such details are inconsequential. Euripides makes detail in this play the legitimate object of the audience's attention; the spectator's heart beats a little faster at the revelation of each material detail.

Identification scenes are a staple of later Athenian comedy, taken over by the Roman Plautus and Terence and making their way into the plays of Shakespeare and some European comedies. Such scenes are akin to the tragic *anagnorisis,* the moment when the hero can say, "Now I understand." Each is a resolution, the one to tragic irony, the other to comic irony. When Jocasta leaves Oedipus for the last time, begging him not to proceed with the investigation (for she has guessed the truth), Oedipus imagines that she fears he will discover that he is slave-born. "But," says he, "I call myself a child of fortune. . . . The months are my brothers . . . and sprung from such as these I should never want to be anyone else." The several ironies here make this proud declaration almost too much to endure. Foundling that he was, exposed in the hills under the sky, he calls upon lunar events as his siblings. He laughs at his wife's fears of slavery in his background, yet enslaved to an oracle's doom, Oedipus is the isolated man, the taboo figure, the man who as king and protector of the city unwittingly curses himself as its polluter. He has struggled toward this fatal moment of recognition, intent, as all heroes in this type of tragic drama seem to be, upon verifying and taking responsibility for his action. It is as though the tragic hero tries to cheat destiny of the satisfaction of manipulating humankind. Tragic recognition is the means to take back dignity that has been cast away from man by mindless and awful fate. That is why Oedipus in ruin will always be so satisfying and not because it is morally edifying to see the great brought low, or patricides and incestuous persons made to suffer. For the ancient Greeks awareness was all important. As Plato has Socrates say in the *Apology*, "the unexamined life is not worth living."

Ion's identification as the son of Creusa comes late in the play, after the delightful ironic exchange between Xuthus and the boy. Xuthus is told by the oracle to greet as son whomever he first meets when leaving the precinct, and so he embraces the lad, who promptly repels him as if he were a pederast. Earlier in the play comes the poignant conversation between Creusa and Ion when she talks of losing her son and he of the temple priestess as his surrogate mother. Xuthus imagines that he must have got some girl pregnant after hearing Creusa's account of Apollo impregnating her.

What each person lacks here is attachment; identification will make them belong to each other in some way. Biological truths and genealogy are the mundane facts upon which this story turns. Yet this story formula exercised an enormously powerful hold on the ancient world for a long time. The world in which Euripides wrote these three plays was a time of convulsion, upheaval, and decline in power and significance of traditional structures in society. These are the circumstances that produce alienation. These plays hold out identification and reunion as the climax, the happy ending. Is this not the grand wish for alienated people, each lost to the others in his own separate existence?

The *Helen* and *Iphigenia in Tauris* are much alike and share with the *Ion* an identification scene that leads to a happy ending. Traditionally, Iphigenia was the maiden whose death sullied her father, Agamemnon's, hands and unleashed her mother, Clytemnestra's, fury. Helen was the wife of Menelaus whose abduction or seduction by Paris led to the Trojan War. In *Helen* and *Iphigenia in Tauris,* however, alternative versions to these stories are presented. According to these, an animal was substituted for Iphigenia at the last moment on the altar, and a deceiving image, a phantom Helen, instead was carried off by Paris to Troy. Both women are caught up and hidden away by gods in remote lands. So it is that their careers are altogether tamer and less consequential. All the bloodshed, sorrow, and dislocation need never have happened; the tragic fact of Greek saga history is an illusion.

In both plays a wicked king holds a princess in his power until she is delivered by a clever stratagem in which a male takes an active part. The male who seeks the woman is in the one case her husband, Menelaus, and in the other her brother, Orestes. In both stories, unrecognizable persons—the shipwrecked Menelaus in his rags, Helen whom he has just lost, Orestes grown-up, Iphigenia grown-up—

carry on tantalizingly ironic dialogue until the scene of recognition. In both plays, the man and woman conspire to steal away from her malevolent keeper by means of an elaborate stratagem. The thrill of recognition that means salvation provides the emotional climax in these plays and is akin to the fear-provoking reversal of truly tragic action.

Many of the elements of these plays reappear in later Athenian comedy, possibly as a result of Euripidean influence. Euripides was very popular throughout the fourth century, and his plays were put on frequently. It would not be too much to assume that the *Iphigenia in Tauris* was especially popular because Aristotle, whose lecture notes on Greek literature are gathered together in a fragmentary work called the *Poetics,* most often illustrates his points with this play or with Sophocles' *Oedipus the King.*

Late Athenian comedy, conventionally called New Comedy, often features young women held captive by a protector and sought out by their young male lovers. Frequently the obstacles to their reunion are removed following a scene of recognition in which persons are identified correctly. The thrill of escape in the finale of the Euripidean plays is the equivalent of the thrill of projected sexual union of the united young lovers at the close of the comedies. This typical New Comedy plot is similar to that of the *Odyssey:* a woman held captive by a man (men in the case of the *Odyssey*) is rescued through a clever stratagem by a stranger who is identified as someone close to her. This similarity supports the argument that a traditional plot may transcend any one author or influence and may simply embody a basic human attitude. This story line can be called the comic theme, just as Aristotle has identified a tragic theme when he says, "Tragedy portrays a better than average man in better than average circumstances going to a worse than average fate or situation."

It is remarkable that literary historians as a rule do not accord to this comic story line the same importance or seriousness they give to the tragic theme. Indeed, very frequently they insist that this type of plot will hold a woman's interest more easily than a man's. This comment usually refers to the ancient novel. It has also been made about the *Odyssey,* however; some critics have even put forth the interesting and attractive idea that the *Odyssey* was composed by a woman. After filtering out the misogynistic subtext in that observation, there remains the possibility of gender-oriented story lines and more importantly, masculine tragedy and feminine comedy, the male saying yes to death as the female says yes to life. Certainly it is the women, Demeter and Persephone, who are the life forces in the well-known myth, and it is the male, Hades, who steals the woman away. The males in antiquity go to war, kill, and plunder; the women stay home, bear children, and grow food.

Eros, or desire, says Plutarch, the second century A.D. man of letters, is the one theme common to all Menander's plays. Whether central or peripheral, a love interest does appear in all the extant plays. The fourth century was a period of shifting political alliances, war, and civil strife. Athens was suffering from the decline in revenues following the loss of the tribute from the Delian League. In the city there were haves and have-nots, in the country a rural proletariat, landless and wandering. Everywhere there was the threat or reality of invading armies, especially from Macedonia. Cities were impoverished. Love was not an escapist theme, but rather the one arena in which an individual could exercise personal control in a world gone haywire. In a fragmented world the lovers' reunion was the only possible kind of integration. Again one may note that the *Odyssey* presupposes a similarly chaotic world for which the travel tales are a metaphor, but which is more directly revealed in the autobiography of the swineherd Eumaeus, born a prince, stolen by pirates, raised as a slave in Odysseus's father's house, and sent to the fields at puberty when he became interested in Odysseus's sister, Ctimente.

The twentieth-century discovery of Menander's surviving plays confirms the idea of New Comedy that developed over the years from the many fragments of fourth-century comedy and from Menander himself. Formal similarities to late works of Aristophanes appear in the use of the chorus, which comes and goes more as something between acts than as actor, and in the low-life characters who are often as direct and abusive in language and action as Aristophanic figures. In addition, Menander employs several stock characters that are the essence of comic theater: the misanthrope, the miserly old man, the stern father, the naive, ineffectual young male lover, and the sweet, helpless young maiden. Another stock character is the keeper of the brothel (*hetaira*), in which young maidens in comic theater, if not in the possession of their fathers, are often detained. (Usually they are born free, but abducted or exposed and sold into slavery until such time as they are happily recognized and gain freedom and their boyfriends.) The faithful family servant and, in a theater that recognizes the importance of sensuality, the cook are frequent characters. Finally there is the parasite as he is commonly called (whom we might call the hanger on, the gofer, the go-between), who effectively manipulates the action with his self-interest in mind, but sometimes ironically and humorously with the reverse result.

The interest in character and type shows a more developed sense of personality than characterized the literature of the fifth century. Instead of vaguely delineated fathers, mothers, daughters, sons, warriors, and maidens, the characters in late comic theater show a variety of idealized personality traits that motivate the action. Aristotle's student and Menander's older contemporary Theophrastus (c. 370–288) was a student of personality and wrote a series of brief essays identifying some prominent types. These essays were not unlike the surveys his teacher did of rhetoric, government, literature, and so on. This interest in particularity, inspired by Aristotle's observation and compilation of fact, becomes increasingly reflected in the plastic art as well. Instead of humans idealized in their perfection, sculptors began to delineate warts, wrinkles, and careless stances (although it may well be argued that these in turn are idealized warts, etc.).

In the third century there appeared a new genre, the romance or novel, which survives only in papyrus fragments from this era, but in five complete works from the imperial Roman period. The one presumed to be earliest is Chariton's *Chaereas and Callirhoe,* which is free of the artificiality, pretentious learning, and intellectuality that occasionally mar the narrative of the others. Papyrus fragments make it clear that these romances were immensely popular.

The origins of this genre are much disputed. Some critics link them with the very popular Hellenistic love elegy because of the pronounced erotic element in the stories. Pastoral poetry, on the other hand, might seem to have been the inspiration for Longus's *Daphnis and Chloe,* the story of two foundlings in a rural landscape who grow up to fall in love with each other. Other critics consider these narratives to be by-products of historiography—sentimentalized, idealized, trivialized historic accounts. The style and diction of Chariton's *Chaereas and Callirhoe,* for instance, owes an obvious debt to the historian Xenophon. Several of the subsidiary characters—Callirhoe's father, for example—are figures taken from history. Generally, the plot centers on a young man and his wife or betrothed whose love and faithfulness are sorely tried in a series of adventures following the mischance of their separation. Surviving courageously through travels and trials, they are finally reunited and live, of course, happily ever after. The characters in such stories are usually superficial, being idealized; the real strength is in the plot, generally well constructed and fast moving, full of twists and surprises that masterfully keep in the direction of the happy ending ahead.

If it is possible to generalize with such limited evidence, one might say that preservation of chastity and sexual reunion are two important ideas of the romance. These are themes as old as the *Odyssey*, of course, but in this genre it seems that they come to be central preoccupations of the principal characters. This is interesting because it shows an enlarged view of self; that is, the self is fulfilled only in reunion with the other. This is a radical change from the traditional selfish, isolated hero of the Greeks.

Many would argue that this change betrays the feminine bias of the typical romance audience: women of the time were emotionally dependent on males, and therefore any satisfactory conclusion to an adventure story had to include reunion. It may also be argued that the woman's strenuous efforts to preserve her chastity relate directly to this dependence. A woman is bound to the man who is her sexual partner. It is a Greek idea as old as Euripides' characterization of Andromache in the *Trojan Women,* who fears that once she has been taken sexually by her captor, she will forget her dead husband, Hector. Against this view, however, one may note that Chariton's male hero pursues his lost wife surely because he needs her as his partner, not as an earlier Greek male might, to retrieve lost goods. Furthermore, his heroine longs for her husband even as she lies in the arms of the second of her lovers. Chariton's novel takes a larger perspective on sex, love, and devotion.

While some of these narratives pause for philosophical asides or elaborated descriptions of art and nature, highly artificial *ekphrases,* the earlier and less intellectually pretentious Chariton has created an exceedingly fast narrative. It is also highly theatrical: first, the story can be broken down into five acts; second, like the audience of the tragic theater of centuries earlier, Chariton's reader is given all the facts that the characters do not possess, so that the narrative is heavily ironic; third, many of the scenes are worked out in a theatrical way, particularly the courtroom scene in which two rivals for the maiden debate their claims in opposing rhetorical styles.

The heroine, Callirhoe, is the victim of her beauty. Courageously and insistently chaste, she is ironically protected by Aphrodite, the deity who sponsors sexuality. A new bride and, unbeknownst to her husband, pregnant, she is kicked by him in a jealous rage (quite unmerited) and seems to die. Once buried, she awakens in the tomb and, fortunately, is saved, but, unfortunately, by grave robbers who steal her away and sell her into slavery to a king named Dionysus. Fortunately, her purchaser falls in love with her, but, unfortunately, she must marry Dionysus, although, fortunately, the marriage provides her with a father for her child. Chaereas meanwhile discovers the empty tomb, learns of her whereabouts, and pursues her, but, unfortunately, is shipwrecked and sold into slavery to another king named Mithridates. Fortunately, his purchaser befriends him, and they write to Callirhoe. Unfortunately, her new husband, Dionysus, intercepts the letters and imagines that Chaereas's purchaser has conceived a passion for his new wife. A trial between Mithridates and Dionysus ensues at Babylon at which Chaereas is named as the true plaintiff against Dionysus. But, unfortunately, the great king who presided as judge falls in love with Callirhoe once he sees her and delays the new trial between the present and the previous husband. Unfortunately, new delays occur when the Egyptians go to war against the Babylonian king, but, fortunately, Chaereas, who fights as a general of the Egyptians, captures the Babylonian king's baggage train with all the women in tow, among whom is Callirhoe, unbeknownst to him. Finally there is a highly dramatic reunion between the two and, after first signing over the baby to Dionysus, Callirhoe goes off with Chaereas, who does not suspect that he is a father.

Very much like the plot development in Sophocles' *Oedipus the King* every move toward solution leads to new catastrophe. As wish fulfillment, this romance is superb. A virtuous woman is able to maintain her reputation for strenuous chastity while at the same time exciting every male she meets with her extraordinary beauty and submitting to a marriage with a handsome, kind, attentive male. Her reward is fame and her original handsome husband, whom she has always loved. It might also be argued that the wife abandoning her baby so that she may enjoy a love relationship with its father speaks to the impossible emotional demands made upon young wives and mothers. This romance could have been entitled "Eat Your Cake and Have It, Too." A précis cannot do justice to the clever interweaving of the several plot developments, the amused tone in which the proceedings are often described, the clarity of the style, and the good will of the narrator toward all the participants in this story.

Critics who fault the romances for their seeming superficiality perhaps do not give sufficient weight to a certain absurdity that attends the proceedings in these pieces. The narrators describe a panoramic view of a much-traveled world in which there is no overarching universal design. Characters travel and crisscross one another's lives, living by chance and coincidence. Attempts to control life through plan and intrigue are doomed to produce reverse results. Buffeted about in such a world, the characters accept the meaninglessness of it all and look to themselves and the love they can generate from within to sustain themselves. A deadly kick in the stomach from one's beloved husband, a baby foisted off on an unsuspecting man while the real father is kept ignorant as well, a beauty so compelling that every encounter becomes torture, the forced marriage and sexual intercourse with a second husband—these are the absurd truths that the erotic passion can keep at a distance until the right ending comes along. And it is in the nature of love and eros to insist that it will.

The Hellenistic world came to be dominated by a belief in the idea of Fortune. This is not the same as Destiny, a concept that stresses the *organization* of the universe. Fortune, rather, is the acknowledgment that people's lives are shaped by utterly random, irrational happenings that cannot be explained by refuge in god or philosophy. Eros is the answer to the despair that such a world view might inspire. Love is an interior emotion that will thrive despite external assaults made upon the person in whom it is enkindled. And because love has an object external to this person, it saves him or her from the dreadful loneliness that the concept of Fortune exacts. It is not too much to say that the idea of love found in the romances is related to the important idea of love that fills the Gospel narratives (which in other ways as well show affinities with this late Greek literary form) as well as Plato's *Symposium*. Love of this sort is finally utterly serious—the means for humans to maintain their integrity and at the same time achieve transcendence. Preserved, protected, and struggled for, love will always produce a happy ending.

CHAPTER EIGHT

The Beginnings of Prose

It is Hecataeus of Miletus who tells this tale. I am writing what follows as it seems true to me. For the stories of the Greeks are both inconsistent and laughable, or so it seems to me.

Hecataeus

Goddamn an eyewitness anyway. He always spoils a good story.

Colonel Crisp as quoted by Harry S Truman

The unexamined life is not worth living.

Socrates

With the invention of writing, epic poetry seems to have gone into decline; poets composed epics, to be sure, but the fragments that remain reveal inferior poems. In the fifth century tragic drama and historical narrative came about, partly in response to needs that epic poems had once satisfied. Tragedy mythologizes epic action; history endows it with motives, space, and time. Tragedy uses a highly stylized poetic language; history uses prose.

Historiography was the first serious prose writing in the age of literacy. Early practitioners of prose were pioneers whose voyages through to the end of a written text were daring experiments. To criticize this writing calls for an appreciation of the hazards and unknowns, for the peculiar aesthetic weightlessness that comes from the absence of a tradition or a recognized standard. In a way, it is remarkable that the very conservative Greeks were capable of this innovation. We have to ask ourselves what needs history writing met.

The earliest surviving large prose pieces are Herodotus's account of Persia and its empire, culminating in the Persian invasion of Greece, and Thucydides' narration of the war between Athens and the major Dorian city-states. The former was completed sometime in the second-to-last decade of the fifth century, and the latter was left unfinished at its author's death around 400 B.C. There are pitfalls to interpreting these two pieces. Immediately, when we use the words "history" and "historian," the modern meaning of these terms prejudices our thinking. Then, too, the fact that these men were near contemporaries and writing in what we take to be an established genre irresistibly misleads us into comparing them. Furthermore, we who are heirs to a rich prose tradition do not always appreciate the novelty of what these two were doing, each in his distinctive manner.

Nonetheless, it is possible to perceive a change in the purpose and assumptions of narrative in Homer and the authors who succeed him. Myth and saga poetry portray an unchangeable, inevitable world that is only tenuously, if at all, related to the time in which narrator and audience dwell. Myth particularly is not susceptible to temporal delineation. *Once upon a time,* one says, events occurred. Moreover, because mythical events are narrated as though inevitable, there is little or no emphasis on causes or on the process and sequence of action. This sense of inevitability comes in part from the constant retelling of the stories, which makes them familiar furniture of the mind. Anyone who has spent time telling stories to children will remember how their preliterate hearers will not tolerate the slightest variation in the narration, for they have a fixed version in their *memory.*

Inevitability is reinforced also by the repeated structures of stories. Consider, for instance, the following three myths reduced to one-sentence summaries:

1. Adonis, who is loved by Aphrodite, is killed by a boar.
2. Anchises, who is seduced by Aphrodite, is crippled by Zeus's thunderbolt.
3. Actaeon, who inadvertently sees Artemis nude, is transformed into a stag, which is attacked and killed by his hunting dogs.

The essence of these three stories is that the sexual, or quasi-sexual encounter between human male and divine female is destructive to him. Ignoring the psychological and theological ramifications of this notion, we may notice that the events of these stories are autonomous. Poets may introduce details to establish a kind of cause and effect: Adonis is killed by one of Aphrodite's jealous divine consorts; Zeus punishes Anchises for publicly boasting of his liaison; Artemis's anger at being seen nude caused Actaeon's transformation. But because there are so many stories on this pattern, it is the pattern rather than the details of any particular story which governs our perception of the whole. The pattern justifies the actions.

Homer acknowledges temporal relativity when he notes that his heroes can lift stones that no one of his own time can. Similes that refer to implements made of iron are set in a narrative where the heroes use bronze. Thus does the oral poetic tradition reflect the chronological evolution of metallurgy from bronze to iron. Hesiod proceeds further in the direction of antiquarianism, first by adding an age of heroes to the traditional ages of man based on metals, then by distilling the truths, as it were, from the traditional genealogy stories. His account of the Muses telling him that they speak both falsehood disguised as truth and the truth is the earliest representation of the scholarly mind that is bent on the discovery and accumulation of fact. Of course, it may be claimed that the author of the *Odyssey* has already addressed the distinction between truth and falsehood, fiction and reality, in his poem. Xenophanes, the philosopher-poet who complained about the ethically corrupt stories of the gods and who noted their anthropomorphic character, was trying to separate truth from traditional fiction. The sixth-century Milesian writer Hecataeus endeavored to retell traditional stories cleansed of their more fabulous, unlikely characteristics, as well as to make divergent accounts cohere. These reactions to the authority of traditional oral narrative, saga, or myth are the groundwork on which Herodotus and Thucydides build their works.

Since Cicero first said it, Herodotus has been styled "the father of history." Thucydides for his part has been considered the first "true" historian, at least in modern times. In their ceaseless quest to establish symmetries or antitheses the ancients have left us only these two historians. To judge from the surviving fragments of the many other Greek historians who wrote throughout antiquity, Herodotus and Thucydides seem to be the best.

Being so nearly contemporary, they are often compared. Thucydides himself invites comparison by insisting on the difference between himself and the older man. "Perhaps the absence of story-telling will be displeasing," he remarks about his work (1.22) in a frosty, condescending manner that may have moved later ages to consider Herodotus garrulous, lightweight, and, as a narrator, definitely self-indulgent. Strangely enough, Thucydides is not mentioned by many of his immediate successors, such as Plato, who surely should have known him and must have read his work, as the parody in the *Menexenus* implies. Yet later centuries preferred him to Herodotus as the more sober, "scientific" historian. In the second century A.D. Plutarch wrote an essay protesting Herodotus's malevolence, as though he were no more than a gossip, the Anthony Trollope, as it were, of historians, an opinion that survived the ages. In the last few decades, however, Herodotus has received considerably more serious attention. His garrulity, the self-indulgent need to give every anecdote and fact that came his way, is now valued as the historian's obligation to reveal all his sources to his reader or as the ethnographer's to display a culture's variant stories. Thucydides, who hitherto was praised for his objectivity, is now faulted for so severely shaping his account, thus obscuring his sources, and manipulating his reader from behind his assumed mask of impartiality.

It is as idle to compare two such disparate figures as it is to judge them against contemporary standards of historiography. Why, indeed, call them historians? Historians are professionals who adhere to or deviate from a common standard, who are judged and may assess themselves against the performance of their colleagues. Herodotus and Thucydides were innovative. They followed no rules and met no standards other than those they imposed upon themselves. Above all else, it is in the artistry of their very personal styles that they differ from twentieth-century historians, whose attempts at being "scientific" usually result in minimalist prose made opaque by baroque jargon. In Herodotus and Thucydides, the narration is often the highlight; the style is as important as the content in any critical assessment of them.

Both historians betray in their narratives certain habits of mind imposed on them by the culture in which they were born, habits quite the opposite of those that inform contemporary history writing. For example, the impulse to generalize and to typify all action is very strong in both writers, while today's historians believe in the singularity of every act, moment, and situation. Epic poetry, which was the major antecedent model for Herodotus and Thucydides, made all action typical, every character a stereotype. Tragic drama also is grounded in archetypal figures and situations. The aphorisms and typical phrases characteristic of Hesiod are to be found as well in Solon's maxims and in Pindar's generalizing images.

Working in this tradition, Herodotus exploits the personages of his history for their typicality, making Solon, Croesus, Polycrates, and the others into examples. Thucydides, too, makes the very few figures whom he mentions emblems of their society and sets up events in the first part of his work that seem to be rehearsals for what occurs later, just as Herodotus seems to linger over Croesus so that the audience will recall Croesus when they come to the portrait of Xerxes, as though history were repeating itself. Both authors' descriptions immediately engender reflections on the nature of human behavior. The Greeks had little love of the uniqueness of things.

As we have discussed earlier, there is a strong bias against the idea of change in epic, and in tragic drama because the tragic sense of life depends on the inevitability and immutability of things. It was no doubt the influence of epic and tragedy that led Herodotus and Thucydides to present events as manifestations of a rhythm or cycle that will inevitably repeat itself. Modern historians, on the other hand, tend to see history as linear, leading from the past into an unknown future in the great passage of time.

Of all things it is time that is most peculiarly treated in the narratives of Herodotus and Thucydides. Like their fellow Greeks of this period, they lacked a strong sense of time. For Greeks of the fifth century B.C. a strict chronology was not available. They did not number the hours. They did not count the passing days. They made little use of months. They did not number their years. Temporal calculations were made on the movements of the moon and of the sun, and these are not synchronized. There was no reasonable calendar. The lunar calendar that all city-states used was 354 days. At random intervals an intercalary month of 30 days was inserted. Not only was this extra month not rigorously scheduled, but it was not added universally at the same time in all city-states. There were yet other temporal oddities. At Athens, for instance, the *boule* operated on a solar calendar when apportioning the year into prytanies, whereas the older magistracies were held for the period of the lunar year, so that the affairs of the city government were not at all synchronous.

How do Herodotus and Thucydides handle these discrepancies? The former tries to make do with very little chronology. Certainly he does order events of the Persian War into some sort of time scheme, but of absolute chronology he has no notion. Once he mentions an Athenian official (8.51.1), who, because he gave his name to his year of office, makes that year identifiable in the sweep of time, but there is nothing more. One often has the impression that in this narrative— as in epic poems—events happen *once upon a time*.

Thucydides, on the contrary, struggles mightily with chronology. Certain lists had already been verified and published by the chroniclers—lists of priestesses, of public officials in Athens and in Sparta, of victors in athletic contests—indicating the relative date of the tenure or the victory. Fighting began in spring and ended in autumn, and Thucydides often identifies events by the season in which they occurred. He tries hard, as we can see (for example, 2.2.1; 4.133.2–3; 5.191), and he is aware of the problems (5.20).

Herodotus, it is commonly remarked, has an epic poet's sense of size. The vast landscape of Persia's dominions, the long passage of almost a century, and the barrage of names, places, and events all combine to give a grand overview. In the same panoramic way, Herodotus digresses, seemingly assuming everything into his narrative. Then, too, Herodotus, like an epic poet, is at some remove from his subject. He deals with strange peoples and remote places. Furthermore, he must have been a boy at the time of the Persian War, which is the climax to his account,· and he begins his account with events seventy-five years antecedent to the war. In an age marked by the absence of significant written record such a span of time takes on vast proportions. Because Herodotus does not mention contemporary events, it is as if he were assigning the events of his history to another temporal setting, to the never-never land of saga or to the *once upon a time* of folktale. He begins with an advertisement that recalls the epic poets. "I am writing so that the amazing feats of both the Greeks and the non-Greek peoples shall not lack their fame." Herodotus lived at a time when legend, folktale, and epic poetry—the products of an oral culture—were probably disappearing. Like any ethnographer on the site, Herodotus may have wished to preserve these materials. His statement recalls the nexus of action, glory, fame, and immortality that dominates the heroic world. It is also possible that he aspired consciously to replace the oral epic tradition. Certainly his style has real affinities with the Homeric epic narrative.

Herodotus uses the word *historia* for his particular intellectual activity. The root means "to see" or "to know" (by seeing). It appears in the noun *histor,* meaning "a judge." Possibly *historia* implies coming to know things by analysis, by sifting the evidence and sorting things out. Much of Herodotus's source material was what today would be categorized as legend or gossip, all of which, it is clear, needed going over in order to separate the fabulous from the fact. He does just this kind of sorting in his opening pages as he introduces a series of traditional stories that account for the enmity between the East and the West. Both Herodotus and his predecessor Hecataeus tell of the travels they made to verify details in stories of faraway places. For example, when Herodotus wants to ascertain the facts about the Egyptian worship of the god Heracles, he "sailed to Tyre in Phoenicia to a very old temple there, because I wanted to get some clear information on these matters" (2.44).

Herodotus may be called the father of history because he created a mode of awareness about past events; that is, he arranged these events so that their juxtaposition in a time scheme makes particular sense. Moreover, this arrangement is relevant to the contemporary reader. Herodotus is wise, however, not to allude to his contemporary world. Because his subject matter derives from the oral tradition, it is true in a certain way that the facts of his own lifetime are not true. Contemporary facts, on the other hand, can be verified by second-hand experience. Oral tradition may be true to certain notions a people entertain of themselves and others, but not factual. For an example from twentieth-century American culture, it is now a documented fact that the great blues singer Bessie Smith was not refused admittance to an exclusively white hospital in Mississippi and did not tragically and ironically bleed to death before its doors. Rather, she was fatally injured in a car crash and was heroically, if vainly, aided during her last moments by a white doctor. The true version, however, is far less satisfying than the legend that used to circulate about the event. We want to maintain our vision of the American South in the first half of the twentieth century. Neither does it sustain the Good-Evil dichotomy or enhance the conception of the powerful black woman as doomed. We want our blues singers to live out and die their blues, as, for instance, Billie Holiday did. Therefore on every count the earlier, untrue version is "truer": Edward Albee's play *The Death of Bessie Smith* is true to the untrue "truer" story. We live in an age when it is possible to determine far more precisely whether any information is true or false than could Herodotus, who lived in a time when anything beyond one's experience reposed in the culture's memory, enshrined there, authenticated by the culture's needs. Very likely it was instinct that told Herodotus to leave out the verifiable material from his contemporary world because it would be incongruous with the traditional stories.

It puzzles some modern historians that Herodotus introduces material that he himself does not believe to be true. Perhaps he does so on the ground that he wants to share his evidence with his reader, the kind of evidence that today would appear in an appendix. But perhaps not. Herodotus does not have to believe a story to introduce it. Rather, he may do so because it is true in another sense: it is true to the culture—a legitimate datum. As Herodotus remarks more than once (e.g., 7.152.3), "My job is to write what has been said, but I do not have to believe it." Here he seems to be rather boldly and clearly setting out the two levels of cultural fact with which he is dealing.

When he says, "As to what the Egyptians say, let him believe it who finds it believable" (2.123), he means to say that this oral tradition is what defines Egyptian culture; in that sense it is true. Whether the stories told are objectively true or are literally believable is something else, to be decided by each reader for himself. Elsewhere, in a discussion about a goddess, Herodotus says, "I should imagine, if one must take a stand concerning things divine. . ." (9.65). By this he means he is reluctant to decide about the truth or falsehood of the goddess's action because it is irrelevant to the kind of truth he is establishing.

His motive in writing, as he says in his introduction, is to keep alive the memory of great and amazing deeds. It often seems that he includes unusual events or people simply because they are unusual, as indeed he himself admits (4.30). He begins his long discourse on Egypt by saying, "I shall say more about Egypt because there are more extraordinary things there and monuments beyond description are everywhere" (2.35). Certainly he is very good at finding extraordinary things to narrate, whether fantastic customs or fantastic natural history (3.98–109). He is particularly keen on the madness of Cambyses; the narration is one of his best (2.27–37). Similar to it is the long account of the self-mutilation of Zapyrus (3.154–60), a story so horrible, so extraordinary, so well told that it remains in the memory forever. When chronicling Persia's imperial expansion Herodotus selects the data for inclusion on the same basis ("Most of his [Cyrus's] minor conquests I shall say nothing about, but mention only those of his campaign which gave him the greatest trouble and are in themselves interesting" [1.177]).

Often enough, however, what may seem a gratuitous anecdote will turn out to have greater significance. In mentioning a large and calamitous shipwreck with its loss of life and treasure (7.190), Herodotus concludes by saying, "This wreck turned out to be a good thing for a certain Magnesian, named Amenocles, the son of Cretines . . . for he picked up on shore [various valuables are mentioned]. This made him a very rich man, though in other respects he proved less fortunate; for, in spite of his luck with the treasure, he came to grief over some distressing affair with the murder of his son." Anecdotes of this sort function much as Homeric similes do. The story of the man on the beach who grows rich from the spoils gives scale to the immensity of the gold and the calamity of the shipwreck. The allusion to Amenocles' later misfortunes underscores the ebb and flow of man's affairs, which returns the reader to what is finally important about the shipwreck of the treasure. While much of what Herodotus writes seems like village folklore and traditional gossip, his purpose seems to be to show the extraordinary range and diversity of human beings. The attitude of the small-town gossip that fills these pages is humanistic and life-affirming, despite—or perhaps because of—Herodotus's penchant for settling on the perverse and the bizarre in human events.

In the modern view, Herodotus's rather impulsive willingness to halt the narrative for observations on still one more fantastic person or event seems self-indulgent or naive. This habit can most probably be attributed, however, to the oral mentality, which, despite the advent of writing, must still have been influential. As is true of most ancient writers, nothing is known of how Herodotus composed, but it is worth bearing in mind that certain commonplace features of modern-day writing were altogether impossible for him. He had no good paper, erasers, scissors, or glue, for instance. His papyrus was, for all practical purposes, continuous. How could he easily find the places he wished to reread and revise? How was he able to insert new material at its proper place? Probably only with the greatest difficulty.

There is evidence in the text that he composed without stopping to rewrite. For instance, at the beginning when introducing Croesus (1.6), he states that this monarch was the first foreigner to have dealings hostile or friendly with the Greeks. A few sections later (1.14–15), however, he contradicts himself by listing the military expeditions against Greek cities in Asia Minor mounted by Gyges and later by Ardys, two kings who are seven generations earlier than Croesus in the royal line. But he does not correct his earlier misstatement. True to the oral mentality, which concentrates upon the moment, he restates it and continues.

The same mentality has left its mark on the marvelous story of Phaedime, who discovers that the man with whom she is sleeping is not the man he claims to be (3.68ff.). Herodotus tells it in the manner that still prevails today, that is, with the denouement or punch line coming the third time around. Phaedime's father tries three times with three messages to devise some way for her to identify this man. In the third message he says, "Check to see if he has ears. If not, you will be sleeping with Smerdis the Magus, not Smerdis the son of Cyrus." At this point, quite anticlimactically and false to the rhythm of this kind of story, Herodotus breaks in to say, "I should mention here that when Cyrus was on the throne he had the ears of Smerdis the Magus cut off as punishment for something or other." This information seems to belong to an earlier place in the narration; any literate person working with a readily accessible text would have been able to add it in revision. Others, of course, might argue that this piece of information is by way of a footnote that in the age of printing would drop to the bottom of the page or to the end of the chapter.

In any case it is fair to assume that Herodotus wrote with the idea of saying his piece aloud; that is, he was writing down words meant to be spoken, so that all the normal practices of an oral performance would come naturally to the printed page. His style is consistent with the oral mentality. Called *lexis eiromene* (speech strung together), the style is paratactic in construction. It is similar to the appositional style in epic poetry: an idea or action is described, redefined, and expanded through the addition of words, phrases, and clauses in apposition. It is not hard to imagine that Herodotus may simply have taken his notes in hand, begun from the beginning, and continued stringing one piece to another until he had used them all.

Herodotus's *Histories* is divided into nine books. It begins with a description of Lydia and her last independent king, Croesus (1.1–94), then proceeds to a description of Lydia's captor, Cyrus, his kingdom, and its people, the Persians (1.95–140). Thereafter, Herodotus describes in an extremely diverse and extended narrative that fills several books the imperial encroachments of the Persian kings Cyrus, Cambyses, and Darius (1.178–5.27). This description allows him to give lengthy accounts of Egypt (almost the whole of the second book), Scythia (4.1–144), Thrace (5.1–27), and Libya (4.145–205), which are the lands conquered by the Persians.

Having reviewed the territorial expansion of the Persians throughout the East, Herodotus narrows the focus and becomes more detailed as he turns to the hostility between Persia and mainland Greece, beginning with the revolt of Ionia (5.28–38; 5.97–6.42) and the invasion of Marathon (6.94–120), together with the background information on Athens and Sparta. In the seventh, eighth, and ninth books Herodotus narrates in greater detail Xerxes' plans for the invasion of Greece and the invasion itself, recounting the battle of Thermopylae, which was fatal to the Greeks (7.196–239), and then their brilliant victory at Salamis (8.40–112) and finally the decisive Greek land victory at Plataea (9.1–89) and sea victory at Mycale (9.90–106).

The *Histories* seem lopsided; the several books devoted to describing Persian expansion and the peoples the Persians conquer do not seem to be in exactly the same style as the description of the Persian invasion of Greece. The problem appears in microcosm in the first book, which is meant to be an account of the reign and campaigns of Cyrus. The first ninety-two sections, however, are an elegant and self-contained narrative of the rise and fall of the Lydian king Croesus. What ought to be nothing more than a side glance at one of the territories conquered by Cyrus instead overwhelms the subsequent narrative by virtue of the artistry of its presentation as well as the philosophical filter through which the events are observed. In the same way the more ethnographic, anthropological descriptions of the middle books cannot compete with the story of Xerxes' invasion of Greece, so rich in character and idea, all of it solidified by myriad details deftly fitted together for a sustained effect.

The Croesus narrative, it becomes clear, is given such importance in the text because it dramatizes a philosophy, a theodicy, that underlies subsequent events in the history. Most of all, Croesus functions as a paradigm for the career of Xerxes with which the work ends. Herodotus, in his disposition of his material, has responded to the narrative imperatives of the oral epic style as it is found in the *Iliad*. The Meleager story of the ninth book of the *Iliad* is an example that comes immediately to mind. Meleager is a paradigm for Achilles, his behavior a rehearsal of what lies in store for the Achaean hero in the *Iliad*. Similarly, the three quarrels of the opening of the *Iliad* set up the basic theme of the poem much as the dialogue between Solon and Croesus establishes the way the audience should view the events of Herodotus's account. The Croesus story and the Xerxes story, because they parallel each other in so many ways, may be said to stand in symmetry, one at the beginning, the other at the end of the work. This structure is analogous to the ring composition technique of the epic poems.

After Herodotus finishes his account of Croesus and before he starts on Xerxes, the principal organizing device is the chronology inherent in narrating a royal succession. That is, he passes from the reign of Cyrus to that of Cambyses to that of Darius. For instance, the description of the Massagetae and Babylonians, whom Cyrus conquered, comes first. The discussion of Cambyses succeeding his father and invading Egypt follows. The narrative of the stories of Croesus and Xerxes, however, is markedly different from the material of the central portion of the *Histories*. The Croesus and Xerxes stories are dramatic, by turns heroic and philosophic; by contrast, the central portion of the *Histories* is an excellent and far-ranging ethnographic review, far more loosely organized. The middle section just falls short of being a miscellany.

The informing principle is Herodotus's curiosity. He wants to know what people create and how they behave. Herodotus seems to have understood that culture is inherent in the natural order. He can speak of the flow of the Nile, certainly a complex kind of natural hydraulics, in much the same way he details burial customs and marriage customs of a people. In his treatment, both appear to be patterns of behavior and aspects of nature. Culture is the human response to being just as the flow of the Nile is water's response to being. At one point he pauses in his extraordinarily rich offering of the range of social behavior to quote a line from the poet Pindar to the effect that custom is the master of us all. His wide-ranging descriptions of peoples do, indeed, seem to reinforce the notion that in the midst of the remarkable diversity of human performance there exists the tendency to normalize human behavior, which is culture.

Herodotus's interest in culture or cultures would have been natural to him. He was born in Halicarnassus, a community in Asia Minor which seems not to have had a homogeneous population. The city originally participated in the festivals of Doric-speaking Greeks but was later associated with Ionic culture, although a majority of the citizens had non-Greek names. Later Herodotus traveled in Egypt, the Levant, and southern Italy; he may also have spent time in Athens. From his earliest years he must have had a naturally cosmopolitan outlook far different from the narrow outlook of the Athenians, who only in the fifth century were beginning to discover cultural relativism.

Immigration and increasing trade in the sixth century gradually awakened the Athenians to the fact that alternative ways of life, equally authentic, existed throughout the Mediterranean. The easy parochialism of the Greek city-states, fostered by the near isolation caused by ubiquitous, almost impassable mountain ranges, led the people of the mainland to assume that local behavior was innate in the human species. Thus did they overemphasize human nature (*physis*). As acquaintance with the larger world showed the Greeks that other people did things otherwise, they grew to ascribe more importance to custom (*nomos*).

In Athens throughout the fifth century the debate ranged over the relative strength of these in the makeup of humankind. Clearly the class whose behavior was validated by its grip on the power in the community was committed to the supremacy of nature over custom, whereas anyone advocating anything new would more likely opt for the superiority of custom. The controversy is important in the pages of Herodotus because he is describing a great range of human behavior, and relatively impartially, as is to be expected from his use of the quotation from Pindar. By showing how people arrange their affairs in one society after another, Herodotus manages to demonstrate that in fact custom is nature—that is, mankind's instinct to forge culture (*nomos*) is natural (*physis*). He might have left it at that, but instead, his account of Xerxes' invasion of Greece is fashioned by him into a testament to the superiority of Greek culture. If he would not call it superior, then certainly more successful—witness the Persian defeats at Marathon, Salamis, Plataea, and Mycale—judged by the criterion established long since by the heroic epic poem, that is, triumph on the field of battle.

With Herodotus begins the tradition of the great division between East and West, between the Greeks (for which thereafter substitute Romans, then Europeans, finally the "Western world," so-called) and the barbarians. This last is a Greek word, originally meant to signify onomatopoetically (*var-var-var*) someone who could not speak Greek and who spoke instead some foreign gibberish. It is Herodotus himself who begins to endow the word with its pejorative connotation. Throughout the books devoted to the Persian conquests to the east, Herodotus's penchant for describing some of the more bizarre and perverse doings of humankind is marked. Such stories combine eventually to qualify the whole of the Eastern world as excessive and fabulous. No such terrible or wonderful anecdotes characterize the Greeks.

While describing the Persian invasion of Greece, Herodotus includes one incident after another that reinforces the distinction between the Greeks and the barbarians. For example, Herodotus tells us that the Persians bury people alive (7.114), Xerxes commanded Pythius's son to be split in two (7.39), a man was forced to castrate his own sons (8.106), and a father gouged out his six sons' eyes for disobedience (8.116). Such anecdotes are answered with descriptions of Greek customs. There is the occasion when the Persians see the Spartans stripped for exercise and combing their hair, which inspires Demaratus to discourse on Spartan virtue (7.208f.); there is Xerxes' wonder at hearing that the Greeks compete for nonmaterial rewards (8.26), and there are speeches in praise of Greek freedom (8.14ff.) and Greek poverty (9.80ff.). The contrast illustrated by these tales is finally verbalized by a king of Sparta, who has been encouraged to insult the corpse of the Persian Mardonius as revenge. "No, no," he replies, "that is much more in the style of the barbarian way of doing things than the Greek, and we even find fault with them for such acts" (9.79).

Xerxes appears in the story as the very embodiment of all excessive and mad energy that fills the descriptions in the middle books. His challenge to the Hellespont, his violent rages and cruel punishments, his sudden tears, his colossal army, and his pompous progress through to Greece are barbarian. Yet at the close of the work, when this excessive and grand man has gone to his defeat and Herodotus recalls Cyrus's admonition to the Persians to stay lean, hard, and poor, he means to offer another lesson perhaps. For the defeated Xerxes is set up as a contrast to Athens and Sparta, victorious in their simplicity and poverty. One wonders whether Herodotus was warning the Athenians about their imperialistic pretensions of the second half of the fifth century. Nothing is more ironic than the way Athens in these later years played out a drama for which Herodotus might have written the scenario.

Such a warning, if indeed intended, would come from Herodotus's conviction that permanence in human affairs is dubious at best. As he says early in the work, "I'll go along telling the story of great cities and small. Most of those great were once small and vice versa—it makes no difference whether the city I write about is great or small, since in this world nobody remains prosperous very long" (1.7). The demonstration of this proposition is perhaps the most important feature of the central books of the *Histories,* apart from the sheer amassing of fact. Indeed the reiteration of examples of this truth gives the mid-section a certain coherence that it otherwise would not have. What distinguishes the Croesus episode and the account of the Persian invasion in the last three books is the style, the control, and the polish of the narration. These episodes are philosophical and dramatic, just as the other parts are factual and expository. The difference may arise from the circumstance that both Croesus and Xerxes suffer tremendous reversals in their lives. These reversals make the dramatic narration more exciting, something that an assemblage of facts, even when presided over by a Cambyses, cannot do. The ethnographic parts lack a hero. It is questionable whether Herodotus or any author at this time could manage the organization and the necessary overview of his material without using a hero. Such is the legacy of epic from which Herodotus has not altogether escaped.

In other respects he has managed to put distance between himself and the epic tradition. Historical speculation grows out of reaction to the myth and saga tradition. Xenophanes debunks anthropomorphism and wants ethically superior deities; Pindar insists on "cleaner" versions of myth. Rationalizing the myths began with Hecataeus and continued with Herodotus's contemporary Hellanicus, who stated that the fight between Achilles and the river god in the *Iliad* really represents nothing more than a spring flood in a river fed by melting mountain snow. Herodotus denies that a cleft in the mountain is, as the natives claim, Poseidon's handiwork, but says it is rather the result of an earthquake (7.129). Elsewhere he asks how Heracles, no more than a human, could have killed, as alleged, tens of thousands of people (2.45).

Herodotus also questions the validity of some contemporary events. For instance, he denies the evidently famous story that Xerxes returned to Asia Minor by sailing directly across the Aegean (unlikely because navigational exigencies demanded that ships hug the islands). At the very start of his work Herodotus treats his audience to a masterful demonstration of his ability to rationalize in a great display of claims and counterclaims by the parties to the historic dispute between the East and the Greeks. The stories of Io, Medea, and Helen are stripped of their fabulous character so that Herodotus can get at the facts. Instead of the loves of Zeus, Jason, and Paris, the three women are described as being abducted by anonymous sailors or other adventurers.

Herodotus clearly intends to do more than give the facts. In the last part of his introductory statement he says, "My aim is . . . to show what kind of cause it was that made these people war with one another." For a great many critics Herodotus's singular achievement has been to order events in a scheme of cause and effect. Far removed from the *Iliad*'s "and the will of Zeus was accomplished" (1.8), this ordering of events is the true sign of the beginnings of history.

But a closer inspection of the *Histories* shows that Herodotus is very selective in choosing what kind of cause to include and that his explanations are in some cases not far from irrational. He begins with the traditional stories but discards them after his demonstration of the "truth" of Io, Medea, and Helen. He then proceeds to more contemporary causes of conflict, naming Croesus and Gyges, who moved against Greek territory. He does not, however, offer motives for the action of either of these two; it is the result of their action which interests him since it is a cause of East-West enmity. Again, as he proceeds with the story of Persian expansion, he does not indicate the reasons for it. He concentrates on the "how" and ignores the "why." We may note that no sooner does he mention Croesus than he launches into a lengthy narrative of his rise and fall. This account is illustrative of his dictum on the mutability of cities, but has little to do with establishing causes for Persian expansion, other than to suggest that Cyrus, once provoked, moved against Lydia.

The Croesus story, however, seems to be the vehicle with which Herodotus can demonstrate a philosophy of history that will explain all subsequent events in the *Histories*. It is because it defines an immutable rhythm to human events that it is given such prominence in the work. The collapse of great cities and the rise of small ones becomes as natural as cell division, but they are finally not subject to analysis in the search of causes.

Like epic poets who deal with stereotypic characters and typical scenes, and like the tragic dramatists who distill action into abstracted episodes, Herodotus, who must confront a mass of detail, often imposes the logic of the storyteller upon events. Consider these two minor events that he describes. Polycrates, tyrant of Samos, blessed with prosperity and happiness, is advised by his friend Amasis, king of Egypt, that his success invites trouble. Amasis encourages him to do something to break his run of good luck. Throw away whatever you value most, he advises. Polycrates takes this advice to heart. He selects a great emerald signet ring, takes it aboard ship, and when far from shore flings it into the ocean. Days later a fisherman catches an extraordinarily large fish, which he presents to Polycrates. It is brought into the palace and cut open, and the emerald ring is found inside and returned to Polycrates, who, says Herodotus, recognizes that something supernatural is intervening in his life. Polycrates writes of this event to Amasis, who immediately breaks off all relations with the tyrant, saying that he could not endure the distress he would feel as a friend when calamity befell Polycrates. Sure enough, Polycrates is subsequently lured to his death, and his corpse is hung on a cross (3.39ff.; 3.120ff.).

The second event is as follows: Croesus receives at his court a fugitive fratricide, Adrastus. After ritually purifying him of this murder, he keeps the man by him as a favorite at the court. Shortly thereafter the young men of the court organize a posse to go after a great boar marauding in the neighboring farmlands. Croesus's son, Atys, a young man newly married, wishes to join in but is prevented by his father, who once dreamt that his son would be killed by an iron weapon. Croesus relents, however, when Atys argues that a boar has only ivory tusks, no iron. The king asks Adrastus to accompany the young man as a safeguard. Adrastus demurs with the argument that he, unfortunate as he is, should not accompany someone blessed with youth, marriage, and royal station, but is finally persuaded by the king, who reminds him of the kindnesses he has received. In the fight with the boar Adrastus hurls his spear and inadvertently strikes and kills Atys.

Both stories are of a type in which the irony is so palpable that the reader knows in advance the direction events will take. It is the tone of the story, its commonplace succession of events, that makes the reader anticipate the ending. There is no appeal to cause and effect here. Adrastus *must* accompany Atys; Croesus against his better judgment *must* allow the boy to go; the fisherman *must* find that particular fish and bring it to Polycrates. This reading of human events is expressed throughout the *Histories*—for instance, in the observation "since things were bound to go wrong for him" (4.79) or "the Pythia [the prophetess at Delphi] said that Miltiades was bound to end up unhappily" (6.135), or, as Herodotus reports from a message, "There never was and never will be a man who was not born with a good chance of misfortune—the greater the man, the greater the misfortune. . . . Xerxes is human and is sure therefore to be disappointed in what he hoped for" (7.203). Wise men are those such as Cyrus, who saves Croesus from the burning pyre at the last minute because "he [Cyrus] realized that he was in fact a human being and treating another human being in this fashion, a man once no less prosperous than he now was, he feared some kind of retribution; what is more, he calculated that there was no way that a man's affairs could be secure and stable" (1.86). A wise man this Cyrus, who a few years later is to meet his own end, his severed head flung into a vat of blood by an avenging queen (1.214).

Those who review the past are caught between perceiving events as unique and imposing a pattern onto them. The former allows for the play of free will; the latter emphasizes destiny. Free will is the companion of forethought; destiny is the product of hindsight. Herodotus, as we have seen, tends to narrate events so that the force of destiny is never far from them. Yet he insists that men act freely as well. When Croesus at last finds himself on the pyre and all seems to be lost, we can conclude with Herodotus that the Lydian king's downfall came about because the family of Gyges was doomed since first Gyges slew Candaules, because Croesus quite foolishly misunderstood an oracle that prophesied disaster if Croesus attempted to go to war against Persia, and because Croesus's prosperity and pride of position made him excessively vulnerable to some kind of divine reaction. Herodotus presents all three explanations as true. The first is a result of destiny; the second is an act of free will; and the third is a fatal circumstance, not unlike the conditions favorable to the incubation of disease.

Herodotus, in fact, seems to prognosticate after the fashion of medical people when he describes Croesus's rise and fall. It is as though Croesus's prosperity were a disease. Pride is a condition arising from exceeding prosperity, which may be defined as the unusual absence of periods of misfortune. Amasis seems to know the danger of pride when he advises Polycrates to throw away what he values most. Pride is fatal to Croesus as Solon, the Athenian lawgiver and sage, warned him it would be (1.32–33). Herodotus introduces Solon as the wise counselor, a figure common in tales of this sort, who admonishes the king to behave in a certain way. The king ignores the admonition, naturally to his peril. Hector's brother, Poulydamas, who appears in the *Iliad* only to offer Hector advice that he sometimes takes but finally rashly and fatally ignores, represents the same device of storytelling, inserted far more arbitrarily than Solon into the narrative. What Solon describes is acted out time and again by the men of Herodotus's *Histories,* nowhere better or more completely narrated than in the careers of Croesus and Xerxes.

This apprehensive regard for excessive good luck is probably agrarian in origin. Farmers who every day must face the prospect of unseasonable frost, flash floods, hail, drought, insect invasions, and the like understand that survival is a fragile business. Because they are used to natural catastrophes interspersed in the growing process, a prolonged absence of bad luck makes for anxiety. Ancient farmers who endowed the forces of nature with personalities and made them divinities presumed a kind of malignant indignation animating these deities when their carefully tended fields, crops, or herds were struck.

Unremitting prosperity is dangerous not only because in the natural flow of things it must finally be balanced with an equally strong dose of misfortune, but because it leaves its benefactor vulnerable to overconfidence. It is as though prosperity destroys the soul's immune system. The Greeks talked of prosperity (*olbia*) or satiety (*koros*), which exhilarate a person so that normal expectations give way to greater. This psychological state they labeled *hubris,* which is often translated as "pride," although the word "pride" can be misleading, holding as it does such an important place in the Christian canon of sins. There is no sin here, simply exuberance that impels one on to extraordinary daring and other excessive behavior. We could liken *hubris* to the state of intoxication or the manic swing. People in this state are prey to every stimulus that acts as a seduction. The seduction the Greeks called *ate*. It is *ate* to which Agamemnon assigns the blame for his arrogance toward Achilles. In Herodotus's narrative the flushed, prosperous man thinks to act on the inflated terms of his successful self, and he misjudges. The Greek word for miscalculation is *hamartia,* derived from the verb which means "to miss the bull's-eye." *Hamartia* engulfs the fellow in catastrophe (*nemesis*).

Croesus, as Herodotus portrays him, is an obvious paradigm of this nexus of actions and psychological states. Rich beyond measure, he imagines himself to be the happiest man alive. He proceeds to act out his greatness and prosperity by invading Persia. The intoxication, seduction, and miscalculation are revealed in the story of his seeking and misunderstanding the oracles. At last he finds himself a prisoner of war upon a pyre. Herodotus shows that all these events and attitudes are inherent in the psyche of the prosperous man. Prosperity is not the cause, but merely the outward symptom of a doomed man. Prosperity, euphoria, and miscalculation are all aspects of the same state, as is, in a less obvious way, catastrophe or divine retribution—or however we wish to style *nemesis*.

The range of this state of *hubris-hamartia-nemesis* resembles clinical descriptions of manic-depressive behavior: the euphoria or overstriving followed by the downturn and depression. One of the more moving moments in the *Histories* occurs when Herodotus relates Xerxes' reaction to the assembly of his fleet and army at Abydus. Herodotus's language is nowhere more expressive. Literally translated the passage reads: "When the time came that the entire Hellespont was by ships covered over, all the heights and the plains of Abydos filled with men, then Xerxes called himself blessed, but after that he burst into tears" (7.45). The moment described is the very instant when the upswing is transformed into the downturn. This is not unlike the *peripateia,* or reversal, which Aristotle names as one of the essential ingredients in tragic action. It is the moment when the Homeric hero stands in triumph on the field of battle, realizing himself to the fullest, just before he walks into the embrace of death at the hands of his adversary. It is the moment conveyed in the well-known statue called *The Discus Thrower,* sculpted with his throwing hand drawn back to its fullest in the swing that will at this very second begin its return, pendulum-like, to hurl its burden. The Greeks called this moment *kairos,* the critical moment or crisis moment. It is akin to the idea conveyed by Wallace Stevens in the line which concludes stanza six of "Sunday Morning": "Death is the Mother of Beauty."

Throughout the early centuries of Greek history until the end of the fifth century this nexus of prosperity, overweening pride, seduction, miscalculation, error, and downfall stands both as the explanation for evil and as the metaphor for death. This is not at all like the Christian notion of sin, which is a knowing transgression of clearly established divine laws. The Christian sinner acts out of free will and is utterly responsible for his action. This belief in free will supports the idea of villainy. There are no real villains in the ancient view of things. Motives, causes, human responsibility, and divine rules are all much more obscure. This lack of human responsibility not only frees mankind of the overriding sense of guilt that characterizes the Judeo-Christian psychology, but also allows for a belief in the essential goodness of human beings.

Herodotus seems to be using the Croesus story as a general explanation of human action. Placed first and exaggerated in importance by its length (relative to other elements in the story of the reign of Cyrus), it is an introduction to his *Histories.* Solon is central to the story because he provides an abstracted explanation of events. Solon is a kind of Euripidean Sophist or a tragic choral counterpoint to the action, objectifying Croesus's action. Herodotus takes over from epic the convention of developing ideas in dialogue.

Solon's advice to Croesus is to count no man happy until he has died, for then he is no longer vulnerable to the hazards of life. In prosperity, Solon warns, a man should look to the envy of god, *pthonos tou theiou.* This phrase seems to describe the cosmic rhythm of balancing excess and want rather than the anthropomorphized response of something supernatural. If a man takes on too much or becomes too great, if a tree grows too tall, some kind of retribution or redistribution is required.

The narrative of Xerxes' invasion of Greece has many similarities with the Croesus story. Xerxes' two advisers are to some extent analogous to the Delphic oracle and Solon. Like the responses the priestess at Delphi gives to Croesus, who both is seduced by them and misunderstands them, Mardonius's advice incites Xerxes into lusting after power, treasure, and glory of revenge that an invasion of Greece would provide. Xerxes' uncle urges caution just as Solon tries to put a brake on Croesus's unrealistic appraisal of his own good fortune.

It is in the nature of folktale of this sort that the good adviser is ignored as the hero succumbs to the temptation offered from the other. When the oracle tells Croesus that a great empire will be destroyed if he invades Persia and he assumes that this prophesies his victory without once considering that the "great empire" might be his own, it is clear that Croesus has made a fatal error in judgment. Xerxes' situation is more complicated. First encouraged by Mardonius, later repenting and siding with his uncle, Artabanus, Xerxes is prudent. Subsequent dreams sent both to him and to Artabanus force them to change their minds and to adopt the dangerous plan of Mardonius. As Polycrates of Samos realized when he so coincidentally recovered his large emerald ring, there is clear evidence of divine intervention. As the apparition that appears to Artabanus says angrily, "Are you the one who is trying to keep Xerxes from the invasion? . . . You cannot stop either now or later that which must be" (7.17).

Xerxes, however, is more than a creature of the gods or a victim of destiny. To this point in the narrative Herodotus has shown us on the one hand a prideful, successful, ambitious despot, vulnerable to the experience that befell Croesus, yet on the other hand a prudent man who can listen to reason, and still further, a man who is, like Polycrates, hedged into his situation. In mingling the motives so thoroughly, Herodotus suggests that Xerxes is a prisoner of the logic of the story, yet that he is capable of an act of free will, and finally that he is the unwitting victim of divine malice.

Thereafter Herodotus describes Xerxes' steady increase in power, pretension, and expectation until more than anything else he becomes a latter-day Croesus. His exaltation and pride reach a peak when he punishes the Hellespont for allowing the storm upon its waters to destroy his bridge (at which point Herodotus enters the narrative [7.35] to call the act both foolish and not Greek). This magnificent, detailed scene is set between two others: Xerxes' reception by a local magnate, Pythius, who in the abject fashion of the Persians before their king offers him all of his fabled wealth, and Xerxes' arrogant, wrathful decision to cut one of Pythius's sons in two in anger at his host, who had asked that one of his many sons be excused from the army. This extravagant narrative leads to the moment on the hill at Abydos when Xerxes burst into tears. The observation Xerxes makes afterwards is true to the Greek view of things. Asked why he cried, Xerxes replies, "There came to me as I was contemplating a great feeling of pity at how short man's life is, how none of the men present here will be around a hundred years from now" (7.46).

The subsequent narration of the encounter between the Greeks and the Persians in battle is informed by these scenes to the very end of the work. The Greek victories over the Persians were unexpected and thus amazing. Herodotus, however, does not really present the war as a Greek success story. While he does offer occasional observations on the Greek way of life which imply its superiority, his account of the Persian War is more Xerxes' failure than a Greek triumph. To look at the war in this way is characteristic of the tragic sense of life that dominated thinking in fifth-century Athens. Explanations can be found in defeat, but not in victory.

For Herodotus the workings of history are the reenactment, the reiteration, the rehearsal of action. The facts of Xerxes' invasion of Greece are given meaning as they re-create the Croesus story. Herodotus has a mind that is habituated to the mythic mode, a mind that yields the particularity of events to the structure of a story. Historical cause and effect become evident in the emergence of a pattern or shape or outline of story in the events. Herodotus gives the story of a king's fall in brief and then makes that the perspective by which to control the massive detail in the growth and spread of the Persian empire. Finally, he returns to the original story—the fall of a king— with Xerxes' invasion of Greece. Through the storyteller's art he has made sense.

At the outset Thucydides emphasizes the distinction between himself and Herodotus by announcing that no storyteller's art will embellish his narrative (1.22). He was Herodotus's younger contemporary by only two or three decades, but his narrative style and his intellectual manner are far different. His prose is dense and complex; it seems highly idiosyncratic, although not enough examples of his contemporaries' prose survive to substantiate this idea. Nonetheless, if an artificial continuum of prose style from Herodotus to Plato and the other fourth-century writers were created, Thucydides' writing would appear peculiar and highly personal.

In the latter half of the fifth century prose finally became an art form as poetry had been for centuries. The great significance of speeches in Herodotus, Thucydides, and Plato surely reflect the inheritance from Homer's epic, in which speeches are as important as the third-person narrative. It also reflects the great role of tragic drama, but perhaps most of all it reflects the influence of the law courts. Rhetoric, as taught by the Sophists, became more and more a considered habit of the mind. The Sophists' recourse to analytical argument spills over into later tragedy (the debates between Jason and Medea in Euripides' *Medea* being a prime example), rendering the essentially divisive nature of tragic action into the naturally dichotomous, adversary relationship that develops in legal and intellectual controversy.

We can assume that tragic drama was the most important influence on Thucydides. Throughout the fifth century it was an institutionalized way of presenting communal ideas. Thucydides was in exile from Athens after 424 for almost twenty years. While it is not known whether he did his writing during this time or after, it is nonetheless fair to say that in the years of isolation, away from the changing currents in Athenian intellectual life, tragic drama would remain a powerful inspiration for him.

He would naturally be vulnerable to the tendency to idiosyncrasy that flourishes in an artist's isolation. Thucydides' prose style is strange enough to encourage that view. There may, however, be more to it. He composed toward the close of a centuries-long period when oral communication was predominant. Even what was written was meant to be read aloud. It is arguable that with the extremely complex, dense, often barely manageable style that Thucydides contrived at his most serious moments, he represents the first thoroughly liberated *writer*. That is, Thucydides, a man alone in exile who did not have an audience available to read to, wrote to be *read*. Simplicity is the hallmark of what was composed to be recited. Perhaps the most notable feature of Thucydides' dense prose is that it needs to be worked out through *close reading*.

The much-discussed chapter (1.22) in which Thucydides analyzes his method shows a high degree of self-consciousness. Concern over diction, style, and meaning in prose was a product of the increasingly intellectual climate introduced into Athens by the Sophists. The exaggerated antitheses in the speech at 1.70.2ff. probably reflect this concern, as does the rhetorical speech at 1.120ff. and the verbal parallels between Pericles' speech at 2.60 and Cleon's speech at 3.37ff. The arrival of Gorgias in Athens in 427 and his speech making there were said to have dazzled the Athenians and brought on a new and furious exaggeration of rhetorical technique. Thucydides presumably was caught up in this development. He may well have begun his writing by that time, shortly before he was to go into exile.

Perhaps more than anything else Thucydides should be considered self-consciously experimental. This experimentation would account for his being so uneven. He uses dialogue only once, and then extremely well and at great length in the so-called Melian Dialogue (5.84ff.). There are no speeches in books five and eight and yet a cluster of them in the first half of the work (two-thirds of the forty speeches are in the first four books); he uses a flat, noncommittal style for the battle narrative (in contrast to the richly subjective speeches) until the ironic, resonating account of the battle of Syracuse; in addition, there is a sudden, peculiar intensity to the description in the plague passage (2.47ff.) and the sailing for Sicily (6.30ff.). In terms of the commonplace Greek aesthetic based on symmetries, one may say that there is something tentative about the writing.

In the first book particularly Thucydides seems to be trying a variety of styles to show some of the possibilities of narrative. It is an ingenious way to introduce both his technique and his subject. Thucydides manages to establish his principal ideas on war, political power, naval power, Sparta, and Athens while at the same time displaying rather fully how he proposes to narrate his material.

He begins by arguing that the war with which he will be dealing is the single most important event and the greatest war in Greek history. It seems a naive point of departure, even if, as some critics insist, he is only making the point that his work is more important than that of Herodotus. What he does with the argument, however, seems finally more impressive than the argument itself. Perhaps the true significance of sections 1 through 21 is that they give him a chance to display his technique. Moreover, he means to set up a contrast between his own closely reasoned analysis of earlier times and the opening section of Herodotus's *Histories* (the rationalization of the myths of Io, Helen, and Medea), a passage that is by comparison to Thucydides' writing not a little banal and simplistic.

He recounts the emergence of the Greek people as a political entity. To do so he depends, of course, on oral history, much deriving from saga. He is penetrating in his analysis of the legends of Agamemnon and the Homeric account of the Trojan War, isolating truths, generalizing from the frail evidence that the early stories provide. Notice, for instance, his intelligent observation about the hazards of determining power and prosperity of earlier societies on the basis of their material remains (1.10). He justly points to sea power as the essential ingredient in all Aegean empire building. Everything in this section is a masterful synopsis of a great period of time. Nothing could be further from the mere narration of events. Herodotus can analyze the flow of the Nile or patterns of behavior and generalize from them, but not human action because action seems to lead him immediately into dramatic narrative.

Thucydides concludes this portion by remarking how uncritically most men accept and hold to the oral tradition (1.20). Men cherish legends and give credence to misinformation that investigation would dispel. He seems to be opposing what in Herodotus we have been calling "cultural truths," distinguishing them from verifiable fact. "On the whole," he says, "he who accepts my analysis on the basis of the inferences which I have made will not be led astray. He will not have to put his faith in the poets who are more concerned with art nor in the storytellers who are more interested in audience response than in purveying truth." The statement sums up the author's sense of authority, which has been buttressed by the display of intelligence, the use of logic, and the ability to grasp essentials. Surely Thucydides' primary concern has been to create an advertisement for himself.

He next turns to contemporary events over which another kind of control must be exercised. But the point has been made that his habits of mind offer the surest proof of the authenticity of his material. He therefore proceeds first to analyze the methods he has employed to gather, check, and select contemporary information. This self-conscious revelation of his intellectual manner is further evidence of his interest in technique and style.

> As to what each party said both before and during the war, both I and my various informants had difficulty establishing an accurate rendition of the actual words. Therefore I created the speeches by keeping as closely as possible to the general tenor and sentiment of the actual remarks, but also on the basis of what each party would necessarily in each one of these situations be bound to say. As to the tangible facts of warfare I did not think it right to base my account on whatever any informant who happened along said, but rather, on the basis of the evidence offered me by others as well as the evidence I amassed of the events to which I myself was party. I have gone through a point-by-point analysis as carefully as possible. My results did not come easily since the various eyewitnesses did not all say the same thing, either because of varying capacities of memory or because they were moved by prejudice.

In this passage Thucydides poses a puzzling dichotomy between words and deeds. He proposes to allow a contrivance, an idealization, to the speeches that he will not allow for the military action. This dichotomy may reflect the influence of contemporary tragic drama, made up, as it is, of alternating passages of choral lyrics and iambic dialogue spoken by the characters. The action of the play takes place or is considered in these dialogues while the choral odes comment on the action. In general Thucydides' speakers comment on the events of the Peloponnesian War in an abstract, thoughtful way that recalls the manner of the tragic choral ode in contrast to the passages that narrate action. Because Thucydides inveighed so sternly against the machinations of the storyteller, one is hard put to justify his deliberate fictions in the speeches. It is not enough to assure his readers that he will hew to the general content, and certainly it is confusing when he confesses that he has made his speakers say what "they would be bound to say." The speeches themselves seem so well fit to the moment that they betray in every instance the efforts of the artificer. Furthermore, they are too consistent in high intelligence and cerebral style to be the expression of a variety of persons.

It is doubtful that Thucydides would have been troubled by what so vexes the modern. Beneath the surface of any utterance there lies greater meaning to be prized out by the percipient, and contexts will always enrich the sense of what is said. Thucydides has simply enlarged upon and altered the reported speeches to include in them what he believes to be their significance. The examples of Homer, Herodotus, and tragic drama lay behind him. A century later Aristotle would say in his *Poetics* (1451b) that poetry is at once more philosophical and more serious than history because it gets at the universal truth, while history deals only with the particular. The speeches come from the poetic tradition; by convention they report another kind of truth. Thucydides was creating history as he wrote, and the speeches represent an intellectual medium that functioned as a rather grand and profound version of modern-day appendixes and footnotes.

Following his discussion of method, Thucydides settles into a narration of the earliest events that provoked the war. As is often observed, Thucydides omits to mention both here and elsewhere the Athenian decrees banning Megarian trading throughout the Athenian empire. Megara, a neighbor to Athens on the northwest, was a Dorian city and thus a natural ally of Corinth and Sparta. The decree, as we know from other sources, was an obvious factor in the mounting hostilities between the two sides. That its implications were well understood by the Athenians seems clear from the allusions to the

decree in Aristophanes' comedies. Some call Thucydides' silence na-
iveté, some calculated misrepresentation. Perhaps neither explanation
is quite valid.

Perhaps he limits himself at this point to describing military situations, that is, the affair of Epidamnus and the affair of Potidaea,
because these are illustrations of what he had so recently defined as
the "tangible facts of warfare," which together with the speeches
constitute the stuff of his narrative. It could also be argued that the
Megarian economic war would have been considerably harder to
narrate. Perhaps he did not have the diction, the way of phrasing for
such a narrative, for he may have boxed himself in when he emphasized the distinction between words and deeds. This distinction is in
its traditional and narrow sense as old as Homer. The deeds were war
deeds, anything calculated to produce physical mayhem. While the
conflict and strategies of economic warfare may have been perfectly
well understood, they are neither words nor deeds in the traditional
sense and therefore perhaps unmanageable.

The speeches subsequent to the narration of these two military
events reinforce the impression that Thucydides is contriving a display of the techniques he has analyzed earlier (1.68ff.). It could be said
that he offers specimen speeches just as he offered specimen military
narration. These speeches, however, more than simply exhibiting
technique, offer a perfect introduction to the psychological climate in
which the ensuing war flourished. The situation here described is a
gathering of allies at Sparta faced with the prospect of war. Hence the
speeches are naturally anticipatory. Yet it is remarkable how free they
are of passion and shortsighted urgency. Indeed they are unusually
abstract. There is the sensation of reading introductory chapters that
offer a masterly summation of the situation.

Thucydides notes that an Athenian delegation happened to be in
Sparta when the Corinthians and the Spartans met and indeed was
permitted to speak. This fact allows for the possibility—however
unlikely it may be, considering the difficulties of writing and hence of
taking dictation—that he was given verbatim versions of the speeches
by the returning delegation. Many other speeches in the work are not
so fortunately supported. Thucydides has said he tried to create
speeches that would reflect "what each party would necessarily in
each of these situations be bound to say." His Greek is so abstract that
endless meanings have been imposed upon it. The nature of these and
other speeches suggests that what he meant by the words "situation"
and "necessarily be bound" was the dictates of the structure of his

narrative. The parley in anticipation or apprehension of a great war has been transformed by him into an introductory survey. Even if the Athenian delegation had memorized the speeches, something not altogether unlikely in a society with limited access to writing, those that Thucydides has given us here do not resemble occasional discourse.

The Corinthians who are the first to be quoted, as it were, by Thucydides speak of the personalities of Athens and Sparta. What they say is highly analytical, delivered in pungent, epigrammatic fashion. The Athenians follow with what is a historical defense of their imperialistic behavior, but what is as well an explanation of the psychological characteristics the Corinthians have imputed to them. The Spartan king Archidamas answers the Corinthians and the Athenians with an analysis of naval warfare and of the Spartan character. The fourth speech, put in the mouth of a Spartan ephor, is, unlike the others, an appeal to the emotions. Also unlike the others, it seems to arise from the occasion and thus returns the reader to the realities of an assembly of men on the verge of war. This passage from textbook to dramatic scene—from dispassionate, abstracted speeches to terse, angry energy—seems to be, as well, a product of art rather than simple recorded fact.

At the conclusion of the speeches a vote is taken, and the treaty between the Lacedaemonians and the Athenians is declared to be broken. War comes a little closer. Thucydides neatly parallels the end of the exposition of his technique with this major shift in the relations between the city-states. As a kind of summation he states that the Spartans voted to break the truce because of their fear of the Athenians. After the manner of epic poetic ring composition the idea of fear as the motive is repeated from the very beginning of this section (1.23.6), thus all the more apparently outlining it.

The rest of the first book is made up of passages markedly different from each other both in intent and in the manner of their execution. But Thucydides has made his material cohere by cross-weaving. He introduces four major items here: (1) a chronicle of events in the fifty years' interval between the Persian and the Peloponnesian wars, (2) another speech from the Corinthians (1.120), (3) biographical anecdotes about the early fifth century Athenian and Spartan leaders Themistocles and Pausanias, and (4) a speech by Pericles with which the book concludes. Before he begins his first item, Thucydides tells the anecdote of Themistocles and his role in the rebuilding of Athens' walls, which occurred at the beginning of the fifty years of Athenian history he is describing. In the course of the story he mentions Pausanias. By enclosing the account of the fifty-year period with references to Themistocles and Pausanias, Thucydides seems again to be using the ring composition technique of the epic poets, tying the fifty years into the narrative. Similarly, because the speeches of the Corinthians and Pericles parallel each other so exactly, it seems Thucydides has positioned them to form a kind of ring around the second Themistocles and Pausanias anecdotes. This intertwining makes disparate items cohere.

The description of the fifty years between the wars is in yet another style. A record of events as they happened year by year, it resembles the chronicle style of a contemporary of Herodotus and Thucydides named Hellanicus, whose work survives only in fragments. Hellanicus composed a chronicle of events in Attica from the earliest times to his own. Thucydides, in fact, who is not given to acknowledging others, names him at this point (1.97), if only to criticize him for the inaccuracy of his chronology and his brevity. Thucydides, however, is sparse himself, even if he has cleared up the order of the events. This section, so unlike the opening analysis of early Greek history or the detailed close-up of events at Epidamnus and Potidaea, represents another style and another intellectual manner. Thucydides has positioned it between the anecdote of Themistocles and the rebuilding of the walls and the speech of the Corinthians as though he wished to distinguish three styles: he assigns the anecdotal style to the Persian War period and to Herodotus, the chronicle style to the mid–fifth century and to Hellanicus, and the speech technique to the period of the Peloponnesian War and to himself.

Having established these distinctions Thucydides seems to enlarge upon them by recounting two lengthy anecdotes about Themistocles and Pausanias. Many critics have said that these are irrelevant to everything else in the first book, but this is not so if they are seen as representations of a style of narration, namely, that of Herodotus. Thucydides asks his reader to associate this style with all prior time that for his contemporaries was not as accessible as current events and hence bordered on the fabulous, just short of myth or saga.

Thucydides finishes with another piece of cross weaving, giving a speech of Pericles, which answers point by point the second speech of the Corinthians (1.120ff.). His continuity throughout the first book comes from the exposition of style and not from chronology. What Pericles has to say points up the artificiality of all Thucydidean speeches because it is a deliberate rebuttal of a speech Pericles surely never heard and of which he very likely had only the merest notion, if any. This very unlikely link between the two speeches serves notice that they stand as something other than the product of disinterested reportage.

For all his self-consciousness Thucydides keeps himself pretty much out of the narrative, unlike Herodotus, whose style seems downright conversational by contrast. Thucydides' modest reference to himself (4.104.4) as a participant in battle is self-effacing, yet reminds us that he is not only the recorder, but often the observer. His descriptions are much like some of the pieces of medical writing that survive from antiquity, a few from the fifth century, all of them gathered together and passed on under the name of Hippocrates. Thucydides seems to have been influenced by the medical writers not only in his masterful account of the plague at Athens (2.47ff.) but in his use of technical terms that do not occur in ordinary prose. Medical reporting at the time was an exposition of the progress of a disease through a description of the successive symptoms that its victims displayed. The emphasis fell upon describing the fatal course of the disease rather than on the explanation for it. This was only natural for people who were largely ignorant of physiology—who, for instance, did not understand either the blood system or bacteria and who were particularly subject to malaria and typhoid. Characteristically, Thucydides scarcely touches on the causes and origins of the plague before he dismisses that line of inquiry. He emphasizes symptoms so that the plague might be *recognized* if it came again (2.48). Recognized, not cured, disease must have its own tragic *anagnorisis*.

While it seems natural that the limited state of medical knowledge led the ancient Greek medical writers to elevate prognosis over diagnosis, it is also fair to say that prognosis is true to the culture of the time, disinclined as it was to thoughts of change or progress or alteration. Thucydides transfers the Hippocratic method of describing symptoms to political action, thereby suggesting that human behavior, like the body, is immutable. His description of the revolution in Corcyra (3.70ff.) reads like a clinical presentation of symptoms. He then generalizes these observations to fit the rest of the Greek states, describing with his usual brilliant, epigrammatic thrusts the progress of horror, betrayal, and infamy that beset them. He makes no attempt to diagnose the condition in terms of social, political, or economic motives, but rather looks to immutable psychological needs of the human soul: greed and ambition. "Horrible things . . . happened," he says, "and will always happen as long as human nature stays the same" (3.82). He qualifies this statement by observing that the prosperity of peace obscures what war, "a stern teacher," brings out in people. There is a hint in these words of the pernicious doctrine that humans are truest in moments of stress and adversity.

In employing this method of description for narrating military matters Thucydides has eschewed the speculative content of his speeches for the factual. This emphasis on fact may be why he declines to discuss strategy. He describes one military engagement after another, but never reveals why each is included, other than—presumably—that it happened. Those who insist there must be some special meaning to the length of his description of the Athenian occupation at Pylos (4.3ff.) quite miss the point. He was well supplied with details concerning the event, and because details *qua* details are significant in the Hippocratic medical view that he seems to have adopted as his intellectual habit, he conscientiously introduces as complete an assemblage of these details as possible.

The peculiarity of this style becomes the more apparent when judged by the standard of the speech (6.89ff.) delivered by Alcibiades before the Spartan assembly in which he advocates among other things establishing a permanent presence in Attica. This speech is unusual because it portrays an intelligent military mind addressing strategy. True enough, it seems to be characteristically Greek to be more thoughtful about the hypothetical, as any future event by its very nature is, then about reality. Elsewhere in the work, of course, Thucydides is dealing with what has already taken place. And yet why this isolated passage? It is tantalizing to consider. Was Thucydides perhaps a poor strategist? He was not a military success himself. Was he deep down uninterested in war as war? Compared to the speeches with their profundity of thought, his military narration seems to show such lack of interest. Alcibiades was supposed to have been very intelligent. This speech may be his own words or very close to them, somehow come into the possession of Thucydides. If it is true that he wrote his *History* over a long period of time, then perhaps as he got further into the work, he grew to realize that speeches could be used to indicate strategy—which is the philosophy of war—just as he used speeches for philosophizing about human existence.

His fascination with military and political events proceeds from his single-minded concentration upon the human desire for power. From the very first, in his analysis of the early Greeks, and thereafter Thucydides measures peoples and persons in terms of strengths and weaknesses. The standard is always material it seems, because Thucydides nowhere acknowledges the immense cultural, artistic, intellectual creativity in Athens of the fifth century. He says nothing about the architecture, the vases, or the drama, to name but a few specimens of Athenian excellence which have caught the imagination of the world over the last twenty-four centuries. When Pericles says in the funeral oration that Athens is the teacher of Greece, he does not mean what moderns take it to mean. Athens is considered today to be the inspiration, the model, for many of the cultural attainments of the Western world, but Pericles seems to mean that Athens showed the way politically and socially. This kind of leadership relates directly to power, to the city's ability to impose on subject cities a political system and a way of life deriving from it. Behind his remark lies the struggle between democratic and oligarchic factions in the city-states: the differences between Athens and Sparta and the quasi-ideological underpinnings to Athenian claims to hegemony.

Striving for power manifests itself in war and politics; empire is the furthest extension of power. Each military action or political event, therefore, must be recorded as an expression of this power. That legitimacy of power was a subject for debate in the late fifth century seems to be reflected in the well-known passage in the first book of Plato's *Republic* in which the Sophist and rhetorician Thrasymachus is introduced to defend the proposition that might makes right. There is nothing to show, however, that this proposition is an article of faith with Thucydides. His neutral descriptions of war and politics simply acknowledge as a fact that the strong dominate the weak, just as the medical men acknowledged certain physical facts to be true.

The predominance of battle narration also plays to the ancient Greek obsession with competition. Striving to be the best is an aristocratic ideal as old as Homer, but the contest system both then and thereafter demanded that for every winner there must be a loser. Competition is a social expression of the deeply ingrained Greek habit of seeing things in antitheses. As we have remarked in the first chapter, their sentences are structured on oppositions, but antithesis is everywhere—in Aristotle's law of the excluded middle, in post and beam architecture, and in the form of tragic drama, to name a few instances. Shortly before Thucydides went into exile, the Sicilian rhetorician Gorgias was dazzling Athens with his exaggeratedly antithetical speeches. Everyone in Thucydides' work speaks in elegantly balanced antitheses, so much so that Dionysius of Halicarnassus, the first-century B.C. author and literary critic, complains that Thucydides gets carried away with antithesis. But it is more than his speeches; antithesis seems to be fundamental to his view of things.

Throughout the work he seems deliberately to set up numerous polarities, some of them more exaggerated and artificial than others. As adversaries, Athens and Sparta, for instance, seem less likely than Athens and Corinth, the two great seagoing trading powers of the time. Some critics call Thucydides' suggestion of Sparta's fear of Athens as a cause of war irrelevant. The Spartans, an isolated land power, seem too remote, too little concerned with the outside world, unlike the Corinthians, for whom the Athenian navy, commerce, and empire would be immediate sources of anxiety. Were Athens and Corinth not the real rivals in the late fifth century?

It is surprising how little Thucydides tells us about Corinth; he mentions no Corinthian by name, and he does not outline the role played by Corinthian money and ships throughout the war. Perhaps for Thucydides' purposes Corinth was too much like Athens in outlook, being yet another seagoing commercial power. Sparta, on the other hand, as the speeches of the Corinthians and King Archidamus in the first book made clear, was altogether the opposite. As Thucydides and his audience knew full well, there were many other points of real antithesis between Athens and Sparta: their political systems, their treatment of slaves, their creativity in the arts and literature, for instance. But what seems truly important, what the speeches in the first book show, is that they are temperamentally opposites.

Thucydides is able to personalize Athens and Sparta in a way he could not personalize Corinth. It is the legacy from heroic saga that dictates that history shall be told through the actions of individuals. The rivalry between Athens and Corinth must have been essentially economic; otherwise the two cities would have been much the same. But Thucydides could create a true antithesis by treating Athens and Sparta as personalities.

Some critics think Thucydides naive for doing so, for instance, when he says (1.25.3) that the Corinthians (like jilted lovers) "hated" the Corcyreans for their indifference or that they "hated" the Athenians for fortifying Megara. Modern-day critics, however, are thinking of foreign-office bureaucrats or other power elites, who presumably do not react with such vehemence. Perhaps Thucydides confers such personalities upon his city-states because he sees them through the perspective of democratic assemblies in which issues such as these would have been aired in a highly charged emotional atmosphere. Ongoing deliberative assemblies do develop a personality. Nonetheless, when Thucydides has the Corinthian delegation speak of Spartan sluggishness, timidity, and caution as though these were inborn character traits, he misses the point, which is that Sparta's behavior was governed by her continuing fear of slave revolt.

Only occasionally does Thucydides introduce individuals into his narrative, and then he uses them as antitheses. The Athenian Themistocles and the Spartan Pausanias in the first book are examples. Themistocles is shown to be clever, cool, and ambitious, and Pausanias crazy once he moves beyond his provincialism. They are the Good Hellene and the Bad Hellene, as it were, and embody the personalities of Athenians and Spartans earlier described by the Corinthians and King Archidamus. Later he will juxtapose Brasidas, the Spartan general whom he admires and who represents all that is good about the conservative military mind of Sparta, and Cleon, the Athenian, a political figure Thucydides despises and who represents all the excesses of the Athenian democracy for him.

Cleon is an important figure in a narrative that describes relatively few named persons. He is most often juxtaposed to Pericles, who by contrast represents the virtues of Athenian democracy. It is in the mouth of Pericles that Thucydides puts the eulogistic speech about Athens, and it is Pericles whom Thucydides in his praise makes into a kind of symbol of all that was good in Athens toward the beginning of the Peloponnesian War. He then paints Cleon, the successor to Pericles, as the major force in the assembly and as loud, vulgar, flamboyant, and corrupt ("roughest public figure of the time" [3.36]). There is evidence—Aristophanes' caricature for one—that Cleon may have had personality traits that would offend someone of Thucydides' stamp, but nothing suggests that Cleon was not upright and honest. Certainly Cleon's memory was respected in the century that followed. But idealized in this fashion, Pericles comes to stand for Athens at its apex, Cleon for the beginning of her decline. In the same way Thucydides introduces Alcibiades and Nicias in debate over the expedition to Syracuse. Alcibiades is young, ambitious, and unscrupulous (6.15.2–4); Nicias, old, cautious, and decent. Thucydides fails to mention Alcibiades' intelligence, concentrating instead on these qualities, just as he does not suggest what part lack of judgment or ineptitude played in the calamities that beset Nicias.

One antithesis that runs fairly consistently through the work is the conflict between hope, always simply named, and an attitude we might call awareness, realism, cynicism, or *Realpolitik,* depending on the value we wish to assign it. Thucydides himself is altogether non-

committal. It is a collision that occurs regularly in Euripidean tragedy. Consider the high tone Phaedra adopts in the face of her lust for
her stepson and her nurse's speech on the importance of sexual freedom and health; or consider Tyndareus's attack on his grandson's
defense of matricide in the *Orestes;* or Pheres' condemnation of his
son for accepting his wife's self-sacrifice in the *Alcestis.* In each instance the traditional, idealistic position is adopted only to be demol-
ished by the intervening character.

The Athenians' argument for their city's supremacy at the parley in
Sparta in the first book stems from an idealization of her role (as
Greece's savior from the Persian menace). Pericles' funeral oration
maintains the same tone. They contrast vividly with Pericles' speech
to the Athenians at the moment they have tired of war (2.60ff.), a
speech that describes what it means for them to be an imperial tyranny from which there is no quick or easy way out once the exploitation and enslavement of subject people has got under way. Cleon says
the same thing more bluntly in the debate over Mytilene (3.37), a
speech that often verbally echoes that of Pericles so that Cleon's
speech seems suddenly a bad dream come true. Speech after speech
analyzes human motives and actions. But rather than being interpreted in the traditional heroic-aristocratic context, these actions
are given a new, cynical, realistic interpretation. It seems fair to say
that Thucydides purposely emphasizes this antithesis between hope
and realism because he is able to use it with great irony in the latter
part of the history when Athens, cool and wise, becomes the victim
of her own fevered delusion.

The Melian Dialogue in the fifth book (5.84ff.) is the culminating
realization of this antithesis. The conference on the island of Melos
between its inhabitants and an Athenian delegation that has come to
offer them the choice of abandoning their neutrality or being killed or
enslaved is the only occasion when Thucydides adopted the dialogue
form. Because the speeches of Thucydides seem so frequently to
answer each other, some critics believe that he composed them first as
dialogues and then reworked them into individual speeches. On this
theory the Melian Dialogue is an unfinished draft. It seems more
likely that the dialogue form here, recalling tragic drama, emphasizes
the antithesis between hope and cynicism.

The Melians, who do not have the military strength to withstand
the Athenians, resist joining the Athenian alliance and base their resistance upon a certain ethical stance. They claim they cannot do
otherwise because they think themselves to be right and believe that

rightness will prevail. The Athenians respond with a realistic, cynical analysis of the Melians' motives and prospects. The Athenian response is a breathtaking exercise in the coldest, boldest *Realpolitik*. The Athenians particularly deride the Melian reliance on hope (5.103). Athenian rationalism, the hallmark of every speech in the work, has never been more chillingly displayed. Just as the speeches in the first book set up the contrasting personalities of Athens and Sparta, here the Melians and the Athenians verbalize and dramatize two ways of getting on with the world, two justifications for existence. Finally the Melians are destroyed.

The subsequent preparation for the expedition to Sicily is a marvelously ironic portrait of Athenian wild hope and deluded expectation which is particularly well developed in the mood of the assembly (6.25). The moment of departure is reminiscent of Herodotus in the profusion of details; it recalls as well the Herodotean predilection for fastening on the mood of adventure, enthusiasm, and extravagance. The experienced reader will feel he is being set up for a downswing that will follow this euphoric moment. A similar mood of deluded expectation is created by the juxtaposition of the funeral speech and the description of the plague in the second book. The one conveys all that made Athens the principal city and model in the mid–fifth century, and the other reveals the dark shadows that forever lurk on the fringe waiting to overwhelm and obscure whatever shines bright. Here, as in Herodotus's portrait of Xerxes at Abydus, the essential manic-depressive attitude is unmistakable.

When the Athenians' position at Syracuse begins to collapse, they have only hope on which to rely. Nicias can say, "My life has been one of devotion toward the gods; there has been much justice. I have not offended against other men. Therefore, I have a strong hope for the future" (7.61.3). Coming so soon after the Melian Dialogue, the irony is unmistakable. It is part of the larger irony that the Athenians were the fifth century's entrepreneurs, for it is the entrepreneur who feeds on expectations; like the gambling man, he pretends shrewdness and nothing more, but is always looking to the future with hope.

It is possible that Thucydides arranged his events—the funeral oration next to the plague, for instance, and the dialogue just before the sailing of the expedition—to create a kind of tragic nexus of events. In the earlier books the Corinthian estimation, the history of Athens between the wars, and the funeral speech all describe Athens at the pinnacle of her power. Later the city is brought to defeat. It is a political reversal but also a tragic reversal. One might say that in their prosperity the Athenians exhibited the kind of dangerous pride of which Herodotus speaks so eloquently when they forced the Melians cruelly and cynically, and that they were seduced in their pride by a Herodotean Bad Counselor, Alcibiades (who plays Mardonius to Nicias's Artabanus at this point), into their *hamartia,* making a fatal misjudgment, the expedition to Sicily, for which they were visited by *nemesis* in the form of their utter defeat. Here are the tragic ingredients *hubris, ate, hamartia,* and *nemesis.* Unlike Herodotus, who clearly wishes this nexus to be understood as the cause of events, Thucydides, through Pericles, makes the less precise, more general comment, "All things are born to diminish" (2.64.3). One of the curious facts of this very curious century is that Athens's rise and fall, so to speak, parallels that of so many tragic heroes. It is natural that whoever recorded the events of the time would unconsciously or consciously look to tragic drama as a model for narration. Beyond that one wonders to what extent a society that lives in the spell of tragic drama shaped attitudes and actions so as to make events conform to the expectations aroused by it.

The other great prose stylist whose pieces survive from a slightly later period is Plato, who was born around 429 at the time of the plague, shortly before Thucydides was sent into exile, and died about eighty years later in 347. He wrote more than twenty-five dialogues and one monologue (*Apology*) over a period of about fifty years. In addition there are also thirteen letters that have been handed down under his authorship, which is much disputed by scholars.

Plato is the earliest author of Greek antiquity about whom much biographical detail exists; as a teacher he was the inspiration for numerous students, principally Aristotle, who devoted considerable thought to elucidating and criticizing what Plato had taught. Because so many of Plato's dialogues purport to represent Socrates as he conducted himself in disputation with various notable Sophists and other members of the cultural establishment, and because Socrates, who seemed to have despised the written word, has not left anything in his own words, the writings of Plato constitute what amounts to a sacred text for people who revere Socrates as the founder of what is a kind of theology of humanism.

Plato has a major claim on the attentions of the heirs to Western culture. It was he who began the process of systematizing philosophical speculation, a task continued and much enlarged by his pupil Aristotle, who was both less original and more systematic. Plato's dialogues address questions of ontology, epistemology, and ethics that are still current among philosophers today. He was the principal influence upon Plotinus (A.D. 205–270), who was himself a major influence on the early Christians who wished to develop an intellectual basis for their faith. In many ways, therefore, Plato is the father of Christian theology. His predecessors' works in the fields of philosophy and science survive only in the merest fragments, showing that he eclipsed the field in fame and that his apparent compatibility with Christian teaching made him that much more prized.

His indisputably genuine works excite enormous controversy and speculation, deriving largely from the peculiar form in which they are presented. That is to say, Plato seems to have invented the dialogue for the exposition of serious thought. What his purpose was is much argued. There is little dispute, however, over the brilliance of his prose style. Only about a century and a half after prose began to be used for serious communication, on its way to supplanting poetry, Plato's dialogues achieve a level of clarity, suppleness, and energy which set the standard forever after. What is more, he has made a contrivance that appeals to educated, cultured people at their ease. The style is intelligent, never pretentious, never learned, grammatically alert, but yielding to demands of expression. Plato is witty, serious, honest, and yet, of course, self-deluding, as all humankind is when asking the big questions.

And the style is so simple, so deceptively simple. It is a style that drives professional philosophers berserk. But then Plato is something other than a philosopher, and certainly not a professional. It is not that he, like Herodotus and Thucydides, lived before the age of professionals in his field. There had been a great company of professional teachers and thinkers in Athens, the Sophists, who were enough associated to constitute the intellectual class. Plato, however, like his teacher, Socrates, stayed aloof from this group, and was resolutely opposed to their professionalism, as his dialogues show. There is never the self-aware tone that is found on every page of Aristotle's works. Aristotle gave to philosophy the structure and categories that it has possessed ever since.

Why Plato wrote these dialogues is not clear. Taken together, they do not set forth a doctrine. Nonetheless, they often refer to each other. In the *Phaedo,* for instance, when Socrates talks about the memory the soul possesses of things from some previous existence, the knowledgeable reader will recall that in the *Meno* Socrates demonstrates this kind of memory by cross-examining an uneducated slave, who is made to reveal an understanding of higher mathematics.

There are innumerable instances of this kind of tacit cross-referenc-
ing. Sometimes the connections are very visible; some dialogues are
almost chapters in a larger, unfolding story. At the conclusion of the
Theaetetus, for instance, Socrates announces that he must be off to the
Royal Stoa to answer charges preferred by Meletus. The setting of
the *Euthyphro* is the porch of the Royal Stoa, where Socrates has
arrived for his legal business with Meletus. This business, of course,
is the very prosecution against which he defends himself so forcefully
in the *Apology.* The negative jury verdict about which Socrates speaks
at the close of the *Apology* results in his imprisonment. In prison he
receives a visit from his friend Crito, related in the *Crito,* and before
his execution, he spends his last moments with his friends, a visit
Plato recounts in the *Phaedo.* The *Theaetetus,* which has been called a
basic text of Plato's theory of knowledge, was composed relatively
late, yet Plato, by associating it dramatically with the early days of
Meletus's legal action against Socrates, makes it an introduction into
the drama just as it is an introduction into his thought. In the same
way the setting of the *Euthyphro,* the porch of the Stoa, is an architectural statement of introduction suitable to the moment when the
drama of Socrates' martyrdom gets under way. It is regrettable that
the critics concern themselves so with the chronology of the composition of these dialogues just to get at the presumed "development" of Plato's thought. They might better occupy themselves considering the creation of a story line in these dialogues, altogether the
great novel of ideas which Plato has created, composing various
chapters at various times in his life.

It is remarkable that the theory of the Ideal Forms which underlies
so much of what Socrates says and to which there is constant allusion
in so many of the dialogues is never fully described or formally
presented to the reader. There are naturally enough conflicting theories as to what exactly Socrates (and Plato) was trying to describe in
his preoccupation with Forms. In essence Socrates (and Plato) make
the distinction between the perceived world and its immaterial rep-
lica, which is the source or motive or cause for the former. In the
commonplace example there is the table we all see and then the ideal,
immaterial table that exists independent of the circumstances of this
physical world. The table of this world owes its form and existence to
the idea of table or to what might be considered the heavenly tem-
plate. Plato came to this notion from mathematics and from the
mystical, religious teachings of Pythagoras. The number two, for
instance, exists independent of the presence of two items before our

eyes. Two plus two will equal four in all the realms of this universe, enduring as a truth that cannot be overthrown, even as Zeus on Olympus reigns eternally. Plato's search furthermore derives from the Milesians, who were concerned with identifying the unchanging material basis of the natural world. Socrates (and Plato) denied any permanence to this world, and in so doing made a distinction between knowledge and opinion. The latter is what is gained in learning from the perceived world, while the former is awareness of the greater reality, the ideal world of forms that have given shape to what we see.

Not only is the doctrine of forms never fully explained, but it seems to be disputed and partially refuted in the *Theaetetus* and the *Parmenides*. The uneven representation of the teachings has provoked some critics to argue that the dialogues are meant to be in the nature of position pamphlets based on the detailed oral teaching of Plato's school, the Academy, addressed to a wider community of interested intellectuals who presumably knew the basics. This idea seems far-fetched, more a conception inspired by the twentieth-century behavior of intellectuals who live by commercialism and hucksterism than an imaginative reconstruction of the life of the mind in the early fourth century B.C. It is probably more to the point that Plato, like all really original minds, is playing games in these dialogues. Only the epigones insist upon creating airtight systems as we can see in the case of the disciples of Jesus or Marx or Freud, or, for that matter, Plato himself.

Socratic cross-examination, which is at the heart of most of the dialogues, is itself highly problematic. The questions he puts to the slave boy in the *Meno,* for instance, are so leading that the fact that the boy is able to understand something of mathematical concepts will strike the reader upon reflection as the product of Socrates' subliminal coaching as much as anything else. Any lawyer would object, and any judge would surely sustain the objection to much of the direction of Socratic questioning. The questions prejudice the answer and lead the witness. Time and again the reader will draw up in dismay as Socrates forces his opponent to answer a question that any thinking or wary respondent would parry or dismiss. It is testimony to the literary genius and shrewdness of Plato that the reader becomes so caught up in the intellectual struggles in these dialogues that he succumbs to the realism of the setting. After all, these are only essays, more or less, addressing certain problems in thinking. Who has read the dialogues, however, and not retained for life the scene of Protagoras and Socrates at that intimate Sophists' soiree or the men lying about talking of love after dinner or Socrates among some of his despairing and crying favorites bidding them farewell? The dialogues are like so many Ivy Compton-Burnett novels, lacking only her absurd and manic tone. Indeed, it may well be said that Plato's dialogues constitute the first harbingers of that genre, the novel.

The handbooks on ancient literature tells us that the literary antecedents of the Platonic dialogue are obscure. Aristotle mentions Sophron, a fifth-century Sicilian writer of mimes whom Plato is said to have admired. There is a tradition that Plato began his career writing dithyrambs and tragedies that he destroyed when he came under the spell of Socrates and turned to philosophy. This theory may be no more than an acknowledgment of the very dramatic quality of the dialogues. In fact, though, dialogue is at the heart of ancient Greek culture, whether the responsion be verbal, plastic, visual, or intellectual.

There is not enough evidence to be sure, but perhaps the fifth-century Sophists wrote something similar to Platonic dialogue. Herodotus, for instance, introduces what is more or less a dramatized essay on theory of government when he has three men speak on the relative virtues of democracy, oligarchy, and monarchy (3.80ff.). While there is no dialogue, there is a kind of implied intensity of interaction. The three are conspirators who have assassinated the ruler; what they say, therefore, is consequential to their own power and their future role in Persia. When they decide to restore the monarchy, it makes sense that Otanes, who had urged democracy, asks not to be considered as a candidate for king and that Darius, who spoke last and most convincingly on the virtues of monarchy, should be appointed king.

Herodotus claims somewhat belligerently that there are those who doubt these speeches took place. The doubt is justified because such a disquisition and such a subject in that setting are utterly unlikely. It is as though the Persian court had gone to an Athenian Sophist for schooling. But, although the passage is artificial in its setting, it would have been far more incongruous to have introduced an expository essay on the subject. Herodotus, whether adapting a Sophistic technique or looking back to something like the triadic speeches of entreaty in the ninth book of the *Iliad* or indeed building upon the essay through speech that he himself creates in the mouth of Solon, has made something not unlike, say, Plato's *Symposium*.

Thucydides comes even closer to Plato in the Melian Dialogue.

While Thucydidean speeches are meant to be public oratory, (although, as we have said, it seems certain that they do not represent the very words or even the manner of the several speakers from whose mouths they issue), the Melian Dialogue is specified as having taken place away from public scrutiny. The result is a certain harshness; there are no rhetorical embellishments as palliatives when the two sides argue for the life or death of the inhabitants of the island of Melos. But the harsh, naked, cynical view is no more remarkable than the continual appeal to ideals. Finally, it is hard to believe that active men confronting the political and military crisis that was unfolding at Melos spoke in this fashion. Thucydides has in fact made an essay on the nature of power and imperialism, the corruption attendant upon these, and the illusion, delusion, and strength offered by these. It is interesting that Thucydides chose the dialogue form, which in Plato's hands becomes a sustained investigation into similar abstracted positions.

In addition to these antecedent attempts at something like Platonic dialogue, Plato's contemporary Xenophon, who was equally an admirer and student of Socrates, also composed dialogues in which Socrates appears. His prose style is more even and less exciting than Plato's, as befits his well-defined conservative, pro-Spartan position. His dialogues are probably the best example of the superior standard of prose writing of the early fourth century. To read Xenophon is to gauge the positive evolution from the prose of Herodotus, the extreme idiosyncrasy of Thucydides, and the real creative genius of Plato. Xenophon's motives for writing dialogue are more immediately apparent than those of Plato. He remarks that there are essays in circulation both favorable and hostile to Socrates. Aristophanes' use of Socrates in the *Clouds* reveals Socrates' celebrity as well as the public's very real ambivalence toward him. Clearly Xenophon admires great men. His account of Cyrus, *The Education of Cyrus,* is essentially a historical novel with didactic intent, even hagiography. Socrates enters the pages of his *Memorabilia* to similar applause; Xenophon apparently composed his account of Socrates about twenty years after Socrates' death as an antidote to the hostile memory of his teacher.

The task is to determine what is true and what not. Xenophon seems clearly to have been able to use Socrates as Herodotus uses Solon, that is, as a historical figure in a fictive situation. His *Symposium,* for instance, in which Socrates is the important figure, seems clearly to be fiction—simply a device to gather together a diversity of opinion. His *Oeconomicus,* or *The Good Householder,* again introduces Socrates as the main character, but the purpose of the piece is to exhibit the virtues of a country gentleman; the character Isomachus, a representative of the species, soon becomes obviously the real hero. Curiously enough, Xenophon and Plato both mention one somewhat similar detail. In Xenophon's *Apology* Socrates strokes the head of his disciple Apollodorus, in Plato's *Phaedo* it is Phaedo who gets his head stroked by the master. Is this coincidence or a deeply impressed but slightly mistaken remembrance or a kind of topos, like the convention of John with his head on Christ's breast in scenes of the Last Supper?

While it is not possible to date the writing of Plato's dialogues with certainty or to know whether Plato began his writing during Socrates' lifetime or later, the order of their composition has been established to some satisfaction on the basis of a statistical investigation of trends and changes in his style of writing. Over time there is an obvious decline in the importance of Socrates as a dramatic figure in the dialogues. The early dialogues center upon him. In them Plato seems determined to present to the world a portrait of the beloved man, almost a saint, who became a martyr to his beliefs on the occasion of his execution (by suicide, so that the city would avoid the pollution inherent in murder) in 399. Pieces such as the *Protagoras* or the *Ion* show Socrates demonstrating that persons who hold to the belief that they know something in fact know nothing. This he does through question and answer, resolutely and quite courageously breaking down established beliefs through the process of definition and redefinition of concepts. It is not unlike the terribly painful process of psychotherapy. In the *Theaetetus* Socrates likens himself to a midwife who assists at the birth, an equally painful experience.

Here the famous Socratic irony, wit, good manners, and geniality are at play. That Socrates is highly manipulative, and in ways that no one other than a self-demeaning student would tolerate, is true. But the form, its allegiance to fiction instead of documentary, makes the reader obediently suspend his disbelief. Aristotle remarks (*de sophisticis elenchis* 183^b), "Socrates asks but he does not answer, for he agrees that he knows nothing." Like the midwife, Socrates assists with birthing, but does not bear himself. Assisting at creating but not creating is both ironic and highly manipulative. The *Euthyphro* is a charming illustration of Socrates at his pedagogic best, confessing ignorance at the beginning, ensnaring young Euthyphro in the toils of confusion, but maintaining his ignorance through to the end. The piece is slightly mocking surely, for when finally Socrates begins yet another tortured investigation of the definitions of the words of their discourse, Euthyphro claims pressing business elsewhere and departs. Socrates confesses in his defense before the Athenian jury in the *Apology* that he is guided by an inner voice that comes to him from time to time and that dissuades him from various courses of action but never encourages him to any. That admission alone reveals the essentially destructive nature of Socrates, reason enough for any community to rid themselves of him. For people survive upon their prejudices, their *idées fixes,* their myths, all of which, like old friends, fit them and sustain them. No one needs a consistently negative thinker.

The gradual departure of Socrates from the center position of the dialogues is accompanied by the emergence of Plato's more developed thought, hardly a coincidence. In the relatively early *Protagoras* Socrates sternly insists upon dialogue despite Protagoras's predilection for and attempts at sustained speech. But in a later dialogue, the *Symposium,* every speaker is allowed his say in a series of speeches that arrange themselves as partial answers to the definition of love, which is finally completed in the lengthy speech of Socrates. In the *Republic,* in which Socrates' fellow speakers are limited to mouthing a variety of assenting interjections, the dialogue structure is exceedingly tenuous, the dramatic form has been more or less discarded, and what remains is purely narrative; the last bit of action in the entire ten books occurs in the fifth (449^b). In the *Parmenides* Socrates yields the floor to Parmenides, and in the *Sophist* it is the stranger from Elea who does the talking while the deferential Socrates listens. Socrates does not even appear in the *Laws,* composed toward the end of Plato's life, a thinly disguised essay in dialogue form on the subject of the codes that are necessary for the ideal state.

The dialogue form is not suitable to the presentation of a complete philosophy. The nearest approach to it, apart from the relatively extended exposition of a legal system in the *Laws,* are the development of the theory of state in the *Republic* and the account of the physical world in the *Timaeus.* The dialogue form has the virtue of obscuring the formal inadequacies of Plato's logic as it makes arguments more convincing. Diogenes the Cynic is said to have remarked that Plato's *diatribe,* "discourse," is really *katatribe,* "disguise." The competition inherent in dialogue is very much like that in the stichomyth of tragic drama; the reader looks no further than the immediately subsequent response that will exceed or defeat the efforts of the preceding speaker.

In the *Phaedrus* Socrates says that he objects to the written word, preferring oral discourse. The context for this observation is a walk into the countryside in the company of the beautiful young Phaedrus, for whom he is developing his ideas. Phaedrus has brought along a written text of Lysias on love which Socrates answers viva voce. The remarks on love and the nature of the lover and the beloved are subjects to which Plato will return in the *Symposium,* in which Phaedrus appears as well.

It is not too much to say that Socrates' preference for the spoken word has a sexual element in it. The dialogue or delivered speech requires a partner, the hearer, just as sexual intercourse requires two people. In both instances the partners work energetically to create something greater than their separate selves. Speech, like sexual desire, works outside of the body; the two are splendid expressions of the transcendence of the flesh, an idea so important to Plato. The dialogue form, therefore, was most likely adopted by him not simply to mask certain inadequacies, but because of this very transcendence.

In the very early dialogue *Lysis,* the homoerotic nimbus is never dispelled throughout. Socrates and some handsome young men go to a newly built exercise park where they see a group of boys at their athletic activities. Two, Lysis and Menexenus, break away and shyly join Socrates, who proceeds to seduce them with his dialogue as they discuss the subject of friendship until at the close the boys' chaperones (an established institution in ancient Athens similar to the duenna in Spanish countries), who suspect the worst, angrily come over and take them away. Plato plays to the perfectly normal interest older men took in beautiful boys in ancient Athens, insisting on the fundamental eroticism of the transaction throughout. For instance, the very last words, so charmingly put by Socrates, are "Oh, Lysis and Menexenus, we have become a joke, you two and me, the old guy. For the bystanders will go away and say that we thought we were friends—yes, I put myself right there as one of you—when all along we never even managed to define what friendship was."

The setting of the *Lysis,* the landscape with athletic boys, is an integral part of the drama worked out in the dialogue. The *Lysis* and the *Phaedrus* are the only two pieces to take place beyond the walls of Athens. The countryside did not normally appeal to the ancient Athenians and certainly not to Socrates, who remarks on the novelty of the setting in the *Phaedrus*. Plato has created his most vivid background in this dialogue with extended description of the landscape. Away from his usual haunts, outside the city, under the spell of the natural beauty, Socrates is poetic and inspired as he proceeds to make lengthy speeches ex tempore, not at all his usual style.

Most dialogues do not have so elaborate a background; only the *Protagoras* matches or indeed exceeds the *Phaedrus* in this respect. In the *Protagoras* Socrates recounts that he was roused in the early morning gloom and went off to the house where the visiting Sophist was staying. The movement is from darkness into light, the commonplace shift from ignorance into knowledge used often by the ancient dramatists, notably Aeschylus in the *Agamemnon*. Arriving at the house, Socrates makes out a number of Sophists, some lying about, some pacing the courtyard in conversation. As Socrates describes seeing these men, he uses the words Homer puts in the mouth of Odysseus when he describes the spirits he saw on his visit to the Underworld. It has been suggested that Plato wishes to indicate (or Socrates, really, since it is he who makes the image) that the Sophists are to be compared with Socrates and that they are mere shades next to his solid, substantial teacher. More likely, the image of Odysseus in the Underworld which the language calls to mind has to do with the goal of his journeying there, namely to consult with Tiresias, for here Socrates, who professes himself to be enraptured with Protagoras, comes to see him as though to the font of all knowledge. Of course, Socrates is being ironic as usual, because Protagoras, like every other establishment figure, proves to be fundamentally ignorant. There is nonetheless throughout this dialogue the impression of Socrates' real respect for Protagoras.

Yet here as well Plato is not afraid to make clear how manipulative Socrates can be. When Socrates cannot get Protagoras to argue after the fashion he prefers, he prepares to leave, claiming an important prior engagement: "Since I have no free time and can't hang around with you going on at such length—I've got to be somewhere else, you see—I'm going" (335c). (One can almost see the discreet, well-mannered pout.) The idea of Socrates' departure so upsets the gathering that Protagoras is emotionally blackmailed really into agreeing to Socrates' demands. The engagement is entirely a fiction, of course, as Socrates himself has already indicated at the very beginning of the dialogue (310a). When he tells his companion that he has just come from Protagoras, the companion asks Socrates to tell him all, saying, "Why don't you tell me about the whole encounter, if you've got nothing pressing?" To which Socrates replies: "Great! I'd be delighted." So much for no free time!

The *Republic*, which is so much longer than the other pieces, takes on, as it were, epic dimensions. True to the epic size, Plato has created the dialogue in a structure of ring composition so familiar to the audience of the Homeric poems. The discussion of the Underworld with Cephalus in the first book is balanced by the myth of Er in the tenth. The discussion of poetry appears in books one through three and again in the tenth book. The just soul is defined in the fourth book, and a portrait of the death of the soul appears in the ninth. The state is the subject of the fourth book and again of the eighth. In the middle of the piece stands the long consideration of the philosopher king. Socrates so dominates the talking that the *Republic* is almost a narrative. The brothers Glaucon and Adeimantus, who share the dialogue with Socrates, function as little more than devices to signal a change in topic, as they alternate in giving their pallid assent to whatever the master asserts.

Most persons associate the *Republic* with Plato's doctrine of the Ideal Forms. As has been said, however, the thesis is always assumed, never demonstrated. It is connected with his ideas on the independence and immortality of the soul. In the opening conversation of the *Phaedo* Socrates states rather than argues that the soul exists independent of and prior to the body, that it survives at death, and that it is chained down by the bodily appetites and pleasures. It is clear that Plato was as much impressed with Pythagoras's belief in reincarnation as with his mathematics. Furthermore, while he accepted Heraclitus's belief that everything in the sensible world is subject to change, Plato had to believe in some permanent reality that would be immaterial, something accessible to the mind. This he found in mathematics, which he extended by analogy to moral forms. The memory that could recall these forms was not personal, but an attribute common to all humans. The proof was the kind of recollection Socrates practices with the slave boy in the *Meno*. These things are there in the mind; we might have an intuition of them, but by working through, much as the slave boy was made to do by Socrates, we arrive at a knowledge of them.

The doctrine of the Ideal Forms, as we have said, establishes that everything in this sensible world is only an imperfect manifestation, an accidental copy of an abstracted, perfect version. Intellectually, Plato is working his way through to the nature of conceptualization. He is also building a bulwark against the inevitability of death. The ancient Greeks were obsessed with dying as all their literature shows. They did not have a well worked out antidote to it. A belief in immortality was not commonly held. Plato's attachment to Forms, then, is a way of denying death; it is, on the other hand, in its dismissal of the value of the perceived world, of life as lived, an equally powerful denial of life. In the evolution of his thought through the dialogues Plato does not arrive at the premise of not knowing as Socrates does. Instead he discovers a metaphysical world. Plato goes beyond knowing as he proceeds beyond being. He avoids the final truth, particularly in his use of The Good. He never spells out what exactly he means by this term, yet in the communion between Socrates and the others in the dialogues and with the readers, there is a kind of shared sensation of the meaning of The Good. That in itself is transcendence. As Socrates says in the *Apology,* the poets are inspired and speak, but they do not know what they are talking about. Socrates or Plato may disapprove of using enthusiasm or inspiration or intuition as a substitute for knowledge, but in the use of the dialogue, in the various highly imagistic myths in these pieces, by the creation of the various personae, especially that of Socrates, Plato is doing the same thing.

Despite the evident debt to his literary past, Plato is hostile to poetry. When Socrates determines that the poets shall have no place in the ideal city, he alludes to "the ancient feud between poetry and philosophy" (*Republic* 607ᵇ). The Platonic/Socratic objection to the great literary tradition of the Greeks is always astonishing. The criticism so often expressed—in the *Ion,* for instance—that the poets describe material objects and techniques and yet do not create these things or teach others to do so seems grotesquely naive. Yet ignoring the literal argument, Socrates is, as usual, concerned with the power of language—what it can do and what it cannot—and concerned with the relationship between a material object and its description. Moreover, he is concerned with the relation between the object imagined by the poet and that imagined by the auditor or reader via the word.

Furthermore, Plato and Socrates were heirs to a poetic tradition that used myths which, if taken literally, were offensive to a refined system of morals and ethics. Xenophanes and others already raised objections to the extreme anthropomorphism in myth, to the portrayal of gods as flawed humans. One can understand the Platonic/Socratic objection to a poetic tradition based on myths which ascribe the inherent indifference of nature to various psychological reactions of the anthropomorphized deities. For nature, when anthropomorphized, can only seem vicious, whimsical, or uncaring. It is also true that tragic drama and the *Iliad* presume a world in which death triumphs, in which the good man is inevitably destroyed despite whatever he might do. Now, Socrates invariably posits an essentially benign universe, one in which right choice leads to happiness and in which man is by nature good. The search for The Good would make no sense if Socrates predicated human action upon the tragic sense of life. Thus the tragic poets—and it is against them that the animus is largely directed—must leave the ideal city.

The larger objection to the tragic poets certainly rests upon the conflict between what Plato was trying to do and the claims made by literature in the culture of the Athenians. The tragedians were acknowledged as public teachers; Homeric epics were memorized in the schools. Before the rise of logical discourse and analytic prose, poetry was *the* medium for the expression of ideas. Apart from the inevitable limits imposed by the diction and style of poetry, there remains the considerably more significant problem that oral epic and tragedy demand instant and unquestioning empathy from their audiences. Empathy such as this inhibits the development of self-awareness so necessary to an intellectual's thought process. It is the very opposite to the unending search for a refinement in definition which marks the Socratic method.

Yet one cannot help feeling that at the very bottom of Plato's combativeness lies jealousy. The dialogues are not all that different from the literature he objects to; they, too, take the reader in and demand that he submit to Socrates, who is as manipulative as any contrivance of the theater. Yet as Plato gradually eliminated him from the dialogues, it is possible that he grew to understand the danger in the seductive metaphor that Socrates presented. One of the most memorable scenes of any dialogue is the concluding one of the *Symposium,* itself the most exciting literary piece of them all. The narrator has been asleep after having drunk too much at a late night party. He awakens toward dawn to find everyone passed out except for Socrates, Aristophanes, and Agathon, the tragic poet. The three of them were sitting together, Socrates in the middle, drinking out of a common goblet, which they passed back and forth. Socrates was holding forth with the argument that the genius of comedy was the same as that of tragedy and that the true artist of comedy was an artist of tragedy as well. The other two were too sleepy and drunk to argue, and as they slowly drifted off to sleep, they drowsily agreed. The truth of the assertion is, of course, the *Symposium* itself.

The tragic protagonist and antagonist become in Platonic dialogue

Socrates and his opponent Sophist. Tragic Necessity (*Anangke*), which finally is so horribly revealed as the inflexible rhythm of events which brings the hero to his destruction, becomes the divine reason, the first principles, which exist immutable and independent of humankind, like mathematics, there to be apprehended through dialectic. The young men who are disembarrassed of their illusions in dialogue after dialogue are like the tragic heroes who, brought to ruin from their high and prosperous estate, must say at the end of the action, "Now I understand." Yet the amused tone Socrates brings to the proceedings, his loving irony as he skirmishes with his discomfited opponents, brings to mind the jousting between the young and the triumphant old in Aristophanic comedy. As Socrates dismisses the commonly held notions of the day, going further and further from what seems probable, the pursuit of The Good is no different from the elusive, wacky schemes pursued by the comic hero. Socrates is somewhat like Don Quixote except that what seems to be a chimera is finally shown to be—at least to those who will courageously launch themselves on the wings of reason—the inevitable truth of the matter.

The *Symposium* commences in an unusual way. Apollodorus is speaking to an unnamed auditor (who must become the reader), and he is telling him that a friend, Glaucon, had once asked him to describe the speeches made in praise of love at an evening drinking party at the house of Agathon. Glaucon had heard of them from a certain Phoenix, but the account had been poor. Apollodorus had to tell Glaucon that these speeches had been made in the days of their youth, that he knew them himself only through the account of Aristodemus, the very same man who had told Phoenix, but that he had later checked some of the details with Socrates. At Glaucon's request, Apollodorus is willing to recount what he remembers having heard from Aristodemus. Thus the reader is not only two removes from an event far distant in time, but is continually reminded of it by the grammar of the dialogue. The Greek language habitually expresses indirect statement in a manner relatively obsolete in English, that is, "He heard him to have said." Apollodorus is telling what he told Glaucon, which Aristodemus had told Apollodorus. The sentence structure employing so many infinitives marks distance between the reader of this dialogue and the actual long gone event.

The deliberate air of mystery imposed by this method of narration works well with the underlying structure of the piece. A series of men give speeches in praise of love; each speech has a different viewpoint, but moves the group along to a fuller understanding of love until finally Socrates, who is the last speaker, gives a lengthy account of the words of Diotima, a wise woman of Mantinea. Now the reader has what Apollodorus told Glaucon he heard from Aristodemus, who had heard from Socrates what Diotima said. It is as though these were the stages of initiation, and finally the mysteries are delivered by the high priestess. Note that it is a *woman* at this typically all-male gathering who delivers the authoritative account. The initial speech was in praise of homoerotic love naturally, and throughout the love of beautiful boys is an unspoken assumption. The movement from earthly love to the transcendent desire for beauty and The Good is a transformation accomplished by the entrance of a feminine presence. The sanctity of the reproductive process, whether of crops or of babies, was enshrined in representations of women in ancient Greece. Thus it is both natural and religiously true for the essence of the ineffable combination of desire, creation, beauty, and goodness to be expressed through the words and understanding of a woman.

Agathon, in whose home the evening reception takes place, is a tragic dramatist who has just won the prize. The victory celebration has taken place the night before, and many of the guests are hung over. Therefore the evening—at least the first part of it—is devoted to talking seriously rather than to drinking and humor. Flute girls and courtesans are sent away. This will be an all-male conversation. Agathon is a figure known through Aristophanic parodies, this account, and various other notices. While it is hard to determine, one might say that, unlike the majority of his compatriots who take on the obligatory young male beloved, he is what is today considered gay, having a lifelong erotic interest in males. Phaedrus and Pausanias, who are also present at this evening party, are lovers from the days of their boyhood, but probably in conventional Athenian terms; that is, their physical relationship and friendship represent masculine bonding, which does not inhibit their regular pursuits of heterosexual life. Alcibiades, who appears at the close, has for a long time been enamored of Socrates, who in turn has found the handsome, brilliant, passionate, if self-indulgent and wayward young aristocrat highly attractive. The paradox is that Socrates and Alcibiades evidently do not engage in sexual relations and that Alcibiades, who is young and beautiful, loves the old and ugly Socrates. Of course, the relationship is exactly true to how Plato/Socrates describe the transcendent experience of desire for the eternal, immaterial good and the beautiful. That is, Alcibiades loves Socrates' soul with a passion not unlike holy enthusiasm.

Toward the start, when Socrates arrives, he is invited by Agathon to lie down next to him. Men typically reclined on low benches around serving tables at Athenian eating and drinking parties. There were two men to a bench and, as ancient vases suggest, it was common for an older man, shown to be bearded, to share the bench with a beardless youth. Given the values of Athenian culture, the inherently erotic nature of this arrangement is obvious, especially when the evening was given over to drinking. The beautiful Agathon flirts with Socrates, saying that he wished that in touching him he might acquire some of his wisdom. Socrates responds by taking up the idea of filling up another person with wisdom as one fills a vessel. Again the inherently erotic setting of the evening, as well as the reader's knowledge of the common practice of an older man ejaculating into a younger man in anal intercourse, gives the words special meaning.

With these words the utterly serious idea of the relationship between physical desire for a fine male's beautiful body and the spiritual desire for transcendent beauty and goodness begins to be established. The reader is engaged erotically by this scene as well as by the final scene. In this way he himself may experience the pangs of carnal desire that are translated into cerebral imaginings, themselves transcendent over the physical events, because he is not involved in a physical experience but rather aroused by words, passed through the mouth and ears of so many over so long a span of time to reach him.

The scene builds to Socrates' account of Diotima's speech. She describes the journey of the soul from the carnal love of a beautiful boy to the transcendent love of beauty and the good. This has been the journey of the evening as each speech has added a nuance in describing love. Dramatically, however, the climax follows with the arrival of the drunken, glamorous Alcibiades, whose love for Socrates drives him mad. Socrates remains coolly and amusedly ironic and detached throughout. The last we see of him is during his morning drinking with Agathon and Aristophanes. Apollodorus's account of Aristodemus's account ends with, "First Aristophanes nodded off, then at the break of dawn, Agathon. Socrates laid them out to sleep, got up and went away. . . . At the Lyceum Socrates took a bath and passed the day as usual. In the evening he went to his own home to rest."

Like Oedipus who meets his destiny in the grove at Colonus in a thunderclap, Socrates, the tragic hero, comes courageously to the final truth as revealed by Diotima. Like the comic old man who triumphs over all others, Socrates drinks Aristophanes and Agathon under the table. Like transcendent goodness and beauty, he receives the attentions of the drunken Alcibiades but will not submit to him. He continues into the day without sleep, without a hangover, in complete control, like the mathematical principles laid up in heaven which cannot be changed by the accidents of this terrestrial experience. As Plato conceives him in these dialogues, Socrates himself is an ancient Greek version of the Incarnation.

CHAPTER NINE

Alexandria: The New Athens

in Egypt, land of diverse tribes, graze
many pedants, fenced in, hugely arguing
in the Muses' wicker cage.

fragment from a poem by Timon

The failure to win the war with Sparta canceled Athenian pretensions to greatness. Athens lost an empire and the tribute money that
had provided the material support for its cultural vitality. The ever-
incomplete evidence seems to show a real decline in production in all
the arts. It is often supposed that this is due to a loss of faith in the
city-state, the Olympian gods whose cults had supported it, and the
public festivals that had articulated it, brought on by the loss of the
war and the decline in prosperity.

It is common to mark the distinction between the fifth and fourth
centuries and to forget that this arbitrary system of numbering the
years is based on the much later Christian era. For the Athenians of
the time, the turning point was the onset of the Peloponnesian War
(431); they looked back with nostalgia to the time before it. The
period thereafter was all the same, a succession of power plays and
land grabs among the city-states which grew more hectic and weari-
some after Athens's defeat. Sparta's attempts at control brought in
Persia as her silent ally; Thebes grew stronger and entered the arena;
Athens recovered and tried to reclaim her losses. The arrival of Philip
of Macedon in the area of these city-states (350) eventually put an end
to their wars and to an identifiable period that had begun with the
Peloponnesian War. Athens was no longer a place for celebration.
Like many another great city in later centuries, the city turned inward
and backward and, as time went by, became a quiet university town
patronized by the sons of the Roman ruling class.

The remarkable feature of what is designated the fourth century is the emergence of the philosophical schools. This should not be neatly tucked into the fourth century either, however. Socrates, who inspired so many of the school men, lived his entire life in the fifth century, and Plato was about thirty when Socrates was executed in 399, at the very beginning of this so-called new century.

Athens exhausted its resources utterly in the decade 415–405. First came the loss of fleet and experienced crew at Syracuse in Sicily. The fleet was rebuilt, but there was never again such a crew. Persia funded a fleet for Sparta, which put Athens's overseas food supply lines in jeopardy and gave her tributary cities the courage to revolt. Despite some naval victories that recovered these cities, the destruction of the fleet at Aegospotami was simply the final depletion. The Athenians were forced to surrender.

Athens, of course, continued to be a great city after the battle of Aegospotami partly because the Spartans, who are too frequently cast as the ancient world's thugs, vetoed the urgent pleas of the Thebans at the conference of victors to sack and destroy the city. Athens survived but changed considerably. In the last years of the war the frequently precarious fate of the fleet while away from home port meant that the political strength of the absent rowers was undermined. It was they who were the beneficiaries and thus the most ardent supporters of the open democracy, which was now beset with oligarchic schemes to overthrow it in favor of a government with considerably more limited suffrage.

An eloquent expression of the hostility of the propertied class to the common man is preserved in a document known as *The Old Oligarch,* authorship unknown but commonly ascribed to Xenophon, whose writings betray a similar, if less vehement, class bias. (It was Xenophon who said that anyone whose occupation forced him to work "seated and in the shade was liable to be weakened in body as well as soul" [*On Household Affairs* 4.2].) The old gentleman complains about the hurly-burly of downtown Athens, where slaves push the gentry to the side and where one can hear a bastard mix of dialects common to no city. At the same time he ruefully acknowledges the extraordinary energy of this commercial seaport. Athens was a society of rich and poor with very few in the middle. Rich and poor of the time were pretty well defined by work; those who worked were poor; those who did not were rich. The bourgeois idea of work as an obligation undertaken as self-justification or self-expression was not an ancient Athenian conceit. Centuries earlier Hesiod pointed out in his *Works and Days* that Zeus made man work for his survival as a punishment, and no Greek ever appeared to challenge that notion.

The collapse of the empire diminished the economic life of Athens. At the same time agriculture declined throughout mainland Greece as soil was depleted and as invading armies of various city-states ravaged farms as they tried to fill the vacuum of power created by Athenian losses. The fourth century was as filled with war as the fifth, but there was more shifting of power centers. Mercenary soldiery was a significant new development of the time as the males of the impoverished rural population rented themselves out to foreign armies. This phenomenon was related to the increased professionalism of the military everywhere. The generals in Athens in this time were nothing like the amateur Pericles, Cleon, or Nicias, this last whose irresolute leadership at Syracuse was largely responsible for the heavy Athenian losses. And when in exile, as they so often were, these truly professional military men formed the leadership required in the mercenary armies.

Despite evidence for a real decline in the cultural life of the *polis* and in its economic and political strength, the constitution of Athens was stable during this period of time. Changes to it, such as the introduction of payment for attendance at the assembly, were few and on the whole beneficial to the democracy.

Much of fourth-century literature survives in fragments; we have names but no texts. The survival of great numbers of speeches designed for the law courts or for the assembly suggests that the real flowering of this period was not in the genres associated with the fifth century but in rhetoric. Thus it is customary to call this the century of prose as the fifth century was the century of poetry. These speeches are without question of the utmost importance for the glimpse they give of the everyday life of the time. It is remarkable how very perilous public life was; few men escaped trial and eventual condemnation, whether in the form of fines, exile, or death, in the political maneuvering in Athens.

The speeches of Demosthenes, who warned against the territorial ambitions of the Macedonian king Philip, are passionate pleas for liberty which have become classic by virtue of their influence on the Roman Cicero and through him Europeans of the Enlightenment. The reputation of rhetoric, which suffers so under the scorn of Plato in his dialogues, is amply restored in these speeches, which are testimony to the intelligence, aesthetics, and moral sensibility of the men who composed them. It is doubtful, however, whether Macedonian hegemony was the novelty or threat that Demosthenes made it out to be. The city-states had ample experience of overlordship from the times of Croesus, who had made himself master of the Greek cities in Asia Minor. Athens itself ruled over the islands of the Aegean, or at least exacted tribute and demanded political conformity, for much of the fifth century. As it turned out, the Macedonians never dominated the mainland cities to the extent that their local civic character was extinguished. Their rule was nothing like that of the Ptolemies in Egypt or the Seleucids in Asia Minor. But Philip will ever have his reputation because of the eloquence of Demosthenes.

In particular the virtues of rhetoric were championed by Isocrates, who was by profession a rhetorician, speech writer, and teacher of oratory. Because he was born with a weak voice, he had no career in the assembly or law courts himself, but was forced to withdraw, first as a writer for other men, then as their teacher. He founded a school in 393, which presumably gave him the chance to form a more objective, intellectual view of the rhetorician's role. At its worst, rhetoric is paid hack writing. At its best, it is the art of verbal clarification—of explaining, persuading, and revealing the truth as precisely as possible.

Speeches and essays survive from Isocrates which demonstrate an overriding concern with the fate of Hellenic civilization. Hitherto the Greek city-states, which had their own local religious cults, dialects, and other manifestations of parochialism and were furthermore at war with each other, acknowledged few things in common beyond the Olympian gods, Homer, and their language. The important fact of the fourth century is the decline of the city-state and the resultant political fragmentation. The move to consolidate Greek-speaking peoples into one self-conscious cultural and political entity, a rudimentary nation, was a natural result of the invasion and dominance of the Greek mainland by Philip, the king of Macedonia, who achieved through political, diplomatic, and military stratagems what Isocrates was endorsing in his writings—Panhellenism. To the horror and disgust of Demosthenes, Philip was the specter, the self-serving tyrant, who would end the liberty of the city-state; to Isocrates, Philip was the savior and the rejuvenator of Greek civilization, which was in danger of being dominated by the Persians. Isocrates was the first to refine and elaborate what can be sensed in the pages of Herodotus; he is, in fact, the first person to articulate the idea of civilization or the culture of a people.

Although Isocrates was a student of Socrates, his perspective came to be very different from that of his fellow student, Plato. The fragments of his *Against the Sophists,* for instance, seem to show that Isocrates objected to Plato and Socrates for their bias toward metaphysical solutions or definitions and for their indifference to the facts of this world and to the givens in the human condition. That Isocrates had been a writer of law court speeches shows up in his emphasis on pragmatics and on the facts of the contemporary situation. It was this approach that Isocrates translated from the law court in developing a conception of Greek civilization that he sets up in opposition to that of Persia. He undertook to define the way of life of the Hellenes and to abstract it for its values, rather than pose some ideal human and an ideal life. In this way he made the Greek cultural experience the ideal, which in turn led the way to its elevation over all others. When Philip's son Alexander took over the throne and began his conquest of all the peoples from Persia through to India, the stage was set for Greece to become part of a much larger world system. The survival of Greek culture in the succeeding centuries is owed in part to the ideology of civilization with which the ruling and intellectual elites were imbued by figures such as Isocrates.

Creating an abstraction of the city in the idea of civilization is but one of the several responses to the fact of the decline of the city-state. Much of Plato's surviving philosophical works indicate his intense concern for the failure of the city-state. Born into an aristocratic Athenian family in 429, Plato by rights should have been an important figure in the assembly. The debacle of the Peloponnesian War, his family's close involvement in the failed aristocratic takeover of 411, and his own aversion to the workings of an extreme democracy combined to make him reject this ambition. Instead he turned his back on the city and moved to the suburbs, where in a park dedicated to the god Academus in 387 Plato established a school, known to the world as the Academy, which survived until A.D. 529, when it was permanently closed by the zealously Christian emperor Justinian.

Plato writes political theories into many of his works. In the *Crito* he has Socrates argue for the total allegiance of a person to the laws of his community, urging that the superior rights of the state are coincident with the birth of its citizens. In effect it is Sophocles' Creon from the *Antigone* gone completely respectable, arguing against the ethically suspect Crito, Plato's Antigone. This identification of citizen and city supports the notion in his *Republic* that an examination of an ideal or actual city will reveal the workings of the human soul and intellect. The identification of person with state is further cemented in his *Laws,* which is an idealized law code designed to represent in its encouragements and prohibitions the true and ideal behavior of any person. Unlike Isocrates, however, Plato does not argue from observable custom or the evolved political experience of his people, but rather from a series of *a priori* truths. In describing an ideal city-state Plato does not betray any awareness of the true decline of the city-state or of the emergence of larger units of governance and society. For his purposes the city-state of his youth, and—as time dims actual memory—of his imagination, remains the only model structure on which he can build.

While starting out possessed of an otherworldly bias he never altogether lost, Aristotle, Plato's most famous student, made observation and description the cornerstone of his methodology. He may have learned these intellectual habits from his father, who was a doctor, because they characterize the medical writings of the so-called Hippocratic School. Born and raised in Macedonia, Aristotle entered Plato's academy as a student and stayed on as a resident scholar until Plato's death in 347. Four years later he was invited by Philip of Macedon to tutor his son, Alexander, at the court in Pella. Thereafter he returned to Athens and founded his own school in 335 near a grove sacred to Apollo Lyceius, from which comes the word "lyceum."

Aristotle's dialogues have not survived; much of what does amounts to "in-house" pieces. Aristotle's work is far different from Plato's. His own work on cities, for instance, shows the different approach. Tradition tells us that he parceled out among his researchers the task of gathering data which were made up into monographs on the governance of the major Greek city-states of his time. Apart from the *Constitution of the Athenians,* the authorship of which is much disputed, these do not survive. On the basis of the information that was gathered for him, he wrote a work entitled *The Workings of Cities (Politics).* Despite what this title suggests, Aristotle, like Plato, did not think in terms other than the city-state, this despite his personal experience of the Macedonian court. Yet his observation in other matters was far-ranging; he studied and described the function of the body, plant life, human ethical systems, language, logic, and so on.

Aristotle also studied the literature of the Greeks. His *Poetics,* which, unfortunately, survives only in part, is the first extended discussion of literary production. It is an ambiguous document, written in so abbreviated and cryptic a style as to seem more like his lecture notes or what some student took down in class than a polished essay. It is hardly a masterful survey of literature. On the subject of tragedy, for instance, Aristotle frequently uses Sophocles' *Oedipus the King* and Euripides' *Iphigenia in Tauris* to illustrate his points. This habit has had the particularly unfortunate result of leading later readers into thinking that Sophocles' *Oedipus* is *the ideal* tragedy when it is, of course—as Aristotle, the scientific observer, would surely have been the first to acknowledge—only one specimen among many. The probable cause for Aristotle's persistent reference to these two plays is that they were revived in his time and were thus useful illustrations because everyone in the lecture hall was familiar with them (keep in mind that reading materials were minimal).

Whatever confusions Aristotle's style may engender, there is one monumental misunderstanding of the *Poetics* that is solely the product of its readers. As in his other writings Aristotle describes literary production, principally epic poetry and tragic drama (other parts of the treatise have not survived). What he does *not* do is to prescribe. Everything he says is offered without judgment, on the basis of observation. Such, however, is the authority of tradition, of texts, and of Greek antiquity that centuries of writers and critics have felt the obligation to subscribe to the usage he presents noncommittally as though it were law. They do so no doubt in part because of the strictures on genre classification and on decorum which were laid down by the Alexandrians and which the Romans took up and bequeathed to the Western world.

Platonic metaphysical speculation and Aristotelian science were two reactions to the decline of the *polis* and the increasing obsolescence of the state gods. There is fragmentary evidence of other disenchantment with the legacy of the city-state. The commonplace question "What city are you from?" is reported to have elicited the entirely unorthodox response, "I am a citizen of the universe." "Nature did not make a slave, but man and his society," is another comment of the times. The culturally defined inferiority of women was being questioned, something at which Euripides hints already in the late fifth century. So far does Aristotle stray from the normal Athenian imperatives of the fifth century that he concludes his *Nicomachean Ethics* by declaring that a life of contemplation is to be valued over the social and political life.

Considerably greater alienation can be found in the behavior and sayings of Diogenes, who was called "the Cynic" (derived from the Greek for "dog") for his rejection of all convention and his freedom from shame. His contempt for public opinion was outrageous; his wit and independence truly admirable. His sayings recorded in the pages of Diogenes Laertius are often as clever as they are intelligent, and always shocking, set against the conventional attitudes of the time. He did not found a philosophical school or make a theology. He preached that freedom from suffering came when dependence on externals was jettisoned. By his example, as a beggar in rags, living the life of poverty, he taught his followers. His asceticism, however, did not include chastity. He acknowledged sexual desire and wanted it freed from social, economic, and political constraints.

Diogenes' follower Crates was the teacher of Zeno, who founded the single most important philosophical system of the ancient world, one that became almost a religion to the thinking class in the Roman world. Stoicism was simply the most notable in a trend toward personal philosophies that appeared late in the fourth century. Epicureanism was the other principal philosophy which, along with Stoicism, constituted the major theology of the Greeks in subsequent centuries, flourishing side by side with magic, astrology, and various mystery religions.

Stoicism is the name given to the teachings of the Phoenician Zeno, who came to Athens in 313 as a student and stayed on to lecture. This he did in a public hall in a gallery called the Stoa Poikile (whence the name Stoicism) because as a foreigner he could not buy land where he could establish a school. Stoicism was very popular from the start; Zeno even attracted the friendship of King Antigonus Gonatas. Disciples of Zeno brought the doctine across the Mediterranean. In Rome, where the ethical propositions of Stoic doctrine found greater support, this doctrine became almost a personal religion. Stoicism colored all native Roman attempts at philosophy, as can be seen again and again in the texts of Cicero. So fragmentary, in fact, are the original Greek sources for the modern knowledge of Stoicism that historians must rely on the Latin materials. The question arises, how much has Greek Stoicism been Romanized?—a question for which there is no easy answer.

Zeno, although he created a complete philosophical system, was most influential in his ethical doctrine, especially at Alexandria and among the Romans. His ethics are based on a belief in a universe that is governed by *logos* (reason), which traditionally was identified with the gods or destiny or some kind of fire. Everything in this universe possesses to some degree something of this divine fire or *logos*. At the core of every human, therefore, is something of the divine. Wisdom is all; to live in harmony with this divine *logos* is the only good. Nothing else matters. No person, therefore, is to be influenced by pain or death or riches or poverty or joy or sorrow or sexual fulfillment or sexual denial. These are merely accidents to the outer shell, the body, which houses the divine spark, fire, or essence. Clearly enough, Zeno was influenced by Plato/Socrates in his search for some absolute that would not be subject to the accidents of the empirical world and by the Milesian School in trying to save matter.

Epicurus, whose name is given to his system of beliefs, settled in Athens a decade after having been a student there. In 307 when he was in his early thirties he bought a house with a very large and beautiful garden, which became the headquarters of his teaching and the residence for his followers. They were a determinedly private group who excited envy and derision by virtue of their exclusiveness and their supposed never-ending search for pleasure and the good life. In fact, they practiced considerable asceticism as part of that very pursuit of pleasure. The group was also highly unusual in that it included women and slaves. The doctrines of Epicurus are poorly preserved, and one must turn to the Roman Lucretius, whose *De Rerum Natura* is both an attempt to introduce the Romans to Epicurean doctrine and an attempt to use it as support for a number of propositions put forward by himself. Thus one is never sure of what is Epicurus and what is Lucretius.

Epicurus founded his thinking upon the atomic theory of Democritus, who argued that the universe is made up of indestructible and unchanging atoms that rain down in a never-deviating, never-ending course. Epicurus did not deny the existence of the traditional Olympian gods, but argued that they lived beyond the universe, indifferent to its workings or the human beings who inhabited it. Man's supreme obligation is to find pleasure so as to live happily. This he will do by avoiding pain, which comes principally from want. Thus it behooves one to limit his wants, hence the asceticism. Furthermore, a quiet and retired life frees one from the emotional shocks of ambition and aggression. A belief in a mechanistic universe frees one from fear of death and from the arbitrary interference of deity. Contemplating pleasure surpasses realizing pleasure; hence a contemplative life is superior to an active life.

Both Stoicism and Epicureanism address inevitability and helplessness, hallmarks of the emergent era. As Alexander pushed his conquests to the East and brought Greeks into an ever-widening circle of experience, the comfortable horizon of village and neighborhood disappeared. The parochial identification between an individual and his city-state diminished even as local dialects began to give way to *koine*, the one common language. The cities themselves underwent a physical transformation with the development of city planning. A rational grid of streets which defied the natural contours of the land replaced roads formed from traditional pathways. What is more, the new urban design could be exported, laid down anywhere; excavated remains show that Hellenistic cities looked alike. These trends produced a certain impersonality before which the individual was beginning to feel lost.

The monarchies that sprang up following the death of Alexander produced an impersonal political arrangement. The Greeks who had either been settled in Egypt by Alexander or had migrated there were heirs to the city-state government by assembly and committee and now had to live in an absolutist political system utterly foreign to them. The Ptolemaic dynasty had taken over the systematic exploitation of the people and the land which the Pharaohs originated. It was an extraordinarily pervasive system of control, extending from the centralized royal court through a vast network of royal agents to the smallest hamlets. An efficient bureaucracy of staggering proportions made the system run. These arrangements did not provide an arena for the significant individual act. How distant to the men of the third century the traditional hero figures must have seemed. Those epic and tragic characters were autonomous, lonely individuals whom poets celebrated and gods loved or hated and whose actions fell like stones in water, making a circle of reaction ever extending further.

This distance between centuries-old literary pieces and the new audience was reinforced in the intellectual and creative life of Alexandria by the establishment of the Library and Mouseion, which gave impetus to the further objectification of the literature. These institutions were the creation of Demetrius of Phaleron, who was invited to Alexandria by Ptolemy. The city of Alexandria in the third century became the new center of literary production for the Greek-speaking people, a city deliberately fostered in its cultural ambitions by Ptolemy.

After Alexander conquered Egypt, he undertook in 331 B.C. to build a city in the very west of the Nile delta, a superb location between Lake Mareotis and the sea. He named it Alexandria. From the start it had a Greek population alongside native Egyptians. It attracted other ethnic groups, such as Jews from the lands to the northeast, and soon became polyglot as well as prosperous. At Alexander's death in 323 his general Ptolemy seized the power in Egypt for himself, and in order to rule it effectively, he created a royal dynasty modeled on the centuries-old native Egyptian tradition of the Pharaohs. The Ptolemaic line survived until 31 B.C., when Cleopatra VIII committed suicide after the battle of Actium along with her paramour and political and military colleague, Antony, in order to prevent her people from rising up in rebellion against their new Roman master, Octavian Caesar, later better known as Augustus.

Ptolemy I wanted a city that would rival Athens in its greatest moments. Here in a vast sea of Egyptians, not to mention the other non-Greek populations, a small coterie of Greeks produced a literature for the relatively small community of their fellow immigrant Greeks. Its reference was to the Greek world outside of Egypt and to the past. This colonial culture ignored the locals; as in other colonial cultures in other times, its creators were incestuous, introspective, elitist, and alienated. Instead of life lived, their preoccupation was with culture perceived.

The consequences for the Western world were great. In the middle of the third century there came to Rome one Livius Andronicus, a Greek from the Greek city of Tarentum, located in what is now southern Italy. As a schoolmaster he despaired of any proper literary models for his schoolboys and undertook to translate the *Odyssey* for them into Latin. Thus began Roman infatuation with things Greek and the Romans' initial oppression by the vastly superior Greek literature.

As they became masters of the Greek world, the Romans eventually outgrew their feelings of inferiority and became proud of their many and pervasive cultural achievements. Still, much that they took from the Alexandrians stayed with them, not least a self-conscious attitude toward literature. Subsequently their adoption and transmission of so many of the principles of aesthetics and criticism formulated by the Alexandrians found their way through the Italian Renaissance into the mainstream of Western thought. These ideas were the backbone of Western literature until the Romantics cast them aside in the nineteenth century. This was not long after their political counterparts, the French revolutionaries, killed their king, thereby effectively ending an equally ancient tradition, the philosophy of the divine right of kings. This, too, had its origin in Alexandria in the third century B.C., when philosophers were attempting to help their fellow Greeks stomach the idea of Alexander's merely human general, Ptolemy, becoming a god as Pharaoh of Egypt.

The Mouseion (our word "museum"), which Demetrius of Phaleron founded, was a cult center for the Muses, an institution already having a long history in Greece, where the association of the Muses and literature was as old as Homer and Hesiod. Functioning somewhat as a medieval monastery or a twentieth-century think tank, the Mouseion provided a workshop and a place of association for men in the service of literature.

The Library, however, was relatively novel. At Athens, Demetrius had studied with Aristotle's successor as head of the Lyceum, Theophrastus. Far more pragmatic than Aristotle, Theophrastus had abandoned the pursuit of first principles and final causes to concentrate upon the accession of knowledge. Aristotle left behind a vast array of factual material, the data for his published treatises, which needed codification. Furthermore, warfare was growing more dependent upon machinery and technology, which in turn depended upon research. These were the imperatives of the Lyceum under Theophrastus's direction. This was the model for the Library, which along with the Mouseion, Demetrius founded in 297.

The Mouseion provided collectivity and intellectual intimacy. This is the atmosphere in which a coterie, with its demands of exclusiveness, loyalty, and obedience, often develops. The tradition of the quarrel between Callimachus and Apollonius and their penchant for quoting or referring to each other betoken the kind of incestuous relationship that is the hallmark of a coterie. The fragment of Timon with which this chapter begins is an expression of this. Two of Theocritus's poems, the thirteenth and the twenty-second Idylls, closely parallel passages at the end of the first book and the beginning of the second of Apollonius's *Argonautica,* showing the cooperation, emulation, or competition in a closely knit literary group. Given the fragmentary nature of the evidence for literary production at the time it is not unreasonable to assume that there was a great deal more similarity between the works of Mouseion frequenters. The Mouseion may have been the Alexandrian Bloomsbury.

The Library was much enlarged under Ptolemy II and at its greatest contained several hundred thousand papyrus rolls. To get some idea of its size, remember that each book of the *Iliad* was copied onto a roll; the Homeric poems would fill forty-four rolls in the Library. This great Library was one of the acknowledged wonders of the ancient world; Athens had no large civic library until the second century; nor did Pergamon, the cultural center of the Attalid dynasty, and that which finally was built never contained more than two hundred thousand rolls. The Alexandrian Library was also a reflection of the enormous rise in a reading public that characterized the Hellenistic age.

With the invention of the alphabet at the end of the eighth century B.C., writing commenced. The first evidence for it is the publication of decrees inscribed in stone; an at least modestly literate public must be assumed for this practice. Nonetheless the evidence suggests that what was written as literature was invariably meant to be delivered orally. Written texts for individual readers do not seem to have been at all common before the end of the fifth century. Euripides was supposed to have had a personal collection of books. Socrates in the *Apology* tells his jury that they can find out the difference between his ideas and those of Anaxagoras by reading about the latter's in a book to be obtained from a bookseller. But reading probably was not common practice.

By the mid–fourth century, however, Aristotle mentions books that were meant to be read, not recited. Evidence from papyrus finds and excavated small private library buildings demonstrates that in the third century education became more and more widespread. At the same time readers were divided between the truly well educated and the class of general readers. In response to the needs of the latter group, there appeared for the first time the man of letters, the critic, persons who wrote because it was pleasant and profitable, not because they were driven to it by high seriousness or holy enthusiasm. Markets were large; a reading public and patron kings made writing prestigious. The names of more than a thousand writers from the Hellenistic centuries survive. Oddly enough, very little of this enormous literary production survives with them. Most writers fell victim to the same spirit that had elicited the increase in writing in the first place. That is, those who read as a narcotic pastime tended to want it easy; hence the era was marked by the spread of abridged versions, anthologies, school texts, and the like. Much was truncated, much discarded, on what canon of taste we really do not know.

One of the principal works associated with the Library was a list entitled *Tables of Persons Eminent in Every Branch of Learning Together with a List of Their Writings,* a work of scholarship undertaken by the poet Callimachus. This encyclopedic catalogue was part of the process whereby the Alexandrian Greeks began to bring their literary past under control, to gain a mastery of it and an awareness that marks a turning point in Western literary history. Although Callimachus's *Tables* is lost, ancient scholarly references to it suggest that Callimachus was very particular with his classifications as well as his verification of the authenticity of the works he listed. The keys to understanding the literature of the Alexandrian Age are facts, authenticity, and classification.

The scholarship of the Library centered on the Homeric texts. Because the *Iliad* and the *Odyssey* enjoyed such widespread popularity, many cities, wealthy individuals, aristocrats, and kings possessed texts of the poems. These texts were not at all identical; extra lines appeared in some, lines were missing in others, and there were variations in dialect, diction, and spelling. Scholars at the Library proceeded to create authoritative texts of the poems. The establishment of a genuine text depends upon a sure and intuitive grasp of the Homeric manner, what was true to it, and what was not. Only a glimpse remains of the preoccupations of these third-century scholars from marginal comments left on the manuscripts by subsequent generations. It is clear that propriety is the overriding consideration. But then it is not altogether clear whether propriety means what Homer would or would not have been likely to say or what in the opinion of any particular critic ought or ought not to be said in epic poetry.

There were many criteria. When the scholar Zenodotus altered lines in which Achilles indicates that his personal glory is the paramount consideration in letting Patroclus go into battle for him, evidently he believed that such naked egoism was false to the spirit of the poem or unsuitable to the ethos of epic poetry. The scholar Aristarchus removed lines describing action that seems to him unduly brutal. Zenodotus offered a two-line substitution for a ten-line passage which had been repeated verbatim from another part of the poem, faithful to the aesthetics of written rather than oral poetry. Aristarchus rejects the lines in which Thetis advises her grieving son to sleep with a woman to get over the loss of Patroclus as unseemly. The great array of citations make clear that the literary circle at Alexandria had very fixed ideas about epic. These changes reflect their preoccupation with genre classification, good taste, and authenticity. It was an age exceedingly self-conscious about literary production. And this self-consciousness is reflected in their poetry. The true subject of Alexandrian poetry is poetry.

It seems that the spokesman for the avant-garde was the poet Callimachus. Born around 305 in the North African city of Cyrene halfway between the Nile delta and present-day Tunisia, he made his way to Alexandria as a young man and taught school in one of its suburbs. Shortly thereafter he was given a position at the Library, where he undertook to make his catalogue. This must have been a stupendous task; the finished work is said to have filled one hundred twenty rolls. More than a simple catalogue, it was literary history, a scientific system of classification and an exhaustive inventory of the Library's contents on its way to being a universal history of recorded knowledge.

Callimachus was productive as a writer. The ancients assert that he composed eight hundred pieces ranging from compilation of fact and scholarship to a variety of experimental poetic pieces. In the surviving fragments of his poems Callimachus calls for poetry made up of only a few lines, a muse peeled down to the subtleties of essence, a sound clear and pure. These notions fit with his use of the images of the clean path, of the priestesses bringing their water from the clear spring and not the muddied river, of the path untrod by the many, of the narrow path where the carts cannot go. The following fragment from his *Aitia* expresses this preoccupation.

> Judge poetry by some critical technique
>   not with a Persian measuring tape.
> Don't expect from me a big-sounding poem;
>   Zeus thunders, not I. . . .
>   [Apollo said to me]
> "Feed the sacrifical beast until fat,
>   keep the Muse fine.
> This I command: where carts have not gone
>   walk there. Drive your chariot
> not in the tracks of others, not on the wide road
>   but on unworn roads, even if your way is narrower."

Homer he calls *eskhatos,* extreme, probably in the sense of beyond comparison; therefore he is not to be imitated. Callimachus disdains the long narrative poem; certainly that is a road too well traveled. The continuous narrative unified by chronology is not for him either ("I hate the cyclic poem"). He wants no epic grandeur ("Zeus thunders, not I"). Hesiod, whom he calls "honey-sweet," is his constantly preferred model. No reasons are given, but the absence of continuous narrative, the brevity relative to Homeric epic, and Hesiod's factual subject matter would recommend him to Callimachus.

Alas, the poetry of Callimachus is poorly preserved, and one must try to form judgments from the necessarily ambiguous fragments. His major piece was the *Aitia* (*Causes*), a poem of seven thousand lines on the subject of the origins or causes of things. Seemingly free of any organizing principle, episodic, a series of vignettes, more a grand catalogue than anything else, the poem reveals the antiquarian mind of the poet, the collector of lore and curiosities. The *Aitia* looks back to Hesoid's *Theogony* in its cataloguelike deployment of information, the loving attention to facts, the play with history. It is the icon of an age in which myth has been displaced by fact, story by list, hero by fate.

The ancients were highly enthusiastic about Callimachus's *Hecale,* which was an experiment in creating what moderns call the *epyllion,* or mini-epic, a literary form that grew to be a favorite among the Romans. In about one thousand lines of hexameter, using a modified form of the diction of Homer, Callimachus tells the story of Theseus killing the bull of Marathon. But that is not really his subject, merely the mythical thread with which to weave quite a different pattern. The story is that Theseus, on his way to kill the bull of Marathon, stops off at the cottage of an old woman named Hecale to seek shelter from a heavy rain. She feeds him and gives him shelter for the night. The next day he continues on, kills the bull, and on his way home stops at Hecale's cottage again only to find that she has died in the interval. In his grief he vows to repay her hospitality by establishing various institutions in her honor.

Traditional epic practice would have required the focus to remain on the male hero and his triumph over the bull. Instead, Callimachus has put these in the background and brought up the old woman, thus changing perspective somewhat. even going so far as to describe fully the meal she served Theseus, in a passage, incidentally, much cherished in antiquity. A brief portion that survives records the conversation of two crows, an exchange more like a moment in fairy tale than a device of the epic convention. Callimachus, by bringing the nonheroic into the poem in the very presence of the hero, is domesticating his narrative. The scene is much like Apollonius's scene of the sailing of the ship *Argo* when he notes that the Centaur Cheiron's wife holds up the infant Achilles to wave good-bye to his father. It is a commonplace fact of myth that Cheiron reared and taught Achilles. Here, startlingly enough, the woman who changes his diapers and feeds him appears in the scene.

Apart from a number of epigrams, six Callimachean hymns survive. They are remarkable for what might be called an amused tone.

This tone could as well be defined by the word *wit* as it was used in the seventeenth century to refer to the elegant or stylish juxtaposition of the incongruous.

The *Hymn to Artemis* is the most obvious example of this manner. Callimachus fashioned his hymns more or less on the model of those known as the Homeric Hymns. These had certain fixed elements: an invocation to the god to whom the hymn is devoted complete with several of his epithets or titles, a description or narrative account of the god's birth, and a list of his powers or attributes. The *Hymn to Artemis* begins as a charming portrait of a little girl (Artemis) on her father's (Zeus) knee, first asking for as many epithets or titles as her brother Apollo has (6–7). She then asks for arrows, ritual title, clothing, maiden attendants, and a city. In this way the poet manages to introduce a variety of the conventional hymnal elements. And he puts in enough homely details to create a portrait of the chatty little girl, too small to reach her father's beard (26ff.), sweet enough to palliate Zeus's problems with dreadful Hera (29–30), yet a tough little miss who once pulled out the hair on the chest of one of the Cyclops. Only the Homeric Hymn to Hermes even begins to approach the amused tone here, and it remains altogether serious, whereas the Callimachean hymn is consistently playful, emphasizing the ridiculous or the absurd. Callimachus is, partly at least, laughing at his medium.

In the *Hymn to Demeter* Callimachus goes still further, combining wit and seriousness. Erysichthon cuts down a tree sacred to Demeter and is punished. This is yet another variant of the myth of the great female goddess and the young male who is destroyed. Demeter punishes him by causing him to hunger without relief. The hymn begins with a reference to the sacred basket and then to Demeter's refusal to eat or drink when she searches for her daughter. It turns from full belly to empty belly. Erysichthon begins to eat without cease. What could be a horror story is made to be immensely funny. Callimachus describes Erysichthon's mother making excuses for her son's disappearance from his friends while he is in the back room gorging. The cooks and the butcher must finally say no to Erysichthon's requests for more food because everything has been cooked, "even the cat before whom the mice used to tremble" (110). The worship of Demeter derives from the very real fear of famine in early societies. Callimachus has given us a harsh, cruel portrait of a compulsive eater, which is also exceedingly humorous to a generation that is not threatened by hunger.

Callimachus's ideal of poetry was fulfilled by Aratus, whose *Phae-nomena,* a poem of 1,154 lines of dactylic hexameters, was essentially the versification of the work of Eudoxus of Cnidus on meteorology. The first part is a description of the heavenly bodies, their names, and celestial positions; the latter part is a curious disquisition in verse on how animals, birds, and nature in general foretell storms. There is a certain charm to this part, whereas the earlier portion seems to depend for its strength on the *tour de force* of versification whereby so much factual information, particularly the intractable proper names, is made to fit into metrical patterns. The unending stream of names generally strikes the modern reader as tedious, but the poem was exceedingly popular among the Greeks and the Romans, probably because of their renewed interest in astrology. Or the appeal may have been the Hesiod-like devotion to hard fact, which was probably what won the approval of Callimachus, who says in one fragment, "I sing nothing false."

Aratus was no isolated phenomenon. Poets wrote cookbooks, books on fishing and medical practice, and compilations of extraordinary rivers. Two poems of Nicander have survived—one on snakes and the treatment of their bites and the other on poisons and their antidotes. The names of snakes and herbals provide a marvelous, exotic sound amid the commonplace poetic diction. Strange visions of reptiles and the vastness of botanical learning make the poems compelling after a fashion. In an age when prose writing had after two centuries become supple enough for any use, it seems odd for prose subjects to appear in verse. Yet Alexandrians must have had a special fascination with fact. The Library was the first repository of fact, the first archive. Fact as fact must itself have offered a means to take control, especially valuable in an age of vastness and impersonality. Fact then would stand beside astrology, magic, mystery religions, and even quietist philosophies or doctrines of resignation as something on which a stance could be made. In any case poems that purveyed fact proliferated.

The Library also encouraged erudition, as is reflected in the 1,474-line epic poem of Lycophron, marked by strange names and queer sounds. Called *Alexandra,* it relates the description by a slave of a prophetic utterance of Cassandra (here called Alexandra). The poem is remarkably obscure. Fifty percent of Lycophron's vocabulary is rare words, ten percent words that occur nowhere else in the extant Greek literature. The patience and tenacity with which the poet assembled the mass of alternative, arcane names for obvious mythological figures is matched by that which the reader must employ to comprehend them. "The centipedes, fair-faced daughters of Phalacra" is a nice image for ships, for instance, but that they were for Paris would be known perhaps only to an encyclopedist who would recognize that Phalacra is the place near Troy where Paris got the wood for his ships. Similarly "the maiden-slaying Thetis" might not be recognizable as the Hellespont except by the pedant who would work out that Thetis, daughter of Neleus, the old man of the sea, stands for the sea here and that "maiden-slaying" refers to the maiden Helle, who drowned in the sea waters presently known as the Hellespont.

Erudition and preciosity can fill important roles in the life of colonials who are in a minority. They provide a formidable barrier to the intrusion and potential takeover by anyone not completely acculturated; they bind the members of the group together tightly; and they make the members of the group self-conscious about their cultural identity. Furthermore, in the larger world scheme where Greek was confronting non-Greek in ever greater numbers, the accumulation of fact in the Library represented the sum total of the Greek experience not to be matched by the bookless, library-less people to the east. It signals the beginning of the triumph of Higher Culture, of life perceived over life lived.

The only glimpse into popular culture of Alexandria comes from seven mimes composed by someone named Herodas or Herondas. Although they are literary compositions (which means among other things that they were composed in Greek), they are said to imitate the very common street mimes of the time. These were small dialogues, witty bits of social commentary, caricature, parody, and extravagant emotion. They must have been like the vaudeville or radio sketches of the early part of the twentieth century. The remarkable feature of Herodas's art is his finished verbal portrait of various characters within these dialogues. He may have been influenced by Theophrastus's study of typical character or something like it.

In his second mime, Herodas portrays a pimp at court trying to exact damages from a man who tried to steal one of his girls. In the fourth, two women are represented as tourists going about in awe at the temple of Asclepius at Cos (one is reminded of the first chorus in Euripides' *Ion* or Theocritus's fifteenth Idyll). In the seventh, Herodas paints a brilliant portrait of a shoe salesman. What Herodas created was far more direct, more obvious than anything in the works of what might be considered the Alexandrian avant-garde. Perhaps they held him in contempt for this directness; fragments of another mime seem to refer to an unhappy reception of his pieces by hostile critics. Many of the street mimes had a strongly Egyptian flavor as did stories of the times. These were naturally in the Egyptian language, but some of them were also in Greek. Critics have wondered why a Greek would have wanted to read this very clearly Egyptian sort of literature. Apart from the obvious chauvinist bias toward Western culture which is inherent in the question, the answer must be that the suffocation of emotion and moral value imposed by the tastemakers of the Library was stultifying and that the average reader of culture and taste wanted something with which he could empathize more easily.

Some of the poems of Theocritus, who was born around the beginning of the century and lived forty years or so, resemble the mimes. Many of his pieces are dramatic sketches portraying simple farmers in a rural setting, which is established with a wealth of detail. He is, however, far more artificial. The collection that survives is curious in that the themes and treatments are quite diverse; indeed, not all of the pieces, which are conventionally known as Idylls, are thought to be by this poet. The eclectic nature of the collection shows a poet who in the best Alexandrian manner is being experimental. The most important are his first eleven poems, which are unified around country themes and constitute the first examples of pastoral poems, which were probably, in fact, Theocritus's invention. This is the penultimate literary invention of the ancient Greeks, the very last being the romance or novel, which is presumed by some scholars to have its origins in this same period, but of which the first example, *Chaereas and Callirhoe,* dates to the late first or early second century A.D.

Theocritus had no institutional position in Alexandria, but his poetic adulation of Ptolemy II Philadelphus implies that he was on some kind of royal stipend. Idyll seventeen, a poem in praise of Ptolemy, is the kind of thing poets in pay turn out. Callimachus, who was a salaried employee of the Library, is far more restrained in his reference to Ptolemy in his *Hymn to Zeus* (85–90). Theocritus in his sixteenth Idyll openly seeks money from Hieron II, tyrant of Syracuse, and at the same time paints a rather nice picture of the unsuccessful mendicant Muses (5–12): "His Graces," as he calls them here, "come home barefoot, complaining. . . . Dejected, they sit, heads between cold knees, down in the empty bottom of his coffers."

Theocritus was a native of Syracuse in Sicily, from which he seems to have gone first to southern Italy, then to the island of Cos in the eastern Aegean, where he spent some time before entering the service of Ptolemy in Alexandria. His Idylls are diverse—some like very small epics or hymns, some like mimes, and some love poems. The most important are the pastoral or bucolic poems because of their novelty and because they have been so influential in the tradition of Western poetry. His successors, Bion and Moschus, if the fragments are any substantial evidence, more consistently exploited the theme of countryside, landscape, rustics, animals, love, and desire and were therefore more influential on such successors as the Roman poet Virgil. Theocritus, however, seems to have invented the genre, and, more important, his pieces survive.

While pastoral as a genre or as a sensibility has never been satisfactorily defined, these first eleven poems share several characteristics. They are miniature dramas. The two rustics who address each other are young, usually beautiful, and usually lovesick for some girl or boy or for each other. They are playful and gentle as they compete with each other in singing or talk over their loves or flirt with one another. Instead of describing passion enkindled, these poems glow with soft beauty. Instead of the heat of eroticism there is the warm bath of sensual contentment even as they bemoan their unrequited love. Yet Theocritus occasionally reminds us of the harsh, efficient sexuality of teenage boys when he puts coarse language in their mouths ("Is the old man still milling that woman?" [Idyll 4.58]; "When I was doing it to you in the ass, you were really in pain. . . . Yeah, well, don't try to bury it any deeper than you did at that session" [Idyll 5.41ff.]).

The descriptions of nature and animals highlight the sharing of experience between man, animal, and nature which diminishes the importance of the human ego, something new to the Greek way of seeing things. There is a kind of neutrality achieved in these poems as though a scrim were placed between the reader and all the objects his imagination is called upon to conjure up. Everything of which Theocritus writes is suffused with poetry. The most distinctive of the pastoral Idylls, known technically as amoebaean, are structured as contests of song between two persons. This structure recalls the commonplace agonistic, dichotomous nature of tragedy or of the Platonic dialogue as well as many other manifestations of antitheses and competition so central to Greek thinking.

Theocritus uses the dactylic hexameter, which is associated with Homer and Hesiod. The ancient literary historians and scholars called Theocritus's pieces "epics," although there is no way of knowing what they meant by that. It could be a classification based on metrical similarity. More probably, though, they are called epics because Theocritus often sets up miniature dramas in his poems with dialogue. It is clear that they are not in the least inspired by Hesiod's *Works and Days*. The harsh realities of farm life have all but disappeared in Theocritus's poems. Nature is celebrated for its beauty rather than its brutality. The pastoral poems express the Epicurean sense of detachment; the emotions, the conflict, and the resolutions are all tamed to the smooth movement of the poetic development. They are a part of it and no more. A similarly insistent artificiality is found in the language Theocritus created for some of these poems. He uses epic dialect at times and also Aeolic and Ionic, dialects with a long literary history. But, more remarkable, for many of his pastoral poems he creates a dialect that is Doric, yet made up of words and forms drawn from the many dialect variations found in Doric. No one ever spoke or sang the Doric he invented. The inherent artificiality of his creation is all the more pronounced in an age when dialects had surrendered to the emergent common Greek language (*koine*). It is a thoroughly Alexandrian literary experiment.

A similar experimental quality marks his first Idyll, which betrays a pronounced Alexandrian self-conscious use of parts to create an unanticipated whole. Thyrsis meets a goatherd who promises him an elegant cup among other things if he will sing a song of Daphnis. Thyrsis agrees, sings the song, and the cup is handed over, all in the brief space of 152 lines. The Daphnis song is eighty-two lines (64–145); the goatherd makes his offer in forty-nine (15–63), of which thirty-four describe the cup (27–60). Theocritus has made a poem that is a diptych. The description of the cup balances in several ways the Daphnis song. The description is far more complex and verbally and imagistically more intriguing than the song. The cup is *worthy* of the song.

The description of the cup, a piece of *ekphrasis,* of which the ancients in general and the Alexandrians in particular were very fond, is as verbal technique the equal of the Daphnis song, which is rendered in a much simpler style, having among other things a refrain. The images on the cup elucidate the prevailing emotion of the Daphnis song. Daphnis is dying of love, but he denies himself out of conviction and so dies. In the song he bids good-bye to the landscape, the wild animals, and love. The mood is one of yearning, and the scenes on the cup reinforce this mood. There are three scenes: a girl set between two courting suitors; an old man angling for fish; and a young boy fashioning a cricket cage beset by two foxes—one after grapes, the other after the lunch in his rucksack. Each of the scenes has to do with appetite. Even the goatherd wants the song, and Theocritus has made the cup so beautiful that the reader and Thyrsis yearn for it. Theocritus has ignored the demands for symmetry which the classical age imposed. He has taken the relatively small account of the cup, structurally less significant than the Daphnis song, and by the richness of his description has given the cup all the focus. It is the cup that establishes a perspective on the rest of the poem. The extreme detail in this poem is akin to Theocritus's characteristic Alexandrian attention to fact. It has been pointed out that there are references to far more plants and trees in the Idylls, and most of them in the pastoral Idylls, than in the whole of Homer. What is more, Theocritus is remarkably accurate in describing both the nature of these botanical specimens and their locale.

In his twenty-fourth Idyll Theocritus uses wit as Callimachus does in his hymns. The twenty-fourth Idyll is meant to be a heroic narrative of the infant Heracles vanquishing the serpents in his crib. Instead it is an amusing and homely account of the behavior of Heracles' father, Amphitryon. He is awakened by Alcmene, rushes to the children's bedroom, and sees that Heracles is in fact not hurt. Then, like any father who has to get up for work the next day and whose wife and children have roused him for nothing from his sleep, "back he went to his bed; he concentrated on his sleep" (63). Theocritus has focused upon the person here as Callimachus does, for instance, in his poem "Bath of Pallas," in which Athena puts out Tiresias's eyes because the lad has seen her nude at her bath. Athena's best friend is Tiresias's mother, Chariclo, and the poet emphasizes this relationship (57–67). When the goddess has blinded the youth, the poet turns to the interesting reaction of Chariclo to her erstwhile friend's ugly gesture and Athena's subsequent response to Chariclo. Here again the Alexandrian sensibility shines forth. The great female goddess, the youthful male's sexual advances (in this myth translated to an innocent glance), and his destruction (here simply blindness) are commonplaces of a myth type; it is the kind of myth that belongs in a hymn such as this. But Callimachus's narrative is really about two friends whose friendship is destroyed.

Theocritus experiments with epic by creating the manner of the very large poem in a few lines. Like Callimachus, he rejects the kind of unity and scale Aristotle describes in early epic poetry. In his thirteenth Idyll, a short piece of only seventy-five lines, he tells how

Hylas, the beloved of Heracles, is snatched away by water nymphs and thereafter sought in anguish by Heracles. Despite the very small scale, Theocritus opens the poem up occasionally to give the sense of epic magnitude—for instance, in the following iterations:

> Heracles never parted from him [Hylas], neither when midday came,
> nor when white-horsed Dawn rode up to the house of Zeus,
> nor when the chirping chickens looked to their bed,
> their mother's wings flapping on the smoke-stained perch.
>
> [10–13]

In the following he uses commonplace epic poetry phrasing to denote the crowd:

> So when Jason, son of Aeson, sailed after the Golden
> Fleece, the best men followed along with him,
> and with them came also to rich Iolcus the man
> of labors, son of Alcmene, queen of Midea.
>
> [16–20]

These and several more epic allusions fill the field in this short poem, leaving small space for the dramatic moment when Hylas is taken away by the nymphs. But Theocritus suddenly departs from the prolix epic style of narration and instead uses an epic simile to impress in one image so perfectly the sense of Hylas's rape that the real lack of action in the poem goes unnoticed. As the nymphs drag him down into the pond, Theocritus says:

> Down he fell, headlong into the dark water
> as a flaming star falls from the heavens
> headlong into the sea, and some sailor says to his comrades:
> "Get your gear together, boys. It's a sailing breeze."

The introduction of the sailor and his urgings is excellent. It mimics the Homeric simile in its tendency to inaugurate a drama of its own, yet the sailor in calling for departure not only conveys the finality of the rape of Hylas but also signals the departure of the *Argo*. This Idyll perfectly illustrates the Alexandrian sensibility that creates literary forms by allusion, reference, and suggestion. It demands an audience, however, that is both educated and self-conscious.

Theocritus is equally characteristic of his age in his concentration on love, or more specifically, desire. The latter, called *eros,* made into the deity Eros, was not in the least condemned or despised, but accepted as a madness or sickness, however sweet to experience, which no one chooses but which is inflicted. The image of Eros shooting the unsuspecting, naive young virgin Medea in Apollonius's *Argonautica* expresses human helplessness as well as the fundamental malignity of the erotic condition.

Love and desire were the common subjects of the most popular Alexandrian poetic piece, the epigram. As the Greek word implies, epigrams were originally cut into stone, elegiac pieces usually found on funeral markers. The Alexandrians considerably widened the scope of the genre; the epigram was no longer confined to stone or to thoughts inspired by death. It became the medium for the occasional poem, for a versified thought, most of all for thoughts on love and sex. Vast numbers of epigrams have survived, most of them strikingly similar, many of them in fact serious imitations of or variations on one another. Many were gathered together into anthologies in the third century and later. What remains from these has been collected into what is called today the *Greek Anthology*. Reading through the *Anthology* reinforces an impression of their general banality and at the same time high technical quality.

Love is *the* metaphor for the human condition in the Alexandrian period. It is no coincidence that Aphrodite, mother of Eros, is the most popular subject in art. The deity is more than a goddess of love, she is emblematic of the phenomenon of reproduction, something the ancients associated more with the breasts, the fleshy body, and the menstruating orifice, giving only a certain due to the erect penis. The English word "love" is vague because it is used to describe a wide range of feeling. The ancient Greek had *philia* for friendship, *agape* for affection, and *eros* for desire. Each suggests a different degree of selfish need and altruism.

It has been suggested that love became so important in the third century because as the frames of reference for the individual faded, as the support system of polis, religion, and society failed, as the individual increasingly lost a sense of scale in his life, sensual experiences alone continued to validate him and make him feel a sense of self. Hence desire, even translated into love, was a constant preoccupation. The surviving epigrams often employ detailed physical descriptions of sexual relations as one might expect from a people who were neither prurient nor shy about the reproductive process. The significant change in Alexandrian times is the appearance of women as the legitimate object of desire and love in poetry. While male poets continued to display their strong passions for boys and young men, they also wrote of their women. There are also love epigrams from the women's point of view, as in Theocritus's second Idyll, the subject of which is a lovesick girl who tries to win back her man through love charms. Apollonius makes Medea the very equal of Jason in his *Argonautica,* again expressing the new heterosexual sensibility founded on the elevation of desire to a position of seriousness.

It was a love-minded audience for whom Apollonius Rhodius was writing. Born in Alexandria shortly after the beginning of the third century and living on for more than half of it, Apollonius was a student of Callimachus. He became director of the Library from c. 260 until 247, in which position he was also tutor to the crown prince. The appellation Rhodius comes to him because after 247 he is supposed to have spent time on the island of Rhodes, where he went after an unsympathetic reception of his epic poem. Following some revisions, so the story goes, he returned and triumphed. This account is bound up with the tale of a furious quarrel between himself and Callimachus over the destiny of literature. Callimachus had said: *mega biblion, mega kakon,* a marvelous saying in the Greek which means literally "big book, big evil." As the fragments of his poetry and critical theorizing indicate, Callimachus was opposed to literary forms already too much exploited, and he was opposed to lengthy narrative poems. Apollonius is said to have composed hexameter poems on the founding of cities and some epigrams, but all that survives is his 5,834-line epic poem on the sailing of Jason and his comrades to recover the Golden Fleece.

Set beside the much larger Homeric epics, a 5,834-line poem is scarcely a *mega biblion.* As has been pointed out, the quotation and allusion between Callimachus and Apollonius in their poems implies friendship and respect rather than the opposite. Aristotle said that the successful new-style epic poem must be far shorter than the typical ones (*Poetics* 1459b). It should be fit rather "to the size of tragedies performed at one hearing." If he means the time allotted to three tragedies and one satyr play in the term "hearing," then the *Argonautica*'s four books, each of them approximately the length of a typical tragedy, would satisfy his definition.

Apollonius certainly did not tread on the well-worn path in making his poem. It is revolutionary in almost every way, which is one reason it found so little favor with critics in the nineteenth and early twentieth centuries who were concerned with Homeric standards of decorum. But for an age that has witnessed the experiments of a

Picasso, a Pound, or a John Cage, the bold departure from the manner of the Homeric epic makes the poem far more appealing. And it is this avant-garde quality that makes it so Callimachean. One cannot imagine that the teacher was not pleased with his pupil's creation, unless he was a little jealous.

From the start Apollonius stresses the difference between his epic and Homeric epic. He introduces Jason without sufficient detail to indicate what his significance is. After minimal attention to the plot direction, he turns abruptly to a lengthy catalogue, which retards the action before it has truly gotten underway. In so doing the poet builds his story without plot in a series of impressions, true to his teacher's disapproval of chronologically developed narratives. And indeed the first and second books of this poem do not develop chronologically; the logic resides in the mood and idea, not in time. Thus it does not matter which episode precedes or follows another; there is no cause and effect here. The reader does not ask, "What happens next?"

Unlike the ever self-effacing Homeric poet, Apollonius keeps himself in the narrative, then takes himself out of it when he addresses deities from the narrative, as though he were joining them far above the action. At the very end (4.1773–76) after the fashion of the Homeric Hymns he steps aside and says farewell to his characters, putting a kind of frame on the action and saying in effect, "Now then, it is done." From time to time he halts his narrative to ask why he continues telling what he tells, as if to say he must not be too generous in the telling or too garrulous; he even has some of his characters worry about their compulsive narrative tendencies.

He addresses his readers when he advises them how they are to imagine certain effects he is describing. He bombards them with facts of contemporary marvels, a constant reminder that they live in the same time in which he lives, far removed from the characters who people the tale. The arrival of the narrator into the narrative is a development owed to the new possibilities offered by the written text. The poet and audience in the oral performance are bound together mouth and ear in an unbreakable symbiosis. The writer, however, must relinquish his text; the reader must re-create it. So it is that the writer-narrator enters the text himself to be present at the re-creation.

The Homeric narrator put in all details or gave the illusion that he was doing so. Apollonius is remarkable for leaving them out. At the very beginning, Jason arrives with one sandal on. Why didn't he go home and change? What does it mean that he has only one sandal? These are details Homer would never omit from his account, but Apollonius won't tell. A little later as the chieftains are assembled at the beach for the sailing, Argus and Acastus are described as arriving late. Why? Apollonius does not say. Instead he remarks enigmatically, "Just the same Jason forebore to ask them any details." Why not? What was going on in his mind? Again, Apollonius won't tell. The reader has the sense that the narrator does not know, that he is not omniscient as the Homeric narrator is, and that these characters have lives of their own, independent of the narrator.

The same effect is achieved in the famous monologues of Medea in the third book. Previously in Greek literature when a character talked to himself or herself, it was in the form of a polished address delivered out beyond the speaker to an imaginary second person. Medea speaks to herself with all the confusion and self-deceit normally associated with the psychological state of internal thinking. Her speeches do not tell the reader everything about the state of her mind because the mind itself is vague in its formulations in the monologues. In this way she becomes deep and mysterious, interior and private.

Apollonius furthermore plays games with the shape of his poem. Because the book divisions in the *Iliad* and the *Odyssey* do not always define the episodes, it is thought that the Homeric poems originally were not divided into books. The *Argonautica* was written by Apollonius as four books (papyrus rolls, of course). The first book begins with an apostrophe to Apollo, god of song. That seems conventional enough. At the twenty-third line in the first book the Muses are politely invoked for their support in telling the names of all the heroes and of the voyage to Colchis. The third book begins with an address to Erato, a Muse of love song. Because that book begins the account of the love affair of Jason and Medea, this apostrophe makes sense as well.

The second book, however, simply proceeds with the events subsequent to the close of the first book as though there were no book division at all. What is more, the first book ends with *sunrise* whereas, of course, it is nightfall that signals the end to an episode in Homer. Indeed, it is a natural expectation at least in this culture for night to herald the end, as indeed we find at the end of the third book of the *Argonautica*. The fourth book, strangely enough, begins with an apostrophe that alludes to the beginning of both the *Iliad* and the *Odyssey* because it includes some of the significant language of both.

This heavyweight start to the fourth book, however, is not symmetrical with anything else. What is the poet up to?

The invocation to Apollo at the start of the first book signals the beginning to the entire poem. Twenty-some lines later when he seeks the Muses' aid to help him remember both the heroes who went along and the voyage to Colchis, Apollonius is in fact indicating the plot of the first two books. This apostrophe to the Muses is answered symmetrically by the appeal to Erato at the beginning of the third, for she is asked to help tell how Jason brought back the fleece to Iolcus with the aid of Medea, which constitutes the plot of the third and fourth books. The fourth book begins with a heavy invocation, but one that asks a simple question: Did Medea leave home because she was in love with Jason or because she was afraid of her father? In other words, Apollonius has cheated the expectations of his reader with this grandiloquent invocation, for it asks about only the merest subsequent plot development.

In fact, the poet ties the third to the fourth book in the same simple narrative way he brought the reader from the first to the second. Apollonius mentions Aeetes, Medea's father, by name at the close of the third book, and in the sixth line of the fourth he writes ". . . now he . . . ," the pronoun referring to Aeetes. Each of these narrative details provokes, stimulates, and causes the reader to consider the nature of narrative, to compare Homeric usage with Apollonian. It makes the poem much more a meditation on narrative art than a story about Jason and Medea.

Jason himself becomes a most unlikely hero in Apollonius's work. First, he is surrounded by a crew who are all important figures in the myth tradition. Most of them, as Apollonius is careful to make clear in the catalogue, are endowed with magical charms, special strengths, and so on, which make them in every way the equal and rival of the nominal hero Jason. Odysseus's crew, the learned reader will remember, was a group of faceless, unimportant, weak, and vacillating men completely dominated and victimized by the hero of the poem. How weak and impotent Jason seems in contrast to the autonomous, independent, and cheerfully lonely Odysseus!

Second, Jason is constantly betrayed by the narrator and made to seem ridiculous. There are little details, such as the scene in which Medea meets her aunt, Circe, and as the poet points out, the two of them converse in their native Colchian. It is hard to imagine a Homeric hero caught in a similar predicament, having to stand by twiddling his thumbs while aunt and niece talk in a language that he, the hero of the poem, does not understand. There are also bigger moments—for instance, the scene early on in the poem when the crew choose their leader. It begins inauspiciously for Jason. The crew stand to meet him as he arrives at the beach. The scene is a typically Homeric center stage for Jason when suddenly Argus and Acastus arrive late and effectively upstage him. Shortly thereafter Jason calls for a vote to determine the leader. The traditional myth tells us that Jason is the leader. Apollonius has set up the first few hundred lines of his narrative in such a fashion that the reader knows that formally Jason is the leader. To the reader's surprise and unrestrained laughter (and, it must be imagined, Jason's profound embarrassment) the crew's response to Jason's command is to shout out in unison, "Heracles!" Humiliated, betrayed, and rejected by his narrator, Jason must travel alone in this narrative. He does not even have a close male friend as might be expected. No wonder he cries as they leave his native shores while, as the ever-unfriendly narrator is quick to point out in the very same scene, Heracles makes the boat sink slightly in the water beneath his might!

The negative impression of Jason is completed with a tragicomic scene at the island of Prince Cyzicus, a gentle young bridegroom, his friend and coeval, whom he mistakenly kills in a nighttime battle for which Apollonius employs all the language of Homer's fighting scenes so as to heap on the irony and humor. For Jason it is better to make love than war. This he does for the first time on the island of Lemnos when he meets the Queen Hypsipyle. Striding up to her castle at her invitation, he comes on like the traditional warrior of the *Iliad*. In a simile, Apollonius compares him to a baleful star, just as Homer describes Achilles making his mad dash toward the walls and the waiting Hector in the twenty-second book of the *Iliad*. Jason has a splendid cape with splendid scenes embroidered on it. The poet lavishes enough attention on the cape, nudging his reader with some allusions to the shield passage in the eighteenth book of the *Iliad,* to make us see that Jason's cape rivals Achilles' shield and that in an ironic and humorous and yet deeply serious way Jason himself rivals Achilles. It is immensely funny, this deflowering of the naive young man, but it is also cheering to see the new heroism of the Alexandrian Age, for Jason is a love hero.

Apollonius dramatizes that notion in a scene that sends Heracles forth out of the narrative and with him all the values he carries. Heracles has a tentmate, the boy Hylas, who, as Theocritus makes clear in the thirteenth Idyll, which tells the same story, is Heracles' loved one. He is a youth who serves as Heracles' steward among other things; so it is that he goes to get the water for the campsite. At the spring a nymph falls in love with his beauty and drags him down into the pool over which he is bending for water and into her arms. For a young boy who has previously been the passive partner in anal intercourse with his older lover the nymph's rape stands as the *rite de passage* from boyhood to manhood, from the anus to the phallus. The pool into which he sinks is the perfect metaphor for this adventure.

Thereafter he is lost to Heracles, who storms out of the narrative in an impassioned, almost erotic search for the boy. The first book ends, and with it end Jason's inadequacy and Heracles' superiority. This poem is to be about the adventures and conquests of heterosexual love and not about the traditional male-oriented violent adventures of a hero of epic. Yet Apollonius is not simplistic, nor does he make facile judgments. Throughout the poem the memory of Heracles is invoked again and again to remind the reader of what has been lost in what has been gained. What has been lost is Heracles' courage, honesty, and strength, ugly in murder, rape, and pillage, of course, but sorely missed in the fawning, timid, self-deceiving boy, Jason.

It is in the third book that the theme of heterosexual love is realized in the meeting between Jason and Medea. The third book has always been the most popular and the best known of the poem, often excerpted as though it were a story complete and entire on its own. Apollonius surely has made this unity to be a paradox. Formally the third book has a beginning, middle, and end, except that Jason's yoking the furious bulls of Aeetes is not really the end because the fleece is still to be won. The connection between the third and fourth books plays to this contradiction between a real ending and a pause in the action. Night falls; the bulls are yoked; one senses a definite end. Yet the long invocation to the Muses that seems to introduce the fourth book simply pulls the narrative forward from book three to book four and binds them together as the grammar does on the intimate level with the pronoun "he" in the fourth book going back to Aeetes in the third. With the fourth book necessarily being assumed into the third to make one larger narrative, the character of Medea suddenly looms up as the equal of the Jason figure. Suddenly the narrative of the single central hero is transformed into the story of the couple. As the wandering commences in the fourth book, its obvious parallel with the voyaging of the second attaches the second book to the narrative of the third and fourth books, and the panorama grows larger. This paradoxical widening of the narrative circle continues as the poet brings Jason, Medea, and the reader back to the beginning when he has reached the end.

The action of the third book is perfectly plotted. Every movement of every person is accounted for, just as though the action were being played on the comic stage with timed entrances and exits. As Eros moves through the sky to Aeetes' palace to shoot his arrow into Medea's breast, Jason moves across the earth to the same destination. Later, when he leaves the palace and continues back to his comrades at the ship, Medea's thoughts go with him. At every moment the reader is kept informed of the space in which the action takes place. In the same way the poet plots the mounting tension in the breast of Medea and the fear and apprehension in Jason. The meeting between the two when the charm is exchanged is the erotic climax of the book, which parallels the action climax shortly thereafter: Medea charms and subdues Jason just as he will overcome the bulls.

Jason goes to meet Medea glistening in his beauty, as the poet says, accompanied by two of his crew. This group reminds the reader of the threesome who went along the shores to Achilles' tent in the ninth book of the *Iliad.* Thus the scene becomes an ironic version of the embassy scene, but because Medea has already been compared to Artemis with the very same simile used to compare Nausicaa to Artemis in the *Odyssey,* it is also reminiscent of the moment when the naked Odysseus came up on the beach and sought the aid of the stalwart young girl. Nausicaa wanted to marry the stranger but discreetly held back when he seemed reluctant. Not so Medea. In an hilarious passage Medea and Jason demand, parry, and negotiate until he ends up with the charm, and she gets an offer of marriage. The ethos of this exchange has been expressed much earlier in the book when the baby Eros, about to do his mother, Aphrodite, a favor and make Medea fall in love with Jason, hands her his dice to keep while he is gone and first *very carefully counts* them. Eros (desire) trusts no one. As Apollonius shows throughout the narrative, Eros is completely self-serving.

Apollonius includes a description of the lovers' physical reaction to each other's presence in the tradition of Sappho's celebrated description of her body's reaction to seeing and hearing her lover. In the midst of this ecstasy Medea withdraws the charm from her bodice and hands it to Jason. The exaggerated pleasure with which he receives it, the love it excites, and her mounting ecstasy and wish to give more transform this transaction into some metaphorical sexual intercourse. Apollonius remains true to this rule of epic: the sexually explicit scenes of epigram poetry violate the decorum of epic as does the depiction of a male's sexual excitement. In this scene Medea loses her virginity, figuratively speaking, by giving up the charm in seduction. A little later Medea instructs Jason how to use the charm, and he is then described preparing himself. He strips and in the dark of the night immerses himself in a pool. Hecate, the infernal goddess, appears to him, and many of the same details encountered in the Artemis simile are used to describe her, making her a kind of infernal counterpart to Artemis-Nausicaa-Medea. Jason's immersion reminds one, too, of Hylas's disappearance into the pond. It is a kind of baptism that changes him forever. Nighttime and the presence of Hecate suggests that sexual excitement has ended in something fatal. Jason took his glamour to the meeting in the temple and spoke as a practiced, "fawning" courtier, as Apollonius remarks. He got what he wanted, but he paid a price. And that is what love is all about.

The slightly sinister quality noted here is augmented by the strange duality in Medea's nature. She is, on the one hand, a sweet young virgin, innocent of men, deeply and naively in love with Jason; on the other hand, she is a sorceress, a witch practiced in the use of loathesome drugs and in hunting out corpses for her enchantments, as the poet expressly tells us. The fearful truth of Medea simply fulfills the awe, dread, and foreboding that drench the narrative of the voyage in the second book. The crew pass scenes suggestive of the Underworld, they must undergo frightening trials, and Jason grows disheartened, yet he is told that all will depend on him and that he must put his faith in the goddess Aphrodite. Clearly, although love will win the day, Jason is afraid and weak. In the larger context the poem describes a male who has left the security of the male-male relationships so valued in his culture and embarked upon a meeting with a woman who is his equal. The encounter with a woman is the meeting with the unknown and with the other. It is as frightening as this voyage into the unknown with all of its infernal associations.

The ambiguity of Medea's Dr. Jekyll and Mr. Hyde character is equal to that which the poet has created in Jason, who is a leader, but tearful and passive, a loving man but also a fawning diplomat and a manipulator and exploiter. Perhaps no innovation of Apollonius equals the excitement of this complex character. The Homeric and tragic heroes are monolith figures who express one attitude throughout their career; one thinks of Odysseus's paranoia, Achilles' self-pity, Aeschylus's Clytemnestra's obsession with revenge. In Medea and Jason Apollonius has combined the ambiguity, complexity, and uncertainty that are true to human character.

In his creation of Medea, Apollonius plays on his reader's expectations, which are built up from their familiarity with other myths and other narratives. The significant epic and tragic characters from these myths are:

1. Ariadne, the girl who betrays her family and helps her lover and is abandoned on Naxos.
2. Penelope, the wife who waits and helps by keeping the house intact. She is in effect abandoned by her husband and the narrator of the *Odyssey* once she and Odysseus have gone to bed upon his return.
3. Euripides' Medea, a tragic female figure who must destroy her child, who is almost herself. Yet she is also a witch and malevolent figure because she survives her evil deed, unlike the purely tragic Sophoclean Dejaneira, who dies.
4. Homer's Circe, who enchants men to their doom. She is a malign witch goddess figure who is sexually dangerous for males on the model of Aphrodite (Adonis perishes in his relationship with her) and Artemis (Actaeon perishes in his quasi-sexual relationship with her) as well as many others.
5. Aeschylus's Clytemnestra, who seduces Agamemnon into entering a warm bath where he is stabbed to death. She is the paradigmatic threatening mortal woman whose power to kill is directly related to the intimacy of the matrimonial chamber.

Very rarely does one find a male-female relationship that is explored in depth. Usually males either seek a woman to exploit and discard or are drawn into a woman's power and destroyed. Apollonius has created a reciprocal relationship with two equally powerful people. For its construction the poet depends on his readers' knowledge of their shared literary past. Without that knowledge, his poem could not exist. This is the consequence of the establishment of the Library, the burgeoning scholarship of Alexandria and the rise of the reading class. Literature would never be the same again.

In the fourth book Apollonius is again highly original in depicting the aftermath of an event. Jason's getting the fleece is not enough; Apollonius must get his couple back to Greece and show them falling out of love as horrendously as they had so passionately fallen into it.

Medea must betray her father to go with Jason; Jason must offer her marriage to get the fleece. It is no wonder that when her brother Apsyrtus follows them, she is afraid that Jason will give her over to him. Trapped, the both of them, there is only the murder of Apsyrtus as a way out. The amused tone with which the narrative began has grown ever darker until the climax in the unheroic, ugly murder of Apsyrtus. Apollonius paints the mood of depression of the ill-starred lovers in some stirring descriptions of a mysterious distant landscape that mirrors the emotions of the crew and the principals. No bird is able to cross the water, spreading out its fragile wings. In mid-course it falls into the flame of the lake, fluttering. Daughters of Helios enclosed in poplar trees stand around the lake crying a sad lament; from their eyes fall tears of amber. The heroes lose their desire for food and drink; they have no joyful thoughts. All day long they are strung out, weighed down by a dreadful smell. All night they have to listen to the shrill cry of the daughters of Helios wailing in a sharp voice. As they cry, their tears are borne upon the waters like drops of oil. Somewhat later their depression increases, and they sail into a place where:

> Everywhere there are shoals, everywhere thick seaweed from the bottom and the foam of the wave lightly flows over them. Sand stretches out until the eye mistakes it for air. Nothing creeps there, nothing flies. . . . Pain overcomes them as they gaze at the air and the broad expanse of earth looking like air, stretching far away without end. No watering hole, no path, no shepherd's enclosure could they see anywhere. Everything is held in a dead calm. [4.1237ff.]

Apollonius portrays a universe in which the gods are so indifferent to humankind that the ugly murder of Apsyrtus makes not a ripple on Olympus. Medea and Jason are adrift in a world altogether of their own making. Elsewhere Apollo is described as striding nearby the heroes, majestic in his divine epiphany. The practiced reader expects that he will engage some one of the heroes in conversation just as the Homeric gods talk to the heroes. But Apollo goes on by without a word exchanged. At the beginning of book three Apollonius depicts Hera, Athena, and Aphrodite as nothing more than three silly society ladies—catty, selfish, and finally inconsequential. There is no retarding action from on high in this poem—no Poseidon, no angry Hera. No host of gods or even one helps Jason on his way. True enough, Hera is favorable to him because of his previous kindness to her. It is she who sees to it that Aphrodite sends her son Eros to make Medea fall in love with Jason and thus help him get the fleece. But this relationship is not like the Athena-Odysseus relationship.

Finally the gods do not matter in the world of humans. This is a truth Achilles communicated to Priam in the jars-of-Zeus speech in the twenty-fourth book of the *Iliad*. But there is a great difference between the Homeric concept and the Alexandrian world view. Homer's heroes saw themselves as abandoned, if not betrayed by the universe and by a system of gods formidable in their stature. These were the proper counterparts to men who saw themselves as proud and grand creatures. Apollonius's Jason has no such illusions, either about himself or his universe. It is a petty universe. For the Theocritan shepherd the sensual pleasure of beauty will provide some comfort against the cold loneliness of the age; for the Callimachean aesthete comfort will come from style and structure; for Apollonius, from irony and wit.

The legacy of the ancient Greeks to later centuries in the West is vast. They seem to have invented the eternal questions that every generation must ask, however unanswerable they remain. In the face of a universe they saw as indifferent, if not hostile, the ancient Greeks constructed a view of man and his entirely humanistic heroism which must make any human beholder proud and glad to be alive. Different generations of Greeks approached this indifferent universe in different ways and in different media. But their solution was always the same—the portrayal of a male person who was intelligent and courageous, attuned to the beauties and sonorities of the sensual life. Statuary depicted the same figure described in the literature. So it is that ancient Greek literature remains alive in the Western world, and no doubt will as long as people can read, as a source of strength and affirmation for the pitiful creatures who live out their destiny under the relentless sun.

Further Reading

And how one can imagine oneself among them [the Greeks]
   I do not know;
  It was all so unimaginably different
   And all so long ago.

                   Louis MacNeice, *Autumn Journal,* part nine

Every age has the renaissance it deserves.

                   Frank Kermode

    Ancient Greek literature became the object of scholarly pursuit from the time of the establishment of the Library in third-century Alexandria. Over the centuries scholarship has become quite an industry. For most of the twentieth century the vast outpouring has been recorded in the French publication *L'année philologique* (Société d'Edition "Les Belles Lettres"), edited first by Jules Marouzeau and then by Juliette Ernst. Here in volumes issued annually one will find cited every book and article in every language of the world concerning every conceivable subject having to do with classical antiquity. The publication is overwhelming, but exhilarating, and it is easy enough to find one's way through all the lists. Sections are indicated by rubrics in the French language, but the vocabulary is recognizable to almost any English-speaking person (e.g., Histoire, Mythologie, etc.). Titles of books are listed with reviews; titles of journal articles are accompanied by a précis in French, German, or English (this last used, naturally enough, for most English-language articles). *L'année philologique* is fun to browse through because it provides a kind of commentary on what has interested professional classicists and historians over the decades of this century.

    An annotated review of scholarship in specific areas of classical studies can be found from time to time in the pages of *The Classical*

World, a journal published by the Classical Association of the Atlantic States. An index to these surveys appears in vol. 67, no. 4 (February 1974), 221–24, and again in vol. 73, no. 5 (February 1980), 275–90. An overview of scholarly positions on a variety of subjects is presented in a series of essays gathered together in *Fifty Years (and Twelve) of Classical Scholarship,* ed. Maurice Platnauer, rev. with appendixes (2d ed.; Oxford: Blackwell, 1968).

The history of classical scholarship from its beginnings to the middle of the nineteenth century has been set out by Rudolph Pfeiffer in two volumes. The first, *History of Classical Scholarship* (Oxford: Oxford Univ. Press, 1968), is a thoughtful survey of the awakening of a historical consciousness among the Greeks toward their cultural past ending with the rise of scholarship in the Hellenistic Age. The second, a much slighter and less rewarding volume, *History of Classical Scholarship from 1300 to 1850* (Oxford: Oxford Univ. Press, 1976), suffers from a rather narrow focus on the doings of professional classicists. The scholarly viewpoint is his subject, of course, but in many ways one gets a better sense of how classical antiquity was perceived by studying the artistic and intellectual reception of the classical literary tradition in successive centuries. The literary tradition itself, of course, depends on the material survival of the texts. The best account of how pieces of ancient literature survived to our time is contained in L. D. Reynolds and N. G. Wilson, *Scribes and Scholars* (2d ed.; Oxford: Oxford Univ. Press, 1974).

Pfeiffer's volumes must be supplemented by J. E. Sandys's *History of Classical Scholarship* (3 vols., reprint; New York: Hafner, 1958), a dull but useful survey through the nineteenth century. Sandys's work is much improved if read in conjunction with Gilbert Highet's magisterial review of classical literature as perceived by Western authors titled *The Classical Tradition* (New York: Oxford Univ. Press paperback, 1957).

Today students of the classics are as interested in the way later ages perceived antiquity as they are in the actual remains of the ancient works. Indeed, naming this interest is a problem. Are we more interested in "the classical tradition," "the remains," or "what survives"—what the Germans call *Nachleben?* More and more scholars tend to use the German term *Receptionsgeschichte,* a term for which there is no easy English equivalent, to describe this kind of study. Literally "reception history," it means the history of how successive centuries came to know, understand, and assimilate the stuff of classical antiquity that survived. Thus it is not how Sophocles' *Antigone* affected Jean Anouilh's *Antigone* which is so interesting, but rather the way Anouilh plays off the Sophoclean version and what he assumes his audience will understand. For rather than passively altering the ancient play, Anouilh has assimilated traditional materials into a new work. In this sense all contemporary classical scholarship is simply an instance of the twentieth-century reception of classical literature and ancient history.

It seems likely that classical studies will move more and more in this direction. See, for instance, J. K. Newman, "Graduate Studies in Classics: Have They a Future?" *Illinois Classical Studies* 10 (1985), 157–65, who argues for scholarship that accepts the inevitability of a dominant contemporary point of view and, what is more, acknowledges that the ancient text can mean no less than what the subsequent centuries have made of it. In sum, you can't go home again. See also P. L. Schmidt, "Reception Theory and Classical Scholarship: A Plea for Convergence," in *Hypatia: Essays in Classics, Comparative Literature, and Philosophy Presented to Hazel E. Barnes on Her Seventieth Birthday* (Boulder: Colorado Associated Univ. Press, 1985), 67–78. Meyer Reinhold and E. A. Hanawalt have begun a series of bibliographies that will document the new interest in this area. See their "Bibliography of the Classical Tradition for 1980–1982," which fills *Classical and Modern Literature* 5, no. 3 (1985). This is the first major effort of the Institute for the Classical Tradition, which they direct.

In any case, antiquity is finally no more than what it seems to be in the eye of the beholder. Considering the degree to which it has been interpreted and reinterpreted over the past twenty centuries, it is not unfair to say that the history and literature of classical antiquity stand alongside the Judeo-Christian religious tradition as the major mythology of the Western world. I have addressed some of the issues deriving from this viewpoint in three articles: "The Morass of Pedantry," *Boston University Journal* 16 (1968), 7–13; "Extra Ecclesiam Non Est Salus," *Parnassus: Poetry in Review* (spring/summer 1982), 76–98; and "Classical Baggage Left in the Unclaimed," *Southwest Review* 5 (1984), 390–412. See also R. R. Bolgar, *The Classical Heritage and Its Beneficiaries* (Cambridge: Cambridge Univ. Press, 1963).

Yet another and very personal view will be found in *History of Classical Scholarship* by Ulrich von Wilamowitz-Moellendorff, trans. Alan Harris (London: Duckworth, 1982), newly prefaced with an essay by Hugh Lloyd-Jones, who explains the author's perspective and offers his own observations on the role of classics in the contemporary world. A professor at Berlin in the early decades of this century, Wilamowitz is generally conceded to be the most original and important classical scholar of that time; certainly he taught an extraordinary number of brilliant persons, many of whom emigrated to the English-speaking world to escape the Nazi persecutions. One of his students, Werner Jaeger, himself long a distinguished professor at Harvard University, has left an interesting description of the profession of classics and the life of the humanities in Berlin in the twenties and thirties in *Five Essays* (Montreal: Casalini, 1960). This may be set against W. M. Calder III, "Werner Jaeger and Richard Harder: An Erklärung," *Quaderni di Storia* 17 (1983), 99–121, an essay about the seduction of the ideology of the Third Reich for German classical scholars.

Wilamowitz has left us his memoirs (English trans. by G. C. Richards) titled *My Recollections, 1848–1914* (London: Chatto & Windus, 1930). He stops his account at the beginning of World War I, an event that was for so many of his generation the beginning of the end. But his pages give a vivid insight into the culture that helped shape his view of classical antiquity. Germany's obsession with Greek antiquity is the subject of E. M. Butler, *The Tyranny of Greece over Germany* (Cambridge: Cambridge Univ. Press, 1935), which begins with Johann Joachim Winckelmann's formulation of an antique aesthetic based on his first view of the Roman copies of Greek statuary in the Vatican Museum and continues into the nineteenth century. See also Hugh Trevelyan, *Goethe and the Greeks* (reprint; Cambridge: Cambridge Univ. Press, 1981), and Michael Ewans, *Wagner and Aeschylus: "The Ring" and the "Oresteia"* (Cambridge: Cambridge Univ. Press, 1983). Meanwhile, in the eighteenth century the English Lord Elgin journeyed to Greece and removed the Parthenon frieze to England, where it sits to this day in the Duveen Room of the British Museum. The story is told in William St. Clair, *Lord Elgin and the Marbles* (Oxford: Oxford Univ. Press, 1983).

British philhellenism is surveyed in Richard Jenkyns, *The Victorians and Ancient Greece* (Oxford: Oxford Univ. Press, 1981), and F. M. Turner, *The Greek Heritage in Victorian Britain* (New Haven: Yale Univ. Press, 1981). These might be read alongside Warren Anderson's *Matthew Arnold and the Classical Tradition* (Ann Arbor: Univ. of Michigan Press, 1965). Arnold was, so to speak, the English equivalent of Nietzsche; that is, both these nineteenth-century figures sought to import into the cultural chaos brought on by the French Revolution and the Industrial Revolution something of the definition and security of the ancient Greek world.

Matthew Arnold was important among late nineteenth-century

teachers of classics and their successors in the early and middle twentieth century who taught classics as though it were a religion. One has only to read Gilbert Murray's introductory essay, "The Value of Greece to the Future of the World," in *The Legacy of Greece and Rome,* ed. R. W. Livingstone (Oxford: Oxford Univ. Press, 1921), to see how the historical phenomenon of Greek antiquity can be made into a transcendent truth or a mythology with all the authority of a religion. The study of the ancient languages and cultures in nineteenth-century England also had an important social function—it was the mark of a gentleman.

It is interesting and sometimes amusing to get a glimpse of English classical scholars from both the earlier centuries and our own. C. O. Brink, *English Classical Scholarship: Historical Reflections on Bentley, Porson and Housman* (Oxford: Oxford Univ. Press, 1986), looks at some distinguished textual critics. Francis West's biography of Gilbert Murray, *Gilbert Murray: A Life* (London: Croom Helm, 1984), on the other hand, is a rather harsh view of a man who was famous for his vegetarianism, his pacificist views, and his role in the League of Nations, as well as for being the most prolific and important popularizer of classics in the first half of the twentieth century. He is supposed to be the model for Adolphus in his friend George Bernard Shaw's play *Major Barbara.*

An equally important figure in the lives of many celebrated English people in decades past was Cecil Maurice Bowra. Warden of Wadham College, Oxford, Sir Maurice was more than a literary historian and collector of fact; he was a good literary critic. He is said to have been the model for Evelyn Waugh's character Anthony Blanche in *Brideshead Revisited.* After his death a collection of essays about him were gathered together by Hugh Lloyd-Jones. The collection is titled *Maurice Bowra: A Celebration* (London: Duckworth, 1974). His near contemporary, E. R. Dodds, has left an impression of his times and his friends in *Missing Persons: An Autobiography* (Oxford: Oxford Univ. Press, 1977). All these books demonstrate that once upon a time classicists played an important role in the intellectual and cultural life of their country. That they do not any longer either in Britain or in the United States is the result partly of the decline in humanistic and historical learning (not to mention the absolute departure of Latin and Greek from school and college curricula) and partly of their own retreat into mandarinism as a reaction to the rise of science and to the increasing cultural power of the consumer society masses.

It is altogether relevant that Americans note the English bias to the subject of classical antiquity. While American classical scholarship was for a long time influenced much more by Germans than by the English, this situation eventually turned around, if for no other reason than that the study of foreign languages in this country has declined so precipitously that neophyte classicists are hard put to get sufficient Latin and Greek let alone the ancillary languages of scholarship, such as French and German. Then, too, the overproduction of classicists in England has resulted in their wholesale exportation and thus a remarkable number of English professors on American classical faculties. As a result, there is a very distinct English flavor to the study of classics in the more influential universities, that is, belletristic, liberal, and humanist, with a subtextual belief in power, maleness, hierarchy, cultural imperialism, and colonial exploitation. The situation has been somewhat redressed by the American assumption of French critical approaches to the study of antiquity—that is, structuralism, semiotics, deconstruction, and the like—and of such novel perspectives as, among others, Marxist, feminist, and gay perspectives, and now, perhaps, *Receptionsgeschichte*. See, for instance, the journal *Arethusa,* which has devoted whole issues to various of these approaches—e.g., feminist, vol. 6, no. 1 (1973); psychoanalytic, vol. 7, no. 1 (1974); Marxist, vol. 8, no. 1 (1975); contemporary literary critical theory, vol. 10, no. 1 (1977); feminist again, vol. 11, nos. 1 and 2 (1978); and semiotics, vol. 16, nos. 1 and 2 (1983). See also E. B. Holtsmark, *Tarzan and Tradition: Classical Myth in Popular Literature* (Westport, Conn.: Greenwood, 1981), and Jon Solomon, *The Ancient World in Cinema* (New York: A. S. Barnes, 1978), neither of which American books would have occurred to the Brits.

In the following paragraphs I list some of the more important, provocative, or conventional studies on the various subjects I have introduced in the earlier chapters. I have not attempted to be complete. Pieces cited are in English, and I have cited articles only from the more accessible journals. I have also tried to select pieces in which the authors use little or no Greek script—or at least translate when they do. In every instance, these bibliographies should be sufficient to cover the subject thoroughly. Anyone who wishes to pursue the subject of classical antiquity more fully should acquire *The Oxford Classical Dictionary,* ed. N. G. L. Hammond and H. H. Scullard (2d ed., Oxford: Oxford Univ. Press, 1970), a reference work that offers brief definitions of everything of consequence in the ancient world. It is invaluable and belongs, as they say, in every home.

The reader who wishes a complete survey of ancient Greek literature would do well to acquire H. J. Rose, *A Handbook of Greek Literature* (3d ed.; London: Methuen, 1948), which in its crisp, unadorned, and uninteresting way has all the facts but has peculiar emphases (for example, there are only brief remarks on Herodotus). Albin Lesky, *A History of Greek Literature* (2d ed.; London: Methuen, 1966), translated from the German by J. Willis and C. de Heer, has perhaps more than one wants to know and a bibliography that is principally German. More recently there has come out *The Cambridge History of Classical Literature,* vol. 1, *Greek Literature,* ed. P. E. Easterling and B. M. W. Knox (Cambridge: Cambridge Univ. Press, 1985). The first volume of Werner Jaeger's *Paideia* (Oxford: Oxford Univ. Press, 1945) is an account of the transmission of Greek culture through literature, a kind of history of ideas of the eighth through the fifth centuries, treating much the same ancient authors discussed in these pages. There are those who were initially inspired to take up the profession of classics after reading this work; some who have reread it in the recent past agree with Hugh Lloyd-Jones's observation that at this date it (or its author) seems woolly-headed. This view is consistent with the often-expressed opinion that English scholars tend to think the Germans are prone to vague and fuzzy generalizations and that the French ignore the facts in their formulations of theory, whereas the scholars of these two nations view their English counterparts as exceedingly small-minded and cautious.

Classicists are trained as philologists first, historians second, and rarely as literary critics. Thus they tend to treat ancient literary pieces primarily as documentary proof of a linguistic or historical phenomenon. This subject has been addressed by C. P. Segal, "Ancient Texts and Modern Literary Criticism," *Arethusa* 1 (1968), 1–25; R. P. Sonkowsky, "Scholarship and Showmanship," *Arion* 1 (1962), 102–7; H. D. F. Kitto, *Poesis: Structure and Thought* (Berkeley: Univ. of California Press, 1967); and Stephanus Kresic, ed., *Contemporary Literary Hermeneutics and Interpretation of Classical Texts* (Ottawa: éd. de l'Université, 1981), among others.

This book begins with some remarks on the Greek language. It can be learned without monstrous difficulty and at home by following F. J. Kinchin-Smith and T. W. Melluish, *Teach Yourself Greek* (London: Hodder and Stoughton for the English Universities Press, 1947). The next step is to find a suitably easy text. One might try Arrian's *History of Alexander* or Plato's *Crito* for starters. Or one might dip into Euripides' *Alcestis,* which is poetry, to be sure, and thus harder; nonetheless it has some of the prosiest poetic dialogue to be found.

Texts in the Loeb Classical Library translations published by Harvard University Press, which have Greek on the left and an English translation on the right, are just the thing for the beginning student learning on his own. The translations are sometimes awful, but if one compares the Greek and the English and asks why the translator says what he says, eventually one can develop a working knowledge of the literary language. Everyone will want to go on to Homer, of course, and in so doing will have to get used to another dialect, which is very hard and disconcerting at first. Ultimately, though, reading Homer is a most rewarding experience because the repetition in Homeric epic finally makes one comfortable with the language. So deep, complex, and compelling are these two poems that one can spend a lifetime going over them and reading them anew. At this point it would be well to look into L. R. Palmer, *The Greek Language* (Atlantic Highlands, N.J.: Humanities Press, 1980), to get some understanding of the history, growth, and structure of the language. Read also G. E. R. Lloyd, *Polarity and Analogy* (Cambridge: Cambridge Univ. Press, 1961), which contains important observations on the antithetical—I suppose we must now say "binary"—habit of the ancient Greek mind.

Accounts of the history of ancient Greece will always go out of date as new discoveries are made, as can be seen from the varying degrees of authority which can be assigned to the essays in the many volumes of the *Cambridge Ancient History*. For what we know of the Mycenaeans read E. T. Vermeule, *Greece in the Bronze Age* (Chicago: Univ. of Chicago Press, 1964). C. G. Starr, *Individual and Community: The Rise of the Polis, 800–500 B.C.* (Oxford: Oxford Univ. Press, 1986), might be read to supplement the early part of J. B. Bury, *A History of Greece,* 4th ed., revised by Russell Meiggs (New York: St. Martin's Press, 1975), and N. G. L. Hammond, *A History of Greece to 322 B.C.* (2d ed.; Oxford: Oxford Univ. Press, 1967). P. M. Fraser's vast *Ptolemaic Alexandria* (Oxford: Oxford Univ. Press, 1972) takes up with considerable detail where most histories leave off or thin out—that is, with the death of Alexander in 323 B.C.

HOMER

I have discussed Homeric scholarship in some detail in the final chapter of my *The "Iliad," the "Odyssey," and the Epic Tradition* (Garden City: Doubleday, 1966), which has been reprinted with an enlarged bibliographical chapter (see pp. 234–67) by Gordian Press

(Staten Island, 1976). Some of the observations in the chapter on Homer in the present book come from my "Male and Female in the Homeric Poems," *Ramus* 3 (1974), 87–101, and "Repeated Similes in the Homeric Poems," *Studies Presented to Sterling Dow* (Greek, Roman, and Byzantine Studies, monograph 10; Durham, 1984), 7–14, and "The Epic of Gilgamesh, the Bible, and Homer: Some Narrative Parallels," *Mnemai: Classical Studies in Memory of Karl K. Hulley* (Chico, Calif.: Scholars Press, 1984), 7–20.

Twentieth-century views on the Homeric epics derive largely from the writing of Milman Parry, who worked out the theory that the *Iliad* and *Odyssey* are oral poems. Since that time scholars either have reacted against the theory and attempted to disprove it or searched for further evidence to validate or modify the theory. Parry's writings are gathered together in *The Making of Homeric Verse: The Collected Papers of Milman Parry* (Oxford: Oxford Univ. Press, 1971), edited by his son, Adam, who prefaces the collection with an important essay discussing the strengths and weaknesses of his father's theory. With the typical zeal of the discoverer, Parry carried his theory to its logical conclusion, which is that the inherited phraseology, type scenes, stock characters, and so on preclude the notion that any one individual made meaning out of the arrangement of words. Parry stressed the *mechanics* of oral poetry and suggested a rather mechanical performer in place of what the Western world has come to call a poet. Parry *fils* suggests that this position is neither correct nor necessary. Many who accept the oral theory have now become concerned with demonstrating the individual poet at work in making the poems out of traditional materials.

Parry died young as he was beginning to study surviving oral poetic practice among the Yugoslavians. The fieldwork was completed by his student Albert Bates Lord, who has devoted his life to refining and strengthening the conception of the Homeric poems as oral. Lord's *Singer of Tales* (Cambridge, Mass.: Harvard Univ. Press, 1960) is an essential study of the Yugoslavian material and how it can be applied to Homer. See also Lord's "Homer as an Oral Poet," *Harvard Studies in Classical Philology* 72 (1967), 1–46, which is an answer to the argument against the oral theory. R. H. Finnegan's *Oral Poetry: Its Nature, Significance and Social Context* (Cambridge: Cambridge Univ. Press, 1977) is a survey and evaluation of oral poetic practice the world over. Finnegan finds several instances of mixtures of orality and literacy which the strict Parry-Lord school would wish to deny, but which give comfort to those who believe that Homer exercised total control over his poem(s), however much he was true to the techniques of oral narration. The always stimulating, original Gregory Nagy has an interesting, if hard to read, essay in *Critical Exchange* 16 (1984), 32–54, titled "Oral Poetry and the Homeric Poems: Broadening and Narrowing of Terms," on the question of making a text into the definitive poem in the ongoing fluidity of oral performances.

One of the very best introductions to the poems is Howard Clarke's *Homer's Readers: An Historical Introduction to the "Iliad" and the "Odyssey"* (Newark: Univ. of Delaware Press, 1981), which surveys all the ways the two poems have been understood and interpreted since antiquity. H. A. Mason, *To Homer through Pope* (New York: Barnes and Noble, 1972), does something of the same thing on a much smaller scale. See also G. deF. Lord, *Homeric Renaissance: The Odyssey of George Chapman* (New Haven: Yale Univ. Press, 1956). See also Kirsti Simonsuuri, *Homer's Original Genius: Eighteenth Century Notions of the Early Greek Epic* (Cambridge: Cambridge Univ. Press, 1979). J. K. Newman, *The Classical Epic Tradition* (Madison: Univ. of Wisconsin Press, 1986), traces the re-creation of the epic form or idea throughout the centuries from Homer to Tolstoy.

D. C. Young in "Never Blotted a Line? Formula and Premeditation in Homer and Hesiod," *Arion* 6 (1967), 279–324, argues with historical analogies for a lesser role of tradition and greater control of the text on the part of the very poet or poets who created the *Iliad* and *Odyssey*. Pages 55–101 of G. S. Kirk, *The Songs of Homer* (Cambridge: Cambridge Univ. Press, 1962), comprise a lucid examination of the question whether such complicated, integrated, strikingly individual poems can be the product of a tradition. Paolo Vivante in his *Homeric Imagination* (Bloomington: Indiana Univ. Press, 1970), supposes that every detail in the two poems betrays the thoughtful intent of a single poet.

Eventually the argument about who created the poems and how becomes tiresome because there will never be any way of verifying one position or another, and everyone's opinion requires an act of faith. The last line of the first book of the *Iliad,* for instance, reads "and then lay down beside Zeus Hera of the golden-throne." One can argue that the epithet "golden-throne" is inappropriate to the moment and that it is no more than the mechanically suitable metrical filler attached to the name Hera. Or one can argue that because the divine couple has just argued bitterly, the bulky piece of furniture the poet has given Hera in her bed is a marvelously subtle indication on his part of the estrangement of the two. Or one can argue that because the line can be so interpreted, the interpretation is now true or always was subconsciously so.

Collections of essays—*The Language and Background of Homer,* ed. G. S. Kirk (Cambridge: Heffer, 1964); *Essays on the "Odyssey": Selected Modern Criticism,* ed. C. M. Taylor, Jr. (Bloomington: Indiana Univ. Press, 1963); and especially *Approaches to Homer,* ed. C. A. Rubino and C. W. Shelmerdine (Austin: Univ. of Texas, 1983)— offer good examples of the variety of ways of reading these poems. J. A. Russo and Bennett Simon in "Homeric Psychology and the Oral Epic Tradition," *Journal of the History of Ideas* 29 (1968), 483–98, make important observations about the public nature of Homeric characters and the relationship of the poet and the audience. B. E. Perry in "The Early Greek Capacity for Viewing Things Separately," *Transactions of the American Philological Association* 68 (1937), 403–27, discusses Homer's seeming ignorance of features of his story. Albert Cook's "Some Thoughts on How to Discuss Epic Poetry," *Helios 10 (1983), 85–91,* is useful, as is R. B. Rutherford's "Tragic Form and Feeling in the *Iliad,*" *Journal of Hellenic Studies* 102 (1982), 145–60. Justin Glenn's "The Polyphemus Myth: Its Origin and Interpretation," *Greece and Rome* 25 (1978), 141–55, is a psychoanalytic interpretation of the myth to be read in conjunction with D. L. Page's discussion of the Polyphemus myth in his *Homeric Odyssey* (Oxford: Oxford Univ. Press, 1955). See also in this connection R. M. Newton, "Poor Polyphemus: Emotional Ambivalence in *Odyssey* 9 and 17," *Classical World* 79 (1983), 137–42.

Jasper Griffin, "The Divine Audience and the Religion of the *Iliad,*" *Classical Quarterly* 28 (1978), 1–22, emphasizes the role of the gods as spectators. An emphasis on religion also marks Griffin's book *Homer on Life and Death* (Oxford: Oxford Univ. Press, 1980), which is also interesting for the way he applies parallels from the Old Testament and other Near Eastern religious texts, suggesting a kind of community of outlook between these Greek pieces and the other texts. Homer and the Near Eastern connection is also the subject of T. B. L. Webster's *From Mycenae to Homer* (London: Methuen, 1958). Two other recent books on the *Iliad* are Martin Mueller's *The "Iliad"* (London: Allen & Unwin, 1984), in which the author's critical position ignores the oral theory and thereby suggests a poem no different from any other long literary piece, and S. L. Schein's *Mortal Hero* (Berkeley: Univ. of California Press, 1984), in which the author's very personal reading of the poem depends on the oral theory of composition. See also J. M. Redfield, whose wordy and jargon-filled *Nature and Culture in the Iliad: The Tragedy of Hector* (Chicago: Univ. of Chicago Press, 1975) has inspired quite a following as a social anthropologist's explanation of why the *Iliad* still appeals (and is in itself not an unsympathetic reading of the poem). Rigorously following the tenets of Freudian psychology, T. W. MacCary exhumes a pre-Oedipal psychology in adult males in *Childlike Achilles: Ontogeny and Phylogeny in the Iliad* (New York: Columbia Univ. Press, 1982).

M. I. Finley in his *World of Odysseus* (rev. ed.; New York: Viking Press, 1978) reads the poem for its sociological and historical data. The revised edition has two new chapters: one on the possibility of determining for fact that there was a Trojan War and the other on the criteria for testing the validity of the Homeric world.

Poems as popular and influential as the Homeric epics have created a veritable scholarly industry. Time was when the annual production of scholarly works on Homer simply overwhelmed the student, but nowadays computers have made it possible to keep some kind of control on the outpouring. D. W. Packard and Tania Meyers's *Bibliography of Homeric Scholarship, Preliminary Edition, 1930–1970* (Malibu, Calif.: Undena Publications, 1974) has every Homeric study categorized and organized.

THE ARCHAIC PERIOD

A. M. Snodgrass, *The Dark Age of Greece: An Archaeological Survey of the Eleventh to the Eighth Centuries B.C.* (Edinburgh: Edinburgh Univ. Press, 1971), and his *Archaic Greece: The Age of Experiment* (London: Dent, 1980) are more detailed and recent than A. R. Burns's *Lyric Age of Greece* (London: St. Martin's Press, 1960), which does, however, emphasize the poets in their historical context, or M. I. Finley's *Early Greece: The Bronze and the Archaic Ages* (New York: Norton, 1970), which is more sociological. P. N. Ure, *The Origin of Tyranny* (Cambridge: Cambridge Univ. Press, 1922), and Antony Andrewes, *The Greek Tyrants* (New York: Harper, 1963), discuss the causes and effects of the distinguishing political and economic facts of the period. Bruno Snell, *The Discovery of the Mind,* trans. T. G. Rosenmeyer (Cambridge, Mass.: Harvard Univ. Press, 1953), is a very original account of the development of a sense of self in the Greeks of this period. See especially pp. 1–89 and 136–52.

The *Works and Days* and the *Theogony* present as many problems as the two Homeric poems. Are they oral? Were they created by the same author? To what degree is the Hesiod who introduces himself into the poems a historical figure; to what degree a *topos,* or conventional figure? What is the relationship between these poems and Near Eastern poems with similar themes and values? Are the two Hesiodic poems in fact coherent wholes or pieces stitched together from inherited patches? And so on and so forth.

The reader may find a fuller account of my conception of the *Works and Days* in my "Rhythm of Hesiod's *Works and Days,*" *Harvard Studies in Classical Philology* 76 (1972), 23–43. In this connection consult Seth Benardete, "Hesiod's *Works and Days:* A First Reading," *Agon* 1 (1967), 150–74; Donald Sheehan, "Hesiod's *Works and Days:* An Introduction," *Arion* 3 (1976), 452–82; Michael Gagarin, "*Dike* in the *Works and Days,*" *Classical Philology* 68 (1973), 81–94; Michael Gagarin, "*Dike* in Archaic Greek Thought," *Classical Philology* 69 (1974), 186–97; and C. J. Rowe, "Archaic Thought in Hesiod," *Journal of Hellenic Studies* 103 (1983), 124–35.

Piero Pucci's *Hesiod and the Language of Poetry* (Baltimore: Johns Hopkins Univ. Press, 1977) proceeds from the paradox of the Muses' (and thus poetry's) claim to be able to speak both lies and the truth. For Hesiod's relationship to the Near East see Peter Walcot, *Hesiod and the Near East* (Cardiff: Wales Univ. Press, 1966). See also C. H. Gordon, *The Common Background of Greek and Hebrew Civilizations* (New York: Norton, 1962). For Hesiod's position in the history of early Greek philosophy read D. J. Stewart, "Hesiod and the Birth of Reason," *Antioch Review* 26 (1966), 213–231, and E. A. Havelock, "Thoughtful Hesiod," *Yale Classical Studies* 20 (1967), 59–72. The thoughts of Aeschylus and Hesiod are traditionally held to be especially close. See, for instance, Friederich Solmsen, *Hesiod and Aeschylus* (Ithaca: Cornell Univ. Press, 1949), and Eirik Vandvik, whose curious *Prometheus of Hesiod and Aeschylus* (Oslo: Dybwad, 1943) makes Hesiod into a kind of Christian moralist. See as well M. B. Arthur, "Cultural Strategies in Hesiod's *Theogony:* Law, Family, Society," *Arethusa* 15 (1982), 63–82; L. S. Sussman, "The Birth of the Gods: Sexuality, Conflict and Cosmic Structure in Hesiod's *Theogony,*" *Ramus* 7 (1978), 61–77; T. P. Feldman, "Personification and Structure in Hesiod's *Theogony,*" *Symbolae Osloenses* 46 (1971), 7–41; P. A. Marquardt, "Hesiod's Ambiguous View of Woman," *Classical Philology* 77 (1982), 283–91; and M. B. Arthur, "The Dream of a World without Women," *Arethusa* 16 (1983), 97–116. On Hesiod's style see T. G. Rosenmeyer, "The Formula in Early Greek Poetry,"

Arion 4 (1965), 295–311; Cora Angier, "Verbal Patterns in Hesiod's *Theogony,*" *Harvard Studies in Classical Philology* 68 (1964), 329–44. For Hesiod's persona see M. S. Jensen, "Tradition and Individuality in Hesiod's *Works and Days,*" *Classica et Mediaevalia* 27 (1966), 1–27, and Mark Griffith, "Personality in Hesiod," *Classical Antiquity* 2 (1983), 37–65. Gregory Nagy places Hesiod's work in the context of Indo-European linguistics, archaic thought patterns, and oral performance in his stimulating essay on Hesiod in *Ancient Writers,* ed. T. J. Luce (New York: Scribners, 1982).

So fragmented are the remains of the works of the Archaic Age that a realistic critical stance toward them can scarcely be taken. C. M. Bowra's *Greek Lyric Poetry* (2d ed.; Oxford: Oxford Univ. Press, 1961) and *Early Greek Elegists* (Cambridge: Heffer, 1960) are more compilations of the details of the poets' lives than anything else. But, as M. R. Lefkowitz has demonstrated well in her *Lives of the Greek Poets* (Baltimore: Johns Hopkins Univ. Press, 1981), the biographical material that survives from antiquity is largely fiction, scarcely to be given credence. See also her "Critical Stereotypes and the Poetry of Sappho," *Greek, Roman, and Byzantine Studies* 14 (1974), 113–23. C. M. Dawson, "*Spoudaiogeloion:* Random Thoughts on Occasional Poems," *Yale Classical Studies* 19 (1966), 37–76, emphasizes the archaic poets' reaction to the Homeric and Hesiodic corpus by drawing attention to the allusions and adaptations. This is perhaps the only possible critical approach given the fragmentary material. See, however, G. M. Kirkwood, *Early Greek Monody: The History of a Poetic Type* (Ithaca: Cornell Univ. Press, 1973); the essay on Sappho in Richard Jenkyns's *Three Classical Poets* (Cambridge, Mass.: Harvard Univ. Press, 1982); A. J. Podlecki, "Three Soldier Poets: Archilochus, Alcaeus and Solon," *Classical World* 63 (1969), 73–81; H. D. Rankin, *Archilochus of Paros* (Park Ridge, N.J.: Noyes Press, 1977); and Gregory Nagy, "Theognis of Megara: The Poet as Seer, Pilot, and Revenant," *Arethusa* 15 (1982), 109–28. On what the Greeks themselves thought of their poetry see G. B. Walsh, *Varieties of Enchantment: Early Greek Views of the Nature and Function of Poetry* (Chapel Hill: Univ. of North Carolina Press, 1984). See also W. B. Stanford, *Enemies of Poetry* (London: Routledge & Kegan Paul, 1980) on the false criticism of ancient literature.

The Greek myths have inspired an enormous scholarly literature. H. J. Rose, *A Handbook of Greek Mythology* (4th ed.; London: Methuen, 1950), gives the most common versions of the stories with the dates. It is crucial to bear in mind that what remains of these myths is known from literary pieces dating over many centuries. Thus extreme and self-conscious contrivance and chronological distinctions forever preclude getting at the myth pure and simple, as anthropologists can sometimes do when studying living cultures. Robert Graves in *The Greek Myths* (Baltimore: Penguin, 1955) recounts the myths, at the same time attempting to suggest possible sociological or psychological truths encoded in them. See also Joseph Fontenrose, *Python: A Study of Delphic Myth and Its Origin* (Berkeley: Univ. of California Press, 1959), and *Orion: The Myth of the Hunter and the Huntress* (Berkeley: Univ. of California Press, 1981). M. P. O. Morford and R. J. Lenardon's *Classical Mythology* (2d ed.; New York: Longman, 1977) is valuable for its quotations from the literature as well as for information on later adaptations and transformations of these myths. See also E. A. S. Butterworth, *The Tree at the Navel of the Earth: Some Traces of the Pre-Olympic World* (Berlin: de Gruyter, 1970), who speculates on the religion of the area prior to the arrival of the Indo-Europeans—a good book until the author begins to dissect the *Odyssey* too literally.

G. S. Kirk, *Myth: Its Meaning and Function in Ancient and Other Cultures* (Berkeley: Univ. of California Press, 1970), introduces a structuralist interpretation to the study of ancient Greek myth. As the heading over the review of this book in the *Times Literary Supplement* said, "Lévi-Strauss without tears." When comparing Greek culture with other cultures, Kirk complains that the ancient Greeks washed the animal and other fantastical elements from their mythology. It may be that this is exactly what makes the Greeks so remarkable in their culture—that they either jettisoned the nonhuman in their conception of the universe or never even imagined it. Two important works from the so-called French school, which seeks to employ anthropological methodology in the investigation of ancient Greek culture, are J. P. Vernant's *Myth and Society in Ancient Greece* (Sussex: Harvester Press, 1980) and his *Myth and Thought among the Greeks* (Boston: Routledge & Kegan Paul, 1983). In these books the author shows the social value of myth to the Greeks and how it encodes facts and behavior essential to their social functioning. Of particular interest is the chapter "The Reason of Myth" in the former volume, pp. 186–242, and "Myth Structures" and "From Myth to Reason," pp. 1–72 and 341–74 in the latter. See also Paul Friedrich's *The Meaning of Aphrodite* (Chicago: Univ. of Chicago Press, 1978), which argues that Aphrodite myths are part of the collective wisdom about sexuality and emotional relationships. F. M. Cornford, *From Religion to Philosophy* (New York: Harper, 1957), describes the evolution of religion into philosophy. The translated text of the remaining fragments of the very earliest thinkers are contained in John Burnet, *Early Greek Philosophy* (4th ed.; London: Black, 1930).

Pindar and Bacchylides are well-nigh impossible to discuss without recourse to the Greek text because it is the contrivance not the content that makes them important artists. See M. R. Lefkowitz, *The Victory Ode: An Introduction* (Park Ridge, N.J.: Noyes, 1976), who analyzes the six odes of Pindar and Bacchylides commissioned by the tyrant Hieron. See D. C. Young, "Pindaric Criticism," *Minnesota Review* 4 (1964), 584–641, now reprinted in W. M. Calder III and Jacob Stern, eds., *Pindaros und Bakchylides* (Wege der Forschung ser., no. 134; Darmstadt: Wissenschaftliche Buchgesellschaft, 1970), 1–95. Here one will also find an account of the theories of E. L. Bundy, whose *Studia Pindarica I–II* (University of California Publications in Classical Philology vol. 18, pts. 1 and 2, 1962) laid the basis for the modern interpretation of Pindar. Bundy in essence argues that the Pindaric ode is highly conventional and that its parts and its so-called ideas are all there to serve the form and to establish the praise for which Pindar was being paid. Bundy's work is a valuable antidote to the work of those critics who, rather than develop criticism, simply sum up what passes for "thought," particularly in Pindar. J. H. Finley, *Pindar and Aeschylus* (Cambridge, Mass.: Harvard Univ. Press, 1955), reminds us that the two poets were contemporaries, speaking in some sense to a common Greek audience. C. M. Bowra, *Pindar* (Oxford: Oxford Univ. Press, 1964), tends toward literal meanings, readings that emphasize the historical connection. C. A. P. Ruck and W. H. Matheson, *Pindar: Selected Odes* (Ann Arbor: Univ. of Michigan Press, 1968), have written interpretive essays that compare musical composition to the creation of a Pindaric ode. This idea accounts for the peculiar lack of continuity of thought in the odes, as though the language were there only to provide texture and tonalities, rather than to signify anything. The essay that prefaces F. J. Nisetich's translations in *Pindar's Victory Songs* (Baltimore: Johns Hopkins Univ. Press, 1980) as well as the introductory remarks before each ode are the very best introduction to this exceedingly difficult author.

D. S. Carne-Ross's *Pindar* (New Haven: Yale Univ. Press, 1985) is one of those old-fashioned armchair tours through selected poems of Pindar wherein the author tries to make his reader experience the poems by narrating and interpreting them altogether subjectively as he goes along. See also M. A. Grant's *Folktale and Herotale Motifs in the Odes of Pindar* (Lawrence: Univ. of Kansas Press, 1967), which locates Pindar's work in the saga and oral traditions. See also R. W. B. Burton's *Pindar's Pythian Odes: Essays in Interpretation* (Oxford: Oxford Univ. Press, 1962); D. C. Young's *Three Odes of Pindar* (*Mnemosyne* suppl. 9, 1968) and *Pindar Isthmian 7: Myth and Exempla* (*Mnemosyne* suppl. 15, 1971). Kevin Crotty's *Song and Action: The Victory Odes of Pindar* (Baltimore: Johns Hopkins Univ. Press, 1982), takes the position that Pindar is not only highly original in his manipulation of the traditional elements identified by Bundy, but also that he speaks both to the increasingly anachronistic aristocracy and to the emergent bourgeoisie as well.

ATHENS IN THE FIFTH CENTURY

The physical city of Athens is described in R. E. Wycherly's *Stones of Athens* (Princeton: Princeton Univ. Press, 1978).

Standard handbooks—for example, Alfred Zimmern's *Greek Commonwealth: Politics and Economics in Fifth-Century Athens* (5th ed.; Oxford: Oxford Univ. Press, 1931) and M. P. Nilsson's *History of Greek Religion* (2d ed. rev.; New York: Norton paperback, 1952)—have been to some extent superseded or at least supplemented by the new sociological and anthropological perspectives. See S. C. Humphreys, *Anthropology and the Greeks* (London: Routledge & Kegan Paul, 1978); L. Gernet, *The Anthropology of Ancient Greece,* trans. John Hamilton and Blaise Nagy (Baltimore: Johns Hopkins Univ. Press, 1981); M. M. Austin and Pierre Vidal-Naquet, *Economic and Social History of Ancient Greece: An Introduction,* trans. and rev. M. M. Austin (Berkeley: Univ. of California Press, 1977); A. W. Gouldner, *Enter Plato: Classical Greece and the Origins of Social Theory* (New York: Basic Books, 1965), the first part of which has been separately issued as *The Hellenic World: A Sociological Analysis* (New York: Harper Torchbook, 1969); and Walter Burkert, *Greek Religion,* trans. John Raffan (Cambridge: Harvard Univ. Press, 1985). These books have in common the altogether laudable intent to demystify classical antiquity, thus denying it the privileged status it enjoys in Western civilization. Rather, the behavior of the ancient Greeks is simply another insight into the repertoire of human responses to existence. This viewpoint coincides nicely with the new interest in *Receptionsgeschichte,* mentioned earlier. Thus the mystification that has built up over the previous twenty-odd centuries can be seen as the successive centuries' projection—as psychologists use the term—of their own problems and tendencies onto the tradition. The principal objections to this new sociological, anthropological interpretation are, first, that the evidence is so scanty that the generalizations and extrapolations about ancient social practice are generally rather flimsy and, second, that the language in which the observations are couched is so obscure as to defy analysis. Then, too, one often has the feeling in some of these studies that the theory was first created and then the facts or what passes for them were assembled to support it. Nonetheless, there are many insights in these books which make their study imperative for anyone who wishes to understand the ancient Greeks. B. M. W. Knox has an excellent review article discussing all the major pieces of the so-called French school in "Greece à la française," *New York Review of Books* 30, no. 3 (Mar. 3, 1983), 26–30.

W. G. Forrest, *The Emergence of Greek Democracy* (New York: World Univ. Library, 1966), is a lucid account of the political evolution of Athens. Not to be missed is J. W. Headlam's *Election by Lot at Athens* (2d ed.; Cambridge: Cambridge Univ. Press, 1933), which in a convincing argument for the relative weakness of the ten generals and the strength of the assembly and the rotated offices makes Athenian democracy to be the purest ever (overlooking, of course, those who were denied suffrage), and perhaps by the same token the most absurd. Gustav Gilbert's *Constitutional Antiquities of Sparta and Athens* (London: MacMillan, 1895), although outdated in details, is highly interesting on the workings of governments that in the abstract have so inspired countless subsequent societies.

M. I. Finley, *Politics in the Ancient World* (Cambridge: Cambridge Univ. Press, 1983), explains ancient history as a struggle between the rich and the poor: democracy flourished when the people acquiesced in their lot. G. E. M. de Ste. Croix, *The Class Struggle in the Ancient Greek World: From the Archaic Age to the Arab Conquests* (Ithaca: Cornell Univ. Press, 1981), takes a Marxist view of things. Andrew Lintott, *Violence, Civil Strife, and Revolution in the Classical City, 750–330 B.C.* (Baltimore: Johns Hopkins Univ. Press, 1981), takes a more moderate stance, talking of legal forms of repression and the philosopher's reaction to *stasis*. See also M. I. Finley, *Studies in Ancient Society* (London: Routledge & Kegan Paul, 1974), and *Economy and Society in Ancient Greece* (New York: Viking, 1982). M. T. W. Arnheim, *Aristocracy in Greek Society* (London: Thames & Hudson, 1977), argues for the enduring strength of the aristocracy, at least its values. See also Walter Donlan, *The Aristocratic Ideal in Ancient Greece: Attitudes of Superiority from Homer to the End of the Fifth Century B.C.* (Lawrence:

Univ. of Kansas Press, 1980). E. A. Havelock, *The Greek Concept of Justice from Its Shadow in Homer to Its Substance in Plato* (Cambridge, Mass.: Harvard Univ. Press, 1978), concentrates mostly on the example set in Homer and maintained through the educational system throughout the fifth century.

The disenfranchised can be studied in S. B. Pomeroy's *Goddesses, Whores, Wives, and Slaves: Women in Classical Antiquity* (New York: Schocken, 1975), in which the author has gathered together the slim evidence for Athenian women's lives. See also *Reflections of Women in Antiquity*, ed. H. P. Foley (New York: Gordon & Breach, 1981), and *Women in the Ancient World: The Arethusa Papers*, ed. John Peradotto and J. P. Sullivan (Albany: State Univ. of New York Press, 1984). Unfortunately, the new and long overdue interest in the role of women in Greek antiquity suffers from the paucity of the evidence; thus it is so easy to read into it. W. K. Lacey's *Family in Classical Greece* (Ithaca: Cornell Univ. Press, 1968) is a comprehensive collection of the evidence for this basic structure of Athenian society. P. E. Slater, *The Glory of Hera: Greek Mythology and the Greek Family* (Boston: Beacon Press, 1968) is a highly original account from a psychoanalytic perspective of the family in literature, myth, and actuality. For slavery see W. L. Westermann, *The Slave Systems of Greek and Roman Antiquity* (Philadelphia: American Philosophical Society, 1955), and M. I. Finley, ed., *Slavery in Classical Antiquity: Views and Controversies* (Cambridge: Heffer, 1960).

K. J. Dover's *Greek Homosexuality* (Cambridge, Mass.: Harvard Univ. Press, 1978) is an authoritative account of one of the more remarkable and controversial Athenian institutions. In this connection one might read the opening chapter of John Boswell, *Christianity, Social Tolerance, and Homosexuality* (Chicago: Univ. of Chicago Press, 1980), who argues on the basis of the Greek evidence that prior to the harsh Judeo-Christian prohibitions homoeroticism was simply one of a number of natural and equally neutral ways in which humankind found sexual, emotional, and sentimental satisfaction. See also Georges Devereux, "Greek Pseudo-Homosexuality and the Greek Miracle," *Symbolae Osloenses* 42 (1968), 69–92, who (committed to the Freudian view against the "normalcy" of homosexuality) argues that the institutionalized homosexuality of Greek males up to the age of thirty freed them long enough from adulthood's responsibilities to make for a larger than average pool of creative persons. See also Paul Cartledge, "Politics of Spartan Paederasty," *Pacific Coast Philological Studies,* n.s. 27 (1981). One would someday like to see this subject discussed by someone who finds the passive role in anal intercourse highly pleasurable instead of a dimly remembered furtive moment of searing pain from boyhood. See also Thorkil Vangaard, *Phallos: A Symbol and Its History in the Male World* (New York: International Universities Press, 1972); W. M. Clarke, "Achilles and Patroklos in Love," *Hermes* 106 (1978), 381–96, which is disputed by D. S. Barrett, "The Friendship of Achilles and Patroklos," *Classical Bulletin* 57 (1981), 87–93. See also Niall Rudd, "Romantic Love in Classical Times," *Ramus* 10 (1981), 140–55, and Otto Brendel, "The Scope and Temperament of Erotic Art in the Greco-Roman World," in *Studies in Erotic Art,* ed. T. R. Bowie and C. V. Christenson (New York: Basic Books, 1970), 3–108. Volumes 78 and 79 (1984, 1985) of *Classical World* contain a review by N. B. Crowther of all the recent studies on the subject of athletics in ancient Greece.

Athenian imperialism is the subject of Russell Meiggs's *Athenian Empire* (Oxford: Oxford Univ. Press, 1972), which should be read together with Donald Kagan, *The Outbreak of the Peloponnesian War* (Ithaca: Cornell Univ. Press, 1969). See V. D. Hanson's *Warfare and Agriculture in Classical Greece* (Pisa: Giardini, 1983), an excellent study of the connection of strategy to the growing season. A good introduction to Sparta is Plutarch's *Life of Lycurgus.* Already in antiquity Sparta was becoming more myth than historical reality. See E. N. Tigerstedt, *Legend of Sparta in Classical Antiquity* (Stockholm: Almquist & Wiksell, 1965), and Elizabeth Rawson, *The Spartan Tradition in European Thought* (Oxford: Oxford Univ. Press, 1969). The historical reality, however, as we can reconstruct it, can be found in J. T. Hooker, *The Ancient Spartans* (London: Dent, 1980). See also J. B. Salmon, *Wealthy Corinth: A History of the City to 338 B.C.* (Oxford: Oxford Univ. Press, 1984).

On religion, in addition to the excellent *Greek Religion* of Walter Burkert, mentioned earlier, there are the older accounts of M. P. Nilsson, *A History of Greek Religion* (2d ed.; New York: Norton paperback, 1952), and W. K. C. Guthrie, *The Greeks and Their Gods* (Boston: Beacon Press, 1955), then more specialized works, as for instance, Hugh Lloyd-Jones's *Justice of Zeus* (Berkeley: Univ. of California Press, 1971); W. K. C. Guthrie, *Orpheus and the Greek Religion* (New York: Norton, 1966); B. C. Dietrich, *Death, Fate and the Gods* (London: University of London Athlone Press, 1965); Walter Otto, *Dionysus* (Bloomington: Univ. of Indiana Press, 1965), a stimulating but crazy book; H. W. Parke and D. E. Wormell, *The Delphic Oracle* (Oxford: Blackwell, 1956); and H. W. Parke, *The Oracles of Zeus* (Cambridge, Mass.: Harvard Univ. Press, 1967). An antidote to the conventional wisdom that the Greeks were first and foremost rationalist in everything including their religious experience is E. R. Dodds's *Greeks and the Irrational* (Berkeley: Univ. of California Press, 1951), which, when it was first published, changed the way fifth-century Athens was studied.

H. I. Marrou's *History of Education in Antiquity* (New York: Sheed & Ward, 1956) is a witty, intelligent discussion of the evidence for educational practices; the section on Greece deals mostly with education in Athens. Volume 3 of W. K. C. Guthrie's exhaustive *History of Greek Philosophy,* titled *The Fifth Century Enlightenment* (Cambridge: Cambridge Univ. Press, 1969) has been reprinted (1971) by the same press as a paperback, *The Sophists.* See also G. B. Kerferd, *The Sophistic Movement* (Cambridge: Cambridge Univ. Press, 1981), who places the movement in its historical context and describes the Sophists' participation in the *nomos-physis* controversy and their influence on ethics, politics, and religion. The surviving fragments together with the sparse and random biographical details of the Sophists have been collected and translated by Kathleen Freeman, *The Pre-Socratic Philosophers* (3d ed.; Cambridge, Mass.: Harvard Univ. Press, 1966). E. A. Havelock's *Preface to Plato* (Cambridge, Mass.: Harvard Univ. Press, 1963) is one of the truly brilliant books of the last few decades; in it the central fact of the orality of ancient culture is discussed in all of its ramifications. See also the first chapter, "Common Sense to Science," in Marx Wartofsky, *Conceptual Foundations of Scientific Thought: An Introduction to the Philosophy of Science* (New York: MacMillan, 1968). The Sophists seem to have held a more optimistic view of things than what generally appears to be the case in classical antiquity. This view is explored by E. A. Havelock in *The Liberal Temper in Greek Politics* (New Haven: Yale Univ. Press, 1957). See also J. B. Bury, *The Idea of Progress: An Inquiry into Its Origin and Growth* (New York: Dover, 1955), and E. R. Dodds's title essay in *The Ancient Concept of Progress and Other Essays on Greek Literature* (Oxford: Oxford Univ. Press, 1973). See also Martin Robertson, *A Shorter History of Greek Art* (Cambridge: Cambridge Univ. Press, 1981), which is an abridgment of the excellent 1975 book.

TRAGEDY

The surviving tragedies are for the most part so abstract and so spare that successive generations of critics have been able to bring all kinds of meaning out of them, individually and collectively. The criticism of tragedy perhaps more than anything else reveals the power for creative mythmaking inherent in the classical tradition. For instead of a critical position on the genre accruing from the succession of essays and books written on each play or tragedy, there is a myriad of competing ideas.

Taking the long view, however, one can see fashions of opinions and trends from century to century, even sometimes from decade to decade. Sophocles' *Philoctetes,* for example, has inspired a wide range of interpretation. In the title essay of his *The Wound and the Bow: Seven Studies in Literature* (Boston: Houghton Mifflin, 1941), Edmund Wilson, in his characteristically magisterial fashion, glamorizes or sentimentalizes human defect in a fashion common to the thirties. The Greeks, who sympathized with the gods laughing at the crippled Hephaestus limping about in the first book of the *Iliad,* might have wondered at Wilson's ideas. There is my own "Sophocles' *Philoctetes* and the Homeric Embassy," *Transactions of the American Philological Association* 101 (1970), 63–75, which, although published at the beginning of the seventies, betrays the mentality of the fifties, when criticism turned on the hero, and especially in Sophocles on the Homeric sort of hero. See also Pierre Vidal-Naquet, "Sophocles' *Philoctetes* and the Ephebeia," in J. P. Vernant and Pierre Vidal-Nacqet, *Myth and Tragedy in Ancient Greece,* trans. J. B. Lloyd (Atlantic Highlands, N.J.: Humanities Press, 1981), 175–99, who illustrates the now-fashionable tendency to see tragedy as mirroring no more than some Athenian social transaction, describing, for instance, a ritual, a *rite de passage,* or an economic relationship and thus removing the freight of the accretions of twenty centuries of humanism—a tendency much decried by Brian Vickers in his *Towards Greek Tragedy: Drama, Myth and Society* (London: Longman, 1973).

On *Philoctetes* see also W. M. Calder III, "Sophoclean Apologia: Philoctetes," *Greek, Roman, and Byzantine Studies* 12 (1971), 153–74; M. C. Hoppin, "What Happens in Sophocles' *Philoctetes?" Traditio* 37 (1981), 1–30; Victor Bers, "The Perjured Chorus in Sophocles' *Philoctetes," Hermes* 109 (1981), 500–504; P. E. Easterling, "*Philoctetes* and Modern Criticism," *Illinois Classical Studies* 3 (1978), 27–39; and Oscar Mandel, "*Philoctetes*" *and the Fall of Troy* (Lincoln: Univ. of Nebraska Press, 1981), a review of approaches to *Philoctetes* through the centuries. As this selection will demonstrate, the dynamics of making meaning of this play are altogether as interesting as the play itself. One wants to see more synthesis, however. For instance, J. E. G. Whitehome, "The Background to Polyneices' Disinterment and

Reburial," *Greece and Rome* 30 (1983), 129–42, goes outside the play to contemporary burial practice to explain the so-called two burials whereas G. F. Held, "Antigone's Dual Motivation for the Double Burials," *Hermes 111* (1983), 190–201, locates the explanation within the play: religion the first time, love the second. If we were to synthesize these two essays we could say that the burial custom predisposes the audience to expect some kind of double burial to which the poet then can attach his own meanings. Similarly, Aya Betensky, "Aeschylus's *Oresteia:* The Power of Clytemnestra," *Ramus* 7 (1978), 11–25, and F. I. Zeitlin, "The Dynamics of Misogyny: Myth and Mythmaking in the *Oresteia,*" *Arethusa* 11 (1978), 149–84, combine well.

As the title indicates, P. W. Harsh's *Handbook of Classical Drama* (Palo Alto: Stanford Univ. Press, 1944) systematically sets out the few known facts about each tragedy, outlines the plot and action, and suggests major problems in interpretation. Albin Lesky, *Greek Tragedy,* trans. H. A. Frankfort (New York: Barnes and Noble, 1965), sets the plays more deeply into their literary and historical context. Lesky's first chapter, "What Is Tragedy?" is a particularly good discussion of the features common to all extant tragedies.

A. W. Pickard-Cambridge's *Dithyramb, Tragedy and Comedy,* 2d ed., rev. T. B. L. Webster (Oxford: Oxford Univ. Press, 1962) is among other things an authoritative review of various theories of the origin of tragedy and comedy together with the available evidence. See also A. C. Schlesinger, *Boundaries of Dionysus: Athenian Foundations for the Theory of Tragedy* (Cambridge, Mass.: Harvard Univ. Press, 1963). George Thomson, *Aeschylus and Athens: A Study of the Social Origins of Drama* (New York: Grosset & Dunlap, 1968), gives a Marxist interpretation. G. F. Else, *The Origin and Early Form of Greek Tragedy* (Cambridge, Mass.: Harvard Univ. Press, 1965), speculates on the literary influences, particularly the poetry of Solon. See also John Herington, *Poetry into Drama: Early Tragedy and the Greek Poetic Tradition* (Berkeley: Univ. of California Press, 1985). The origin and nature of tragedy as the ancients saw it can be found in Aristotle's *Poetics,* which G. F. Else has studied, translated, and commented upon in his *Aristotle's "Poetics": The Argument* (Cambridge, Mass.: Harvard Univ. Press, 1957). John Jones's *Aristotle and the Art of Tragedy* (Oxford: Oxford Univ. Press, 1960) is a most important book, in which the author insists that action, as Aristotle himself said, and not character, as Christian humanists interpret it, is the main feature of tragedy. This book helped to turn criticism of the time away from the concentration on the Homeric-like hero toward the structure of the action, thus reemphasizing the myth.

The relationship between tragic drama, myth, and ritual is problematic and has inspired a large scholarly literature. See, for instance, Herbert Musurillo, *Symbol and Myth in Ancient Poetry* (New York: Fordham Univ. Press, 1961); R. Y. Hathorn, *Tragedy, Myth, and Mystery* (Bloomington: Univ. of Indiana Press, 1962); J. P. Guépin, *The Tragic Paradox: Myth and Ritual in Greek Drama* (Amsterdam: Hakkert, 1968); Jack Lindsay, *The Clashing Rocks: A Study of Early Greek Religion and Culture and the Origins of Drama* (London: Chapman & Hall, 1965); V. P. Vernant and Pierre Vidal-Naquet, *Myth and Tragedy in Ancient Greece,* trans. J. B. Lloyd (Atlantic Highlands, N.J.: Humanities Press, 1981); Walter Burkert, "Greek Tragedy and Sacrificial Ritual," *Greek, Roman, and Byzantine Studies* 7 (1966), 87–121, and his *Homo Necans: The Anthropology of Ancient Greek Sacrificial Ritual and Myth* (Berkeley: Univ. of California Press, 1983), which have led the way to such studies as Helene P. Foley's *Ritual Irony: Poetry and Sacrifice in Euripides* (Ithaca: Cornell Univ. Press, 1985). See also Joseph Fontenrose, *The Ritual Theory of Myth* (Berkeley: Univ. of California Press, 1966).

The indispensable book for studying theatrical production is A. W. Pickard-Cambridge's *Dramatic Festivals of Athens,* 2d ed., rev. John Gould and D. M. Lewis (Oxford: Oxford Univ. Press, 1968), in which all the evidence is assembled and assessed. The book poses some difficulty for those who do not know Greek. See also T. B. L. Webster, *Greek Theater Production* (2d ed.; London: Methuen, 1970), and Peter Arnott, *Greek Scenic Conventions in the Fifth Century B.C.* (Oxford: Oxford Univ. Press, 1962). David Seale, *Vision and Stagecraft in Sophocles* (Chicago: Univ. of Chicago Press, 1982), discusses production values play by play. D. F. Sutton, *The Greek Satyr Play* (Meisenheim am Glan: Hain, 1980), discusses this often-ignored element of the dramatic festivals. W. B. Stanford, *Greek Tragedy and the Emotion: An Introductory Study* (London: Routledge & Kegan Paul, 1983), studies the way the tragedians manipulated the audience.

The contemporary political reference in tragedy continually beguiles the critics. See Gunter Zuntz, *The Political Plays of Euripides* (2d ed.; Manchester: Manchester Univ. Press, 1963), who discounts any specific topical references; A. J. Podlecki, *The Political Background of Aeschylean Tragedy* (Ann Arbor: Univ. of Michigan Press, 1966); J. H. Finley, "Politics and Early Attic Tragedy," *Harvard Studies in Classical Philology* 71 (1966), 1–13; Jacqueline de Romilly, "*Phoenician*

Women of Euripides: Topicality in Greek Tragedy," trans. D. H. Orroh, *Bucknell Review* 15 (1967), 108–32; and C. W. McLeod, "Politics and the *Oresteia*," *Journal of Hellenic Studies* 102 (1982), 124–44. P. J. Conacher, "Contemporary Politics in Greek Tragedy," *Acta Classica* 24 (1981), 23–35, criticizes reading political references into the plays. The plays are sometimes read against their historical context, as in A. W. H. Adkins, "Divine and Human Values in Aeschylus's *Seven against Thebes*," *Antike und Abendland* 28 (1982), 32–68, and "Basic Greek Values in Euripides' *Hecuba* and *Hercules Furens*," *Classical Quarterly* 16 (1966), 193–219; B. X. de Wet, "The *Electra* of Sophocles: A Study in Social Values," *Acta Classica* 20 (1977), 23–36; H. P. Foley, "The Concept of Women in Athenian Drama," in *Reflections of Women in Antiquity*, edited by her (New York: Gordon & Breach, 1981). T. M. Falkner, "Coming of Age in Argos: Physis and Paideia in Euripides' *Orestes*," *Classical Journal* 78 (1983), 289–300; and A. W. Gouldner's "Death and the Tragic Outlook," in *Enter Plato: Classical Greece and the Origin of Social Theory* (New York: Basic Books, 1965). The plays serve as the basis for drawing a still grander picture in C. P. Segal's *Tragedy and Civilization: An Interpretation of Sophocles* (Cambridge, Mass.: Harvard Univ. Press, 1981), which is a structuralist reading of Sophocles' plays; the first three chapters are on tragic drama and Sophocles in general.

While Aristotle's emphasis of Sophocles' *Oedipus the King* may have made it the most studied play ever (see, e.g., *Twentieth Century Interpretations of "Oedipus Rex": A Collection of Critical Essays,* ed. M. J. O'Brien [Englewood Cliffs, N.J.: Prentice-Hall, 1968]), no two scholars can agree on it. See, for instance, E. R. Dodds's "On Misunderstanding the *Oedipus Rex*," *Greece and Rome* 13 (1966), 37–49, which presents a view quite the opposite of that in Thomas Gould, "The Innocence of Oedipus: The Philosophers in *Oedipus the King*," *Arion* 4 (1965), 363–86.

Freud may have been inspired by Sophocles' *Oedipus the King* for the definition of his Oedipal complex (see Patrick Mullahy, *Oedipus: Myth and Complex* [New York: Hermitage Press, 1948]), but Euripides' *Bacchae* has provided the stuff for any number of psychoanalytic studies, particularly of the character Pentheus. See J. A. LaRue, "Prurience Uncovered: The Psychology of Euripides' Pentheus," *Classical Journal* 63 (1968), 209–14; William Sale, "The Psychoanalysis of Pentheus in the *Bacchae* of Euripides," *Yale Classical Studies* 22 (1972), 63–82, followed by his *Existentialism and Euripides: Sickness, Tragedy, and Divinity in the "Medea," "Hippolytus," and the*

"Bacchae" (Berwick, N.J.: Aureal Publications, 1977); C. P. Segal, "Pentheus on the Couch and on the Grid: Psychological and Structuralist Readings of Greek Tragedy," *Classical World* 72 (1978), 129–48, from which he has gone on to write *Dionysiac Poetics and Euripides' "Bacchae"* (Princeton: Princeton Univ. Press, 1982). See also B. H. Fowler, "Thought and Underthought in Three Sophoclean Plays," *Eranos* 79 (1981), 1–22, which is a Freudian interpretation of subconscious meanings; Georges Devereux, "The Self-Blinding of Oidipous in Sophocles' *Oidipous Tyrannos,*" *Journal of Hellenic Studies* 93 (1973), 36–49; and A. V. Rankin, "Euripides' Hippolytus: A Psychopathological Hero," *Arethusa* 7 (1974), 71–94.

F. I. Zeitlin, *Under the Sign of the Shield: Semiotics and Aeschylus' "Seven against Thebes"* (Rome: Edizioni dell'Ateneo, 1982), has made a very close and elegant reading of the text, which elicits a view of the enormous range and interconnection engendered by Aeschylus's language. In this connection see C. P. Segal, "Greek Myth as a Semiotic and Structural System and the Problem of Tragedy," *Arethusa* 16 (1983), 173–98, and Bradley Berke, *Tragic Thought and the Grammar of Tragic Myth* (Bloomington: Indiana Univ. Press, 1982). See also Jon Knott, *The Eating of the Gods: An Interpretation of Greek Tragedy* (New York: Random House, 1972), which emphasizes the contemporary relevance of the plays. In this connection one might consult B. F. Dick, *"Lord of the Flies* and the *Bacchae,"* *Classical World* 57 (1964), 145–56, who notices how like contemporary thought Euripides' ideas seem, and William Arrowsmith, "Eliot and Euripides," *Arion* 4 (1965), 21–35, who deals with *The Cocktail Party* and the *Alcestis* and along the way with A. W. Verrall's criticism of Euripides. Verrall, by the way, is valuable for his peculiar readings of these plays. He seeks realism and reads the text absolutely literally. His interpretations are therefore often bizarre, but they force his reader to rethink the play in question and generally to come to understand how convention works in the drama. They are contained in *Euripides the Rationalist: A Study in the History of Art and Religion* (Cambridge: Cambridge Univ. Press, 1895), *Essays in Four Plays of Euripides: "Andromache," "Helen," "Heracles," and "Orestes"* (Cambridge: Cambridge Univ. Press, 1905), and *The "Bacchants" of Euripides and Other Plays* (Cambridge: Cambridge Univ. Press, 1910).

One of tragedy's finer critics, of the sort who stay within the text, is R. P. Winnington-Ingram, whose *Euripides and Dionysus: An Interpretation of the "Bacchae"* (Cambridge: Cambridge Univ. Press, 1948) is a detailed, subtle, sensitive, line-by-line reading of the play, just about the best analysis of a tragedy there is. More recently, he distilled a lifetime's experience with tragedy into two excellent books, *Sophocles: An Interpretation* (Cambridge: Cambridge Univ. Press, 1980) and *Studies in Aeschylus* (Cambridge: Cambridge Univ. Press, 1983). An equally gifted critic is B. M. W. Knox, whose *Oedipus at Thebes* (New Haven: Yale Univ. Press, 1957) is a superlative study of the language of the play, showing how the figure of Oedipus mirrors Athens the city. See also his *The Heroic Temper: A Study in Heroic Humanism* (Berkeley: Univ. of California Press, 1964), the first two of chapters of which are the best account of the Greek tradition of the hero from Homer to Sophocles. See also his "Euripidean Comedy" in *Rarer Action: Essays in Honor of Francis Ferguson,* ed. Alan Cheuse and Richard Koffler (New Brunswick, N.J.: Rutgers Univ. Press, 1970), his "The *Ajax* of Sophocles," *Harvard Studies in Classical Philology* 65 (1961), 1–37, as well as his essay on Euripides' *Medea* in the excellent collection of essays on Greek tragedy contained in *Yale Classical Studies* 25 (1977), 193–226. These articles and others by Knox are gathered together in a collection of his essays titled *Word and Action: Essays on Ancient Theater* (Baltimore: Johns Hopkins Univ. Press, 1979).

William Arrowsmith in "The Criticism of Greek Tragedy," *Tulane Drama Review* 3 (1959), 31–57, argues that tragic drama had the capacity to open up the people of Athens to new ideas. It is, of course, debatable whether theater publicly supported and so popular could be anything other than conformist and conventional. The answer to this question makes a difference in how we are to read the plays. See my "Nature's Mirror or Nature's Distillery: The Proper Metaphor for Ancient Greek Tragedy," *Florida State University Comparative Drama Papers* (Washington, D.C., 1982), 1:11–36, for the argument that the choral passages by their lyrical beauty and platitudinizing intervene and erase the tension and conflict engendered by the dialogue passages; thus does art conquer tragedy. Further superior criticism of tragedy is found in T. G. Rosenmeyer, *The Masks of Tragedy: Essays on Six Dramas* (Austin: Univ. of Texas Press, 1963), and *The Art of Aeschylus* (Berkeley: Univ. of California Press, 1982); Michael Gagarin, *Aeschylean Drama* (Berkeley: Univ. of California Press, 1976); Ruth Scodel, *Sophocles* (Boston: Twayne, 1984); J. C. Opstelten, *Sophocles and Greek Pessimism,* trans. J. A. Ross (Amsterdam: North Holland, 1952), who disabuses us of the notion that the Greek tragic view of life was pessimistic; and A. J. A. Waldock's *Sophocles the Dramatist* (Cambridge: Cambridge Univ. Press, 1966), which is a necessary antidote to the works that concentrate so upon Sophoclean thought and piety that one would believe the man to have been a don or a divine rather than a dramatist. *Sophocles: A Collection of Critical Essays,* ed. T. M. Woodward (Englewood Cliffs, N.J.: Prentice-Hall, 1966), eschews the obvious for essays written by Nietzsche, Heidegger, Virginia Woolf, and Oswald Spengler, all of which remind us also of Sophocles' greater importance as a cultural icon.

Euripides' plays, being generally more ambiguous, excite more variant interpretations; see, for instance, J. R. Wilson, *Twentieth Century Interpretations of Euripides' "Alcestis"* (Englewood Cliffs, N.J.: Prentice-Hall, 1968). G. M. A. Grube's *Drama of Euripides* (London: Methuen, 1941) is still the standard survey. What E. M. Blaiklock, *The Male Characters of Euripides: A Study in Realism* (Manchester: Manchester Univ. Press, 1955), does for the males needs to be done for the women who figure so prominently in Euripidean drama. A. P. Burnett, *Catastrophe Survived: Euripides' Plays of Mixed Reversal* (Oxford: Oxford Univ. Press, 1971), tends to literal readings of the plays, ignoring ambiguity, absurdity, and humor, more the current staples of Euripidean criticism. See also C. G. Wolff, "The Design and Myth in Euripides' *Ion,*" *Harvard Studies in Classical Philology* 69 (1965), 169–94; N. A. Greenberg, "Euripides' *Orestes:* An Interpretation," *Harvard Studies in Classical Philology* 66 (1962), 157–92; Hugh Parry, "Euripides' *Orestes:* The Quest for Salvation," *Transactions of the American Philological Association* 100 (1969), 337–53.

COMEDY

K. J. Dover's *Aristophanic Comedy* (Berkeley: Univ. of California Press, 1972) is a good introduction to Aristophanes, dealing with the technical problems of production as well as interpreting the plays. C. H. Whitman, *Aristophanes and the Comic Hero* (Cambridge, Mass.: Harvard Univ. Press, 1964), focuses more on the fiction of the plays, the relation between comic and tragic drama, and the views of man therein. This approach is challenged by William Arrowsmith, "Aristophanes' *Birds:* The Fantasy Politics of Eros," *Arion* n.s. 1 (1973), 119–67, who insists upon the historical background to the plays. Some scholars use Aristophanes' plays as historical documents; see, for instance, Victor Ehrenberg, *People of Aristophanes; A Sociology of Old Attic Comedy* (3d ed.; New York: Schocken, 1962). G. A. H.

Chapman, "Some Notes on Dramatic Illusion in Aristophanes," *American Journal of Philology* 104 (1983), 1–23, remarks on the different relationship established between actors and audience in tragic and comic drama. F. I. Zeitlin, "Travesties of Gender and Genre in Aristophanes' *Thesmophoriazusae*," in *Reflections of Women in Antiquity*, ed. H. P. Foley (New York: Gordon & Breach, 1981), takes up two of Aristophanes' continual preoccupations, and we may presume of his audience as well. Leo Strauss, *Socrates and Aristophanes* (New York: Basic Books, 1962), discusses ancient views of education. See also Martha Nussbaum, "Aristophanes and Socrates on Learning Practical Wisdom," in *Aristophanes: Essays in Appreciation*, ed. Jeffrey Henderson, Yale Classical Studies 26 (New Haven, 1980). David Konstan, "An Anthropology of Euripides' *Cyclops*," *Ramus* 10 (1981), 87–103, talks of the anarchy of the Cyclops as he is presented in the play in conflict with man's social restraints. David Konstan and Mathew Dillon, "The Ideology of Aristophanes' *Wealth*," *American Journal of Philology* 102 (1981), 371–94, describe the play as a conscious attempt to create ideology at a time of considerable political instability in Athens. See also D. F. Sutton, *Self and Society in Aristophanes* (Washington, D.C.: University Press of America, 1980), who also wrote the work on the satyr play noted in the section on tragedy. C. W. Dearden, *The Stage of Aristophanes* (London: Univ. of London, Athlone Press, 1976), concentrates upon production values, whereas D. C. Moulton, *Aristophanic Poetry* (Göttingen: Vandenhoeck & Ruprecht, 1981), looks to the language.

W. G. Arnott, "From Aristophanes to Menander," *Greece and Rome* 19 (1972), 65–80, looks to the change between the so-called Old and New Comedy. B. M. W. Knox, "Euripidean Comedy," in *Rarer Action: Essays in Honor of Francis Ferguson,* ed. Alan Chase and Richard Koffler (New Brunswick: Rutgers Univ. Press, 1970), 68–96, suggests that the comic elements in Euripidean drama are the starting point for the Western comic theater. In this connection see L. A. Post, "Menander and the *Helen* of Euripides," *Harvard Studies in Classical Philology* 68 (1964), 99–118. See also H. E. Barnes, "Greek Tragicomedy," *Classical Journal* 60 (1964), 125–31. My "Alcestis and Her Critics," *Greek, Roman, and Byzantine Studies* 2 (1959), 111–27, takes the view that the *Alcestis* is amusing or unsettling. See also my *Euripides' "Alcestis,"* translation with a commentary (Englewood Cliffs, N.J.: Prentice-Hall, 1974). T. B. L. Webster, *An Introduction to Menander* (Manchester: Manchester Univ. Press, 1974), puts the dramatist into his historical context, while S. M. Goldberg, *The Making of Menander's Comedy* (Berkeley: Univ. of California Press, 1980), is more a critical study of them as literary productions. Consult F. H. Sandbach, *The Comic Theater of Greece and Rome* (New York: Norton, 1977), to see how much we must depend on Roman adaptations of the Greek comedies for our knowledge of the originals.

Sophie Trenkner, *The Greek Novella in the Classical Period* (Cambridge: Cambridge Univ. Press, 1958), discusses the elements in the Greek romances as they appear in fragments in the fifth century. Arthur Heiserman's *Novel before the Novel* (Chicago: Univ. of Chicago Press, 1977) is a marvelously original critical discussion of the romances as well as of Apollonius Rhodius's *Argonautica* as a prototypical romance. B. E. Perry's *The Ancient Romances* (Berkeley: Univ. of California Press, 1967) is, like everything this man writes, intelligent and thoughtful; in this book he analyzes the historical and social milieu from which this new art form sprang as well as each of the extant pieces. See Tomas Hägg's more recent *Novel in Antiquity* (Berkeley: Univ. of California Press, 1983), in which he describes the historical context for the novel, identifies the probable audience (women), speculates on origins (cities), and stresses the epic and New Comedy connection. S. P. and M. J. Schierling, "The Influence of the Ancient Romances on the Acts of the Apostles," *Classical Bulletin* 54 (1978), 81–88, discuss what is currently one of the more interesting aspects of the romances.

THE BEGINNINGS OF PROSE

The first part of R. G. Collingwood, *The Idea of History* (New York: Galaxy paperback, 1956), titled "Greco-Roman Historiography," raises basic philosophical questions about the nature of ancient historiography and along the way makes a devastating attack upon Thucydides. J. B. Bury, whose history of ancient Greece is the standard, writes of his own predecessors in *The Ancient Greek Historians* (New York: Dover paperback, 1958). F. W. Walbank, "History and Tragedy," *Historia* 9 (1960), 216–34, discusses the relation between epic, history, and tragedy. See also Arnaldo Momigliano, "Historiography on Written Tradition and Historiography on Oral Tradition," in *Studies in Historiography* (London: Weidenfeld & Nicolson, 1966), 211–20, and "Greek Historiography," *History and Theory* 17 (1978), 1–28, as well as G. A. Press, *The Development of the Idea of History in Antiquity* (Montreal: McGill–Queen's Univ. Press, 1983).

C. R. Ligota, "This Story Is Not True: Fact and Fiction in Antiquity," *Journal of the Warburg Institute* 45 (1982), 1–13, treats one of the principal philosophical problems in ancient historiography. See also J. P. Vernant's "From Oedipus to Periander: Lameness, Tyranny, Incest in Legend and History," *Arethusa* 15 (1982), 19–38, an analysis of parallels between myth and historical fact in Herodotus. In this connection see Barry Baldwin, "How Credulous Was Herodotus?" *Greece and Rome* 11 (1964), 167–77; J. A. S. Evans, "Father of History or Father of Lies: The Reputation of Herodotus," *Classical Journal* 64 (1968), 11–17. Herodotus had his detractors in antiquity; see Plutarch's essay *Concerning Herodotus' Hostile Prejudice (de malignitate Herodoti)*. F. J. Groten, "Herodotus' Use of Variant Versions," *Phoenix* 17 (1963), 79–87; Martin Miller, "The Herodotean Croesus," *Klio* 41 (1963), 58–94; and Mabel Lang, "Herodotus and the Ionian Revolt," *Historia* 17 (1968), 24–36, all deal in one way or another with the question of Herodotus's veracity.

Richmond Lattimore, "Composition of the History of Herodotus," *Classical Philology* 53 (1958), 9–19, is an excellent reconstruction of the writing materials available to Herodotus and how they helped shape his style. Mabel Lang, *Herodotean Narrative and Discourse* (Cambridge, Mass.: Harvard Univ. Press, 1984), explores the oral techniques of Herodotus. The question of the unity of Herodotus's work preoccupies many of his critics. H. R. Immerwahr, *Form and Thought in Herodotus* (Chapel Hill: Univ. of North Carolina Press, 1966), takes the relationship of the stories in Herodotus to be the key to the unity as well as the source of the meaning of the history. The second chapter, on style and structure, is particularly good. C. W. Fornara, *Herodotus: An Interpretative Essay* (Oxford: Oxford Univ. Press, 1971), also deals with the question of Herodotean unity, besides making interesting remarks on the influence of tragedy on Herodotus. The first chapter is a good survey of the scholarship on Herodotus up to the time. See also John Hart, *Herodotus and Greek History* (New York: St. Martin's, 1982); J. A. S. Evans, *Herodotus* (Boston: Twayne, 1982); David Konstan, "The Stories in Herodotus' *Histories*, Book 1," *Helios* 9 (1983), 1–22; and Stewart Flory, "Laughter, Tears, and Wisdom in Herodotus," *American Journal of Philology* 99 (1978), 145–53, who argues that these form a pattern of narration in several episodes.

V. J. Hunter, *Past and Process in Herodotus and Thucydides* (Princeton: Princeton Univ. Press, 1982) explores the narrative styles of both historians, which demonstrate their contemporaneity rather than their disparate quality. W. P. Wallace, "Thucydides," *Phoenix* 18

(1964), 251–61, describes the way Thucydides manipulates his reader. G. W. Bowersock, "The Personality of Thucydides," *Antioch Review* 25 (1965), 135–46, shows that Thucydides is less objective than he is so often presumed to be. J. H. Finley, *Three Essays on Thucydides* (Cambridge, Mass.: Harvard Univ. Press, 1967), makes excellent observations on Thucydidean style, his relationship to the Sophistic movement, and the unity of his *History*.

R. W. Connor, *Thucydides* (Princeton: Princeton Univ. Press, 1984), after a stimulating introduction that covers the previous important scholarship and raises certain basic questions about the way someone in the late twentieth century will read Thucydides, devotes a separate chapter to each book of the *History*. H. R. Rawlings, *The Structure of Thucydides' "History"* (Princeton: Princeton Univ. Press, 1981), argues that Thucydides planned ten books, the first five to parallel the latter (of which only six through eight were written before his death). V. J. Hunter, *Thucydides: The Artful Reporter* (Toronto: Hakkert, 1973), notices such things as how prescient the speeches are, suggesting that Thucydides wrote them after the fact rather than reporting what was said. See also K. J. Dover, "Thucydides as History and as Literature," *History and Theory: Studies in the Philosophy of History* 22 (1983), 54–63; Marc Cogan, *The Human Thing: The Speeches and Principles of Thucydides' "History"* (Chicago: Univ. of Chicago Press, 1981); and C. W. MacLeod's "Reason and Necessity: Thucydides iii.9.14 37–48," *Journal of Hellenic Studies* 98 (1978), 64–78, which is an analysis of the relationship between Thucydides' own message and the speakers' arguments. G. B. Grundy's *Thucydides and the History of His Age* (2d ed.; Oxford: Blackwell, 1948) is a detailed account of the historical realities Thucydides' readers must know to understand his less than obvious allusions. A. W. Gomme, *A Historical Commentary on Thucydides* (vol. 1; Oxford: Oxford Univ. Press, 1945), 1–88, is an excellent statement of what Thucydides takes for granted, possible reasons for his silences, as well as some account of the other sources for the period of history Thucydides describes. C. N. Cochrane, *Thucydides and the Science of History* (London: Russell, 1929), supports the notion that Thucydides was a "scientific" historian, a hard-nosed fact finder. On the other side is F. M. Cornford's brilliant *Thucydides Mythistoricus* (reissue; London: Routledge & Kegan Paul, 1965), which seeks to show how tragic logic dominated the intellectual activity in fifth-century Athens. Peter Pouncey, *The Necessities of War: A Study of Thucydides' Pessimism* (New York: Columbia Univ. Press, 1980), is especially good on Thucydides' description of man's selfishness and fear as the principal human motives.

Paul Friedländer has written the indispensable study of Plato, translated by Hans Meyerhoff. The first volume is an *Introduction* (2d ed.; Princeton: Princeton Univ. Press, 1969). In volume 2, *The Dialogues: First Period,* and volume 3, *The Dialogues: Second and Third Period* (Princeton Univ. Press, 1964, 1969), each dialogue is discussed singly. For the background to the life and times of Plato see G. C. Field, *Plato and His Contemporaries* (3d ed.; London: Methuen, 1967). For the *Symposium* see Helen Bacon, "Socrates Crowned," *Virginia Quarterly Review* 35 (1959), 415–30; Diskin Clay, "The Tragic and Comic Poet of the *Symposium,*" *Arion* n.s. 2 (1975), 238–61; S. L. Schein, "Alcibiades and Misguided Love in Plato's *Symposium,*" *Theta Pi* 3 (1974), 158–67; Frances Muecke's "Portrait of the Artist as a Young Woman," *Classical Quarterly* 32 (1982), 41–55, in which it is argued that for Aristophanes Agathon's effeminacy is a reflection of his art as well as his personality; Richard Patterson, "The Platonic Idea of Comedy and Tragedy," *Philosophy and Literature* 6 (1982), 76–93; Dorothy Tarrant, "Plato as Dramatist," *Journal of Hellenic Studies* 75 (1955), 82–89; and Stanley Rosen, *Plato's "Symposium"* (New Haven: Yale Univ. Press, 1968). See also Ludwig Edelstein, "The Function of Myth in Plato's Philosophy," *Journal of the History of Ideas* 10 (1949), 463–81; J. N. Findlay's "Myths of Plato," *Dionysius* 2 (1978), 19–34, in which the myths are analyzed to show that they represent serious propositions; Martha Nussbaum, "This Story Isn't True," in *Plato on Beauty, Wisdom, and the Arts,* ed. Julius Moravcsik and Philip Temko (Totowa, N.J.: Rowman & Littlefield, 1982), 79–124; John Tate, "Plato and Allegorical Interpretation," *Classical Quarterly* 23 (1929), 142–54; 24 (1930), 1–10; 28 (1934), 105–14. On the art of the dialogue see Julius Stenzel's *Plato's Method of Dialectic,* trans. D. J. Allan (New York: Russell & Russell, 1964), in which there is an excellent introductory essay by the translator on Stenzel and the subject of dialectic. See especially the chapter entitled "The Literary Form and the Philosophical Content of the Platonic Dialogue"; H. G. Gadamer, *Dialogue and Dialectic: Eight Hermeneutic Studies on Plato* (New Haven: Yale Univ. Press, 1980); the chapter entitled "Dialogue," pp. 154–70 in the introductory volume of Freidländer's work; K. F. Moors, "Plato's Use of Dialogue," *Classical World* 72 (1978), 77–93. See also Dorothea Wender, "Letting Go: Imagery and Symbolic Naming in Plato's *Lysis,*" *Ramus* 7 (1978), 38–45; Thomas Payne's "*Crito* as a Mythological Mime," *Interpretation*

11 (1983), 1–23, in which it is argued that Plato is playing off the ninth book of the *Iliad* in the *Crito*.

On the trial see E. T. H. Brann, "The Offense of Socrates: A Rereading of Plato's *Apology*," *Interpretation* 7 (1978), 1–21, in conjunction with which read Seth Benardete's *Being of the Beautiful* (Chicago: Univ. of Chicago Press, 1984) which is a reading of the *Theatetus*, the *Sophist*, and the *Statesman* taken together as a continuum of Socrates' thoughts as he prepares for his defense; Richard Kraut, *Socrates and the State* (Princeton: Princeton Univ. Press, 1984), who demonstrates Plato's consistent portrait of Socrates' political beliefs through the early dialogues; and E. M. and Neal Wood's *Class Ideology and Ancient Political Theory: Socrates, Plato and Aristotle in Social Context* (New York: Oxford Univ. Press, 1978), which is a relentlessly Marxist approach but a nice antidote to Arnheim's book on aristocracy mentioned earlier in which the author's sympathies are clearly engaged with *hoi kaloi k'agathoi* (a Greek equivalent more or less for "the beautiful people").

ALEXANDRIAN LITERATURE

Most ancient Greek histories end with the death of Alexander the Great. But lots more was yet to come, as contemporary historians are now affirming. P. M. Fraser's *Ptolemaic Alexandria* (Oxford: Oxford Univ. Press, 1972) is the newest vast repository of fact about the third century's most important city. W. W. Tarn and G. T. Griffith's *Hellenistic Civilization* (3d ed.; London: Arnold, 1952) is the standard survey; F. E. Peters, *The Harvest of Hellenism* (New York: Simon and Schuster, 1970), pp. 17–260, concentrates on politics and philosophy; Arnaldo Momigliano, *Alien Wisdom: The Limits of Hellenization* (Cambridge: Cambridge Univ. Press, 1975), discusses the interaction between Greeks and barbarians in the Hellenistic world down to the period of Augustus. S. B. Pomeroy, *Women in Hellenistic Egypt from Alexander to Cleopatra* (New York: Schocken, 1984), describes a period when women began to have some greater autonomy; J. P. Lynch, *Aristotle's School* (Berkeley: Univ. of California Press, 1972), describes the new scholarship; R. K. Hack, "The Doctrine of Literary Forms," *Harvard Studies in Classical Philology* 27 (1916), 1–66, describes the way Aristotle saved the poets from Plato's attack upon them and reworked the doctrine of imitation. See also J. O. Haydon, *Polestar of the Ancients: The Aristotelian Tradition in Classical and English Literary*

Criticism (Newark: Univ. of Delaware Press, 1979). This was the period when scholars began to understand their tradition. For example, look at the opening chapters of W. B. Stanford, *The Ulysses Theme* (Oxford: Oxford Univ. Press, 1954), and G. K. Galinsky, *The Herakles Theme* (Princeton: Princeton Univ. Press, 1957), to see what Alexandrian poets, Apollonius particularly, could expect their audiences to know. See also G. L. Huxley, *Greek Epic Poetry from Eumelos to Panyassis* (Cambridge, Mass.: Harvard Univ. Press, 1969), for what we know of the epic poems written between the time of Homer and Apollonius.

T. G. Rosenmeyer, *The Green Cabinet* (Berkeley: Univ. of California Press, 1969), looks at Hellenistic pastoral poetry in the context of its evolution in the next twenty centuries. D. M. Halperin, *Before Pastoral: Theocritus and the Ancient Tradition of Pastoral Poetry* (New Haven: Yale Univ. Press, 1983), looks at where it came from. Gilbert Lawall, *Theocritus' Coan Pastorals: A Poetry Book* (Cambridge, Mass.: Harvard Univ. Press, 1967), seeks to define Theocritus's pastoral man, a new Hellenistic conception equivalent to epic man or tragic man. See also C. P. Segal, *Poetry and Myth in Ancient Pastoral: Essays on Theocritus and Virgil* (Princeton: Princeton Univ. Press, 1981).

John Ferguson, *Callimachus* (Boston: Twayne, 1980), has written a survey of what we know about this little known but so important author. See also J. V. Cody, *Horace and Callimachean Aesthetics* (Brussels: Latomus, 1976); T. M. Klein, "Callimachus, Apollonius and the Concept of the 'Big Book,'" *Eranos* 73 (1975), 16–25; K. J. McKay's *Poet at Play* (Leiden: Brill, 1962), which may be hard going for the Greekless; and D. H. Garrison, *Mild Frenzy: A Reading of Hellenistic Love Epigrams* (Wiesbaden: Steiner, 1978).

I have written *Epic and Romance in the "Argonautica" of Apollonius* (Carbondale: Southern Illinois Univ. Press, 1982), in which there is a rather comprehensive bibliographical essay on pp. 169–78; one might also read Gilbert Lawall, "Apollonius' *Argonautica:* Jason as Anti-Hero," *Yale Classical Studies* 19 (1966), 121–69, and J. F. Carspecken, "Apollonius Rhodius and the Homeric Epic," in volume 13 (1952) of that same journal.

Important Dates in History and Literature

The history of ancient Greece, particularly its literary history, is so fragmentary that much is unknown. Thus for many authors we have only a birth date or death date but not both. Or we have an approximate date for an author's creative period based on some datable event to which he refers. We have established dates for the first production of some of the tragedies and comedies, approximate dates for the writing of some of the other pieces of literature. Most of this scheme is problematic and arguable, but in general outline it is sufficiently reliable to offer a shape to the history of ancient Greek letters.

The Second Millennium (The Bronze Age)

---

c. 1600–1200. Mycenae dominates the
Mediterranean
c. 1180. Troy destroyed
c. 1000. Dorian invasion

The Eighth Century B.C.

Invention of the alphabet Beginnings of colonization in Sicily	Hesiod composes *Works and Days,* *Theogony* in Ascra (Boeotia) Homer composes *Iliad, Odyssey*

The Seventh Century B.C.

---

c. 680. Gyges seizes the throne in Lydia
c. 675. Sparta crushes revolt of
Messenians and acquires a conservative,
severe constitution

323

The Seventh Century B.C.

c. 650–600. Spread of tyrant governments in Greece c. 640–630. Standardized coinage is begun in Lydia and soon adopted by Greek city-states	c. 650. Archilochus (born on Paros) writes poetry (mentions the eclipse of April 6, 648, in a poem) Second half of the century. Tyrtaeus writes poetry in Sparta c. 630. Mimnermus writes poetry in Asia Minor c. 612. Sappho born in Mytilene on Lesbos

The Sixth Century B.C.

594/93. Solon appointed chief magistrate at Athens to reform the constitution May 8, 585. Thales predicts an eclipse 561. Peisistratus becomes tyrant at Athens 560. Croesus succeeds to the throne 546. Croesus dies c. 540. Polycrates becomes tyrant on Samos	
	c. 556. Simonides born on Ceos 540. Theognis writes poetry in Megara c. 535. Thespis wins first prize when tragedy is first introduced at the Greater Dionysia in Athens
528. Hippias succeeds his father, Peisistratus, at Athens	
	525. Aeschylus born at Athens
c. 523. Polycrates of Samos dies	c. 524. Bacchylides born on Ceos 518. Pindar born in Boeotia
510. Hippias is expelled from Athens 508. Cleisthenes begins his reforms of the Athenian constitution	
	c. 500. Satyr plays are added to the tragic festival

The Fifth Century B.C.

499. Ionian cities in Asia Minor revolt from Persia with Athenian aid	
	c. 495. Pericles, Sophocles born at Athens Herodotus said to have been born "before the Persian War" at Halicarnassus
494. Revolt collapses, Ionians flee to Athens	
	c. 490. Phidias born
490. Persian retaliation; invasion of Greece is defeated at Marathon.	
	488/7. Comedy introduced at the Greater Dionysia festival

The Fifth Century B.C.

487. First use of ostracism at Athens; public officials now elected by lot rather than popular election

c. 485. Protagoras, Euripides born at Athens

484. Aeschylus's first victory

483. Discovery of rich new vein of silver at Laurium; a large fleet is built at the direction of Themistocles

480. August: Xerxes enters Greece; battle of Thermopylae; September: battle of Salamis is a great Greek victory

c. 480. Anaxagoras comes to Athens

479. Battle of Plataea; battle of Mycale; Greeks victorious, Persians withdraw
478–476. Fortification of Athens
477. Formation of the Delian League on the island of Delos

476. Pindar writes Olympian I, Bacchylides writes Ode V

472. Discontent appears in the League: Carystus (472), Naxos (470), Thasos (465) try to withdraw, are crushed and subjugated by Athens

472. Aeschylus's *Persians*

469. Socrates born
468. Sophocles defeats Aeschylus at tragic festival
467. Aeschylus's *Seven against Thebes*
463? Aeschylus's *Suppliants*
Between 460 and 455. Thucydides born at Athens

458. Long walls are built from Athens to the harbor

458. Aeschylus's *Oresteia*

456. Aeschylus dies at Gela in Sicily
455. Euripides first competes at the Dionysia

454. Treasury of the Delian League moved to Athens from Delos

c. 455. Aristophanes born at Athens

447. The Parthenon is begun; Euboea revolts, is subdued and made subject to Athens

444. Herodotus goes to assist in the founding of Thurii in southern Italy
441? Sophocles' *Antigone*
441. Euripides wins first victory
438. Euripides' *Alcestis*
438. Pindar dies
436. Isocrates born at Athens

432. Dorians assemble at Sparta and decide on war with Athens

431. Euripides' *Medea*

430. Plague at Athens
429. Pericles dies; Cleon becomes the major voice in the Assembly

430? Sophocles' *Oedipus Tyrannus*
429. Plato born at Athens

The Fifth Century B.C.

428. Euripides' *Hippolytus*
c. 428. Publication of Herodotus's *Histories*
427. Gorgias of Leontini arrives to create a sensation at Athens
425. Aristophanes' *Acharnians.*
424. Thucydides goes into exile
424. Aristophanes' *Knights*
423. Aristophanes' *Clouds*
422. Aristophanes' *Wasps*

421. Peace of Nicias between Athens and Sparta
421. Aristophanes' *Peace*
c. 420. Herodotus dies
415. Athenian expedition against Sicily
415. Euripides' *Trojan Women*
414. Aristophanes' *Birds*

413. Grave Athenian defeat at Syracuse in Sicily

412. Euripides' *Helen*
411. Oligarchic revolution in Athens
411. Aristophanes' *Lysistrata*
410. Democracy restored in Athens

409. Sophocles' *Philoctetes*
408. Euripides' *Orestes*
406. Euripides dies in Macedonia, Sophocles dies at Athens

405. Battle of Aegospotami; Athens' fleet destroyed
405. Euripides' *Bacchae, Iphigenia in Aulis;* Aristophanes' *Frogs*
404. Athens surrenders
404. Thucydides returns to Athens
401. Sophocles' *Oedipus at Colonus*
c. 400. Thucydides dies at Athens

The Fourth Century B.C.

399. Socrates dies at Athens
394. Battle of Coronea ends Sparta's pretensions to leadership of Greece
388. Aristophanes' *Wealth*
387. Plato starts the Academy at Athens
385. Aristophanes dies
384. Aristotle born in Chalcidice

362. Battle of Mantinea ends Thebes' pretensions to leadership of Greece
356. Alexander born in Macedonia

347. Plato dies at Athens
342/41. Menander born at Athens
341. Epicurus born at Samos
338. Philip of Macedon wins battle of Chaeronea against the combined forces of the Greeks
338. Isocrates dies
336. Alexander succeeds to the Macedonian throne

The Fourth Century B.C.

335. Zeno born in Cyprus; Aristotle comes to Athens, founds school

331. Foundation of the city of Alexandria in Egypt
323. Alexander dies

322. Aristotle dies
307. Epicurus starts his school
c. 305. Callimachus born in Cyrene

304. Ptolemy declares himself king in Egypt

c. 300. Theocritus born in Sicily

The Third Century B.C.

297. Foundation of the Mouseion at Alexandria
c. 295. Apollonius born in Alexandria
c. 290. Menander dies

282. Ptolemy I dies

270. Epicurus dies at Athens
263. Zeno dies
c. 260. Theocritus dies
247. Apollonius steps down as librarian
240. Callimachus dies

Index

Library of Congress Cataloging-in-Publication Data

Beye, Charles Rowan.
  Ancient Greek literature and society.

  Bibliography: p.
  Includes index.
  1. Greek literature—History and criticism. 2. Literature and society—
Greece. I. Title.
PA3052.B4   1987   880'.9   86-47972
ISBN 0-8014-1874-7 (alk. paper)
ISBN 0-8014-9444-3 (pbk. : alk. paper)